Joseph Crowell

The young volunteer

A record of the experiences of a private soldier

Joseph Crowell

The young volunteer
A record of the experiences of a private soldier

ISBN/EAN: 9783337135317

Printed in Europe, USA, Canada, Australia, Japan

Cover: Foto ©ninafisch / pixelio.de

More available books at **www.hansebooks.com**

THE
YOUNG VOLUNTEER.

A RECORD OF THE

EXPERIENCES OF A PRIVATE SOLDIER.

BY

JOSEPH E. CROWELL,

Late Private Company K, 13th N. J. Volunteers and Lieutenant
Veteran Reserve Corps.

F. TENNYSON NEELY,
PUBLISHER,
LONDON.   NEW YORK.

TO MY LIFE-LONG FRIEND,

CAPTAIN CHARLES CURIE,
(Late of the 9th and 178th Regiments, N. Y. Volunteers)

A BRAVE SOLDIER, A GALLANT, A CONSIDERATE OFFICER, A LOYAL VETERAN, A WORTHY CITIZEN, AN UPRIGHT MAN, AND, ABOVE ALL, A TRUE FRIEND IN EVERY SENSE OF THE WORD, THIS BOOK IS HEARTILY AND

RESPECTFULLY DEDICATED.

PREFACE.

WHAT is army life during the time of war like, as seen by "the rank and file"—the men who compose the great majority?

To give an idea of the experiences and everyday existence of the private soldier was the main object in writing this story.

The world is full of books written from the standpoint of the officers, giving the movements of troops and general accounts of great battles, and describing the maneuvers as witnessed from headquarters. They are histories, it is true, as seen by the writers, but they do not portray the life, hardships, trials and sufferings of that portion of the army known as "the men."

There is a great dividing gulf, military and social, between "officers" and "men," and they see the same things with vastly different eyes.

There are very few works relating to the actual experiences of the private soldier, giving his troubles and his joys, and presenting the dark and the bright sides of his life in the army. Hence this story covers a somewhat unbeaten field, and its novelty will proportionately add to its interest.

The story is historically correct, so far as it goes. It is part of the history of the Thirteenth Regiment, New Jersey Volunteers, in the War of the Rebellion. But it is only so in part, for it is merely carried far enough to give the reader an idea of a private's life in the army.

To extend it further would be largely a repetition of the same experiences, for, with topographical and climatic variations, all marches and battles are similar—to the private soldier. Most of the names used are genuine and a majority of the incidents portrayed are the actual experiences of the author; hence for the nearly two years covered it is history.

It may be confidently asserted that nothing has been exaggerated or overdrawn. Nor is there anything in it especially remarkable. Practically it relates the experience of nearly every private soldier who served in the civil war. Thousands and thousands of others could refer to it as their own history, for their experiences were identical with it.

To give the youth of the country a faint idea of real war and real army life; to instil in them sentiments of patriotism; to impress upon them the magnitude of the task of preserving the Union; and to cause them all the more to appreciate the blessings they now enjoy through the patriotism, sufferings and privations of their fathers and grandfathers, were also objects which instigated the story of "The Young Volunteer."

THE YOUNG VOLUNTEER.

CHAPTER I.

ENLISTING.

"Say, Joe, won't you carry this package of cheese around to Mr. Pennington's? The boys are all out, and I promised to send it some time ago."

The speaker was Henry B. Crosby, who kept the big grocery store in Main Street. He was variously known as "The Grocer King" and "The Cheese Prince"—the latter appellation resulting from his custom of buying cheese by the cargo and selling it a lower price than any one else. If I had known then what I afterward knew, I would probably have said "Cheese it," and forthwith "skipped," instead of being a "skipper." If it hadn't been for that pound of cheese I might never have been in the army, and the war might have been going on yet!

Aaron S. Pennington's big stone mansion was a fine old residence and stood on a high hill. The ground was then on a level with what is now the second story, and to this day you can see the former big front door up there in the air. It was surrounded by spacious grounds.

Aaron S. Pennington, like all the old gentlemen of that day, generally did his own marketing. You could see him walking down among the hucksters on Main Street every morning, with a big market basket on his arm. Few of the grocers and butchers had wagons in those days. People bought their own provisions and generally carried them home themselves. How Mr. Pennington came to leave that pound of cheese to be sent home I never knew.

I did not work in the grocery store. I was employed in the *Guardian* office. In the forenoon I set type. In the afternoon I wrote down the war news at the only telegraph office in the city, which was in the old Erie depot. "Jack" Dunning was telegraph operator. "Tune" Dougherty, who was then a wee bit of a fellow, was the sole messenger boy. In the afternoon when the paper was out, I carried a route and sold papers on the street. In the evening I tended office and helped on the books, for I understood bookkeeping. Wages one dollar and fifty cents per week.

Still, my hours were not ironclad, and I had time left to go around a little to pick up local items, and Crosby's grocery store was one of my "loafing" places. There was a considerable degree of familiarity between the boss grocer and myself, and that is how he asked me, as a favor, to carry around the cheese to Mr. Pennington. This introduction is given, therefore, not only as an historical fact, but as an example to show by what insignificant events a man's life is frequently swerved. Many a time afterward I hurled boundless anathemas at that pound of cheese, and wondered why Aaron S. Pennington wanted cheese for supper on that particular afternoon.

I well remember the day. It was Wednesday, August 18, 1862. And right here let me interpolate a little historical data.

It was, so far as the feelings and apprehensions of the North were concerned, the most critical period of the war. The Army of the Potomac had retreated from a position whence they could actually see the seven hills of Richmond, back to Harrison's Landing, on the James River. General Lee was marching with the Confederate army close behind, and even Washington was threatened. The North was, as a consequence, precipitated into a genuine panic. It looked as if, before another month, the Confederates would be in possession of the National Capital. President Lincoln issued a call for three hundred thousand additional volunteers. If enough could not be obtained voluntarily, a draft was to be ordered.

It should be stated that the first rush to arms, in 1861,

had been spontaneous. The first term of enlistment was but for three months. Then it became apparent that the rebellion was not going to be suppressed in three months, and three years' men were called. The ambitious, impulsive youths who are ever on the watch for adventure, constituted the first spontaneous outpouring of robust young patriots, but in '62 it was different. Things had become serious. The people of the country had suddenly awakened to a realization of the fact that they had a real war on hand. And not only a war, but probably a long and stubborn one, against an enemy equally brave, almost as strong, and, perhaps, still more determined.

It would be impossible for the present generation to form the slightest conception of the excitement that prevailed. Public meetings were held everywhere, and the most potent orators in every locality, were urging upon the young men to do their duty by flying to the defense of their country.

I was one of the "flyers." And it was all through that pound of cheese. As I came back from Mr. Pennington's, I saw a big crowd of people in front of the old "bank building" in Main Street. There was a big stone piazza or vestibule on a level with the second story, which was reached by flights of stone steps on each side. On that piazza some one was making a speech.

It was Henry A. Williams, the mayor of the city. He told of the imperilled country and urged on the young men to enlist. Socrates Tuttle, a prominent lawyer, described what a glorious thing it was to fight for one's native land. Colonel A. B. Woodruff, General Thomas D. Hoxsey and others spoke in a similar strain. The result of it all was that half the boys in the crowd couldn't get to the nearest recruiting office quickly enough.

It is a very singular thing that of all these impassioned orators who said it was such a glorious thing, but one enlisted himself! But then, perhaps, it was necessary to have some one remain home to do the talking! One of them, however, who was subsequently drafted, nobly fought and died—by proxy. He sent a substitute, at a cost of eight hundred dollars.

And that reminds me of a thing that has perhaps been forgotten. So afraid were some of the leading citizens that they might be drafted, that they formed a "mutual substitute insurance company." It cost at that time eight hundred dollars to get a man to take your place. (Later in the war the price advanced to fifteen hundred and two thousand dollars.) Well, eight men would chip in one hundred dollars each into a general fund, and if any one of the eight was drafted the money would be used to "buy a substitute." If two of them were drafted, the extra money was raised by an additional assessment; but the drafting process was like a lottery, and as a matter of fact there was seldom more than one "prize" in an association of eight men. I might mention the names of quite a number of well-known citizens still living who belonged to these substitute insurance companies. At political meetings I have often heard some of them shouting "how *we* saved the Union!"

But we poor chaps, who couldn't raise one hundred let alone eight hundred dollars escaped the draft by enlisting. It wasn't fear of the draft, however, that influenced us. I was just past eighteen years old, and "liable," but so far as I was concerned I never once thought anything about being drafted.

Why I, and the other fellows, came to enlist, is something I never could explain. I think I am safe in saying that, at the moment, genuine patriotism hardly entered into the question. Of course there were some who enlisted from patriotic motives; but when one comes down to the bottom facts, I believe a majority of the boys were induced to go from other motives. Most probably it was the general excitement of the times. It was simply a furore to go to the war. To many it was a change from the ordinary humdrum of life. To others it was looked upon as a picnic. And then in every boy's heart there is an inherent spirit of adventure.

The orators on the steps of the old bank building had said the reason the war had lasted so long already was because there were not enough soldiers at the front. But now all that would be attended to in short order. With the great army that was about to be organized, the war couldn't possibly last more than three months longer By cold weather it would all be over. As said before, what particular motive I had in enlisting, beyond an impulse, I don't know, and many of my companions frequently expressed a similar opinion. But enlist we did.

Hugh C. Irish was forming a company for the Thirteenth New Jersey Volunteers. It is in his memory that Camp No. 8 of the Sons of Veterans of Paterson is named. Mr. Irish had been my employer, as one of the proprietors of the *Guardian*. For some reason Mr. Irish sold out his interest in the *Guardian* and embarked in the grocery business. He had been there but a few months when he became convinced that it was his duty to go to war. Mr. Irish was one of the men who entered the service out of pure loyalty and patriotism. In his case the motive was unquestionable.

Mr. Irish had been authorized to raise a company for the Thirteenth Regiment, then forming at Newark, under the president's call, and he was to be the captain. His grocery store was transformed into a recruiting office. The recruits signed the roll on the bottom of a soap box. It was to this place I hastened after hearing the patriotic speeches from the steps of the old bank building. Whatever hesitation I might have had on the way thither was completely knocked out by the tune of "The Girl I Left Behind Me," which was being played on a cracked drum and wheezy fife by two "musicians" in baggy clothes who had just enlisted themselves. They stood in front of the store banging and blowing away for dear life.

Under ordinary circumstances such music would have been rotten-egged. As it was, it was but a noisy echo of the spirit of the times, and filled the heart of the listener with patriotic emotions that were simply irresistible. No one, hearing such martial strains, could resist the war influence! I couldn't. In a very few moments I had signed an eagle-headed sheet of paper which bound me, "stronger than ropes and cords could bind me," to the service of the United States of America, "for the term of three years unless sooner discharged."

I had scarcely signed before I began to be sorry. For

the first time I realized what I had done and began to be frightened. But the sight of so many of my friends and companions around me soon dissipated that feeling. There was "Rats" and "Curt" and "Liv," besides Captain Irish, all from our office. "Rats" was David Harris. "Curt" was Curtis Bowne, whose tragic and singular death at the battle of Antietam will be noticed later on. "Liv" was E. Livingston Allen, now a Methodist minister. He is the only one of the lot who went into the ministry. All those mentioned were printers. Then there were James G. Scott (afterward captain) and Hank Van Orden, Jim Dougherty, Jack Stansfield, Heber Wells, "Ginger" Clark, John Butterworth, "Lem" Smith, John Snyder (with the big nose), "Slaughter House Ick," Dan Wannamaker, John J. Carlough, Sandy Kidd, John Nield, John Anderson, "Dad" Bush, Reddy Mahar, George Comer, William Lambert, Archy McCall, Archy Todd, "Jake" Engel, "Jake" Berdan, W. J. Campbell, W. J. Carlough, John Farlow, Thomas Hardy, Joseph H. Pewtner, Theodore S. Perry, James H. Peterson, and a whole lot of other fellows I had known, and some of whom will come in for further reference during the course of this story.

The immediate association of all these—the fact that so many old acquaintances had enlisted together and would go to war together, relieved the event of the lonesomeness and awfulness of the step. It was simply impossible to remain lonesome and downhearted in company with such a crowd—and many others whose names are now beyond memory's call. And when one comes to look at them, they must have been physically a tough set, for many of them are yet alive, and some of them do not look much older than they did during the war.

There were a number who felt dubious about enlisting in a regiment which was to bear the unlucky number "13," but it wasn't a superstitious crowd, and that was soon forgotten. Nor was it an aristocratic crowd. Nearly all were poor working boys.

A sort of pride fills the heart of the new recruit. He imagines that he has already done something brave, and rather looks down on those who have not signed the roll. When I went to see my girl that night I felt considerably puffed up. As it was a good-by call, I asked for her picture.

"What," exclaimed she, "and have some stranger take it out of your pocket if you are killed? I guess not."

That wasn't very pleasant. Getting killed wasn't in the bargain. I didn't feel a bit comfortable at such a gloomy possibility.

But when I left the house I had the picture of a very pretty girl in my pocket. The girls of those days were patriotic, and he indeed was a poor soldier who had not in his pocket a picture of "The Girl I Left Behind me."

CHAPTER II.

IN CAMP.

A DAY or so later a squad of recruits for Company K, Thirteenth Regiment of New Jersey Volunteers, proceeded to Camp Frelinghuysen, Newark. The camp was along the canal, in the higher portion of the city. There was no railroad then between Paterson and Newark, and our contingent went down by Barney Demarest's stage, reaching camp shortly after noon. Many others had preceded us.

When the stage started from Paterson it wasn't a very jolly crowd. Many an eye bore a redness indicative of recent tears, for the hardest part of enlisting is the parting with one's dear ones at home. There was many an affecting scene in many a home the previous night. Not that parents and sisters and sweethearts were not patriotic; but it was with copious tears that mothers and sisters, while admitting that the sacrifice was loyal and right, bade good-by to the dear boys they might never see again. The mother's tears that had dropped on the soldier's coat sleeves were hardly dry when the boys rode over the Main Street cobblestones in Barney Demarest's rickety old stagecoach, and the influence of the last embrace and farewell kiss was still upon nearly all.

But human nature is buoyant. Perhaps it was to offset the gloomy farewell that the boys soon became boisterously merry, and they made the morning air resound with their shouts and their hurrahs and their song of

"We're coming Father Abraham
Three hundred thousand more."

The stage was gayly decked with flags, the crowds in

the streets shouted a hearty farewell, and all sorrowful thoughts were soon drowned in the noise and racket that was too loud to permit any one to think. A similar noisy demonstration greeted us at "Acquackanonk" (Passaic), Bloomfield and Newark, and a hurrah arose from the throats of the already arrived recruits as we drove past the guards at the entrance to Camp Frelinghuysen. The armed guards and picket line around the camp was another evidence that we were no longer free men; but we did not fully appreciate that fact until later.

And yet the camp presented a picturesque appearance. The colonel's tent stood at the top of the hill. It was a large and commodious canvas house. Near by were similar but smaller tents for the lieutenant-colonel, major, adjutant and quartermaster. Still further down was a long row of still smaller tents, occupied by the captains and lieutenants. Running at right angles from the latter was a row of large, circular tents, occupied by the "enlisted men" of each company. These were known as "Sibley" tents, and resembled an Indian tepee, with a ventilator at the top. These tents would accommodate fifteen or twenty men. In our innocence we supposed that we were to have these tents right along all through the war. For all that we knew, all the soldiers in the army had the same commodious and comfortable quarters. We were undeceived on this point, however, in the course of a very few days.

Shortly after our arrival we were taken before the regimental surgeon for examination. The surgeon was Dr. J. J. H. Love, one of the most brusque-appearing and yet most kind-hearted men that ever lived. Until his recent death he was one of the most respected and prominent residents of Montclair.

"Strip," ordered the doctor.

There were five or six examined at a time. We boys, who never had a pain or qualm in our lives, thought it was a needless formality, but were told that it was "according to the regulations." Then the doctor punched us and pinched us, rubbed his hands down our legs as if we were so many horses, seized us in the groin and told us to cough, and finally said:

"Let's see your teeth?"

"What do you want to see my teeth for?" I asked. "Are we to bite the enemy?"

"Something tougher than that," good-naturedly answered Dr. Love. "You will have to bite hard-tack and chew cartridges, and I guess you will find both tougher than any rebel meat you ever will see."

I didn't know then that hard-tack was the stuff soldiers were mainly fed upon; but I found out before long. For the information of the reader I will explain that a hard-tack is the most deceptive-looking thing in the world. Its general appearance is that of a soda cracker, but there the resemblance ends. You can bite a soda cracker. A hard-tack isn't tender. Compared with it a block of granilite paving stones would be mush. That is the sort of pastry the government fed its soldiers upon. Hard-tack must have been referred to in that part of the Bible where it says "he asked for bread and they gave him a stone." A further corroboration of this conclusion lies in the positive fact that every box of hard-tack that ever arrived in the army was marked:

"B. C. 348,764,"

the variation being only in the figure. The "B. C." was on every box. And judging from the antediluvian toughness of some of the crackers, the prehistoric ancient who stencilled on the figures either accidentally or wilfully post dated the box several thousand years.

What "chewing cartridges" meant, I hadn't the slightest conception of, but learned that subsequently. That my teeth were apparently equal to the emergency of both biting hard-tack and chewing cartridges, however, must have been a matter satisfactory to Dr. Love, for I successfully passed the ordeal of a "surgical examination."

The next thing was to go to the quartermaster's and get our uniform and equipments. What a lot of things there were!

There were undershirts and drawers and thick stockings, all supposed to be of wool, but apparently mainly composed of thistles and sticks—the coarsest things a man ever put next to his skin. And it was midsummer at that! Then there were a pair of light blue trousers, a dark blue blouse, a dark blue dress coat, a heavy, caped light blue overcoat, a knit cardigan jacket, a forage cap, a heavy woolen blanket, a thick rubber blanket, and a pair of heavy brogans. These were the clothes. Added to this were a knapsack, a haversack, a canteen, a cartridge belt, a bayonet belt, and an Enfield rifle.

As the men were called up, the clothing, etc., were thrown in front of each one in a pile, and utterly regardless of fit or size. When the recruits repaired to their tents and donned the uniform, they presented a ludicrous appearance.

"How do I look, boys?" asked Hank Van Orden, as he emerged from his corner.

"Hank" was a sight to behold. Nature had been generous with him as to legs and arms, and as luck would have it, he had got a small-sized suit. The bottom of his trousers didn't come down to his shoe tops, while his arms stuck several inches beyond the end of his blouse sleeves. The shoes were too tight and his cap was stuck on the back of his head in a comical fashion.

"Don't laugh at me. Look at Heber," said Hank.

There stood Heber Wells, dressed up in a suit Van Orden ought to have had. His trousers were turned up at the bottom like a dude's of the present day, while the sleeves of his coat fit like a Chinaman's. His cap came down to his ears.

Robust Abe Godwin couldn't button his clothes about him, while slim Johnny Nield had twice as much uniform as he wanted. In fact, while there were different-sized suits, no man had got a suit anywhere near fitting, and a more incongruous lot of noble soldiers could not be imagined. Falstaff's army was simply nowhere. But the difficulty was in a measure overcome by exchanging suits, an operation that took nearly all the afternoon. Still they didn't fit. But nobody but a raw recruit would spend more than a moment thinking about the fit of his uniform.

The clothes were awfully uncomfortable. The absence of a vest was particularly noticeable. "Enlisted men" in the army never wear vests. There was a nasty smell of dye-stuff. The coarse underclothes tickled and irritated, the heavy brogan, for men who were used to gaiters and Oxford ties, were disagreeably clumsy. And, above all, the wearing of woolen stockings a quarter of an inch thick, in the August dog days, fairly capped the climax.

"Fall in for your rations."

Such was the cry we heard for the first time, about 6 o'clock. None of us knew what "fall in" meant; but Heber Wells, who had been selected as orderly sergeant, told us it was to get into a line, one after the other.

"Forward march!" said Heber.

It is the rule in the army to step off first with the left foot, but we didn't know that. Some started with the left and some with the right, and the whole line came near stumbling over each other. After going to the lower end of the company street, the new orderly cried out:

"File left."

Heber took hold of the leading man and twirled him to the left, and the rest of us followed. Otherwise none of us would have known what to do.

"Where did he learn so much military?" was the question everybody was asking about Wells. We at once began to look to him as a marvel of tactical knowledge. The fact is this was all the tactics Heber knew, and he had just been told that much!

The "cook house," where we went for our rations, wasn't a house at all. It was all outdoors. A couple of forked pieces of wood held a horizontal pole, and on this were three or four big sheet-iron pails or kettles, under which a cordwood fire was burning, with much smoke. There was a similar "cook house" at the lower end of each company street. As each man filed past he was given a tin cup, filled with black coffee (no milk) already sweetened, a tin plate filled with beans and pork, and a hunk of bread. We were told to take care of our "crockery," and bring them to the cook house whenever "rations" were called.

"Where's the knife and fork and spoon?" John Butterworth wanted to know.

"You're a nice fellow," replied Jake Engle, "to think soldiers have forks and spoons. Use your fingers—they were made before forks." Neither were there any napkins.

The men took their rations and sat down about their tents to eat their first meal as real soldiers. Coffee without milk was not very palatable, at the start, but from that time on, for many, many months, the majority of these soldier boys never saw such a thing as milk. Milkless coffee isn't so bad when one is once used to it, and coffee was the mainstay of the army. What a soldier in active service would do without his pint of coffee three times a day, is a serious question.

It was also awkward to eat pork and beans without knife, fork or spoon. But with the aid of pocket knives, and wooden spoons made out of a sliver from a board, the recruits soon learned to eat soldier fashion, and they soon found out, also, that beans spread upon bread was a fair substitute for butter.

What a picnic it was! What a free, airy life! Who wouldn't be a soldier? To tell the truth, the novelty of the thing was interesting.

After supper we heard some sort of a commotion up by Captain Irish's tent. There was a crowd of men standing there, from the midst of which, at frequent intervals, there was a momentary glimpse of a man being projected a considerable height into the air. It was "initiation."

"Come, Joe, you're next," was the salute I got, and before I could remonstrate I was seized bodily and thrown headlong upon a big blanket, surrounded by the men who were holding it. The blanket hung slack in the middle.

"One! Two! Three! Hip!"

The men pulled the blanket taut, and up I was projected, ten or fifteen feet into the air. Coming down, one landed head first or feet first or sideways, just as it might happen, and then, up again! Three times was the ordeal, and the "candidate" was "initiated." Every man in the company had to go through it.

"Now for the captain," cried Hank Van Orden, who seemed to be the ringleader.

"Oh, no," replied Lieutenant Scott, with dignity. "The officers are exempt."

"Guess not," said Hank, and over went Scott into the blanket.

Captain Irish good-naturedly offered no resistance, and he was tossed also. Poor fellow, he little knew that in less than a month his dead body would be in possession of the enemy in one of the bloodiest battlefields of the war.

The same "initiation" was being enacted all along the line, and as there were seven or eight hundred recruits in camp, it may be imagined that it was a lively scene.

Then the boys gathered around their tents, or the cook fire, smoked their pipes, told stories and sang songs, until 9 o'clock, when the "tattoo" roll was called and half an hour later a few single strokes on the drum indicated "taps," and lights were ordered out.

My chum that night was John Butterworth, and when he prepared for "bed" he created a yell of laughter by saying:

"Say, boys, I forgot to bring my night shirt."

The most of us, however, slept in all our clothes, except our coats and shoes. With a blanket under us and a blanket over us, and knapsacks for pillows we were quite comfortable as to warmth, but goodness, how hard the ground was! It was the first time I had ever slept on the ground, and there was an uncomfortable dampness that came from it that was not pleasant, even in midsummer. Through the flaps of the tent and the ventilator at the top one could see the bright stars, and there was a peculiar outdoor "looseness" to the sensation that was quite uncanny.

As for sleeping! Well, with the cat calls and shouts and yells, the snatches of song, and cries of "Get on your own side of the bed," and "Give me half of the sheet, will you?" and such things, the hullabaloo was kept up until long after midnight. And after that the snoring began. All sorts of snores. Double bass, tenor, baritone. Snores like a grandfather bull frog and snores like a sick calf's bleat. Snores that would awaken the dead or make the devil laugh. You never heard such a miscellaneous job lot of snores in your life.

But all things have an end, and even the outrageous snoring finally produced such a soporific effect that we all slept soundly.

CHAPTER III.

"FALL IN."

WE were aroused at an outlandishly early hour by an indescribable conglomeration of discords outside somewhere. All the boys, as they tried to untangle their stiffened limbs from the blankets, rubbed their eyes in an uncertain, mystified way that was very comical.

It was a strange feeling. Where were we? What noise was that? What makes the bedroom look so marvelously unfamiliar this morning? Are we dreaming? Who are all these men lying and stretching about? And all in bed with their clothes on—blue clothes.

Is it a dream? Is the dim remembrance of doing something unusual—of entering into a new life—actual reality, or have we had the nightmare? Let's see. Did we enlist into the army yesterday, or didn't we? The other men are kicking off the blankets, reaching for their shoes, rubbing their half-opened eyes, and grunting and groaning from the stiffness caused by the hard bed and damp earth, and again there is that discordant racket outside.

It is the first attempt of the new fifer and drummer to sound the reveille—the "get up bell" we were destined to hear every morning for three years—"unless sooner discharged." No wonder such an outrageous musical attempt woke us up. It was enough to awaken the dead.

"Reveille—Fall in for roll call."

It was the voice of Heber Wells, the orderly sergeant.

"Refillee? Vot's dot, alretty?" asked John Ick, who was destined to become the funniest Dutchman, most awkward recruit, unceasing and chronic kicker in the company, and yet one of the bravest of soldiers in action.

Poor fellow, he fell early, pierced by a rebel bullet. But John was as ignorant as the rest of us on military orders, and "reveille" was something new.

"I tole you vot dot vash," said he. "Dot vas brekfasht."

And he got his tin plate and cup, and piled out with the crowd. A lot of others were similarly equipped, to the intense astonishment of Captain Irish, who had turned out to see the first reveille roll call.

"Fall in—fall in according to size," was the order.

This meant that the men should get in a line, with the tallest man at the head of the class and the shortest one at the foot. Hank Van Orden thus stood at the right of the line and Sandy Kidd at the left, and the captain told us that ever after we were to get ourselves together in that shape whenever we heard the order to "Fall in."

The roll was called. It was a sleepy looking crowd —there were about ninety—and as a matter of fact the soldiers were always a sleepy lot at reveille roll call. Before dismissing the company, after finding all the members "present or accounted for," Orderly Wells picked out ten men to do "police duty." The rest of us were for the present dismissed.

A matutinal ablution is naturally one of the first duties of every man. Soldiers are no exception. Then we began for the first time to experience the utter inadequacy of the toilet accommodations supplied by Uncle Sam to his brave defenders. There were not many houses provided with the luxury of a bathroom in those days; but the most of us at least had become used to the accommodations of a washbowl and pitcher and a clean towel. We hadn't even the towel. The canal at the foot of the camp, however, afforded an all-sufficient supply of water, and the tails or sleeves of our coats served as towels. Johnny Nield had a pocket comb, and that was passed around.

We went up to see how the new policemen were getting along—the ten men who had been picked out to do "police duty." We naturally supposed that meant to stand guard around the camp and look fierce; but it wasn't. To "police" a camp means to clean it up.

You've seen the street department gang with their brooms and hoes cleaning the dirt out of the gutters. Well, that, in army parlance, is "police duty." If a real policeman were called upon to perform that "duty" he would kick like a steer. Whoever heard of a policeman working?

The new recruits "kicked," too, but it was no use. There was a bookkeeper from one of the mills, two Main Street dry goods clerks with soft hands, a printer and a cotton manufacturer working for dear life in the "chain gang" as they were dubbed, and bossed by a sergeant who used to sell beer in a Dublin gin mill. Oh, but it was galling.

That was one of the hardest features of army life—to fall under the command of an officer who was in every way—except for his straps or stripes—your inferior. Such men, feeling for the first time the pleasures of autocracy, were the most cruel and relentless taskmasters. But they had to be obeyed. Such was discipline. The first duty of a soldier is obedience—no matter if your "superior officer" be an ignorant, boorish bully you wouldn't have recognized in civil life. My old employer had said it was a good thing for me to go into the army, because I needed discipline. I would never recognize a "boss," and was the most independent young American in the United States. That was something the army life would cure me of. My old employer was right. I soon had the independence knocked out of me. I was soon thoroughly "disciplined." But in that respect, doubtless, I have since retrograded.

"Fall in for rations," was the next order, and John Ick made another dive for his tin plate and cup. He was perennially hungry, was John.

"Itsch 'vall in' all de times," said he, "but I don'd mind him a little ven dot means some tings to eat, ain't it?"

The breakfast was like the supper the night before, with the exception that boiled beef was substituted for the pork and beans. Somehow it didn't seem very tasty. We missed the customary muffins and chops and eggs, and the cream in our coffee. But still it went. It had to. It was that or nothing. No sooner was breakfast over than it was again:

"Fall in, Company K!"

This time it was to pick out a detail for guard duty, and the ten men selected were instructed to be ready to fall in again a little before 9 o'clock, "fully armed and equipped." I escaped this "draft," but with the others anxiously awaited the time to see the first "guard mount."

A little before 9 o'clock a drum beat called out the guard detail—and there appeared the ten men "fully armed and equipped." They had on everything the government had given them. Although a midsummer evening, they perspired under their heavy overcoats. They had their knapsacks, haversacks and canteens, their belts and ammunition boxes and their muskets—all ready to go to war. It was a funny sight. Some of the knapsacks were perched upon the shoulders like the hump of a hunchback, while others hung at the bottom of the back, like a "Grecian bend." Two of the men carried their haversacks in their left hands, as if they were satchels.

Even the captain had to laugh. He explained to them that they only required their blouses and arms, and told them to leave their knapsacks, haversacks, and canteens in the tents. After some coaching they were finally arranged right and formed into line.

"Now," said Sergeant Wells, "all you have got to do is to follow your file leader."

"Vot vash dot vile leeder, Mr. Wells?" asked John Ick.

"Don't talk while in the ranks. Don't you know better than that?" asked Wells, with a comical assumption of insulted dignity.

"Dot's all ri-et, Mister Wells. Dot's all riet; but how in dunderwedder we don't know some tings ven we don't ask nobotty already?"

Without deigning to reply the orderly gave the order to "right face," and twirled Hank Van Orden around to the right. Then began the command:

"Forward, march!"

And taking Hank by the elbow, he led him as he would a team of oxen, around the head of the company street and toward the place in the middle of the camp where a fife was tooting and a drum beating, and an already assembled crowd indicated that something was going on. The appearance of Company K's guard detail on that occasion was like a crowd of political heelers marching toward a barroom on the invitation of the candidates. There would be just about as much military precision in the latter as there was in the former.

Here let me explain. The Thirteenth Regiment was recruited in Newark, Orange, Belleville, Montclair, Bloomfield, Caldwell, Millburn, Jersey City and Paterson. There were two companies from Paterson—Company C, commanded by Captain Ryerson, and Company K, by Captain Irish. Not more than two companies were from one place, so that to a great degree the men were strangers to each other. The extent of friendship from previous acquaintance was consequently limited, but nine or ten hundred men who were thus brought together soon became quite well acquainted with each other.

Ten men from each of the ten companies, one hundred altogether, had been detailed for guard duty that day. The other eight hundred or so gathered around as spectators.

Colonel Carman stood on one side of the field, gorgeously attired, with a ferocious look on his face. He had already served some time in an official position in another regiment, and was regarded as a veteran. Before the war Colonel Carman was an humble clerk in some New York store. So he was, I understand, after the departure of his military glory; but he has since then been honored by being made commissioner in charge of the Antietam battlefield.

But the colonel certainly looked ferocious and brave enough that morning to whip the whole rebel army alone. A short distance in front of him was Adjutant Charles A. Hopkins (now New England agent of the Mutual Life Insurance Company, and worth half a million, it is said). Now there is always something fussy and featherish about an adjutant, and Lieutenant Hopkins was no exception; but under his showy exterior there was as true and brave and sympathetic a heart as ever beat against the padded breast of a military officer.

The adjutant is usually the boss of a guard mount. The presence of the colonel, occasionally, is to add impressiveness and dignity. In actual service his place is usually substituted by the red-sashed officer who has been detailed as "officer of the day." He is the general superintendent and high-cock-a-lorum of the camp for the twenty-four hours for which he is appointed. An inferior officer, usually a lieutenant, is similarly selected as "officer of the guard."

But the "guard mount" was about to begin, and we watched the proceeding with all the eyes we had.

CHAPTER IV.

GUARD MOUNT AND DRILL.

This chapter does not purpose to be an accurate description of the details of military tactics. I will only describe the "guard mount" as I then saw it—as it would appear to any person for the first time.

The positions of the principal officers were described in the preceding chapter. Down in the field further, drawn up in a line, were ten fifers and ten drummers playing for dear life. It was the first time they had played together, and the orchestral effects were anything but harmonious. These musicians seemed to be the central cluster or nucleus around which the others were to gather, like a lot of bees swarming.

From every company street there marched, or rather straggled, a squad of ten soldiers, commanded—perhaps I should say led—by a sergeant. The first gang marched around until it came to the musicians. Then another ten would come along until it reached the tail end of the first, and so on, until the whole ten times ten were standing in a row or string.

It would have made an old army officer drop dead to see the way the men were carrying their muskets. They had had no drill. Half of them had never before seen, let alone handled, a rifle. Some carried them on one shoulder and some on the other. Here you would see a gun held up stiff and straight like a flagstaff, and the next man would hold it jauntily in the crook of his elbow. The "line" was about as near being straight as a horseshoe. Somebody yelled:

"Front!"

One of the boys who had once served in a hotel office was at the point of rushing forward, but he could see no counter to run to. No one else stirred.

"Front!" again commanded the adjutant. But still nobody moved, except to look helplessly at his companion. Many of them thought maybe it was the army way of saying grace, or something of that sort. No one had ever heard "Front" before. The adjutant became excited.

"All turn this way, and look at me," shouted the adjutant.

"Vy dond you say dod pefore," cried out John Ick.

"Silence in the ranks. When I say 'Front,' you turn to the front, that's all."

"Dot's all ri-et, Mister Hopkins," replied John Ick. "I'se a lookin' at you, don't it?"

"Silence!" yelled the officer, "or you'll go to the guardhouse."

"Can't a man say nottings all the time?" murmured Ick.

Poor John! He was marched off to the guardhouse, whatever that meant. None of us knew. It must be something awful.

"Dress up!"

Not a man stirred.

"Dress up, I say. Dress to the right!" commanded the adjutant, and stepping up to the end of the string he looked along the edge and gave the order again:

"Right—dress!"

Every man looked carefully over himself. Everybody seemed to have on his right dress! They were all dressed right. They were looking everywhere except to the right.

"What a lot of idiots," shouted Lieutenant Hopkins. "Just turn your eyes this way and get into a straight line." A general shuffle was the result. There was some sort of a commotion in Company K's detachment.

"What's the matter here?" asked the adjutant, coming over. "Why don't you get in a straight line?"

"Can't," replied Davy Harris. "Just look at John Snyder's nose!"

"Silence in the ranks!"

"See here," asked Lem Smith, "am I to take my bearings from Pop Farlow's fat belly, or from that spindle-shanked Anderson?"

"Silence in the ranks, or you'll go to the guardhouse," was the only reply.

Silence resulted. One man was already in the guardhouse, and an awful ignorance of what sort of horrible torture he might at that moment be undergoing made the warning sufficient.

Finally the adjutant got the men tolerably straight, and then the drummers and fifers marched down in front of the line, turned around and marched back again, playing "When Johnnie Comes Marching Home Again" the while. Then the adjutant stepped forward, turned on his heel, turned to the left, marched along to the middle of the parade, turned on his heel to the right, marched a few paces toward the colonel, and then turned completely around as if on a pivot. He gave the order to "Present arms!"

But no pretense was made of obeying it, inasmuch as no one in the ranks knew the difference between present arms and a lame leg. But just as if it had all been done according to Hoyle, or rather according to Hardee, the adjutant turned around facing the colonel, and bringing his sword up to his nose, dropped it with a curving sweep, like a farmer with a scythe. The adjutant said something to the colonel and the colonel said something to the adjutant, and some orders were given which no one understood.

Then with much confusion and trouble the men in the line were twisted around into platoons and marched past the colonel in about the order of a mob coming out of a circus, and then off to the guardhouse. As a military maneuver it was simply atrocious. Had Kaiser Wilhelm been there he would have thrown himself into the canal with ineffable disgust. But the spectators thought it was grand. When the Thirteenth Regiment got to the front and the enemy saw what they could do, the rebellion would be speedily ended! Indeed, had the Confederates witnessed a guard mount like that they would have thought it some new sort of tactics they didn't understand, and would doubtless have immediately surrendered.

The guards were put on duty around the camp. In the army the men go on guard duty for two hours and have a four-hour rest, and then go on again, and so on for the twenty-four hours. The duty of the guards was to let no one out of the camp, without a pass, and no visitors in—except at the gates.

We fellows who were not on guard were congratulating ourselves with having nothing to do when suddenly there was another drum beat, followed by the order:

"Fall in, Company K, for drill!"

The men hastily put on their belts, picked up their guns, and ran out to "get into a string," which we had learned by this time was the proper thing to do on hearing the order to "fall in." A sergeant who had served three months already and was therefore supposed to know all about war, was detailed to instruct us. He was an arrogant brute, as such men usually are, and gave his orders as if we were slaves.

Many a man's face flushed at being called "fool," "idiot," and worse names, when the sergeant became angry with our clumsiness and awkwardness. When we started we thought a "file" was something used by machinists, a "wheel" was part of the running gear of a wagon, and that when the order was to "shoulder arms," it meant to hold our guns on our shoulders, instead of holding them straight up at our sides. It had been "carry" arms, under the "Hardee" tactics, but Casey's revision was just being introduced, and the same movement was designated as "shoulder arms."

But how that relentless sergeant did drill us! He made us handle the guns in different shapes until they seemed to weigh half a ton, and our arms ached. And he marched us up and down and hither and thither until we were completely tired out with the unwonted exercise. It was in dog days, too, and the hot clothing and thick, scratchy shirts made us perspire until we were soaked. Being a soldier wasn't so much fun after all. We were glad enough when finally, at noon, we were dismissed for our dinner.

With the exception of soup for the main dish, dinner was similar to the other meals. We were beginning to get it through our heads that the prospects were bad for any very great variety in the menu. But it "went," for we were hungry, and our post prandial briarwood pipes were hugely enjoyed. Just as we were thinking of crawling into the tent for a snooze, again came that everlasting order:

"Fall in for drill!"

This was too much! What, drill twice a day? We would speak to the captain about it.

But the afternoon drill was worse yet, for it was a regimental drill—that is a drill of the entire regiment together. The colonel, who had seen some service, bossed this job. Now in a regimental drill a fellow has to walk about ten times as much as in a company drill, and we were soon so tired that we couldn't go any more.

The colonel saw this, and gave us some more instruction in the manual of arms, and for the first time showed us how to load the guns.

"Load in nine times—load."

Such was the order. We had been served with blank cartridges, and were told to simply go through the motion of loading. But Sandy Kidd failed to hear this, and before he was discovered he had loaded his guns nine times—that is, put nine cartridges into the barrel. What the nine "times" meant was the nine different motions that are necessary in loading a gun according to the tactics. During the latter part of the drill the colonel thought he would see how the regiment would do in an actual shoot. So he marched us around by the canal and once more went through the process of "loading in nine times."

Then I discovered why Dr. Love had so carefully examined our teeth. One of the orders was to "tear cartridges." Now the cartridges of those days were not the metallic affairs used at the present time. Breech-loading guns had hardly been introduced and our old muskets were loaded at the muzzle, like an old-fashioned shotgun. The cartridges containing the powder were made of paper. It was a thick brown paper, as tough as is used in a hardware store. One had to insert the end of the cartridge between the teeth and tear it open. Nothing but the stoutest teeth could stand this ordeal. And, ugh! how salt and nasty the powder tasted!

But we are finally loaded, cocked and primed. In order to make a grander effect for the assembled audience, we were strung along the towpath of the canal. Then the colonel gave the order:

"Ready! Aim!—Fire!"

Now I had never shot off a gun in my life. I only knew you had to hold it up to the shoulder and pull the trigger. When the colonel said "aim" my hands shook in a manner that would have made it perfectly safe for a man to stand directly in front of the muzzle. When the order came to "fire" I shut my eyes tight and pulled the trigger!

Bang!

Was I kicked by a mule? A stinging blow on my right shoulder nearly knocked me off my feet, and I thought my arm was dislocated. For a moment I feared I was shot myself. I never knew before that a gun "kicked." It was simply the "kick" of the musket on being discharged. But it was a surprise party for me.

The first man to "fall in an engagement" in the Thirteenth Regiment was Sandy Kidd. When the rackety "volley," about as simultaneous as a pack of exploding firecrackers, had stopped, there lay Sandy Kidd, sprawling on his back at the bottom of the towpath.

He had shot off all the nine cartridges in his gun at once!

CHAPTER V.

MUSTERED IN—DESERTED.

Before the regimental drill was dismissed, Colonel Carman had announced that "dress parade" would be dispensed with that afternoon. Goodness, was there anything more? Is a soldier's work never done?

No, never. From that time on, during all the years of service, whenever in camp, there was that same everlasting routine of guard mount, and squad or company drill in the morning, and a regimental or "battalion" drill (as it was more commonly called) in the afternoon, winding up with the perennial dress parade at 4 or 6 o'clock. A "dress parade" is a guard mount on a larger scale, and is the formal display of "the pomp and panoply of war." But so many people are familiar with "dress parades" that it is unnecessary to describe them.

We were awfully tired that night; but we were aroused to interest by the announcement that on that evening we would "elect our officers."

What a farce! No one in the army ever has a chance to vote for officers. The "election" simply consisted in the reading of a pronunciamento or order that Hugh C. Irish had been elected captain; James G. Scott, first lieutenant, and so on, and that the captain had selected "the following sergeants and corporals." And at the end of it was "Approved—Ezra A. Carman, Colonel Commanding; Charles A. Hopkins, First Lieutenant and Adjutant." That is the way we "elected" our officers.

There was little variation in camp life for several days. It was the same old routine of guard mount and drill, and "fall in for rations." We began to get used to the unwonted exercise and the outdoor air and work was hardening the muscles and improving the general health.

There was a constant stream of visitors, including many ladies; and the latter came around to the tents and chatted to "the boys" with an unconventional familiarity and sisterly affection utterly unknown in ordinary life. This was a new phase of existence that was very interesting. They brought us many luxuries, and some of the boys received big boxes from home, containing pies and cakes and other toothsome things that greatly enhanced our bill of fare. And there was a continuous round of pranks and practical jokes and song singing and amateur entertainments in the evening. till at last we were constrained to exclaim: "Well, this is a picnic!"

On August 24, 1862, the announcement was made that on the following afternoon the Thirteenth Regiment would be "mustered in." This was something new, and created great excitement.

When a man "enlists' he, so to speak, gets into his coffin. When he is "mustered," Undertaker Uncle Sam has put on the lid and screwed it down. When a man deserts the service after being "mustered in" he is shot.

About 3 o'clock the next afternoon the regiment was drawn up as if in dress parade. While somewhat improved in military movements from the four or five days drill, yet it was anything but an imposing spectacle from a professional point of view. The line was straggling and broken and uncertain, and there was a painful absence of that self-possessed nonchalance that characterizes the experienced soldier. But there we stood, 937 of us—38 officers and 899 non-commissioned officers and privates, at parade rest, with the perspiration trickling down our faces and we forbidden to wipe it off!

From the knot of officers gathered at the flank of the parade stepped forth one more gorgeous, more self-possessed, more airish than the others. Ah! he was a man who understood his business! He must be a major-general at least!

Bah! The single strip of bullion at the end of his

shoulder straps indicated that he was nothing but a first lieutenant! And yet he was a First Lieutenant with a capital "L" and a still bigger "F."

Maybe you don't understand the awful dignity that surrounded a "mustering officer," like a dazzling halo! As the drum-major of a band is more gorgeous in make-up than the colonel of a regiment, so is a mustering officer more indescribably magnificent in general bearing than the commander of the whole army. The chief qualification of a mustering officer seemed to be his capacity for putting on airs.

The more airs he could put on the better. No soldier ever heard of a plain, unassuming, courteous mustering officer. It is his business to be otherwise.

The irridescent specimen of military grandeur that dazzled our eyes and filled our hearts with apprehension, as if we were the serfs and he the czar, was, we were told, "Louis D. Watkins, First Lieutenant, Fifth United States Cavalry." A regular officer. Phew! A West Point graduate, perhaps. And a cavalry officer too. The cavalry officers always considered themselves so much higher than infantry officers. In reality they were, in the march—about five feet higher—when mounted.

Behind him was a private soldier with his rifle and another carrying the rolls of the regiment, on which was every man's name, the color of his eyes and hair, his height, complexion, color, age, and "previous condition of servitude."

"At-ten-shun!" commanded he, with that peculiar inflexion only attainable after considerable service.

"Hats off!"

"Hands up!"

When, after much confusion, it was arranged that each man held his hat in his left hand and upheld his right, the mustering officer began:

"Repeat after me the following oath: I, Louis D. Watkins——"

"I, Louis D. Watkins," came the grand chorus from the assembled thousand. I don't know how they ever came to do it so well in concert. It sounded as if it came from one gigantic throat.

"No—no—no," interrupted the mustering officer. "Each man say his own name. Now, I, John Smith—or whatever it may be."

A low murmur of many names followed, as each man pronounced his own, followed by "whatever it may be." John Ick was slow of comprehension, and he came out behind all the rest, and it made everybody laugh to hear his

"May pe!"

Lieutenant Watkins pretended not to notice this unnecessary addition to the oath, but went on:

"Do solemnly——"

"Solemnly," chorused the regiment.

—"Emly," from John Ick.

"Swear that I will bear—" continued the mustering officer.

The regiment responded, while loud and husky came John Ick with his

—"Bear."

"True faith and allegiance."

The nine hundred responded on schedule time—all but John Ick, who nearly upset the whole business with his ringing:

"Vatty elegance."

"To the United States of America," continued the mustering officer.

The regiment responded, and so it went on with the rest of the oath, viz:

—"Against all her enemies whatsoever: That I will obey the orders of the President of the United States and of the officers appointed over me, according to the rules and articles of war. So help me God."

And John Ick came in at the tail end about three words behind as usual. But as if that wasn't enough he added something of his own in the shape of a loud "Amen." He naturally imagined that anything so near like a prayer was not quite complete without an "amen" at the end of it.

The oath, although as ironclad as the whole power and force of the United States government can make it, isn't in itself very long, but the slow process of repetition had necessitated our holding up our hands for what seemed an age, and our arms ached. It was with intense satisfaction and relief therefore that we received the orders:

"Hands down! Hats on!"

The pompous mustering officer, with a show of dignity that would have done credit to a czar or a kaiser, then formally and awfully announced, that he, he—with a big H, Louis D. Watkins, by the authority with which he was vested (and otherwise clothed), then and there and here and now did declare that the officers and men of the Thirteenth Regiment of New Jersey Volunteers were duly mustered into the service of the United States, to serve for the period of three years unless sooner discharged.

The nail was clinched.

The colonel then stepped forward and ordered the officers to approach, which they did, and when standing in front of him in a tolerably straight line, he addressed them in a few words that the rest of us could not hear. As the officers came back to lead their companies to their streets, something on their faces told us all that there was something unusually important on hand.

There was. Before the companies were dismissed the captain informed the men that the situation of affairs at Washington was so precarious that the president had ordered the Thirteenth Regiment to come on at once. Similar orders had been sent to every regiment in the country in process of formation.

"Captain," said one of the men, "we were to have a furlough before we started; we wanted to take our citizens' suits back home and bid our families good-by, and we want to get a few articles to take along with us. Wasn't this understood?"

"Yes," replied Captain Irish; "but in times of war any programme may be changed and all that we have to do is to obey orders."

"Is that fair?" asked John Snyder.

"Don't talk in the ranks," said the captain.

"No, you," said John Ick knowingly, "dond you talk by the ranks, or you'll go by the garthous; ven you carry a stick of dot gord wood up and down for an hour, alreaty, you don talk no more by the ranks, by gum."

"Silence!" shouted the captain.

"Gimminney," said Ick, sotto voce, "I pelief I vas talking mine own selluff, and didn't know it."

The recruits broke ranks with much kicking. They had fully expected a furlough before going to the front. There were ominous whispers and knowing winks that night. Something was up.

In the morning there were not a dozen men in camp. Even the guards had disappeared, leaving their guns sticking bayonet down, in the ground.

Practically the entire regiment had deserted!

What an inglorious end to our career as soldiers! And not mustered in half a day yet.

How it all happened the next chapter will relate.

CHAPTER VI.

THE EVE OF DEPARTURE.

As stated in the preceding chapter, the entire Thirteenth Regiment of New Jersey Volunteers had deserted, almost in a body, at the very first intimation of active service. Not that they were like that famous character:
"First in peace, last in war."
Nor even like that historical militia organization whose first by-law read:
"Resolved, that in case of war, riot or other unpleasant disturbance, this company immediately disbands."
No, it wasn't that. It wasn't cowardice. The boys simply "wanted to go home." (They wanted to go home many another time before their three years were up, but didn't have the opportunity.) And we believe it is an historical fact that this was the only instance during the war where eight or nine hundred men deserted and were not only not punished, but were not even reprimanded.

It could hardly be called desertion. The boys simply wanted to go home, and they went. They could hardly be blamed. All had enlisted and hurried off to camp with quite a distinct understanding that they should have a furlough long enough to fix up things at home, and this idea of being so suddenly and unceremoniously projected to the very scene of conflict completely upset them.

The regiment deserted, so to speak, in squads. We had previously arranged our respective coteries; "Davy" Harris, "Pop" Snyder and I were one of the groups arranged in trios, and along toward midnight we marched out of camp. One of Company C's men was on guard at the post we had to pass. It did not take him long to stick his bayonet in the ground and join us.

We took the towpath and walked up to Paterson along the canal bank, arriving there at 4 or 5 o'clock in the evening. It took about twenty-four hours to arrange our affairs and say good-by to our friends for the last time. It didn't take me long to settle up my affairs. I deposited with a relative the new suit of clothes I had just bought, and wrote a letter to my father, who lived in another State, that I had enlisted.

Let me tell you about that suit of clothes. It was in the latest fashion. The coat was of a Prince Albert pattern, but it came down to about halfway between the knees and heels. It was black and white, in squares, each one of the squares being as big as the square of a checkerboard. The length of the coat was something like the dude fashion of the present time. But during the four years I was away fashions had changed to plain, dark colors, and the coat tail had been abbreviated. Had I appeared on the streets in that suit after the war, I would have been mobbed.

The changes in fashions are so gradual that they are hardly noticed. But bury yourself, mentally, for four years, and the change will be startling. We think nothing of the absurd wings the ladies wear now, but had that ridiculous fashion been projected upon us in all its ugliness without an evolutionary endurance—like cutting off a dog's tail by inches—we should have been startled, to say the least. So that stylish suit, which had cost me twenty-one weeks' wages, was utterly useless after the war was over.

But this is a digression. I didn't have to save my money for clothes now. Uncle Sam furnished them. As the late Tune Van Iderstine used to say, there was "Plenty for to eat (usually) plenty for to drink (that is, soft drinks) and nothing for to pay." Besides all this we were paid the munificent wages of thirteen dollars a month—which usually went to sutler or poker, of which more anon.

We straggled back to camp, and in two days every man was back again. We expected to be at least scolded, if not actually punished; but not a word was said to us about our "desertion."

There was a more serious look on the men's faces this time than there was the first time they left home. The farewell had been more sorrowful, for it was known to be the last time they would meet their loved ones for many months—perhaps years—perhaps forever. Somehow it had at first been a sort of picnic—a few days' excursion. Now we began to realize that it really "meant business."

But a soldier's downheartedness doesn't last long. We were kept busy with the final arrangements. We "men" expected to be ordered to start every moment. We were kept in ignorance, in accordance with "army discipline." Only the officers knew we were not to start before Sunday.

On Friday we went through that pleasant and delusive experience that all regiments went through. We were presented with a flag by the ladies. Flag presentations were too common in those days to indulge in silk. It was an ordinary everyday bunting flag. A clergyman made the speech for the ladies and the colonel responded for the regiment.

I think I felt then my first thrill of patriotism. The stars and stripes never before looked as they did then. As the breeze rippled through the folds it seemed as if a patriotic luster emanated from the ensign, and a vague idea that I would some day see that flag dimly outlined through the smoke and fire of battle made the blood jump through my veins.

And the ladies, God bless them! They looked so pretty and sweet, so loyal and yet so tender, that it aroused one's manhood to a sense of duty in defending them. I never was a hero. I was naturally a coward. But I felt brave just then and mentally resolved that I would never do aught to be ashamed of.

A similar feeling must have pervaded the entire regiment, for it gave vent to loud and enthusiastic cheers at the conclusion of the presentation.

"I never saw the flag look so beautiful as it did to-day," said John Stansfield, as he unbuckled his belt.

"Dott all ri-et, you," said John Ick. "But it doud look so beautiful one of dese days, I doud tink. I vash thinking dot plue is like how plue we vill all pe pefore ve gits home alretty, and de ret stripes—dot vash plood. We vas all going to ein schlaughter haus."

Despite this sanguinary prediction, Ick's remarks created a laugh, and from that time on, forever afterward, he was called "Slaughter House Ike."

On Friday it began to look like business; about one hundred men were yet missing and patrols were sent out to capture them, wherever found, and bring them in. The announcement in the Newark *Advertiser* that the Thirteenth was about to start brought crowds of visitors to camp, a large proportion of them being ladies.

On Saturday evening, August 30, 1862, the boys received word that they would start the next (Sunday) morning for the front!

Immediately the camp became a scene of great excitement and hilariousness.

CHAPTER VII.

OFF FOR THE FRONT.

When "reveille" sounded in Camp Frelinghuysen on Sunday morning, August 31, 1862, no one was awakened. Everybody was already up and filled with excitement over the approaching departure for "the front." A busy scene was enacted. Everybody was packing up. The men were wondering how to get into their knapsacks besides the clothing Uncle Sam provided them, such things as canned preserves, towels, looking-glasses, shaving outfits and a hundred and one other things from loving ones at home—even to embroidered slippers!

It was no go. The knapsack would scarcely hold the regular outfit, let alone other things. The parsimony of the government in providing such limited "trunks" was vigorously criticized, little knowing that before long we should be more than convinced that the knapsacks were altogether too large and too heavy.

But the problem was solved by packing the superfluous luxuries into barrels and boxes. We had a vague idea that they would come along with the baggage. Innocent souls that we were. Somebody must have had a feast. We never saw those things again.

We filled our haversacks with "grub" from the "cook house" and our canteens with water from the canal, and when everything was in readiness we tried on our "things."

Phew! Here was another thing we hadn't counted upon. That we were to be "pack mules" had never entered our heads. Contemplate the array:

First, our thick clothes (with the scratchy shirt and

stockings); then a broad leather belt extending from the right shoulder to the left hip; then a body belt, upon which was a leather percussion cap box on the front and a heavy cartridge box on the right hip—a box containing forty rounds of ball cartridges in a tin case—the whole weighing several pounds. Then there was the bulgy haversack, on the right hip, hanging by a strap from the left shoulder, while on the reverse side was the canteen, suspended from a strap which ran over the right shoulder. Then came the knapsack, like the hump on Pilgrim's back, hanging from straps over both shoulders and steadied by another strap that extended over the breast. On the equipments were brass eagles and brass plates with "U. S," upon them. The knapsack was packed as full as it could be, and in straps on the top were the rubber and woolen blankets tightly rolled, while the overcoat was strapped to the back.

This was "heavy marching order." Add the rifle, weighing about nine pounds, and you have the complete soldier. All you can see is his face and legs, and a lot of straps and bundles and bags with a gleaming bayonet sticking up alongside the right shoulder. Thus arrayed and equipped, the load that a soldier had to carry was about sixty pounds. Imagine yourself walking thirty miles a day and carrying sixty pounds of baggage.

A momentary trial of this load was enough. Every man threw off his knapsack completely discouraged.

We were confronted with a condition utterly unforeseen. Had there been an opportunity to test this layout in Captain Irish's recruiting office, the probability is that not a single man would have enlisted!

Poor John Ick expressed the sentiment of Company K when he threw his knapsack down on the ground and exclaimed:

"Mine gott, poys. Dot vash de camel vot proke de straw's pack. I vash going heim. I don'd vant to be a soldier sometimes any more, alretty."

But it was too late to go home now. We were going away from home, and the evidences of our departure were too painfully apparent all around us.

Solemn-faced men were embracing and kissing crying women and children all over the camp, and even some of the men were crying, not so much, perhaps, on their own account, as from sympathy with the really bereaved wives, mothers and daughters. No man likes to see a woman cry, but under ordinary conditions it affects different men in different ways. A woman's tears, to some men, is a signal for immediate capitulation. To others it has an irresistibly irritating effect. But when a woman cries from pure grief—and not from petulance, anger or hysteria—then it strikes a sympathetic chord in the male breast, and he whose eyes are not moist under such circumstances is a brute. In the economy of nature it is only a brute that cannot laugh or cry.

So it was not unmanly to see great, strong men weep, because their wives, their mothers, their sweethearts wept. No one knew when they should meet again. Perhaps never. To some, it was never.

But there is no time for long-drawn-out sentiment in war. The final farewells were terminated by the order to—

"Fall in!"

In a short time the regiment was formed and the order was given to march. A wild huzza arose from several thousand throats as the Thirteenth New Jersey filed out of the entrance to Camp Frelinghuysen, which the soldiers were to see for the last time. The regiment was marched down through Orange Street to Broad, followed by an immense crowd of people. It was a Sunday, but it was totally unlike an ordinary Sunday in Newark, for the whole city was out as if on a holiday.

A short halt was made at Washington Park, for a little rest. And "green" troops that we were, we greatly needed it. The day was atrociously hot. The sun poured down its pitiless rays until the backs of our necks were blistered. The straps from our knapsacks and accouterments had begun to cut into the uncalloused flesh of our shoulders, and the awful load we carried fatigued us greatly. The cobble stones with which Broad Street was then paved seemed unnaturally high, round and uneven.

We were marched to the Chestnut Street depot, where the train was supposed to be ready. It wasn't. No one ever knew of an army train being on time. It was a special, made up of the cheapest, dirtiest, oldest cars of the road—"The New Jersey Railroad and Transportation Company"—a part of the "Camden and Amboy" system. The "Pennsylvania" was as yet unheard of—at least in New Jersey.

There were more farewells. Venders of knickknacks, and particularly of cool drinks, did a thriving business. A milkman came along, and soon his cans were empty. As my father handed me an overflowing glass of milk, I looked upon his face for the last time. Before the war was ended he had given his life to his country.

It was a solemn crowd. The first boisterousness had disappeared. The sorrowful, tearful farewells had a depressing effect. The news from the front was not cheerful. Even at that moment a great battle was in progress, and not very many miles from Washington.

And yet there were laughable scenes. I will tell you one. It relates to James O. Smith, afterward connected with the New York *Commercial Advertiser*. Smith was a Newark boy, a jolly fellow, as he is to this day. He is one of those men who never grow old. Well, Smith's mother and his best girl and her mother were looking around for Jim to bid him a last good-by, and Jim was watching for their expected appearance. Just then a beautiful little German girl came up, and intently gazing upon Smith for a moment, stepped up and asked:

"Vas you going to go avay?"

"Yes," answered Jim, "I am going to the front."

"Vell," answered the little German girl, "I vas so sorry."

And thereupon she put her hands on Smith's shoulders, and leaning her face down upon them, began to cry as if her heart would break.

Now James O. Smith said then, and he says yet, that he would pledge his word of honor as a man, as a gentleman and as a soldier, that never in the whole course of his life had he ever laid eyes on that pretty little German girl before. But imagine his predicament when, just at that particular moment, up stepped his own, his genuine best girl, with her mother!

And before Jim could explain the truth the order was received to board the the train.

With a yell, a hurrah and a general racket the members of the Thirteenth climbed upon the cars. Every window was closely shut, and the air was stifling. As usual, the windows were stuck fast and could not be budged. Then, as if seized with the inspiration that a soldier's duty was to destroy, smash went every window in every one of the fourteen or fifteen cars composing the "special" train. It was done with the butt ends of the rifles. There was plenty of air after that. The officers tried to expostulate, but it was too late.

It took a long time to get on the "baggage" and other things necessary and in the meanwhile the boys were chatting through the broken glass windows with their friends outside. Jim Smith was apparently having much difficulty in convincing his real girl that his encounter with that pretty little German girl was only an accidental meeting. Whether he succeeded in putting himself right no one ever knew.

A long blast of the whistle. A last, superfluous cry of "all aboard." A slight movement of the train. We were off.

"Hurrah for the Thirteenth Regiment!" said some one in the crowd. A wild hurrah from six thousand throats arose in the torrid atmosphere of that hot Sunday noon of August 31, 1862.

"Hurrah for the ladies of Newark!" shouted a soldier. And the cars quivered with the shout.

The people shouted again in chorus, and the air was filled with Godsends and "good-by, Johns" and "good-by, Bills," while outside the cars pandemonium reigned supreme.

And thus it was, with a whoop and a shout, that the Thirteenth Regiment of New Jersey Volunteers started off for that mysterious, that awful, that unknown destination comprehensively termed "The Front."

Alas! If some of them had known what they had to go through ere they again saw the city of Newark, they would have felt disposed to have thrown themselves under the car wheels and been crushed to jelly.

CHAPTER VIII.

WASHINGTON AND LINCOLN.

Those who have been on a target excursion know what sort of a scene is enacted on the cars going to and returning from a day's pleasure. I can liken that journey of the Thirteenth Regiment from Newark to Philadelphia, to nothing but a gigantic excursion. Perhaps there was the more indulgence in boisterousness as a sort of offset to the gloomy features of the farewell. All the songs that the boys knew, and some that they didn't know, were sung, and when the supply was exhausted they were sung over again. There were anecdotes and stories told, practical jokes perpetrated, and whenever any one began to look sober and solemn he was selected as a victim.

It seemed as if we had cut loose from everything, as it were—from the world, the conventional routine of life, from restraining influences, from civilization. And so it was to a greater extent than we knew then, for the fact must be told that away from the influence of society, of woman, man becomes a brute. He loses all the little niceties and amenities of humanity and quickly deteriorates into a savage. Another proof of Darwinism. Who knows, were we all turned out into the woods, how long it would be before tails began to sprout!

No such philosophical turn, however, entered the minds of the boisterous crowd that kept up the racket all the way to the southern boundaries of the State. The train went through Trenton and Bordentown, and entered Philadelphia via Camden. It was about dusk when we crossed the Delaware in ferry boats that sailed between the two halves of Smith's Island, and were at last in the city of Brotherly Love.

"Philadelphia." "Brotherly Love."

How sweet are the memories that hover around these names to every old soldier. No city loved the soldier more, or did more for the soldier, than Philadelphia. Every building large enough was already an hospital. Every fire engine had its ambulance, in the gorgeous decoration of which vehicles the different companies vied with each other until their ingenuity for something more handsome was exhausted.

One of the institutions of Philadelphia was "The Soldiers' Rest." It was a large structure, as big as the train shed at a railroad terminus. When a new regiment passed through the city on the way to the front, it was provided with a meal little short of a banquet. The men were seated at tables provided with table cloths and crockery—real crockery, not tinware. The soldiers were waited upon by young ladies, pretty ones too.

"Oh, my jimminey, put I vas glad I come to de war!" enthusiastically exclaimed John Ick.

John expressed the sentiment of all of us. We began to think that, if the further south we went the better we fared, by the time we reached the front we would have a regular picnic. Alas, we didn't stop to remember that the last thing done to a Thanksgiving turkey is to gorge him with chestnuts.

But, seriously, the old soldier will never forget Philadelphia hospitality. But it was the jumping off place. Between the City of Brotherly Love and Baltimore there was a gap, a chasm. For right there was located somewhere the dividing line, on one side of which a soldier was considered a patriot, a gentleman, and on the other side regarded merely as a soulless machine.

We bade adieu to Philadelphia late that night with a salvo of cheers.

Alas for human consistency. The last man to get on the cars was Jim Smith. In fact he came near being left in consequence of his lingering flirtation with a pretty Philadelphia girl. And so soon after his encounter with his own true love—and that beautiful little German girl.

The ride to Baltimore was through the night. At

Havre de Grace the cars in those days crossed on a big ferryboat. There were no bridges yet. The switches were choked with troop-laden trains, and we had to wait three hours for our turn on the ferry-boat. And, by the way, it was the first time for nearly all of us to see a locomotive and train cross a wide river on a boat. It was morning when we reached Baltimore. Here we had breakfast.

Breakfast? Ugh!

We had passed the "dividing line." We were in a State only semiloyal. Indeed bloody riots had occurred in the streets of Baltimore, caused by rebel sympathizers attacking passing regiments. As we disembarked we were quietly ordered to load our rifles—with bullets! It began to look like business.

But that breakfast! It was in a shed. The coffee was black and nasty—about as much flavor to it as mud. We had soft bread that was slack-baked—half-dough. And the meat! We were formally introduced to "salt horse!"

"Vot sort of meat you calls that?" asked the irrepressible John Ick, who wanted to know everything. The waiter was a soldier who had seen some service.

"Salt junk," replied he.

"Salt yunk. Vot vas dot, alretty?" asked John. "Dot looks like old dried-up liverworst."

John attempted to take a mouthful. There were no knives or forks, and he held it in his hand. It was tougher than sole leather. It was what Rider Haggard would call "biltong."

"Ugh!" exclaimed John, spitting out the salty stuff and pushing the unsavory mess away from him. "Take it avay. Bring me some peefsteaks."

"Eat that or nothing," said the soldier.

"I no eat dot," replied Ick angrily. "You vas ein shysterpoop. You vas a old seseshel, and py gimmeny I can lick you quicker'n——"

John had got up to fight. Sergeant Wells came to see what the disturbance was about.

"Dot old schweinigel, Mister Wells, he told me to eat dot or nothing. I doand like dot, alretty. Look by dot meat, dot—vot he callem—salt yunk. Und ven I ask him to pring me some peefsteaks, he tole me to eat dot or nothing, ain't it."

"You must keep quiet, John," said Wells. "That's the regulation army food."

"I don'd vant no reggellashen grub, I vant some peefsteaks, dot's vat I vant."

"There's no beefsteak here, John. You keep quiet, or you'll get in trouble."

"I'll go straight heim, dot's vot I vill."

"Keep still."

"Vait vounce till I get you outside, you old pumpernickel," shouted the irate Ick, shaking his fist across the table. Then he quieted down, rather to everybody's surprise.

John Ick only expressed the feelings of the others. Oh, for a good, tender, juicy beefsteak. Salt horse, muddy coffee and black bread! What a menu! The coffee was served in tin cups. The bread and meat were laid on the bare board that served as a table and which had evidently not been washed since it was made.

The "Soldiers' Retreat," as this inhospitable place was called, was near the depot. We were compelled to sit or stand around there all day. Armed guards prevented our going out "to see the town." We had to take our dinner and supper—both of which were similar to the breakfast—in that miserable place. About dark we were told that the train was ready.

And what a train! Hitherto we had traveled in passenger cars, poor though they were. Now we were piled into old freight cars. We were getting to a part of the country where war was war and a soldier nothing more than an animated piece of the machinery of war. It was simply "anyway to get there," now. Rough board seats were built across the cars and we were huddled in like so many sheep. Auger holes bored through the sides afforded what little ventilation there was. As it was, we were nearly stifled.

With a series of stops and jerks as the bumpers of the old-fashioned coupled freight cars jammed together, we passed a miserable, restless, sleepless six hours, during which the rebels, the army, the government, the railroad, the officers and everything else were unsparingly anathematized, and we kicked ourselves that we were ever such fools as to enlist. Only for the irresistibly comical vigor of the curses of John Ick, which somewhat amused us, we would have died.

Washington!

We arrived at last. Our first impressions of the great capital were anything but pleasant. It was in the middle of the night. We were marched through and over a lot of switches and sidings, and finally entered what seemed to be a large freight house. Here we spread our blankets and lay down. We were so tired out that we couldn't help sleeping soundly.

I was awakened early, as were my comrades. We found that the place was another of those "Soldiers' Retreats." The breakfast was served *à la* Baltimore. After breakfast I obtained permission to be absent from camp for two hours and with three or four comrades went to see that Mecca of every true American, the capitol building.

The capitol was scarcely like what it is now. The grounds were in a state of chaos. The dome was but partially completed; on its top was a gigantic derrick, just as the workmen left it when the government had other calls for its money than erecting marble buildings and glass domes.

I climbed up into the rotunda, that was comparatively finished—partially in the same shape as now, except that only a portion of the pictures were painted —those pictures that subsequently became so familiar on the back of the national currency.

With opened-mouthed wonder, and mind filled with historical recollections thus so plainly brought face to face, I was gazing up toward the unfinished dome, when I felt a hearty slap on my shoulder.

"Good-morning, my boy!"

I turned to look. I was almost paralyzed. It seemed as if the dead had come to life. Did the reader ever experience the sensation of meeting for the first time some great man whose picture was as familiar as a dining-room clock? It seems as if you had encountered an apparition.

Mind you, it was 6 o'clock in the morning. I was

"only a private." But there at that early hour, standing in front of me, was a tall, gaunt figure whose features were familiar to every man and woman, every boy and girl, in the country.

It was no less a personage than Abraham Lincoln, the President of the United States!

CHAPTER IX.

PRESIDENT AND PRIVATE.

President Lincoln!
Now any one who has been in the army knows that it is a rather extraordinary thing for a mere private soldier to come face to face with the President of the United States, the great commander of the whole army and navy. And it was more extraordinary that such an encounter should occur almost at the moment the aforesaid private soldier arrived in Washington—and at 6 o'clock in the morning at that.

I had, of course, never seen Lincoln before, but his face was as familiar through popular portraits as General Grant's subsequently was. Besides hadn't I, in the fall of '60, fed into the press at the *Guardian* office over forty thousand election tickets bearing the picture of Abraham Lincoln?

There he stood, tall, gaunt, pale, in a somber suit of black. His face wore an anxious look that accentuated that familiar wart on his cheek. And he was indeed anxious. The rebels were, so to speak, almost at the very gates of the national capital. There wasn't much sleep for anybody. The president had hurriedly telegraphed for every available volunteer. He was on hand to see how many had come. He was like a boy who cannot wait for daylight on Christmas morning, but surreptitiously gets up in his nightshirt to take a glance at his stocking by the mantelpiece. This explains why President Lincoln, with one or two other men—I don't know who they were—was at the capitol so early that Monday morning, September 1, 1862.

"Good-morning, my boy," said he as I turned to see who had slapped me so familiarly on the shoulder.

And as I turned and instantly recognized him, as just explained, I was almost paralyzed with amazement, I might say, terror. Who wouldn't be under the circumstances?

"G-g-good-morning," I stammered, "are—aren't you the p-p-president?"

"Yes, my boy," said he, encouragingly, seeing my embarrassment, and taking me kindly by the hand, as a grave smile passed over his pale face. "Yes, I am the president—the president of a distressed country. We want you now, my lad, and a good many like you. You are from New Jersey?"

"Y-y-yes, sir."

"The Thirteenth New Jersey?"

"Yes, sir," I answered, the surprise that he should know the number of my regiment somewhat overshadowing my embarrassment.

"Who is your colonel?" he asked.

"Colonel Carman."

"Oh, yes, I remember," said Mr. Lincoln.

And that he should know or remember the name of our colonel, when there were so many colonels and regiments gave me another surprise.

"How strong is your regiment?"

"About nine hundred, I believe, sir."

"Are there any more troops on the way?"

"Yes, sir; lots of them; but I don't know how many, sir."

"You don't know where they are from, I suppose?"

"No, sir," I replied, "but I heard some of them calling each other 'Hoosiers' and 'Suckers,' so that I suppose they are from Indiana and Illinois."

The president laughed, and a quizzical look passed over his face as he asked:

"So they call the men from Illinois 'suckers,' do they?"

"Yes, sir," I replied, proud of my knowledge of State nomenclature.

"Well, you know I'm from Illinois?"

I thought I would sink through the marble floor of the rotunda.

"Oh—oh—M-m-mister President," I stammered,

while I felt the hot blood rushing to the roots of my hair, "I d-d-didn't mean——"

"That's all right, my boy," he said, with a reassuring smile. "I was only joking."

I had of course heard a good deal about "Abe" Lincoln's jokes; but I never thought he would work one on me. I didn't laugh at it a little bit—at least not just then.

Mr. Lincoln then asked my name, residence and occupation, and seemed to take a remarkable interest in an obscure stranger—nothing but a common private. He took my hand for a good-by, when I reminded him that there were several other Jersey boys standing behind me, who would no doubt feel honored to shake hands with the President of the United States.

"I did not intend to miss them," said Mr. Lincoln. "Every soldier is my friend and my brother. We are all soldiers now, in a common cause. God bless you all."

Then he shook hands and said a pleasant word to every blue-coated recruit in the rotunda. A couple of distinguished-looking officers came in and interrupted proceedings, and after a word or so with them he started off in their company. We followed him to the top of the then unfinished eastern stairway, down which he went and walked over toward the old Capitol Prison.

The familiar, friendly way in which the President had greeted us had captivated us entirely. The magnificent, though unfinished capitol building had no attractions for us after that. We had seen and spoken to a real, live president, and from that moment every one of us felt like giving his life, if necessary, in defense of a country with such a ruler. There is that in every citizen that enhances his loyalty at the sight of his ruler's person.

We hurried back to the "Retreat" to tell of our adventure. Every word of that conversation was impressed on my mind and it is there to-day as fresh as it was on the day it took place. Of course it created a sensation among my comrades. We told it to Company K, and then Captain Irish sent for us and we had to repeat it to him. Then we received a message from the colonel, and were required to relate it all over again for his information.

"The boys who talked with the president" were the heroes of the day. As for myself I think I grew about two inches taller. I thought I ought to be promoted at once, and imagined the colonel would make me a corporal at least. But he didn't.

I met President Lincoln personally several times after that. I would have felt sad just then had I known that the last service I should be called upon to render him would be to stand guard over Abraham Lincoln's murdered body. I did.

I was soon brought down from my sublime height of imaginary importance by hearing Sergeant Heber Wells' order:

"Fall in, boys. We're ordered to go over to Virginia at once."

CHAPTER X.

IN OLD VARGINNY.

There was a good deal of humbug and mild deception in the army, as everywhere else, and one example is the way in which the innocent credulity of nearly every volunteer was played upon. Probably there never was an Eastern regiment that did not start out with a sort of understanding, either tacit or expressed, that it was to be specially favored. It was generally to the effect that the colonel had "a pull" with the powers that were, and that that particular regiment, instead of long marches and hard fighting, was to be detailed for guard duty at Washington or some similar snap, relieving some other regiment of more experience.

Such an impression prevailed in the Thirteenth Regiment, and there seemed to be some ground for it, for surely the government would not send to the front a lot of men who had had scarcely any drilling and the most of the members of which hardly knew how to load and fire a gun. But all this dreamy, pic-nicky prospect was scattered to the four winds by the peremptory order to get ready to march over into Virginia.

"Dot is a shame," exclaimed the irrepressible John Ick. "I'll no go. Dose fellers don't get me by no schlaughter-haus, py hooky."

"Oh, you're always a-croakin'! ye cranky old Dutchman," retorted Reddy Mahar; "shut up wid ye?"

"Whose a granky old Deutschman?" answered Ick angrily, "you are a old Irish red head, dot's vat you vash, und I don't care, needer."

"Ye're afraid, that's phwat ye are," said Reddy.

"You vash anudder, alretty."

"Ye're a coward, ye spalpeen."

"Whose a gowyard, Irish? Don' you gall me dot py jimminy."

"That's phwat ye are," reiterated Reddy, "always prating about slaughter house and sich. Ye must ha' been dhrunk when ye 'listed, or ye wouldn't been here."

"You vas von liar."

Reddy dropped his knapsack and went for "Slaughter House" Ick. The latter had got his arm twisted up in the strap of his knapsack somehow, and was caught at a disadvantage. He was helpless and could not parry the blow that Reddy landed between his eyes. Ick, handicapped as he was, threw himself bodily upon Reddy, and the two went down together. In falling the two belligerents tumbled against Sandy Kidd and the three went down into a heap. Then the others gathered around to witness an exceedingly lively rough-and-tumble fight. Hank Van Orden and some others jumped in to interfere and for a moment it resembled a riot.

Captain Irish rushed up to the scene, furious. It was the first case of disorder that had occurred in the regiment, and he regarded it as an ineffable disgrace to Company K. He was too angry to listen to details, and ordered under arrest not only Ick and Mahar, but Van Orden and Kidd as well, in spite of the latter's protests. The two innocent men were subsequently released, but Ick and Mahar had to carry two muskets for the rest of the day as a punishment. And any old soldier will tell you that it is no fun to carry two heavy rifles, in addition to all the legitimate baggage of a private.

When the matter was reported to Colonel Carman he laconically remarked:

"They'll get over that nonsense. They'll have all the fighting they want before they are home again, I guess."

"But you can put down the fact, colonel," replied Lieutenant Scott, "that Company K was the first in a fight."

The colonel smiled, shifted his "chew," and strode away. Soon after we were on the march.

Our orders were to proceed to "Fort Ward," wherever that might be. None of us knew, of course, except that it was over in "Old Varginny." We marched through some back streets of the capital city until we came to the famous "Long Bridge." And let me say that Washington was not then the magnificent city that it is now. The streets were paved with cobble stones or were mere dirt—not with the asphalt of to-day. What is now the beautiful park back of the White House was then nothing but a swamp. The Washington monument was not half completed. Work had been stopped on it for a great many years. Visitors to the capital now can tell its height then by the dirty appearance of the stone on the lower half. The upper and more recently completed part looks whiter and cleaner.

We crossed the Long Bridge and during the afternoon made our first foot tracks in the dusty roads of Virginia's sacred soil. The general color of Virginia soil is brick red. In summer it is an impalpable dust. In winter it is mud—and such mud! The possibilities of its depth are limitless, while its consistency ranges from paste to dough. When we arrived the dust season was at its height.

We didn't go to Fort Ward, but to Fort Richardson. But it didn't matter. The difference was only in name. It was simply a row of embankments, hastily thrown up. It was on Arlington Heights, just across the river from Washington. These so-called fortifications (still there) were made for the protection of the capital, the idea being then that the enemy was close at hand and that it would be the scene of a battle in a day or so.

It was close enough to the city for visitors and fakirs. The latter's name was legion. They sold all sorts of useful and useless things to the soldier, the only one of which that was any good being a combined pocket knife, fork and spoon. No soldier ever had cause to regret buying one of these useful articles. All the other things were humbugs.

The tintype fiend was also numerously in evidence, and there were few who didn't have "their pictures took" in warlike array to send home to admiring and awestruck friends and relatives.

But where was the baggage? Where were the tents? Not a sign of them, and night was approaching. Jakey Engle cooked our beans and made our coffee on time, but there were no signs of sleeping accommodations. There was a general "kick." The Thirteenth Regiment then and there began the kicking that they kept up till the end of the war. There was an old saying in the army that a soldier who didn't kick was no good. In that particular sense there was no regiment in the army that filled the requirements of good soldiers to a greater extent than the Thirteenth New Jersey.

For the first time in the lives of the most of us we went to bed outdoors on the bare ground, with nothing over us except the stars. It is a singular sensation to wake up in the night, chilled to the bone, and see the bright stars overhead.

Many a man wished that night that he was between the sheets of his comfortable bed at home. Patriotism was at ebb tide, and at heart there were very few who were not sorry they had enlisted.

"Wouldn't you rather be setting type for an extra in the *Guardian* office?" asked Davy Harris.

I honestly confessed that I would indeed.

"Don't get downhearted, boys," said John Stansfield. "We have only 1,087 more days to serve."

"What's that?"

"I say we have only 1,087 more days to serve. You see we enlisted for three years. That is 1,095 days. We have been mustered in eight days. That leaves 1,087 yet to serve."

"Oh, but you know," said Harris, "that we enlisted 'for three years unless sooner discharged,' and as the war won't last three years——"

"Don't calculate too much on that," interrupted Stansfield. "I believe it is going to take more than three years to settle this thing."

This was a dampening remark. I don't believe a single one of the men imagined when he enlisted that the war would last one year, let alone three. Such language was not calculated to make us very cheerful.

And yet John Stansfield was pretty near right. It lacked only a few weeks of three years when the Thirteenth Regiment was mustered out because their "services were no longer required."

As to Stansfield's calculations: I don't believe there

was a soldier in the army who did not, every night, mentally count up how many days had elapsed since his enlistment, and "how many more days he had to serve." This phase of the case certainly shows that army life was not as enjoyable as some people think it was. They counted the days yet remaining before they would be discharged, the same as a convict does the remaining days of his imprisonment.

As we lay there on the hard Virginia soil that night, with the sky for a counterpane and the bright stars for night lamps, not one appreciated the magnitude of the struggle. Not one dreamed that the North would require 1,500,000 soldiers before the rebellion was suppressed; that there would be 300,000 men killed; that there would be between 400,000 and 500,000 wounded; that the number who died from disease or exposure or were included under that wonderful and mysterious heading of "missing," would aggregate some 300,000 more!

These are frightful statistics, but they are approximately true. So sleep on in ignorance of the awful times to come! Dream of home, soldier!

And so we slept.

CHAPTER XI.

A RETREATING ARMY.

In the morning we were awakened by the mighty tread of a moving army. And what an army! Thousands upon thousands of men, whose dirty, filthy clothes made a sorry contrast with our bright new uniforms; men with dirty, unkempt hair, worn out and pinched. None of them carried knapsacks—nothing but a rolled blanket hanging over one shoulder and tied under the arms on the other side with a string. They resembled horse collars. We wondered why this was done—why they had discarded their knapsacks. We learned that later.

There were troops and troops of cavalry and mounted officers. There was an apparently interminable string of flying artillery. And as for the army wagons, each drawn by six braying mules, there was simply no end of them.

But there was something else! Blood!

Hundreds of two-wheeled ambulances came along; glancing in we saw the form of a motionless soldier, or perhaps two of them, and each one wearing a blood stained bandage somewhere. There were soldiers minus legs, soldiers minus arms, soldiers whose heads were so swathed that only the eyes could be seen.

On foot were, seemingly, myriads of soldiers less severely wounded, with bandages on their heads, with their arms in slings, and not a white bandage could be seen without the stain of blood oozing through. John Ick's remark about a "slaughter house" was verified.

We encountered some Paterson boys in the passing army—boys who had enlisted in the earlier regiments.

They were already veterans. Many had "smelled powder." They had seen a battle. In fact they had been in a battle, and had been wounded. The privates didn't know it, but the army was even then on the retreat, and falling back on Washington. The very capital was threatened.

Soldiers who participate in a battle don't know where they are or what it is named. Historians give names to battlefields. The one that had just taken place is now known as "The Second Bull Run." Twice the Army of the Potomac had been defeated on the same ground at Manassas.

This battle was fought on August 29 and 30, 1862.

It was this battle that caused the peremptory telegraphic order for us to leave Camp Frelinghuysen at once.

And on Monday night, September 1st, while we were on the way the maneuvering of the armies precipitated a second conflict between Hill's and Ewell's divisions of Stonewall Jackson's troops on the Confederate side, and the Union commands of Reno, Hooker and Kearny. It was what was subsequently called the battle of Chantilly. History tells us that one of Reno's divisions was forced back in disorder, whereupon the intrepid Kearny sent Birney's brigade to repair the break. A gap still remained on Birney's right, and Kearny galloped forward to reconnoiter.

It was here that the gallant Phil Kearny lost his life. He had already lost an arm in a previous battle, and more than once the soldiers saw him leading a charge with his sword between his teeth, and guiding his horse with his only hand. He was courageous to the degree of recklessness. Unknowingly he penetrated the enemy's lines and was killed. In grateful remembrance of his services the State of New Jersey erected a handsome bronze monument, which for a time stood in the State House at Trenton, but which now stands in one of the parks on Broad Street, Newark.

After the battle of Chantilly the Army of the Potomac fell back within the fortifications of Washington. It was this "falling back" that the Thirteenth Regiment encountered a day or so after they had left their mustering camp in Newark.

It was expected then and there that General Lee and

his whole army would be upon us in a few hours, and we raw recruits were told that we would likely have a battle soon. Was I frightened? Wasn't I? I can't speak for the others, but as for myself I thought surely that my days were numbered. When I enlisted I had a remote idea that I might possibly, some day in the far-off future, see a real battle; but this suddenness was too much, and I was completely upset. The sight of the vast retreating army; the awful spectacle of the blood stained wounded; the prospects of an immediate battle—well, it scared the whole lot of us.

"Scared," is the correct word. We were thoroughly scared. And let me say right here that the man who says he was not scared on the eve of a battle is a liar.

"You'll be sick of it before you're in it long," said one of the veteran Jerseymen.

"We're sick of it already," was the reply.

And we were. If there had been any back way to sneak home, I believe the whole lot of us would have sneaked. Why did we enlist? Why were we such fools? As for myself, I looked back over the previous few days and traced it to the pound of cheese I had carried around to Mr. Pennington's house. I never looked at a piece of cheese without thinking of it. My war experience and cheese are indissolubly connected.

But General Lee and his army didn't chase us clear into Washington. Lee turned his face northward in search of new fields to conquer. Day after day passed, and no enemy appeared, no fighting was done. Doubtless the "big guns" knew what was going on, but we privates were in ignorance. Privates never know anything. They simply do as they are told. From the moment they enlist they are shackled slaves, and some of the officers were worse slave-drivers than ever cudgeled a plantation negro.

The first scare soon wore off. It is always so with an averted or delayed danger. For several days we had things easy. Our belated Sibley tents arrived from somewhere, the weather was fine, and we were comfortable, to say the least. We mingled with the old Jersey soldiers and listened to their stories with interest—and consternation. They soon convinced us that our enlistment was not likely to be "a season of pleasure and victorious conquest," but that we were about to undergo hardships and sufferings then unknown to all but veterans.

Congress was in session, then day and night, and some of us went over on passes and saw the lawmakers at work. I became acquainted with Senator McDougall, previously governor of California. I don't remember exactly how it was, but somehow he took a notion to me, and afterward proved a friend.

It was not all play, however. We were put through much drilling, and kept at work with the pick and shovel throwing up earthworks until our soft hands were blistered. It is a big jump from setting type to digging trenches.

"Sure'n I didn't 'list for this," said Reddy Mahar, one afternoon, "I 'listed to fight the Johnny Rebs, and not to dig holes in the ground. Be jabers, oim going to sthrike!"

Lem Smith was of similar opinion. John Ick thought it was a little better than a slaughter house anyway. Jack Butterworth said it was harder than turning bobbins in Daggers & Row's shop. Curt Bowne thought it a shame. Discontent ruled the whole line.

So an "indignation meeting" was held, and a committee appointed to "wait on the colonel." The colonel said he had nothing to do with privates; all complaints must come through the captain. That was "according to regulations." The committee then waited on the captain.

"Go back to work, or you'll go to the guardhouse," said he. "A soldier has nothing to do except obey orders. Your orders are to dig that trench."

"But," said the spokesman, "we enlisted for soldiers, not to——"

The sentence was interrupted by a peculiar drum beat. The officers hurried to the colonel's tent. In a moment Captain Irish returned and ordered Company K to fall in.

The whole regiment assembled in dress parade. Looking to the other camps we could see all the regiments doing the same thing. The adjutant read an order. It was to the effect that General George B. McClellan has been reassigned to the command of the Army of the Potomac.

We all cheered. I didn't know why. Perhaps because all the other regiments were cheering. A mighty chorus of hurrahs arose from the assembled army. The raw recruits were not aware of the fact that McClellan, no matter how much he might be in disfavor with the "heavy weights" at the head of the government was the idol of the older soldiers. His reassignment to command filled them with enthusiasm, and they cheered; we cheered to be in fashion, if for nothing else.

But there was another order. It involved dropping the pick and shovel, and so it ended Company K's threatened "strike." It was an order to be in readiness to move at a moment's notice.

That afternoon, Saturday, September 6, 1862, it got out somehow that Lee with his whole army had skirted Washington and was over in Maryland making his way as fast as he could toward Pennsylvania. Unless stopped the enemy would soon be through Delaware and in New Jersey, on the way to New York.

Instinctively every man thought of his home and family.

"Why didn't they keep us at Newark?" asked Jack Butterworth. "We would have been of more use there."

"Oh, I guess we'll head them off," answered John Stansfield. "Besides I'd rather be along with the rest of the army than fighting the whole Southern Confederacy with a single regiment."

So thought I. Besides, I rather liked the idea of Lee and his army marching up Main street, Paterson. I'd like to see an attack on the man who ordered that pound of cheese. And I wondered how those patriotic citizens who had induced me to enlist would act when they got a dose of their own medicine.

We talked the matter over that night and speculated on coming events till we were tired, and finally went to bed on our blanket mattresses in the comfortable Sibley tents.

But not to sleep. We had scarcely closed our eyes, when once more that infernal drum began beating in a way we'd never heard it beat before.

"What is that?" we asked.

"It's the long roll," said Sergeant Heber Wells, as he stuck his head through the flap of our tent.

"The long roll? what does that mean?"

"It means to pack up, boys," replied the sergeant, with considerable agitation manifested in his voice. "Pack up at once, get ready for a long march. And be quick about it. There's no time to lose."

What could it mean? Was the enemy unexpectedly upon us, after all?

CHAPTER XII.

A MARCH IN THE DARK.

LIKE the Arab of old we stole away in the night.
But not "quietly." It was with a noise and a clatter, with cheer and jest, as if it were a moonlight excursion. We were loaded like pack mules. Our haversacks were stuffed with three days' rations. Our canteens were filled to the brim. In our cartridge boxes were forty rounds of ammunition, forty ounces of which were leaden bullets. Our knapsacks were packed like Saratoga trunks, and the straps fairly cracked.

All went smoothly enough for a while, and we kept a pretty good line as we crossed the aqueduct bridge into Georgetown. And by the way Georgetown with its surroundings looked then pretty much as it does now. I remember well my last glance at Washington. In the far distance was the Capitol, all lighted up, for Congress was holding one of its usual night sessions. In the rear of the White House was a camp. I think it was the Tenth New Jersey, which was detailed for guard duty. Lucky Tenth! Unlucky Thirteenth!

When I returned to Washington next, it was also in the night. But I didn't see much of it. I was only a wounded soldier, *en route* for the hospital. Never mind now. That comes later, and much comes before it.

Unused as we were to marching, loaded down as we were with superfluous weight, it soon began to tell on us. One by one the raw and soft recruits began to fall by the wayside, utterly exhausted. We were beginning to appreciate the fact which all old soldiers knew by experience, that if there is any one thing worse than a battle it is a long march. Indeed for long-continued suffering, for indescribable agony, both physical and mental, for everything except the horror, marching is vastly worse than fighting.

To the veterans it was comparatively easy. They were hardened, toughened. A thoroughly trained athlete can run five, ten, or even fifteen miles. An untrained man would be fatigued at as many rods. We were like a bicyclist when he starts to ride in the spring, after a winter's rest. And the boys dropped from the ranks like drops from an icicle in the sun.

I was young and wiry and stuck it out. But I was glad enough when about midnight were marched into a big field; our guns were stacked, and we threw ourselves down on the ground, just as we were, for a few hours' needed rest and sleep. Everybody was too tired to jest, too tired to talk. We needed no rocking to sleep.

"Wake up, Joe, wake up! There's no rest for the wicked."

It was John Stansfield, who was lying alongside me.

"What in thunder are you doing?" I demanded angrily; "can't you let a fellow sleep?"

"Get up," he repeated, giving me a punch in the ribs, "we've got to tramp again."

It was too true. We were ordered to fall in; and we hadn't rested an hour. It was a sleepy crowd that formed the crooked line of men comprising Company K. But it was dark and no one to see us. Furthermore the officers were as sleepy as we were.

Now company officers march the same as the "men;" but they have to carry no baggage. That is carried in the wagons. All the foot officers have to carry is their swords—and, generally, a flask! The officers higher than captains rode horseback.

What we were aroused for unless to make us more tired, I don't know. But we were marched up the road and down the road and back again, halted and countermarched, until finally we were once more told to "break ranks" in a field adjoining the first one, and once more we threw ourselves on the ground almost dead.

To a private soldier these mysterious movements were always inexplicable. Every veteran can recall thousands of such experiences which then seemed and seem now to have been utterly unnecessary, and concocted for no other purpose than to fatigue and annoy. The misery, torture and suffering caused by these unexplained maneuvers could never be described.

The next day was Sunday.

"I guess they'll give us a rest to-day," said John Butterworth to me.

"Why?" I asked.

"Because it is Sunday. We haven't heard the chaplain yet. You know he's to preach every Sunday, and of course we can't march and go to church at the same time."

I had forgotten the chaplain. He was Rev. T. Romeyn Beck. He is still living, and is pastor of a church in California. He was a nice sort of a fellow, but didn't do much preaching, if I remember correctly. The chaplain wore a uniform of solemn black, even to the buttons. He rode with the colonel and major and altogether had quite a soft snap of it.

Chaplains didn't do much fighting. They were supposed to administer spiritual consolation on the battle-field; but as a usual thing they, like the old war-horse, "smelled the battle from afar." The rate of mortality among the chaplains was not high. I don't think the life insurance companies classed them as "extra hazardous." I don't say our chaplain was never in a battle; but I can say I never saw him in one. But then perhaps I was generally too scared to see anybody in particular.

But nevertheless Chaplain Beck was a nice man and kind to us soldier boys. The chaplain was usually the regimental postmaster. I forget whether Chaplain Beck or the one who succeeded him was the victim of a cruel joke late in the campaign, which I might as well tell here as anywhere.

There had been no mail for several weeks and the boys were getting impatient to hear from home. They fairly pestered the life out of the chaplain to know when the mail would be in. He couldn't go anywhere or attempt to do a thing without meeting some one with the inquiry about mail. There is a limit to the endurance even of clergymen. Getting tired of answering questions the following notice was posted outside the chaplain's tent:

"The chaplain does not know when the mail will be in."

The boys didn't like this. It was shutting them off too summarily. Finally a wag got a piece of charcoal and made an addition to the sign.

All the boys tittered when they saw it, but sneaked out of sight when they saw Colonel Carman approaching. He gave one glance at the sign in front of the tent, and then stuck his head in the opening.

"Say, cap," said he, addressing the chaplain, "what sort of a notice is this you have out here?"

"Oh," replied he, "the boys are bothering me so much about the mails that I thought I would post a general answer, so that they may all read it."

"But isn't the language rather rough?" inquired the colonel.

"It's all right, isn't it?"

"Just look at it and see how it reads, cap."

The chaplain stepped out, bareheaded, and this is the sign that met his astonished gaze:

"The chaplain does not know when the mail will be in—neither does he care a damn!"

That sign came down, and never again did anything of the kind appear in front of his tent.

But this is a digression. We will dismiss the chaplain by saying that we had no religious services that day, nor for many a long day.

Neither were we allowed to have a rest. Tired and stiff as we were, with our legs cramped and sore, with blood in our shoes from chafed feet, we were relentlessly ordered to fall in to resume the pitiless march.

And never shall I forget that day!

CHAPTER XIII.

SUNSTRUCK.

No, never shall I forget that day—that hot Sunday, September 7, 1862.

The sun rose like a red, burnished copper globe. Not a breath of air was stirring. The atmosphere was torrid, stifling, enervating. It was pitilessly hot. And we were stiff, sore, and filled with strange pains and aches from the previous night's march.

But what mattered that? What were the personal suffering of individuals in a vast army! Cruel and relentless it seemed to us, raw recruits that we were, fresh from the customary considerations of civil life, that we should be forced to resume the terrible march.

And here let me state a curious fact. Any one would naturally imagine that the men who best stood the rigors of an army march would be those who filled the hardest positions in civil life. An express-wagon driver, accustomed to lifting heavy boxes; a backwoodsman, inured to hardships and exposure; a blacksmith or a day laborer—these are the men one would imagine the best toughened for soldier life. But such was not the case. The men who stood it out the best were those who were accustomed to the lightest work at home. Bookkeepers, dry goods clerks, men who never lifted anything heavier than a ledger or a roll of calico—these were the men who could endure the most hardship and fatigue.

Any old officer of the army will tell you that this is so. It is a singular fact. It was often discussed and commented upon, but no explanation was ever given. It was simply so and that settled it.

And so it was on this hot September morning. The men who had been regarded the most hardy seemed to suffer the most. Those who had had the hardest physical labor at home were the stiffest, the sorest, the most complaining. Although I had never had hard work in the printing office and was not naturally robust, I probably suffered as little as anybody, as far as physical ailment was concerned, except for the intolerably raw blisters on my feet, caused by the unpliable brogans and thick coarse stockings, the latter being so much too large that they were as full of wrinkles as the skin of a hippopotamus.

There was one thing that worried me that morning, however. It was the heat, and threatened promise of what we now call "a scorcher." I never could stand the fierce rays of the summer sun; but never dreaded it so much as I did that morning. Was it a presentiment of what was to happen? Who knows?

That morning was our first experience with "hardtack." Hitherto we had had fresh bread; but that "soft stuff" had run out, and we were compelled to draw upon the rations in our haversacks. Now, as explained in a previous chapter, a hard-tack is an innocent- and soft-looking thing. But he who tackles one finds that he is a victim of misplaced confidence. They look like soda crackers. But they are not soda crackers.

When I struck the first one I thought that I had encountered an unusually ancient specimen. I could make no more impression on it than a missionary could on the heart of a Fiji cannibal. I turned to my comrade, Heber Wells, and saw him trying to pull a tooth. At least so it seemed. He was only trying to get a bite out of the hard-tack.

"How does it go?" I asked.

"Don't go at all," he replied. "How do you eat these things, anyhow?"

"I tell you how I did it," said John Stansfield. "I smashed mine between a couple of stones."

"By jimminey," said John Ick, "I tried that, and by jimminey I proke dose stones alretty, and never proke dot, vat you callem, dot hart-tack."

Jake Engle had, however, got a pointer from one of the older soldiers, who had taught him how to made "lobskouse." Now what bread and butter is to a person at home, that is "lobskouse" to the soldier. Here is the way to make the great army dish.

Take a bit of fat pork and melt it over the fire in a frying-pan or tin plate. Break up the hard-tack into small pieces and drop it into the frying fat. Let the whole mess sizzle together until the cracker is saturated with the fat and the result is a product that looks and tastes like pie crust. It is quite palatable. The crackers are softened and you can eat the stuff, and over a million men could testify that it would sustain life. Where all other supplies were unattainable, "lobskouse" was generally available, and scarcely a day passed but that it did not form the principal dish for at least one meal.

Indigestible stuff, you say? Well, who ever heard of a soldier having dyspepsia? Of all the ailments that came along to make the soldier's life miserable, indigestion was one of the things he never complained of. Ye dyspeptics, who swallow nostrums and patent medicines by the barrel, consider the ways of the soldiers and be wise. Go to the war and be shot, and you'll have no more dyspepsia. Nor will you have any more even if you are not shot.

As soon as we had gulped down our lobskouse and black coffee, we fell in and were marched down to the edge of the field near the highway. There we waited for an hour or more, watching the passing troops. Was there no end to them? The line seemed interminable. Infantry, cavalry, artillery, baggage wagons and ambulances, in an endless row—the men and horses four abreast, the wagons and cannons two abreast. They were mostly old soldiers, and, of course, dirty soldiers. They looked like tramps. But few carried knapsacks. They carried their blankets in a roll over their shoulders.

Each of the men carried a quart cup or a tomato can, tied to his haversack. These had wire handles or bales, making them into little tin pails. Each one was as black as a stovepipe from smoke. We did not know then what we learned afterward, that the tin pails constituted the main cooking utensil of the army. On the march and field every man is his own cook.

Some carried frying-pans. At each step the tin pails, canteens and other things rattle together with a "clinkety-clink," "clinkety-clink" that sounded like an orchestra of cracked cowbells. In the still of the night you could hear the clatter of the tinware of an army miles away. All this was new to us raw recruits.

After an apparently interminable wait, we were finally ordered to fall in the seemingly endless procession. The trouble began.

Now those who have never marched in an army know nothing of the most exasperating features. When you see a company or regiment of militia marching up a street you are pleased with the regularity of the step and the nicely maintained distance between the lines. But suppose a train came along while crossing the railroad, or a street car gets into the way, there is a break and delay. When the obstruction is removed, the rear of the column has to march in quick step to close up the gap caused by the forward end keeping on the go while the rear is stopped.

In the army there were such obstructions in the shape of broken wagons or caissons, narrow bridges, or brooks to cross. The front men narrowed the width of the column and marched past, while the rear slowed up. With a few men this amounted to nothing; but when extended down and through a line of thousands or tens of thousands, those in the rear had frequent halts of half an hour or so, and then a stiff race of five or ten minutes to catch up. This was very wearing and fatiguing. Old soldiers knew enough to lie down every minute they could and reserve their strength and endurance. We were ignorant.

As the sun rose in the sky it grew hotter and hotter. It was a perfect broil. The perspiration fell in streams from our faces and rolled down our backs. Our thick underclothing stuck to our skin like wet sheets. Our backs began to ache. The numerous straps on our shoulders cut into the very flesh. Whatever way we carried our guns they seemed heavier than before. It was torture. Nine out of ten men were limping as if lame from the constantly increasing size of the raw blisters on their feet.

We were in Maryland and were to march, it was said, until we reached Rockville. How far was it? we asked the first "native" we encountered. "Right about nine mile, I reckon," he said.

After marching an hour or so longer we asked another Maryland rustic how far it was to Rockville.

"Right about nine mile!"

And so it was. Everybody we asked, no matter how much further we went, "reckoned it were about nine mile."

I saw the other fellows lightening their load and followed suit. First went an extra suit of underclothes. "Every little helps." A while later and I discarded by the wayside a comb and brush, a shaving set, a box of blacking and brush. "Every pound counts." A mile further and I pulled out two cakes of soap, a couple of towels, a pincushion and sewing case. "A little better."

But no use. What the others were doing I would do.

It seemed a pity to throw away the nice overcoat and blouse and dress coat, but they had to go. And finally the knapsack itself followed, leaving nothing but the rubber and woolen blankets. The heaviest thing of all, the cartridge box, we couldn't discard, for soldiers must fight. The most useful things, the haversack and canteen, we stuck to, for soldiers must eat and drink.

The road for miles was strewn with things that cost the government much money. But what odds? Uncle Sam was rich, and we were only doing what every new soldier had done before us and what all soldiers will do hereafter, to the beginning of the millennium when there will be no more war. By noon we were, that is the most of us, down to the lightest marching order of the oldest veterans in the line.

As I intimated, not all of us. Some sturdy fellows stuck to their loads. Sergeant Heber Wells, for instance, who did not discard a single article from his stuffed knapsack, nor that comical fellow "Jeff Davis," who all through the war persisted in carrying two knapsacks.

The pitiless sun shortly after noon began to get in its fine work. One by one the men fell out. Hank Van

Orden was the first of Company K to succumb. His mind suddenly grew flighty, he mumbled a few inarticulate meaningless words, threw up his arms, gave a yell, and fell like a log, senseless. He was rolled to the side of the road and left "for the ambulance to pick up." A moment later Lem Smith raised his hands, clutched the air, and fell. John Snyder dropped like a bullock felled with an axe. Poor John Ick, who had quite appropriately been prating about "slaughter houses" and "shambles," was the next victim. Soon after fat John Farlow staggered to the side path and threw himself down in the miserable shade of a rail fence. Archy Todd reeled like a top two or three times, and fell forward on his face in the dusty road.

And so it went. By 3 o'clock in the afternoon not thirty of the ninety members of Company K were in the line, and it was correspondingly the same in all the other companies of the regiment. There were perhaps three times as many members of the Thirteenth stretched along the roadside than there were in the ranks.

Aside from the suffering from the sun and the torture from the heavy load and from our bleeding feet, there was a marked mental depression, consequent upon the sight of so many of our comrades falling out. It is a well-known fact that when one or two girls faint in a mill or in a school, a dozen will do likewise. Any old factory foreman or teacher will tell you this. To a certain extent the same species of hysteria affects men. I know it affected me.

And as said before, I never could stand the sun. What I suffered that day no man can ever know unless he has been through the same experience.

Along about 3 o'clock I guess it was, I suddenly noticed that the trees and fences were beginning to dance. The soldiers in front of me were turning rapid somersaults. There was a horrible sickness of the stomach and my head seemed about to split open!

For an instant the air was full of stars! Then the sky turned green! Then black!

Then—utter oblivion!

I was sunstruck!

CHAPTER XIV.

AT ROCKVILLE.

"No, he isn't going to die. He'll come around all right."

"It was a close shave, though; wasn't it, doctor?"

"Yes, it was. But the danger is over now. Keep him right here under the shade of this tree, and keep the towel on his head wet with cool water. Don't give him any more of the brandy without letting me know first."

This is part of a conversation I hear, in a dim, hazy sort of a way. It seems afar off, or as if in another room, through partly closed doors. Yet it is distinct, in a certain way. What does it mean? Oh, how my head aches!

Where am I? What has happened? What am I doing here, with my head done up in wet towels, lying on the grass under a tree? For a moment I think I am on my old grandfather's farm, lying in the orchard, as I used to do. But that pain in my head! What does it mean? And I feel so sick—oh, so sick!

I open my eyes and dimly see the men moving about. Ha! There's Liv Allen and Davy Harris. It's the *Guardian* office. There's been an accident somehow, and I've been hurt. I'll ask. But wait. How funny they look, all dressed in blue. Where are their working aprons? I can't think. It's too much. My head! My head! I cannot rest a bit. Let me think. Where am I?

"Fall in for your supper, boys."

What's that I hear? "Boys?" "Supper." "Fall in!" Oh, my head! How bewildered I am! Oh!

In a minute, as if by magic, a veil seems to roll away and I recognized the voice I had heard as Jake Engle's.

Jake! Oh, yes, Jake, who has been appointed company cook, the cook for Company K, when in camp. It's all coming back now. I remember, I enlisted. Yes, that march. The men falling around us, like so many tenpins. The terrible heat, I remember now. Was I too sunstruck?

With an effort I pull myself together and speak. Who was leaning over me but the captain, the kind-hearted Captain Irish—who had less than ten days more to live himself!

"How do you feel, Joe?" he asked, taking my hand.

"Got a terrible headache," I replied. "But what happened? Was I sunstruck?"

"Yes, but you're all right now, the doctor says."

The captain then told me that I had fallen out, like the others, a little after 3 o'clock, and that it was now after 6. I had been picked up and brought along by one of the ambulances. I had been unconscious for nearly three hours, and at one time they thought I was dead.

The captain told me that we were at a place called Rockville, in the State of Maryland, twenty-two miles from Washington; we had only marched fourteen miles that day, but the sun was so hot and the boys so unused to marching that when they reached the camping-place, about 5 o'clock, there were less than two hundred of the Thirteenth present. Out of nine hundred men, only two hundred stood it out. Seven hundred men had succumbed to the fierce heat of that hot September day and fallen by the wayside!

No man ever fully recovers from the effects of a genuine sunstroke. I have suffered from it in more ways than one, ever since. A few moments in the hot sun is sure to bring on symptoms that are danger-singals for precautionary measures. Perhaps that sunstroke has been the cause of many subsequent sins of omission and commission. I trust that my critics will bear this in mind and make allowance for shortcomings!

Captain Irish had in his hand as he spoke to me a box of some sort of salve or ointment. Noticing my inquiring look, he said:

"When they pulled off your shoes, I noticed that your feet were bleeding from the blisters. I had some ointment that Mrs. Irish made. It is from an old family receipt. I think your feet won't hurt you so much now."

"But, captain," I interrupted. "You don't mean to say you have been rubbing my feet with ointment? You did not do it yourself, I hope?"

His answer made a lump come into my throat.

"Why certainly, Joe. Why not?"

I turned my head, because I did not want him to see the tears in my eyes. Just think of it! A captain bathing the sore feet of a private! How many soldiers in the army can recall a case like that? But there was only one Captain Irish. Do you wonder his men learned to worship him in the short time he lived to serve his country? Do you wonder that his old soldiers touch their hats reverently to this day, when his name is mentioned? Not only was he a brave patriot, but a kind, tender-hearted man, beloved as a father by the men in his company.

But no matter what the after effect may be, the immediate recuperative powers inherent in a healthy boy of seventeen or eighteen are wonderful, and with the exception of a slight headache and general played-outness, I felt quite well the next day, and went around pretty much as the others.

The men who had fallen out like myself had returned to the regiment and we again assumed the appearance of a camp.

To enhance our comfort our big Sibley tents arrived from somewhere unknown to us, and we were soon in as good a shape as at Camp Frelinghuysen in Newark, with the exception that there were a number who were still somewhat under the weather from the unaccustomed exposure and the fatigue of the march.

This resulted in the introduction of, to us, a new feature of army experience, the surgeon. Dr. Love and his assistant, Dr. Freeman, had put up their medical tent, and started business. And they were doing quite a business.

The sick soldiers in the army are divided into three

classes. One class includes those who are confined to their tents; the second those who are confined to the hospital; and the third those who are able to go to the surgical headquarters for their medicine. Those in the hospital or tents were visited as often as necessity required—the same as a doctor would do in civil life. With the others it was as follows:

Every morning at 8 o'clock the drummer and fifer detailed at the regiment headquarters would sound the "sick call." The tune played by the fifer was something like "Johnny, get your gun," but the way the boys interpreted it was this:

> " Come, get your blue pills,
> Blue pills, blue pills,
> Come, get your blue pills,
> Blue pills, blue."

The point of this was that it was a tradition in the army that the surgeons had only one kind of medicine, and that was calomel; or as commonly called, "blue pills." If a soldier had a headache or a sore toe, the remedy was a blue pill. If an indiscreet forager had indulged in too much surreptitious green corn, the proper remedy was a blue pill. If in the ordinary course of events the ailment was of a contrary character, what you wanted was a good dose of blue pills. No matter what was the matter, the remedy was blue pills.

I am not a doctor. Whether there was any truth in this story about blue pills being a regulation panacea for all the ills that flesh is heir to, I am unable to affirm. All that I can say is that it was an army tradition, and I appeal to veterans for verification. Hence the familiar words that the boys tacked on to "the sick call."

From the indications surrounding us we privates naturally imagined that we were going to have a long stay at Rockville camp. It was a pretty spot and we were nothing loath. We did not know that it was but a temporary halt of a pursuing army.

General Lee and the Confederate forces were marching up into Maryland somewhere ahead of us. The commanders of the Union army were, it seems, a little at a loss as to just what point Lee was steering for. That naturally involved the route we were to take. There were several roads to select from, but the question was which one would best intercept the enemy in his northward course. The enemy's intentions were therefore an essential requisite.

Such information was obtained by scouts, or by cavalry reconnoisances. To make these investigations and bring back a non-conflicting report, occupied a day or so's time. That was what we were waiting for.

The head officers knew all this, of course; but we privates did not. The rank and file of an army know no more about what they are doing, why they stop here and go there, than so many sheep. We naturally supposed just then that we were going to have a good rest —to "wait till it got a little cooler."

In the light of history we know now that General McClellan ascertained that the enemy's objective point was the great strategic position of Harper's Ferry. Hence McClellan picked out a route that converged with that of the enemy so that the two armies would probably intersect near South Mountain. And so they did! That is just where they "intersected."

While at Rockville we were "brigaded." That means that we were assigned to a particular section of the army. We were put in General Gordon's brigade of General William's division of General Bank's corps. The other regiments of our brigade were the Second Massachusetts, the Third Wisconsin, the Twenty-seventh Indiana, and the One Hundred and Seventh New York. With the exception of the latter and the Thirteenth Regiment, they were all veterans, and ranked with the best fighting troops of the army. Phew! we didn't relish that much!

General Gordon, the brigade commander, was a West Point graduate, and former Colonel of the Second Massachusetts. Colonel Ruger, of the Third Division, was also a West Pointer. He is now a major-general in the regular army.

About noon on Tuesday, September 9, 1862, our hopes of a long rest were suddenly dispelled by an order to fall in at once to resume the march.

This order was accompanied by instructions that seemed to mean business. It was that we would proceed in "light marching order." We were told to leave behind our commodious Sibley tents (which we never laid eyes on again). We were soon told to leave our knapsacks. Most of those had been left by the wayside; but that was the order to be obeyed by those who had stuck to their "trunks."

"What does this mean?" I asked one of the Second Massachusetts veterans.

"It means a fight!" said he.

CHAPTER XV.

A BIVOUAC.

"A fight?"

"Yes."

"A battle?"

"Yes."

"What makes you think so?"

"Oh," calmly replied the Second Massachusetts man, "we old soldiers know the signs. When you have been halted a day or so, and then suddenly along comes an order to get up and git, in light marching order, that generally means that you are going to get into a scrimmage mighty soon, or somewhere pretty near it."

"How does a fellow feel when he gets into a battle?" I asked, nervously.

"Are you scared?" he asked.

"Well, no; not exactly that. But I don't feel comfortable."

"Own up now, like a man, that you're scared."

"Well—a little bit."

To tell the truth my teeth were chattering.

"You'll be scared a darned sight worse, I reckon," said the unfeeling bean-eater. "Scared is no name for it. The man never lived that wasn't scared in a battle. Put that down. But the worst part of it is just before you go in—when you're waiting to go in." (A soldier always referred to entering a battle as "going in.")

"What are your sensations then?"

"Pshaw, pard, I couldn't begin to tell you, except that you're scared, awfully scared. and that's all there is about it."

"Were you ever wounded?"

"No; nor I don't want to be, neither. If ever I'm shot, I want to be plunked dead and be done with it. I've seen enough men wounded not to care to be wounded myself. But it's no use o' my telling you. From the looks o' things I guess you'll know all about it yourself before long."

Now this was interesting talk, wasn't it? It made the patriotism ooze out of my little toe. What with the marching and the hot weather and the horrible prospects ahead, I was rapidly becoming very sorry that I had been such a fool as to enlist.

But soldiers are kept too busy to have much time for reflection, and activity is the best possible antidote for depression of spirits. The preparations for the start engrossed our attention. And after the customary preliminary delay we were again on the march. Quite a number of sick and disabled men were left behind to catch up with the regiment when they had recovered.

In the Union army, as it started on that Maryland campaign, there were about one hundred thousand men. General Lee's army contained about sixty thousand men. We were about five to three of the enemy. Perhaps had we known that then, we would have felt a little better. And then again, perhaps we wouldn't!

The army moved forward in three columns—that is, by three roads. History tells us that the right wing, under General Burnside, comprised the latter's own corps and that of General Hooker. This was on the right. The center column was composed of Generals Sumner and Mansfield's corps, under command of Sumner. General Franklin's corps and General Couch's division were on the left, while General Fitz-John Porter and his troops brought up the rear.

We know all this now. We didn't at the time. All that we knew, was that we were part and parcel of a string of soldiers of apparently countless numbers, marching along toward some fate, we knew not what. John Ick said it was to "a slaughter house."

After a march that was not so fatiguing as that to Rockville, for the weather was slightly cooler and we were getting somewhat used to it, we encamped for the night at a place called Middlebrook. Here we were initiated into the art of "every man his own cook."

I don't know where all the tomato cans came from. Perhaps they were discarded relics of the officers' mess, for the officers' provisions were carried in the baggage wagons and usually comprised a greater variety than the *menu* of the "men." Perhaps it will not be generally remembered that this was before the days of canned goods. Tomatoes and sardines were about the only things put up in tin cans in 1862. Fresh vegetables were not attainable the year round, as they are now.

Some of the boys had provided themselves with little tin pails; I had not, but I was fortunate enough to find a tomato can and a piece of wire, and making a bale of the latter I soon had a little pail. These tomato cans were a good deal better than the "boughten" pails, for, the tin being thinner, you could boil water quicker, and when the can gets too much smoked and burned you could throw it away and pick up another.

Taking some lessons from the older soldiers, we prepared our own suppers. For the edification of housewives and cooks I'll tell you how we soldiers made coffee.

Take a tomato-can pail and fill it with water from the nearest spring or brook. Take a handful of ground coffee from your haversack and sprinkle it on top of the water; the most of it will float. Get a long stick and put the pail on the end of it and hold it over the fire. Of course a dozen or fifteen other fellows are scrambling for the hottest place in the fire with their coffee pails, and you must fight for your chance. You're lucky if you don't get a plunk in the nose. After awhile the water begins to boil, and suddenly the coffee rises to the top, in a creamy sort of a chocolate color. Then quickly dash from your canteen a squirt or so of cold water. Instantly the grounds will settle to the bottom and your coffee will be quite clear. As the orthodox recipes say, "serve hot."

That is the way army coffee is made and it isn't bad either. At least it is as good as coffee can be without cream. We had sugar and "sweetened to taste," and generally drank right out of the tin pail, for cups were a useless bother.

With a bit of fat pork toasted in the fire on the end of a stick, and the hard-tack somewhat softened by soaking in the coffee, it made a tolerably fair meal. And this was the average meal of the Union soldier on the march throughout the war. Somehow we got a knack of cracking the hard-tack with our teeth and they by no means seemed as hard as at first. A hard-tack is similar to the Hebrew unleavened bread of Passover times. In fact it is practically the same. No salt is used in its manufacture, and if kept dry it will last for years. Hence that brand of "B. C." wouldn't be so inappropriate after all.

It must be acknowledged that there could be no more picturesque sight than an army of soldiers in bivouac after a day's march. When the order came to halt, which was generally in the vicinity of some body of fresh water, say a brook or a spring or lake, there would be a general scramble for fuel. The choicest fuel of all was a rail fence. Then the dry twigs that lay around under the trees. Then the trees themselves. Then the boards and shingles from every old house and barn in sight.

An enormous flock of Nebraska grasshoppers could not create such sudden devastation. In five minutes not a vestige of a rail fence could be seen. A pretty strong guard was the only way of preventing the immediate demolishing of a building. In three days' time, should the army stop, nothing but stumps could be seen where there had stood a vast forest. In a friendly section certain restrictions were placed on the troops. In an enemy's country, unlimited license to destroy was the unwritten law.

There were generally one or two camp fires to a company, besides additional ones for the officers, and at the respective headquarters. In the one hundred thousand troops encamped that night there were perhaps two thousand or two thousand five hundred campfires. The encamping army covered ground twelve or sixteen miles square.

Just imagine a grand concourse of soldiers scattered over a tract of land ten or fifteen miles square. Scatter among these two or three thousand bonfires, each one producing a big volume of smoke. Around each fire a crowd of men, cooking their suppers, smoking their pipes, singing and laughing. Add the indescribable braying of the mules, a fife and drum here, a bugle there and occasionally a brass band (there weren't many of them) playing. Imagine all this, and you'll have a vague sort of an idea of the army as it stopped that night at Middlebrook, Maryland.

And the songs the soldiers used to sing! It mattered not how little one knew how to sing, he was expected to join in the chorus. When on the march, and not too tired, the whole army would suddenly break out with that famous old song to the tune of "John's Brown's body:"

> "We'll hang Jeff Davis on a sour apple tree,
> We'll hang Jeff Davis on a sour apple tree,
> We'll hang Jeff Davis on a sour apple tree,
>   While his soul goes marching on."

When sitting around the campfire a different class of songs were sung, such as "Dixie":

> "I wish I was in de land of cotton
>   Cinnamon seed and sandy bottom
> Look away, look away, look away to Dixie land."

Or another to which an additional verse was added for each year the war continued, which ran:

> "In eighteen hundred and sixty-one
>   Free-ball! Free-ball!
> In eighteen hundred and sixty-one
>   Free-ball! Free-ball!
> In eighteen hundred and sixty-one
> The war had then but just begun
> And we'll all drink stone blind,
> Johnny, fill up the bowl."

The latter verse will no doubt cause a smile to appear on the lips of all soldiers who see it, for it will involuntarily recall to their mind the text of some of the others, which would hardly look well in print!

CHAPTER XVI.

A GREEN PICKET.

In the previous chapter I told how the boys were sitting around the Middlebrook camp fires, smoking and singing. But "there were others," as the saying goes, and these were on picket duty. Every night, whether in camp or on the march, a certain number of men are detailed to do picket duty. They are to watch that the enemy doesn't get in, and that the soldiers don't get out.

One of Company K's picket detail was the irrepressible John Ick. The officer of the guard had a hard time instructing John Ick in the duties of a sentry. John's post, by the way, was under a tree at the edge of a wood. It is perhaps hardly necessary to say that there wasn't a "Johnny Reb" within thirty or forty miles. But John took the assignment with great dignity, with as much apparent determination to do his duty as if the woods swarmed with the soldiers of the enemy.

"Now you must be very careful," said Lieutenant Scott, the officer of the guard. "You must not let any one pass without the countersign."

"Vot vas the goundersign, Mr. Scott?" asked Ick.

"It is a word that must be whispered in your ear like this—'Brandywine.' That's the countersign."

"Brandywine. Oh, yes, I'll remember dot; dat is something to trink, like lager beer. I'll just think by ein glass lager beer, and don't forget dot what you call him—dot gountersign."

Lieutenant Scott instructed Ick in the *modus operandi* of treating approaching friend or foe during the night, and particularly enjoined upon him not to let his gun pass out of his hands, no matter who it might be. Nor must he let any one pass without the countersign.

"Not even der captain?" asked Ick.

"No, not even the captain."

"Nobotty?"

"Nobody whatever."

"Now I onderstand, dot's all ri-et," said John. "Iffer everybotty comes by here vot don't des gountersign have, I shoot 'em, eh?"

Later in the night Lieutenant Scott suggested to Captain Irish that he test John Ick while he was on his post. He did so.

"Who comes there, alretty?" demanded Ick. This was the correct salutation, for a wonder, except for the "alretty."

"It's I—Captain Irish," was the reply.

"Oh, dot's all ri-et. How you was, captain? It was a nice night, ain't it?"

"Yes, a very nice night. But say, John, you are not holding your gun right. Let me show you."

Ick handed the captain his rifle.

"You must hold it this way," said the captain, bringing it to a "charge bayonet" and touching John with the point of it against his stomach.

"Don't do dot captain; by gimminey, you almost stick it through me alretty."

"Now look here, John," said the captain severely, "supposing I wasn't Captain Irish. Suppose I was a rebel."

"But you vasn't no reppel, I know'd you was Captain Irish."

"Yes, but suppose it was so dark you couldn't see me, or suppose it was General McClellan?"

"Dot would be all riet, not?"

"But suppose it was some one else who passed himself off under a false name, and after getting your gun, killed you?"

"Mine Gott! I dont't think py dot."

"Now, John," said the captain, kindly, "I only did this to try you. Let it be a lesson. Never let your gun out of your hands while on picket, not even if it is the President of the United States."

"By gimminey, I don'd give dot gun to Kaiser Wilhelm if he comes any more."

John Ick evidently understood this part of the business now. And let me say right here that that identical test was tried on every new recruit in the army, and in five cases out of ten with a similar result.

About an hour afterward the "grand rounds" came along. The "grand rounds" was a regular nocturnal visit, usually about midnight, to test the vigilance of the picket lines. Some high officer, but more generally the officer of the day, accompanied by a small body guard, performed it. As they approached John Ick they were met with the regulation salutation:

"Who comes there?"

"The grand rounds."

"The grand rounds," answered Ick, "I don'd know vat dot grand rounds vas, but you don'd fool me any more alretty like dot Captain Irish. I vas holding dot gun all ri-et, and don'd you forget it."

"What nonsense is this?" asked the grand officer, stepping forward.

"No you don'd do dot," exclaimed Ick. "You don'd got my gun some more, and you don'd got py here ober you don'd say dot gountersign. Say lager beer!"

"What?" exclaimed the astonished officer.

"Say lager beer."

"What is lager beer? What do you mean by that, you stupid blockhead?" demanded the officer.

"Dot vas de gountersign alretty. You dond pass by ober you dond say lager beer."

"Who told you the countersign was lager beer?"

"Mister Scott."

"Who is Mister Scott?"

"Vy, don't you know him? Dot vas Jim, der lufftennant by Company K."

"Did he tell you the countersign was lager beer?"

"Yah."

"Didn't he say Brandywine?"

"Brandywine? Oh, ya! Dot vas it. I forgot him alretty. I know'd it vas something to drink, and I thought it was lager beer, py gimminey. You shust say Brandywine. Dat's all ri-et!"

"How long have you been in the service?" asked the officer.

"Vot service?"

"The army. How long have you been a soldier?"

"Oh, about six week, alretty."

"Been on picket before?"

"Nein. Dot vos de first times."

"I thought so," said the grand officer. And then he proceeded to explain that he must never give away the countersign; that it must come from the person who wanted to get past, and not from the soldier on guard. Although outwardly severe, the officers made all allowances for such green recruits. It was the way they instructed them in their duties. And it made a more lasting lesson than any amount of school class tuition. John Ick learned his lesson well, and was proven to be a faithful picket on many a subsequent occasion.

The incidents just related were duplicated in a thousand instances. The men, taken from all phases of life, were utterly ignorant of military duty. There was not time to put them through a regular graduated course of instruction, and they were taught in this eminently practical way.

The next morning, September 10th, the Thirteenth, with its brigade companies, marched off on a line about parallel to the Baltimore and Ohio railroad. The distance covered on that day and the next was short, and the marches were comparatively easy.

Excitement began to be manifested, however, from the fact that we began to see evidences that the enemy had passed along that way not many days previous. There were signs of camps from the ashes where there had been fires. The rail fences had disappeared. In fact the trail of the military serpent was everywhere visible.

It was evident to all that we were getting into close quarters. There were frequent consultations among the officers, and an increase in their earnestness and in the severity of their orders. A peculiar atmosphere of impending disaster surrounded us that was indescribable. That sensation is a familiar one to old soldiers, but it was our first experience and there was an uncanny weirdness about it that was not at all pleasant.

We were not quite so close upon the enemy, however,

as we private soldiers imagined, although, as it subsequently transpired, a couple of days more marching would bring us in sight of the "Johnnies."

On the 12th of September we suddenly came to quite a good sized stream. We were told it was the Monocacy River.

There were no bridges nor boats; but an army doesn't stop for a little thing like that. We were simply and coolly ordered to "cross the river," and so we did.

Did you ever "ford a river"?

CHAPTER XVII.

A FREDERICK CITY GIRL.

WE were ordered to ford the river.

The Monocacy River isn't a very formidable stream nor is it in the summer season very deep. On this occasion it came up about to the waist at the place picked out as a "ford," although it was deeper above and below. But it was our first experience at fording a stream, and consequently accompanied with much interest.

The irrepressible and original John Ick wanted to take off his clothes and cross in a state of nature; but to his infinite disgust that would not be permitted, as such an operation would take too much time.

The government does not object, when soldiers are marching, to their discarding any superfluous weight in the shape of clothing or eatables. But when it comes to those things that absolutely pertain to war the case is different. One can't throw away guns or ammunition, no matter how heavy such things may be—and they were heavy enough. On all occasions the greatest care must be taken to keep the rifle in good order and the cartridges dry.

In fording a river the cartridge and percussion-cap boxes and belts were unstrapped and fastened at the bayonet end of the guns. By carrying the rifles on the shoulder the ammunition was kept above the water and dry. No matter if the contents of the haversack were ruined. No matter if the blankets and other wearing apparel were saturated. The government cared naught for that, so long as the ammunition was intact.

Even in the summer season it is not pleasant to cross a stream containing two or three or four feet of water in one's clothes. In the winter time, as many of us learned afterward, it is accompanied with little short of torture. In warm weather it is simply a question of discomfort.

Several pounds of weight seem to be added to the soldier's load. The clothing, uncomfortable at the best of times, sticks closer than a brother, and clings and pulls one's legs with a force almost inconceivable. The wet stockings flop about in the coarse aloes with a "ker-sock," "ker-sock" that sounds like a suction pump, and materially assists in the development of additional painful blisters.

As each man emerges on the other side of the stream, he sheds his quota of water, until the ground grows soggy and soft and the mud deeper and deeper until it is soon, not only ankle-deep, but knee-deep. With one's wet clothes increasing the weight, the climb through the sticky mud up the embankment of the stream was a tiresome task. It was also a tedious affair, for there is always considerable delay in fording a river or creek, and then comes that inevitable, wearisome scamper to catch up with those who have gone ahead.

A funny thing it was to see the ammunition mules. Each one of these stubborn but interesting animals had two large boxes of cartridges slung over his back, one on each side. The boxes just cleared the water, if everything was all right. But a mule doesn't like swiftly running water between his legs. It makes him discouraged. And when you discourage a mule his usefulness immediately departs. A discouraged mule invariably gives up and lies down, no matter where he may be.

The mules had no respect for the strict orders about keeping the cartridges dry. One of them lay down in the water, rolled over, and shed his load. The other mules saw this, and at once caught on to the scheme. The practice became epidemic. Mule after mule lay down in the middle of the stream, tumbled off his two heavy cases of cartridges, righted himself again and scrambled up the muddy bank with an expression of countenance that failed to indicate the least compunction of conscience. Those mules must have been in league with the enemy, for I heard one of the officers say that they had dumped enough cartridges in the

Monocacy River that day to fight a good sized battle. Every cartridge that got wet was ruined, of course, for the powder covering was only paper.

Fortunately for us we did not march very far after fording the river, and when we got into camp all the new soldiers took off their wet trousers and stockings and hung them on the bushes to dry. As we cooked our supper that night we resembled the *bouffe* soldiers in a German opera.

Johnny Neild came near getting into a fight with Reddy Mahar by remarking on the cleanliness of his pedal extremities.

"I believe that is the first time you ever had your feet washed in your life," said Neild.

"You're a liar!" returned Reddy.

Neild was going to take it up; but Hank Van Orden stepped between them and prevented a continuation of hostilities.

On the next day we reached Frederick city, and we found that we were getting closer upon the enemy than we imagined, that is, closer than we privates imagined. I suppose the officers knew all about it all along. The rebels had passed through Frederick only the day before. Indeed it is said that some of their rear guards were found in the city still when our advance guard reached the place, and that a few shots were fired. I didn't hear anything of that sort, however, or perhaps I wouldn't have been so unconcerned.

My remembrance of Frederick city is a very pleasant one. The place consisted in that day, essentially, of one large street. I remember being struck particularly with a wonder as to what the people did for a living. Outside of the stores, there seemed to be no business. Brought up within the sound of the hum of the busy mills of Paterson, it struck me that there ought to be some factories or other evidence of industry. But Frederick was a "market town" only, which was something that in those days I did not understand.

Frederick is the city made famous by the poet in the beautiful poem about "Barbara Fritchie." To be sure later historians have said that there never was a Barbara Fritchie in Frederick, and that the flag incident was a pure romance. But that makes no difference; the story of Barbara Fritchie will always remain associated with Frederick city.

And by the way they say that "Sheridan's Ride" was a fake, and lots of other things are false, including the "Charge of the Light Brigade," the flood and the ark, and Adam and Eve in the Garden of Eden. But we're here anyway, and we must have had ancestors, and who can dispute that there was an Adam and an Eve? I frown upon such despicable attempts to disprove facts by new theories. If it keeps on that way, some busybody will even throw out a suspicion that there are romances in this war story. So on general principles I stand up for all the interesting old traditions, including Barbara Fritchie!

The alleged incident of Barbara and the flag occurred the day before we reached Frederick, so that we didn't see it ourselves. But we saw the house from the upper window of which she defiantly flaunted the stars and stripes. At least I saw every house in Frederick, and so can truthfully testify that I saw the Fritchie place of residence.

I don't know how the citizens of Frederick treated the rebel army the day before, but I do know that they treated us "bang up." I went into a store and bought a pipe and some tobacco, and the proprietor wouldn't take a cent. The fact leaking out that cigar dealer's stock was soon completely disposed of on the same terms. The bakers gave us bread and cake. The citizens gave us pies and other luxuries, and pretty Maryland girls stood in their doorways with pitchers of milk.

There could be no discounting the fact of the hospitality of the people of Frederick city. They knew the Union army was coming close behind the rebels, and had made considerable preparation for us. The women of Frederick served us with sandwiches, cakes, pies, roasted chickens, hams, and what not.

During a temporary halt in the main street of the little city the boys were strung along the sidewalks, in front of the stores and residences, partaking of a lunch that was to us a regular feast. It was my good fortune to be served by a very pretty girl of about seventeen or eighteen years. As I stood there, leaning against the fence of the little door-yard in front of the cottage, with a chicken wing in one hand and a glass of milk in the other, I ventured into a little conversation with my fair entertainer.

"Did you do this for the other fellows?" I asked, feeling my ground.

"You mean the rebels, I suppose," said she.

"Yes; I didn't say 'rebel,' because I didn't know how you would take it."

"That's all right," said she reassuringly. "That's what I call them, anyhow. No, we didn't, as a general thing, treat 'the other fellows,' as you call them, in this way. Some of the people did, but not many. You see the most of us are Union folks. Then again, when the rebels passed through they seemed to be in a big hurry. Most of the houses and nearly all the stores were closed up, till it looked like Sunday. We had been told that they were going to clean out all the stores and then set fire to the town. We were much frightened, I can assure you, and we didn't feel safe until we began to see the blue-coated soldiers."

"So you're a Union girl," I remarked.

"Yes, sir," she replied. "And I have a brother in the Third Maryland——"

"The Third Maryland," I interrupted, "why I believe that regiment is in our division—General Williams'?"

"Yes; that's the name," she replied. "Fred wrote me that General Williams was his commander. Perhaps you may meet Fred."

"Very likely," I answered. "But what is his last name?"

"Summers."

"Fred Summers. And what name shall I use when I say I saw his sister?"

"Mabel" (with a slight blush).

"Is your brother older than you are?"

"No."

"What, younger? He must be a mere boy."

"He is neither older nor younger," was her answer, and she blushed again as she said: "We are twins—twin brother and sister."

"That's nice," said I. "And—and if he is anything like his twin sister, Fred must be a handsome fellow."

I was getting along pretty well considering I hadn't known the girl five minutes. But I couldn't help it. I really meant it, you know. I never saw a girl blush so easily as Mabel Summers did. My last remarks suffused her face with carnation. Now I come to recall it, I don't wonder.

"Have you any correspondent in the army?" I ventured.

"Oh, yes; my brother."

"Any one else?"

"Oh, no."

"Wouldn't you like to have one?"

"What do you mean?"

"I think I would make a good correspondent."

Another blush on the part of Mabel.

"I—I hardly think it would be proper. And," with a little show of pretty petulance, "I think your suggestion is a little bold, not to say somewhat impudent."

"I beg your pardon, Mabel—I mean Miss Summers—but you know that soldiers must be bold, not to say impudent."

This play on her words made her smile, and she asked me my name.

"Joe," I replied.

I don't know how much further the promising flirtation would have gone had it not just at this point been interrupted by a sergeant, accompanied by a file of men. The non-commissioned officers asked me what I was doing there?

"Eating and talking and having a good time," said I.

"What regiment do you belong to?" asked the sergeant.

"Thirteenth New Jersey."

"What corps?"

I told him.

"Don't you know," he asked, "that your command started off some time ago? Take him in charge, men" (turning to his companions).

"Who are you?" I asked indignantly.

"The provost guard."

That was the first time I had ever heard of such a think as the "provost guard," but I considered that it was advisable to go along without making any fuss. I was greatly surprised to learn that my regiment had already started off.

I turned to bid farewell to the pretty little Frederick city girl. A spirit of mischief seized me, and I said:

"Good-by, Mabel."

Mabel's blush was on schedule time, as usual, but that did not prevent her taking up the implied challenge, for she coquettishly answered:

"Good-by, Joe."

That was the first and last time I ever saw Mabel Summers. The reader may perhaps think we were both a little "fresh" to indulge in such familiarity on such short acquaintance; but the present generation does not understand the feeling that prevailed at that time toward the soldier boys. The blue uniform of Uncle Sam's service was an open sesame. No one wearing it needed an introduction to anybody. The girls seemed to regard every soldier as a hero. Perhaps it is better for the reputation of some of us that they were never undeceived.

I have often wondered what became of Mabel Summers. Is she living yet? Perhaps, and possibly a grandmother.

But I forgot that I was in the hands of the provost guard—a prisoner!

CHAPTER XVIII.

THE PROVOST GUARD.

Let me introduce the reader to the "provost guard."

The provost guard was what might be called the police force of the army. Their duty was to look after the recreant soldiers, stragglers, camp followers, hangers-on, and the like.

People unacquainted with war often ask how it was that there were not more desertions. How was it that the men, suffering from the fatigue of the march, the hardships and exposures of the camp and the awful horror of the battle, did not escape through the pickets and run through the guard lines and—go home?

It was the provost guard that prevented all this.

Imagine a man in a battle. What is there between him and liberty? Behind him are first, the non-commissioned officers, then the commissioned officers; then the "turkey buzzards." This consisted of a line of cavalry, generally armed with long spears, on the end of which were strips of red flannel, the latter curious insignia giving them the singularly appropriate title of "turkey buzzards." You couldn't get past this line without a written pass, or a show of blood issuing from a wound. So much for a battle.

At other times, and practically in fact at all times, there were regimental and corps guards and outside these the army pickets. Suppose you escaped through all these? Everywhere you went, through every city of the land, you would meet with soldiers of the provost guard, who would arrest you if you couldn't show written authority for being absent from your regiment.

There were provost guards even in Paterson, where I lived, perhaps in uniform, maybe not, and more than one deserter was arrested there and sent back. If a man hadn't a written pass he was considered a deserter. I might mention the names of several now prominent Patersonians in this connection, but will not. There would doubtless have been more if they could have similarly succeeded in getting "through the lines."

Up in the mountains not many miles from many cities there were huts and caves that were utilized by deserters for months in the latter part of the war. These deserters were where the provost guard could not find them, and they were consequently safe. They came sneaking back to town in the night when the war was over.

Not many deserters suffered the penalty prescribed for that offense—being shot. President Lincoln was very tender-hearted in this respect. Scores—I might perhaps safely say hundreds—of deserters who had been sentenced to death were pardoned or had their sentence commuted by the kind-hearted president. In all my experience I saw only two men shot for desertion. That terrible sight I will describe before long.

The worst penalty suffered by a deserter was what might be called the social ostracism to which he was subjected on his return to his regiment. He was ignored, disrespected, and treated with contempt generally in a way that was unbearable. No one sympathized with him in sickness or trouble, he was put to the hardest duties and most menial work, and his life was made such that the poor victim often prayed for death. I heard of two men committing suicide because they could not stand this treatment from their companions when they had returned to the regiment after deserting. It is a singular fact that some of the men who wanted to —or even tried to—desert were the most severe in their treatment of the ones who had succeeded—and been caught.

If I deserted I would a thousand times rather be shot than go back to the regiment.

The offense for which I had been arrested by the provost guard was technically called "straggling." Any man who fell out of the ranks or otherwise got behind his regiment while on a march, unless taken sick or wounded, was called a straggler. It was the most common of all army offenses. It was considered the least serious. The punishment was scarcely ever anything worse than being conducted back to your regimental headquarters, and perhaps receiving a mild reprimand from the colonel or captain.

I did not know this then, however, and felt somewhat nervous as I was waiting my turn to be disposed of at the headquarters of the provost guard when the army halted that night. I began to think that thirteen was an unlucky number for me. I had enlisted in the Thirteenth Regiment and here I was arrested on the 13th of September. What had I done? Had I deserted? Would I be shot?

A comical incident interrupted my reverie. I was in the midst of some old soldiers. The officers were almost as dirty as the men in appearance. Most of them were in their undress uniforms and few of them wore shoulder straps or other insignia of office. A man in a dark suit, which was presumably originally black, was leaning against a tree, smoking a briarwood pipe.

A tall, gawky-looking fellow of gigantic build, being over six feet high and heavy in proportion, with long, bushy, sandy whiskers, stalked up. Some of the men saluted and addressed him as "colonel," although he wore no sign of a silver eagle, the insignia of that office. The slouchy-looking man smoking the pipe did not salute and this seemingly attracted the attention of the other.

The colonel, for such he was, addressed the smoker, and asked him gruffly:

"What are you doing here?"

"Smoking," was the laconic reply, and not very civilly at that.

"Who the devil are you, anyhow?" asked the colonel.

"I am the chaplain of the —th Ohio," replied he. "Now who in h——l are you?"

Such language from a chaplain collapsed the colonel and every one else who stood around. The colonel looked at the chaplain a moment and said:

"Good for you, chaplain; I've got some good 'commissary' in my tent. Come along and sample it."

The colonel and chaplain walked off arm and arm together as sociably as if they had known each other for years.

For the edification of the reader I will explain that "commissary" was the whisky furnished by the government to the army for medical purposes. The staff officers were generally "sick," and this was their proverbial panacea and preventive. We sick privates were fed on blue pills. We never got whisky, unless we stole it—which by the way, we occasionally did. The door on the wine cellar of the officers was nothing more secure than a canvas tent flap, you know!

When my turn came in the line of delinquents I was sentenced to nothing worse than to be sent back to my regiment under guard, and I reached Company K just as the boys were boiling their coffee for supper. A number of others had been similarly picked up by the provost guard and brought back, and nothing was said about it.

I found the boys in a state of considerable excitement. The news had leaked out among them somehow that we were close upon the rebels. There had even been some shooting further out to the front and some slightly wounded soldiers had been brought through to the rear.

The pervading sentiment seemed to be that we would have a battle on the morrow. Who can describe the feelings and emotions of a soldier on the eve of an expected battle? As for myself, my mental sufferings were acute.

I supposed then that it was because it was my first experience, but I subsequently learned that that did not in fact make much difference. I firmly believe that with most men each subsequent battle requires more nerve to enter.

"How do you feel, Rats?" I asked Davy Harris. We always called him "Rats." It was a name the boys in the *Guardian* office had given him. Harris was at that moment very pale.

Just as I spoke there was a sound of distant musketry. It sounded like a far-off explosion of firecrackers. It was only an exchange of picket shots. We didn't know. We could fairly feel a quiver of quiet excitement sweep through the camps. For a moment every one stopped talking and there was a stillness so impressive that the crackling of the camp fires sounded like pistol shots. Then there was a low murmur of many voices. That I had turned pale myself I could feel.

As soon as I could get my self-possession again, and saw that general conversation had been resumed with the cessation of the shooting, I repeated my question to Davy Harris as to his personal emotions at that particular moment.

Davy did not reply for a minute or so. Then he quietly arose, turned his back to me, and emphatically ordered:

"Kick me!"

"What?" I asked, not fairly understanding.

"Kick me!"

"What do you mean, anyhow?"

"Kick me!" Davy answered for the third time, *a la* Amelie Rives when she wrote her famous three-time "Kiss Me!"

Then I saw what he meant. It was his expressive way of indicating his feelings in response to my inquiry as to how he felt then and there on the eve of an expected battle. He offered no explanation of his singular reply, nor was any needed. He simply wanted me to kick him for enlisting. I felt the same way myself. I would have liked to have some one kick me then and there for listening to the persuasive eloquence of the patriotic orators on the steps of the old Main Street bank building in Paterson whose speeches had induced me to enlist. I should also have liked to have kicked those self-same orators!

Some great things had happened that day, of which we privates did not know at the time, nor for a long while after, for it remained for the newspapers and the historians to tell what had taken place.

Some of these things will be related in the next chapter.

CHAPTER XIX.

SIGNS OF A BATTLE.

As said in the previous chapter, some great things had occurred on that day (September 13, 1862), which we did not know about at the time. Upon that day General Lee issued an order directing Stonewall Jackson to proceed to Harper's Ferry by the way of Sharpsburg, where he was to cross the Potomac River and thus make a rear movement, while at the same time General McLaws was to go direct, by the way of Middletown, and seize Maryland Heights, while General Walker was to cross the river below Harper's Ferry and take possession of Loudon Heights. The same order of General Lee contained the information that the remainder of the Confederate army would remain in the neighborhood of Boonesborough or Hagerstown, and stay there till rejoined by the troops detailed for the capture of Harper's Ferry.

Harper's Ferry was, from a warlike standpoint, a most important strategic point. It is a cleft or opening in the mountains, where two rivers join. The letter Y is about the shape of the confluence of the Potomac and Shenandoah Rivers. On one side of the Potomac are Maryland Heights, on the other side, Loudon Heights, and the third mountain is called Bolivar Heights. It is a natural gateway, the only passage through which is the narrow road along the side of the river. The Chesapeake and Ohio canal runs along the river on the Maryland side. It will be thus appreciated, even by the reader who has no knowledge whatever of military matters, that this was a most important strategic point.

If General Lee obtained possession of this it would give him the key to an important position. That is the reason that Harper's Ferry played such an important part in many instances during the course of the war. It is not my province here to dilate upon the cowardly manner in which Harper's Ferry was evacuated in the face of the enemy at about this time.

Well, this important order of General Lee, involving the whole plan and scheme of the rebel army, in some mysterious way fell into the hands of General McClellan a few hours after it was issued. It was said that General McClellan had a copy of it as soon as the generals on the rebel side, to whom duplicates had been addressed. How General McClellan got that order no one ever knew. Some said that it was procured by a scout. Others that it came through the hands of a spy. Still others say that it was sold to the Northern general by a Confederate officer, the same as the secret plans of the French were recently sold to the Germans, for which the traitorous officer was sentenced to imprisonment on an island for life. If this be so, the officer in this case was never captured by the Confederates. If he had been, his bones would have long since been transformed into another shape of elementary substance of a cereal character, for those grounds are now covered with corn and wheat fields.

As said frequently before, this war story is not intended as a military history, but rather as the experience of a private soldier in the ranks; but at the same time this particular circumstance is so interesting and has such a direct bearing on subsequent events, that I thought it would not be amiss to give it. Of course we privates did not know anything about all these things at the time. Perhaps only the very highest officers in the army were acquainted with the circumstances. All that we knew at the time was that there was every indication of a coming engagement of some sort, for that we were in close proximity to the enemy there was every sign.

General McClellan, taking advantage of the important information he had so mysteriously gained, proceeded to make a movement that would head off General Lee. He started his army immediately toward South Mountain, which was a high, rocky hill, between

Hagerstown and Sharpsburg. By doing this he would cut right in the middle of the Confederate army. And there is nothing in the world that is so dangerous to an army as to be divided by the enemy.

To come back to our feelings and sensations on the eve of an expected battle! We had around our campfire that night some of the old veterans of the Third Wisconsin, one of the other regiments of our brigade. Naturally the conversation turned to the coming conflict and the subject of battles generally.

After our visitor had got us pretty well alarmed over the horrors of a battle, and myself in particular in a state of nervousness bordering on hysteria, he asked:

"By the way, boys, have you formed your clubs?"

We asked him what he meant by clubs?

"Well, you see," replied he, "if there is a battle the chances are that some of you will be killed" (and how glibly he uttered the awful word). "In that case it is a good thing to have a club."

I wished somebody would club me.

"The idea of a club is this," he continued, while we were listening with mouths and ears wide open. "The plan is to divide yourselves up in clubs of three men. The chances are that the whole three will not be killed. You give each other your names and addresses of the relatives or friends at home whom you would wish to be notified in case anything happened. Then the fellow that comes out all right can send word at once in case anything happens."

"But don't the officers report all these things. Don't the newspaper correspondents send the list of names by telegraph to their papers?" I asked, with journalistic instinct.

"Oh, pshaw, that don't amount to nothing," was the reply. "These fellows get all the news they can, of course; but they don't get half. In a battle everything is all mixed up. Men are killed and they are stripped of their clothes and everything in their pockets so that they do not leave a trace of who they are. Then fellows get captured by the rebs, and wounded men fall into the hands of the graybacks, and some are left on the battlefield to die alone and no one ever hears what becomes of them. In this case you can write to their friends that they are 'missing.' But as a general thing the three men in a club can keep track of each other, whatever happens. I tell you clubs are a good thing. In fact clubs are trumps."

The idea struck me like joining a suicide club, but at the same time it could not be doubted that it was a good thing. We immediately decided to form ourselves into a club. The club to which I attached myself consisted of Sergeant Heber Wells, John Butterworth and myself. And it is a singular fact that all three of us are alive to-day. There were soon decimations in many of the clubs, but none of our particular three had to send a letter breaking the news of a death in our trio. Two of us were, however, wounded in the battle of Chancellorsville, but the news of that got home quickly enough.

I can't say that this club business was very pleasant. It seemed like writing one's own epitaph, or engraving one's own name on his coffin-plate. It made me very nervous and downhearted. I felt sure that I was the one of our three whose name would be the first to be sent home among the list of killed.

I didn't sleep much that night. I could think of nothing but fighting and being shot. I wondered how it felt to be shot. Did it hurt much? Was the agony awful? I had never seen anything shot but a dog.

A hundred times I recalled the shooting of that dog, how he yelped and writhed, kicked and struggled! Imagine a human being writhing and struggling in that way! Imagine me—me, writhing and struggling in that way, in mortal agony! In fitful dreams I saw the shooting of that dog again, and it seemed as if I were the dog, yelping and writhing and struggling in my death agony.

Then I dreamed that I was at home, in bed, in my little front room in Fair Street, with the aquarium at the window and the canary bird in his painted cage. I dreamed that I dreamed. I dreamed that I awoke from a dream—a horrible dream—that I had been in the army, and that there was going to be a battle. I dreamed that I awoke from the horrible dream and found that it was a nightmare, and that I got out of bed and knelt beside it and thanked God that it was but a dream and nothing worse. Thank heaven, that it was but a dream! Thank heaven, I had not enlisted! Thank heaven, I was at my home, safe and secure, and that the only warlike sound I would hear in the morning would be the bell calling me down to a breakfast of broiled chicken and muffins.

Sleep on, soldier! Pleasant be thy dream! For the morrow ye know not!

CHAPTER XX.

NEAR A BATTLE.

It was not the breakfast bell at my home in Fair Street that awoke me the next morning, but that everlasting drum sounding the reveille that had become so painfully familiar. After the vivid dream of home related in the previous chapter, the awakening to a sense of my surroundings was a severe shock. But there was too much excitement around camp to spend much time in gloomy reveries.

It is perhaps good for the soldier that there is such incessant activity while at the front. It occupies his time and takes all his mind, so that there is not much opportunity to sit down and think. And when night comes the soldier is generally so fatigued that he sinks at once into a leaden-like slumber. It was not often that the soldier dreams as I had dreamed the night before.

"I tole you fellers," said John Ick as he was boiling his coffee, "we got by dot schlaughter haus to-day, and don'd you forgot dot." Then turning to Reddy Mahar, who seemed to be his natural enemy, he added:

"You don'd was so fresh yourselluf, Retty. You don'd vant to fight so much alretty, eh?"

"Be jabbers and I wish I was home, that's phwat I does," answered Reddy very meekly.

"No, you don'd vant to fight so much as you was by Washington, don'd it? I don'd was no cowyard now, ain't it?"

"Shut up, you fellows," said John Stansfield, thinking there was going to be a repetition of the racket between these two in Washington. But there was no danger. There was no fight in either of them. John Ick seemed at the moment to be outwardly the least concerned, but it was evident that it was only put on for the occcasion. Ick apparently wanted to arouse the ire of his old adversary for the purpose of creating some sort of a diversion, but it was a failure. He might have kicked Mahar just then, and I doubt if he would have taken it up.

It was not long before we heard fighting of some sort further at the front. The musket shots started in first in little spurts, two or three at a time. Then there would be a volley that sounded like a rattle—like one of those wooden concerns that the boys hold in their hands and whirl around. Then something else—more warlike than all! Listen!

"Hark! 'Tis the cannon's opening roar!"

I shall never forget the first time I heard a cannon fired in the army. And this was the morning.

Boom!

And the hills echoed and re-echoed with the roar, like lowering thunder.

Whiz—whiz—whiz—whiz—whiz—!

Say it as fast as you can. Start with the voice loud and strong. Then with each reiterated "whiz" let the voice fall, diminishing in force. Try it:

Whiz—whiz—whiz—whiz—whiz—!

That is the sound of the rifled shell flying through the air. Then—

Crash!

At it smashes through the trees, or splinters the rocks, or richochets along the ground. Then, again, another—

Boom!

As the shell explodes, its fragments fly in every direction, scattering destruction and death in its wake.

And if you are near enough to where it struck, and there is any one in the way, there is another sound.

It is the shrieking, the yelling, the cursing of those who have been rent asunder by those terrible fragments, and yet have enough life left to suffer.

Why is it that men curse and blaspheme when wounded, instead of praying?

I am describing here the first cannon shots that I ever heard. The part relative to the curse does not apply to this particular day, but to subsequent experiences. On the day in question we were not close enough to the front to hear the cries of the severely wounded, but we did hear the roar of the cannon and we heard lots of it.

Once the shooting of the cannon had commenced, there was a good deal of it. It was some distance further out in the front, but we could hear it plainly enough. It was a continual "Boom—whiz—crash!" for several hours.

And it formed the bass and baritone for the soprano and tenor of the musket shots. Once or twice, far back as we were, we heard the peculiar singing of a rifle bullet. This can be best expressed in type this way:

"Z-z-z-z-z-z-z-zip!"

The "z-z-z" represents the course of the bullet through the air. The "zip" is the sound of its striking something.

Imagine a mosquito buzzing around, and then the slap on the cheek that puts him (and you) out of misery, and you will have a fair idea, on a small scale, of the sound of a minnie rifle bullet.

That all this shooting further out in the front was no Fourth of July nonsense soon began to be evident, for the wounded soldiers began to stream in.

It was our first sight of the real horrors of battle.

We were too close to the front for any of the wounded to be attended to by the surgeons without passing through us to the improvised field hospitals, designated by small yellow flags on staves stuck in the ground, to the rear of us. Thus it was that we saw the wounded, not with their injuries concealed by neat white bandages, but in all their grewsome nakedness.

Of course these were the men who were "slightly" wounded—those who were able to walk. A wonderful number were shot in the arm and hand. There were lacerated fingers and thumbs; useless arms, held up by the others unhurt; men with the tips of their noses shot off; soldiers with the fragment of an ear hanging down alongside of their necks; men painfully limping from the effects of shots in the leg or foot; officers and privates with blood streaming over their faces from scalp-wounds—the most terrible of all to look at, but in reality the least dangerous. All these hurried to the doctors in the rear.

What struck me was the utter nonchalance of the wounded. Of those able to walk, no matter how desperately hurt they seemed to be, no matter how bloody they were, none uttered a cry or a complaint. On the contrary they seemed to be remarkably cheerful and chipper. Had those men been similiarly injured in civil life they would have indulged in vehement demonstrations of agony.

But when a man is wounded in the army, it seems as if his system, both mental and physical, were nerved up to it. And furthermore there is a feeling of inexpressible exultation over the fact that one has escaped something worse, and the victim is also braced up with the knowledge that for awhile at least he will have no fighting to do, and that there is a good prospect of his getting a furlough to go home and see his family.

I did not appreciate all this at the moment and so was struck with the apparent unconcern of those who had been wounded. When I was wounded myself on a subsequent occasion, I learned to understand these things.

And furthermore, when a man is shot, if it be not in a vital spot, the immediate pain is not severe. The real agony comes later, when inflammation begins to set in, and the entire system is involved with the fever that invariably follows gunshot wounds sooner or later. If you want to know how it feels to be shot through the leg, for instance, let some one throw a stone from across the street so that it will strike you. There will be a sharp sting, followed by a sort of numbness. That is almost exactly the sensation of being shot through a muscular part of the body.

But afterward—when the fever begins! Then there are long and tedious days and nights of intolerable agony.

Pretty soon the more severely wounded began to come through on stretchers, carried on blankets with the sound men holding each corner; or being lifted by the legs and arms in the most primitive way.

We were lying near the town of Boonesborough. Here the wounded were taken. The churches, school-houses and even residences taken possession of as hospitals became at once the scenes of surgical butchery. I use this word in no offensive sense.

And yet, one week previous, the people of Boonesborough had no more idea that they would be in the immediate theater of actual war than had the people of the quietest town in the country. Imagine the feelings of the women and children on seeing their homes suddenly filled with mutilated and bleeding soldiers, spread in rows along the floor of the parlor and dining room! And yet one week—in fact two days—before, there were no more signs of such a thing happening in that particular town than there is to-day, I might almost say.

What were my feelings all this time? I can hardly describe them. We lay there momentarily expecting to be ordered into the thick of the fray ourselves! We did not know at what minute our turn would come, or how soon some of us might swell the number of mutilated human beings going back to the surgeon's knife. As for myself I remember that I was in a state bordering on a panic. I was almost out of my head. In fact I was mentally and physically almost paralyzed. I moved about in a misty, hazy sort of a way, hardly knowing where I was or what I was doing.

There was not much talk among the boys that day. The same listless, despairing spirit seemed to prevade all.

What was going on? We didn't know. What battle was it? We didn't know. All that we knew was that there was a scene of carnage being enacted somewhere out there a little further in front, where human beings were being torn to pieces. And all that we thought of was that our turn to take part in the awful scene would soon come.

"What do you think of it?" I asked Davy Harris as he threw himself on the grass beside me.

Harris was very pale. He replied:

"I think——"

The sentence was not completed. It was interrupted by the order:

"Fall in, Thirteenth!"

Davy Harris and I exchanged nervous glances.

"Our turn has come, Joe," said he quietly.

CHAPTER XXI.

SOME AWFUL FIGURES.

Of course we thought surely that our turn had come and that we were about to be precipitated into a battle. Does the reader wonder that we were demoralized? Consider the situation.

We had barely entered the service. As a matter of fact it was only two weeks since we had left the mustering camp at Newark. The most of us had never fired a gun in our lives with the exception of the single volley over the canal at Camp Frelinghuysen in the battalion drill. We had had no experience, but little drilling, and were practically as ignorant of military movements as we were on the day we enlisted.

We had entered the army with the idea of course that we would some day in the future be precipitated into an engagement, but we did not imagine that we would be thus summarily hustled from our homes to the battlefield without being hardened and prepared for it by degrees, as it were. In the whole course of the war I do not believe there ever was a regiment so suddenly engaged in a battle after entering the service as the Thirteenth New Jersey.

It so happened that we did not get into a fight that day, nor for a couple of days later, but the same remark holds good about the remarkably short time that existed between the time of our enlistment and our experience in actual warfare, in one of the most sanguinary of conflicts.

I believe that if we had really been ordered into a fight that day I would have fainted from terror and nervous weakness. But fortunately, at least for me, we didn't get into that battle. It was only one of those mysterious movements that were so frequent—a change of position. There may have been some reason for these constant changes, and again there may not have been. I still incline to the latter idea. But nevertheless, it did seem as if we were forever changing our position and moving from this spot to that without any sense or reason whatever. That was all it amounted to on this occasion.

And to our intense satisfaction and relief there was a sudden cessation of the firing in the front. Whatever had been going on, it had evidently come to a settlement some way.

What we had heard, as we learned later, was the engagement that has gone into history as the battle of South Mountain. It wasn't a long engagement, but it was an important one, and had it been properly followed up and had the other departments of the army properly co-operated, the result would have been of inestimable value to the Northern army.

General McClellan had captured the South Mountain passes at the engagement at Turner's Gap, although not without considerable loss. The Confederate loss in this engagement at South Mountain has been put down at about 3,000, including some prisoners. The loss on both sides in the shape of killed, wounded and prisoners, was perhaps 5,000. This is not much of a battle compared with some of the fights during the war, but it was a considerable one just the same, even in these days, as will be seen by comparing the number with that of some of the recent engagements between the Japs and Chinese, with all the former's advantage of improved weapons and ammunition.

And by the way, is the reader of this a sufficient student of history to notice the fact that as civilization progresses and the means of killing people are facilited, the losses in battle continually decrease? The accepted theory is that eventually the instruments of wholesale slaughter and death will be so perfected that a fight between two armies will mean nothing less than total annihilation of one or the other; that this will reach such a stage that war will cease to be possible, and that the differences of the future will be settled by arbitration instead of by recourse to arms. But the facts do not bear this out. History tells us that they had a good deal more extensive list of fatalities in olden times than at present, which, if the records are correct, suggest some strange comparisons.

Modern warfare has been aptly described as an improved and scientific way of throwing stones. In olden times a battle was more in the nature of a hand-to-hand conflict and the number of killed and wounded was undoubtedly larger.

At the battle of Cressy the arms of the English Prince of Wales were won by Edward, the Black Prince. Among the killed on the side of the French was the King of Bohemia, whose crest was three ostrich feathers and the motto "Ich Dien" (I serve). At the conclusion of the battle the crest and the motto were adopted by the Black Prince, and have ever since been worn by the Prince of Wales. I interpolate this simply as an interesting fact. What I wanted to say was that at that battle the French went into the fight with nearly 100,000 men and at the close of the day the French king fled with five knights and sixty soldiers. Over 40,000 men had been killed or wounded and the rest of the army had scattered in every direction.

At the battle of Borodino there were 250,000 men engaged, and in one day 78,000, or 31 per cent., had been killed and wounded. Every woman in France wore mourning after that battle. In the Roman army of 146,000 men, the loss was 52,000 or 34 per cent., at the battle of Cannæ. All the prisoners were massacred, and Hannibal, the victor, sent to Carthage five bushels of gold rings taken from the fingers of the enemy's knights that were killed.

As the Battle of a Week, in 732 A.D., in which Martel overthrew the Saracens, there were 550,000 men engaged, of whom 375,000 were killed on the field. This was the bloodiest battle of history, and yet the arms at the time must have been of an extremely primitive character. Among the 140,000 who participated at Waterloo, the loss was 51,000. In the Battle of Nations at Leipsig in 1813, there were 320,000 men engaged, and the loss was 111,000. Of the 320,000 engaged at Gravelotte, the killed and wounded numbered 48,000. At Marengo, in which 58,000 were engaged, the loss was 13,000.

To afford a comparison with our late war, I will cite the battle of Gettysburg as an example. In this engagement there were 140,000 men opposed to each other. The loss in killed, wounded and missing during the three days' fighting at Gettysburg, was—Federal, 28,898; Confederate, 37,000; total, 65,898. That is between 25 and 30 per cent. But this was not only the largest battle of the war, but the loss was proportionately the greatest. The average loss in battle, according to statistical historians who have made a study of "our late unpleasantness," was not over 10 or 12 per cent.

And yet, during the late war, compared with the armies of old times, the troops were equipped with modern and improved arms, and naturally it might be supposed that the mortality would be all the greater.

The records of losses during the last war (between the United States and Spain) are not complete, so that they may be only roughly stated, viz.: Americans killed at and around Santiago, from 260 to 270; wounded, about 1,600. Killed in naval encounters at Bahio Honda and other points on the north coast of Cuba, 5 or 6. Killed at Porto Rico, 5 or 6; wounded 60 or 70. Killed in the capture of Manila and attendant skirmishes, 40 or 50; wounded, about 200. In addition to these, several thousand American soldiers and sailors died of disease in camp, the estimated number being, according to latest reports, about 2,600. A rough aggregate would make the total American loss in the war (including the destruction of the Maine), about 3,236 killed (and died), and about 5,356 wounded. These are believed to be the outside figures. Official and complete reports would probably show a sight diminution.

The Spanish losses may only be estimated, as follows: At Santiago, killed, 2,000; wounded, 6,000. Killed in the destruction of Cervera's fleet, 600 to 700; wounded, 400. How many were lost by the Spanish in the other engagements will probably never be known, for no figures have ever been given out of Spain's loss in the memorable destruction of Montojo's fleet by the matchless Admiral Dewey on May 1, 1898.

The last battles between the United States forces and the Filippino insurgents under Aguinaldo in the Philippine Islands are too recent and the information too indefinite to present very reliable figures. In the battle at Manila in February, 1899, the American losses are believed to have been about 40 or 50 killed and perhaps 250 wounded. The Filippino losses are estimated at from 1,500 to 2,000 killed and about 3,000 wounded. This was really a large battle, for there were no less than 32,000 men engaged—13,000 Americans and 20,000 Filippinos.

The total strength of the American army in the Spanish war was 274,717. The war began on Thursday, April 21, 1898, at 7 A.M. The peace protocol was signed at Washington, D. C., on Friday, August 12, 1898, at 4:23 P.M. The treaty of peace was signed by the joint American and Spanish commission in Paris on December 10, 1898. The treaty was ratified by the United States senate on Monday, February 6, 1899, at 3:25 P.M.

A comparison of the number of men enlisted in the war with Spain and in previous wars by the United States may in this connection be interesting. In the Revolutionary war the number did not exceed 250,000. In the civil war there were 2,320,168 Federal troops, of whom 178,975 were colored and 67,000 regulars. In the war of 1812 there were 471,622, of whom 62,674 were regulars. In the Mexican war there were 116,321, of whom 42,545 were regulars. In the war with Spain our troops numbered 219,035 volunteers (of whom 10,189 were colored), and 55,682 were regulars, a total of 274,717.

I interpolate these statistics here as being interesting and appropriate, inasmuch as they give the reader an idea of the size and extent of the battle of South Mountain. To the private soldier a battle is a battle, and it practically makes little difference to him, as an individual, whether the loss is 1,000 or 100,000. The effect on the army or the country, however, is more or less important, according to the numerical and strategical results

The battle of South Mountain, although not a large one, as battles go, was nevertheless an important one, for it gave General McClellan the opportunity he desired of cutting the rebel army in two and relieving the Federal garrison at Harper's Ferry.

But the disgraceful and utterly inexcusable surrender of Harper's Ferry defeated this purpose. Colonel Miles had 12,000 men, 73 pieces of artillery, and an immense quantity of military stores and supplies, and he should have defended such an important place to the last man. But he surrendered. He saw the signs of the big rebel army, and capitulated without terms or conditions.

The cowardly act, however, met with instant retribution. While Colonel Miles was in the very act of hoisting a white flag in token of surrender, he was struck by a cannon ball and instantly killed. There is an old adage that it is not well to speak ill of the dead. But it was a fortunate thing for Colonel Miles that he was killed as he was, for it blunted the rough edge of popular indignation that was expressed at his conduct. In those exciting days there was little sympathy for a commanding officer who had the reputation of being a coward. Had Colonel Miles lived long enough to have heard the criticism over his surrender of Harper's Ferry he would probably have committed suicide.

Now that Harper's Ferry had been lost General McClellan changed his plans and directed his entire attention to the main army of General Lee, and then commenced the movements that a day or so later precipitated us into one of the great conflicts of the war—the battle of Antietam.

In that bloody battle the Thirteenth New Jersey regiment received its "baptism of fire."

CHAPTER XXII.

EVE OF BATTLE.

AFTER the battle of South Mountain, General Lee, who saw that General McClellan meant business, found what military men would call "a strong position" on the west side of Antietam creek, and proceeded to get his army in readiness to meet the pursuing Union army. In telling this, of course, I am writing in the light of subsequent knowledge. Of course at the time we knew nothing more of what was going on, or what was coming, or indeed what had passed, than so many sheep in a drove.

But at the same time we felt, rather than positively knew, that the army was getting into position for a great conflict. There was a hurrying and scurrying of mounted officers and messengers, an anxious look on the faces of the higher officers over us that we frequently met or passed, and an air of general importance and preparation, not manifest on other occasions, that gave the soldier a knowledge that a battle was imminent. It was evident even to us raw recruits, who had scarcely been a fortnight away from our homes. Much more were these movements and preparations understood by the older and more experienced soldiers.

We all knew, therefore, that we were about to be plunged into a battle, and as practically the whole of the Federal and Confederate armies of Virginia were pitted against each other, it would be a battle royal and a terrible conflict.

And, by the way, speaking of Company K and the other company from Paterson and vicinity, Company C, we had hardly yet become acquainted with each other. We had enlisted in haste, had been hurried off to the front so quickly, and had been kept on such constant movement, that there had been no chance to become acquainted outside of our own immediate coteries, so to speak. We were simply a big crowd of comparative strangers.

Soldiers in the army always divide themselves into couples. Every man has his partner (usually called "pard"), and they were to each other almost man and wife. I will not go into this right here, for my present partner was one with whom I only had a comparatively short connection, and the ordinary relations between "pards" did not prevail. My partner, or bed-mate, just then was Heber Wells, the orderly sergeant of the company. I could not call him a tent-mate, for we had no tents at this time, having left our Sibleys at Rockville, and the "shelter" or "pup tents" had not yet been given out to us. In another stage of the story I will have something to say about the man who was essentially "my partner," John Butterworth, with whom I was thrown in accidentally, as it were, but whom I found to be one of the best of fellows and a "partner" in more senses than one.

Heber Wells was the orderly sergeant. He was the busiest man in the company. He had to call the rolls, attend to all the company reports, and in other respects do the work of the commissioned officers, so that he was kept at it all the while and did not have opportunity to spend much time with the gatherings and groups of the privates. He was always a gentleman, always a good friend, always a brave man, and always carried himself with a dignity that was inborn.

Then there was John Stansfield, always full of fun, but at the same time dignified. Two other characters were also already familiar to the whole company—"Slaughter House Ike" and "Reddy Mahar," the former particularly, not only on account of his perennial wit, but because of his everlasting penchant to get into trouble.

I might also mention my old printer associates, David Harris, Liv. Allen and Curt Brown, and such men as Abe Ackerman, James J. Vanderbeck, James W. Post, John J. Carlough, Daniel S. Wanamaker, Samuel Dougherty, John Anderson, Jacob Berdan, Henry Clark, John Farlow, Alexander Kidd, Archibald Mc-

Call, George Mickle, Henry Speer, Thomas Vanderbeck, Charles Noble, William Lambert, and others who were acquaintances by this time, and the most of whom are living to-day. There were plenty of others in the company with whom I became acquainted afterward, but the above about comprised the limit of personal acquaintances at the time mentioned, and I particularly remember them as we were approaching the place where we were to engage in our first real fighting.

John Ick had the "slaughter-house" fever bad just then. He broke out every five minutes with some remark about the "shambles" and every wounded man that came along was the signal for a fresh outbreak. But there was no reprimand or fun cast at John Ick at this time, for we all felt the same way, and to a great extent he expressed our sentiments.

In speaking for myself in saying that I was in a perpetual state of nervous fright, I think I can speak for the rest. Once when a lad, I had come near drowning. I was under the water long enough to remember everything that I had ever done in my life. I remember to this day how the bad things stood out in the boldest relief. Things that I then considered very wicked perhaps would not trouble my conscience so much nowadays, but the smallest offense seemed a great sin then and it was pictured before me like a panorama.

So it was now. I felt as sure that I was going to be killed as I did when I was under the water when a lad. I thought over my comparatively short life and everything that I had done. I wished that I had not done some things. I wished that I had lived a better life, that I was a member of the church and in other respects better. In fact I thought I was going to die, and I was afraid, not so much of the simple dying, as of the mysterious hereafter. In fact I felt afraid to die, and I am sure that I mentally made up my mind that if I got through with this all right, I would lead a better life. But alas, that is the rule always.

"When the devil was sick, the devil a monk would be.
When the devil was well, the devil a monk was he."

In other words I am afraid that after the big battle

that came and passed I was wickeder than ever. Such is life.

I remember plainly what Henry Spear said to me.

"It is all right for you young fellows, who have no one to depend upon you. But just think of me and the others who have wives and families."

"That's all right," said I, "but don't you suppose we young fellows like to live as well as you older ones?"

"Perhaps; but you have no one depending on you and that makes all the difference. I don't think of myself at all, but of my wife and children."

"That's true," said Heber Wells, who had heard the conversation; "if you had a family depending on you you would feel different."

"And are you not afraid for your own self?" I asked.

"Of course I do not want to be killed," answered Henry Spear; "but that is nothing compared with the thought of family."

I was young then. I had my doubts about it. True I had no family depending on me, but I had bright prospects and—well, I had the picture of a pretty girl in my pocket who perhaps might grieve, and perhaps might not. On the whole I didn't think she would—much. But I was scared for myself, and I honestly believe the others were too. I did not have any family excuse to cover up my fear. And yet, seriously, in the light of later experience, I can appreciate the fact that this must have added materially to the mental sufferings of the men who imagined they were going to their death.

All this time we were marching and countermarching, going hither and thither, as if the commanding officers were not quite satisfied where they did want us to stand. Late in the afternoon on September 15, 1862, the advance troops of our army reached the front of the enemy and preparations were at once made for the big battle that was expected to begin the following morning.

That was not a pleasant night. We were in a state of nervous expectancy, and as we sat around the camp fires we discussed the awful possibilities of the morrow. The little "club" to which I belonged gave each other the directions as to what to do in case anything happened to any one of the three. We carefully went over the addresses of each other's relatives at home, and mutually agreed to stand by each other in case any of us were wounded. In fact we made arrangements that impressed me as being very much like the preparations for a funeral. Which of us would be the corpse? The comrade from the Third Wisconsin who had suggested the idea had told us that there was no likelihood of all three being killed. One might. Perhaps two might. But the chances were that at least one of the three would escape. Who would it be? I hoped that I would be the one, but I had my doubts about it.

Was this cowardice? Was I a coward? Perhaps I was. But I really believe that if I was a coward for feeling this way, then ninety-nine hundredths of the army were cowards. It is not natural that any man, or any animal for that matter, should not be nervous and apprehensive in the face of impending death. If this feeling was cowardice, then truly I was a coward. I guess I was never cut out for a soldier, at least the kind that have to fight. I wished that I had joined the "home guards."

When the reveille sounded the next morning we all arose and looked at each other in a strange way. We did not talk much, but the glance that each man gave the other was a silent inquiry or interchange of feeling. Nearly every man was pale, and everybody's eyes bore the appearance of having passed a wakeful night. In a listless way we prepared and tried to eat a little breakfast, but there was no taste to it, and we had no appetite. And when the order to "fall in" came, we got into the ranks in a slow, despairing sort of way, as if we had given up all hope—the sort of way that a condemned prisoner pulls himself together to walk to the scaffold.

Let a man of that regiment say, if he truthfully can, that he felt differently from the way I have tried to describe.

But we did not get into the battle that day. They say that "hope deferred maketh the heart sick." I cannot say that the delay in this made any of our hearts very ill. But at the same time it was a painful wait, withal. When a man has an aching tooth to be pulled he wants to have it hurried through and be done with, and the same sentiment prevailed now. We thought that we would rather be plunged into the unknown horror of the battle and be done with it than have to much longer suffer this terrible suspense.

I am only endeavoring to describe the feelings of a private soldier on the eve of his first battle. The description is tame and unsatisfactory at the best. I feel that I have greatly underestimated the sensations.

We moved that day with Mansfield's corps, to which we were attached, to the neighborhood of Keedysville, where we remained all day. The preparations for the battle were seen all around us. The troops were getting in line for the conflict, and even to our inexperienced eyes, the reasons for the movements were understood. The artillery was being placed on the hills, the guns unlimbered and turned toward the direction where the rebels were supposed to be. The cavalry were galloping hither and thither to the front. Mounted orderlies dashed up to the corps headquarters with written orders to the generals. When night came we could even hear distant drums and bugles, which were said to be those of the enemy. We were getting into close quarters and no mistake.

Late in the night we received orders to move. The orders were ominous. Instructions were passed around in a whisper, to move as quietly as possible. There must be no loud talking. Our tin cans and coffee pots were to be muffled in some way so that they would not rattle. Under no circumstances must any man light his pipe or strike a match for any purpose whatever, for it was a quiet maneuver in the dark, to be made without letting the enemy know what was going on.

That was enough. Company K wasn't going to let the enemy know where it was, not if she knew herself, and we were as still as mice as we marched here and there in the dark, stumbling over almost everything in the way. We went over fences, through woods, up hill and down, past quiet farmhouses, and crossed a good-sized stream on an old bridge. We learned afterward that it was Antietam creek, made famous the next day by the bloody battle that took place along its banks.

Finally we were halted in a position on the extreme right of the line, and threw ourselves on the ground for a much-needed rest. It was at that weird hour in the morning just before dawn, when it is the darkest.

Scarcely had we laid ourselves on the ground than there was some very sharp shooting in front of us.

The battle of Antietam had begun!

CHAPTER XXIII.

ANTIETAM.

It was the memorable day of September 17, 1862.

As stated in the previous chapter, it was an hour or so before the first signs of daylight, and we had just thrown ourselves on the ground for a short rest after a tedious and fatiguing night's march. Then the shooting began a little distance in front of us.

Hooker's corps had been assigned the position on the right of the Union army in the hope of turning the enemy's left. Our corps was to support Hooker's. The skirmishers on our right had encountered those of the rebels on their left. They exchanged shots, and that was the firing we had heard.

It seems—and this was learned afterward, of course —that Stonewall Jackson's force had made a rapid march from Harper's Ferry and joined Lee during the day. Lee was one of the most able generals and astute strategists that the world ever knew. He seemed to possess a wonderful facility for learning the enemy's movements and as if by intuition knew what they were intended for. Thus by bringing his own troops into the proper position he frequently frustrated the best-laid plans of the Northern generals. In this way on this occasion he had strengthened the weakest point of the Confederate's right, where General McClellan had intended to make his most savage attack.

Although but two weeks away from home, as it were, we had become quite used to the sound of musketry, but never before did the shooting seem to have the same significance that it did now. We knew that we were in for it. We waited for daylight as the condemned murderer waits for the sun to rise on his last day, for there was not one of us that did not regard it as his last day.

"We was by dot schlaughter-haus now, sure, alretty," said John Ick, in the darkness.

"Sh-h!" said Sergeant Wells. And it was the only answer to Ick's lugubrious remark, for we all felt that there was too much truth in it. Even Reddy Mahar, Ich's perennial enemy, said not a word, but hugged the ground all the closer.

The minutes rolled on. Did ever time pass so slowly? Everybody was silent. Everybody was thinking—thinking—thinking! The sun would arise! Would we ever see it set? Alas, some of us did not!

The long-delayed daylight finally arrived. The first gray streaks of dawn disclosed to our eyes a vast army, lying in battle array, all ready for the fight, it seemed.

The first thing done was to serve us all with a ration of fresh beef. This was the universal custom before a battle. Why was it? Was it to make us more savage, like so many animals? At all events it seemed to be the general rule. More than once I have seen an army marching into a battle with a chunk of half-roasted fresh beef in every man's hand. There used to be a tradition that the Confederates gave their men a ration of whisky and gunpowder before a fight to make them savage. I don't know whether there was any truth in this or not.

We lighted fires. There was no use for secrecy now, for each army knew the proximity of the other. We stuck our fresh beef on the ends of sticks, held them in the flames of the camp fires and roasted, or rather toasted them, as best as we could. But before the meat was scarcely smoked we were ordered to change our position.

The Thirteenth was formed in "close column," which is a usual way to prepare for a battle. We had never been drilled in any such movement, and to get us in the right position it was almost necessary for the officers to lead each man by the shoulders and put him where he ought to be. And to tell the truth, most of the officers knew about as little of these movements as the men.

When we were in the right shape we were told that we might again light the fires and cook our meat for breakfast. But that breakfast was never cooked. We had scarcely got the fires started than the firing in the front began again more vigorously than we had ever heard it before. We were ordered to "fall in."

Some of the men ate their beef raw. I was not used to that yet, and thrust my ration into my haversack. I didn't have much of an appetite anyhow!

Then the firing of the rifles in the front became more continuous. That was followed by the artillery. First there was a single shot, as if it were a signal. Then there was an answering roar from a far-off hill. The Union artillery responded, and the rebels answered back. The shooting of big guns extended all along the line, and the scarce risen sun was greeted with a continuous salvo that sounded like ten thousand anvil choruses.

The "boom—whiz—crash—boom" described in a previous chapter, was repeated and repeated a hundred, a thousand, yes, thousands of times, till the skies crashed like a thousand severe summer thunder-storms. It was simply awful! The noise was ear-splitting, and the effect on the nerves was terrible. I really believe that if it were not for the infernal noise of the artillery in a battle it would not seem half so bad.

We were temporarily halted along a piece of woods; I believe that this woods has gone into history as "The East Woods." Then every man was startled by the most unearthly yelling.

None had ever before heard such demoniacal shrieks. They sounded as if they came from a lost soul in the nethermost depths of purgatory. We were all startled. It made our blood run cold.

"What in the world is that man making such a noise for?" asked Sergeant Wells.

"Damfino," replied Hank Van Orden, "let's go and see."

Don't let the reader think that Hank meant to be profane, right there in the face of death. He was so used to that expression that he would have said the same thing if spoken to by the Angel Gabriel. No one ever regarded it as profanity, and even Wells did not notice it then.

So we went over the edge of the woods from whence the unearthly shrieks were coming. Wells made an exclamation of horror. There was no more cool and self-possessed man in the army than Heber Wells, but the sight that he saw was enough to turn the stomach of the most hardened veterans.

There lay a wounded soldier. He was a member of the One Hundred and Seventh New York, one of the regiments of our brigade, and whose face was instantly recognized. He had been struck by the fragments of a bursted shell, and both of his legs were torn off near the knees. The feet and ankles were gone entirely, but there protruded from the lacerated flesh the ends of the bones of the legs in a most horrible manner, making a sight that was simply sickening. Nearly every man of Company K went over to take a look at the wounded man and immediately turned away with a pallid face.

There were plenty of wounded men now passing through to the rear, but their injuries were comparatively insignificant. This was the first time that any of us had seen a man mortally wounded and in the act of dying. I think that did more to upset and demoralize the men just at that moment than anything else in the world, and the fact that he was one of our own men, so to speak, and that the same fate was likely to overcome any one of us at any moment, made an impression that was terrible.

Heber Wells saw that the man was beyond hope and that all that could be done for him would be to possibly relieve his sufferings.

"What do you want, man?" asked Heber, sympathetically.

"Water, water, water!" moaned the wounded man.

Wells reached for his canteen and handed it to the dying man.

"No, no," he said, in a weak voice, as Heber held it to his lips. "No, not—drink. Pour—head——"

The man's head was bursting with the fever of the terrible anguish he was suffering.

"Thank—thank—better—" painfully gasped the

poor wretch, as he felt the cooling draught trickle down his forehead.

An order to "fall in" ended this painful scene. The wounded man must have died a few minutes later, for he was going fast when we left him. He is probably in one of the graves in the Sharpsburg national cemetery marked "unknown." But the dreadful sight had made an unpleasant impression upon us, for nothing that we had yet seen had so greatly unnerved us. I don't think any member of the company ever forgot that sight.

We were ordered to take a slightly changed position, to support Hexhamer's battery, which was banging away for dear life. As fast as the men could load the cannon they were sending shot and shell toward a rebel battery on an opposite hill, and the latter were sending back their shells, which were striking around us in the most reckless manner. The execution done by the enemy just then, to our intense relief, did not amount to much, for the most of the shells went over us, and exploded somewhere further in the rear. When I saw the artillerymen at work then, I began to wish that I had enlisted in that branch of the service, for it certainly looked a good deal safer than the infantry or cavalry.

My subsequent experience corroborated this. Let me advise the reader if there is another war, to enlist in the artillery. When an artilleryman is wounded, he is generally torn to pieces; but taken as a whole the chances of his getting out of a fight alive are a good deal better than in most of the other branches of the service and it is better in other respects.

Suddenly we were ordered to lie down flat, with space between each file sufficient for some one to pass through. This strange order was soon understood, for a moment later, the Sixty-ninth New York, one of the bravest fighting regiments of the war, came running through us in the double quick.

They had been ordered to charge one of the rebel batteries. They went down the hill on the run with their guns on their shoulders, or hanging in their arms, and when they began to ascend the other side of the valley, they brought their muskets to a "charge bayonet!"

A gallant charge they made, but they were repulsed. They were ordered back to their former position. Although a number of them had been killed, although there were some still in the ranks with blood streaming from their wounds, they came back through the Thirteenth with as much regularity as if they had been in a drill, and with a discipline that excited our admiration. It was this sort of conduct that made the Sixty-ninth New York one of the most famous regiments in the war, and no historian could ever praise that regiment too much.

"How do you feel, Heber?" asked Captain Irish of Heber Wells.

"Hungry, just now," was Heber's cool response.

"I don't mean that. You know what I mean, Heber," said the captain.

"Well, to tell the truth," was Wells' reply, "I would much rather be at home."

"Do you know," said Captain Irish, "I feel as if I would never come out of this alive."

"Oh, nonsense," said Wells, "you will come out all right."

"No," reiterated the captain gloomily; "I will never come out alive."

Do men have presentiments of death? Inside of thirty minutes Captain Irish was a corpse!

CHAPTER XXIV.

CAPTAIN IRISH KILLED.

Now comes the Thirteenth's "baptism of fire." And a bloody one it was!

We were ordered forward!

Over eight hundred strong, in battle front, we proceeded. The officers ordered us to "dress to the right," but it was a straggling line.

The "z—z—z—ip" of the bullets could be heard whistling past us. And a moment later the first man of Company K fell. It was Fred King. He was mortally wounded, and died in the hospital about two weeks later. The feeling at seeing one of our own men fall out this way was indescribable. I shall not attempt to do it. But no matter who fell we must obey orders. And the pitiless, relentless order was "Forward!"

The cannon balls and shell struck around us, tearing up the earth, and sometimes ricochetting or bouncing along the ground a great distance, like a flat stone skims across the water of a pond.

Wounded men lay everywhere. Some were writhing and kicking. Others lay still. Some of the human forms were already quiet in death. The number of dead horses was enormous. They seemed to lie everywhere. But it was still "Forward!"

We climbed over a rail fence. It was a road, the old road that yet runs from Hagerstown to Sharpsburg. We did not take the road, however, for the order was still "Forward!"

We climbed over the fence on the other side of the road. We marched some fifteen or twenty feet into what was then a meadow.

We could not see any of the enemy, although their bullets were whistling past our heads. The rebels seemed to be in a woods on the other side of the meadow.

Suddenly something occurred that seemed almost supernatural. A vast number of the enemy appeared to rise straight out of the solid earth, and they poured into us a deadly volley of leaden hail.

It is not believed that there is another geological formation like that particular spot on the face of the earth. Great military men from all over the world have since inspected it, and said that it seemed as if nature, in a savage mood, had made those natural breastworks, simply for the purpose for which they were used on that particular day.

Let me describe that field if I can. On one side, as before said, was a road, flanked by a post and rail fence. On the other side was a little valley, at the bottom of which was a small brook, and beyond this, a woods. About two-thirds of the distance to one side of the field, nearest the woods, there is a sudden drop in the surface of the ground, making a step of about four or five feet in height. The perpendicular side of this step is of ledgy rock. On the upper level, and on the lower level, it is tillable ground. It is as if one-third of the field had simply dropped its level about five feet.

Standing over by the fence the whole field looks flat, without a break in it. No one would ever think there was such a step there. It is one of the most wonderful formations in the world. It extends from one side of the field to the other, a distance perhaps equal to two city blocks in length.

It was behind this singular, natural breastworks that the rebels had concealed themselves, and quietly waited till we had got within shooting distance and then suddenly stood up and fired into us. When standing erect, their aimed muskets were a little above the higher level. It was thus that it appeared as if the enemy had actually arisen right out of the solid earth.

They fired into us a murderous volley.

Surprised, demoralized, we wavered and fell back and made for the first fence, on the nearest side of the road!

Does anybody wonder? Remember that we were green troops. This was the first battle we had been in. It was scarcely two weeks since we had left the mustering camp at Newark. Perhaps there were not half a dozen men in the regiment who knew the least thing about loading and firing a rifle. Under such circumstances, and thus surprised by what seemed like an apparition of the enemy, the most experienced troops would have wavered. What wonder then that the green and inexperienced Thirteenth Regiment broke and with one accord made for the fence.

Most of the officers, to their everlasting honor be it said, were marvelously cool and collected in that terrible scene. They succeeded in stopping the stampede. They re-formed us on the road before we had climbed the second fence, and we were again turned against the enemy.

A cessation, for a few moments, not entirely, but partially, of the firing, enabled us to collect our shattered senses as we gazed over the meadow we had just left.

Then we saw the murderous effect of the volley that had been fired into our ranks by the enemy concealed behind those natural breastworks.

There in the meadow lay nine dead and sixty wounded men of the Thirteenth Regiment—the work of a single volley!

There was but one man there who seemed not to be wounded. It was Heber Wells, one of the bravest men in the battle that ever lived. I wish that I had sufficient mastery of the pen to adequately describe and give proper tribute to Heber Wells' bravery.

Why had he remained behind in the storm of bullets that were whistling past him, when everybody else had fled?

He had remained beside the body of his dead captain.

Captain Irish had been killed!

When the captain saw the company wavering, he raised his sword aloft and cried out the words that have made his memory famous:

"Rally, boys! Rally!"

And just as he said this, he fell, pierced by a bullet.

Sergeant Wells saw him fall and returned to his side. Wells imagined at first that the captain had been shot in the head, but could not find the wound.

"Captain," said he, "are you hurt?"

"Heber, I'm killed!"

Captain Irish pressed his hand on his right breast, glanced gratefully at his faithful friend Heber, gasped painfully—and was dead!

And thus died one of the bravest, kindest-hearted men that ever lived. Thus died my old friend, my old employer. When the members of Company K realized what had happened they were paralyzed with horror. The poetry of war, however, had been verified, for the first man to be killed was the captain, while in the brave act of rallying his wavering men.

Heber Wells tore open the captain's coat and shirt, and found a small wound near the right nipple of his breast. There was not a particle of blood oozing from it. But it had reached a vital spot. Wells put his ear to the captain's breast, and heard the last fluttering of his stilling heart.

Then Wells searched the pockets, taking from them the captain's watch, the papers and memorandums, and unfastened his sword. He tried to get the pocket knife and other things on the other side, but could not, on account of the way the body was twisted around. There was imminent danger of the Union troops being repulsed and the body falling into the hands of the rebels, and Heber did not want any of the contents of the captain's pockets to fall into the hands of the enemy.

Then Wells made up his mind to rescue the body. The bullets were still whistling about his ears in a dangerous fashion, but he seemed to care naught for that. Picking up the things he had removed from the captain's pockets, and his sword, he took them over to the road and called for volunteers to rescue the captain's body. There were plenty of responses of this noble, yet sad duty, dangerous though it was. Of the volunteers, Wells selected Jacob Engle, Lewellen T. Probert and Jacob Berdan, and the four carried the captain's body over the fence and laid it in the road.

Word was sent home as soon as possible and a delegation came on and took charge of the remains. They were brought home and Captain Irish's funeral was one of the largest ever seen in Paterson. Business was suspended, the streets were hung with banners bearing the last famous words of the dead captain, flags were displayed at half-mast, all the public and many private buildings were draped with mourning, and an immense concourse of people followed the body to the grave at Sandy Hill, where it was buried.

Captain Irish was a member of the First Baptist Church of Paterson, and a handsome memorial tablet was set in the walls, and is there yet. Later, when the Sons of Veterans were organized, the first post started in Paterson was named "Captain Hugh C. Irish Camp, No. 8."

Captain Irish was not the only one of Company K who lost his life in that battle. The others were Frederick C. King, Curtis Bowne, John B. Doremus, Robert Gammall and Abraham Margoff. The latter was killed instantaneously. The others were mortally wounded and died afterward. The case of Curtis Bowne was very peculiar, as will be described a little further on.

Company C, the other Paterson company, also suffered severely, there being three who were fatally shot, namely: Peter Arlington, John M. Sheperd and George Meyers. All these were Paterson boys.

Altogether in the regiment, however, as before stated, there were nine killed and some sixty wounded, and the whole thing occurred in that one murderous volley, which did not take more time than it does to write this sentence.

The captain being dead, the command of the company fell on First Lieutenant Scott. But he was *hors de combat* too.

The lieutenant was not killed, but sick—very sick. When Sergeant Wells went to look for him, he found the lieutenant lying alongside the fence, doubled up with cramps and vomiting like a dog. Sergeant Wells ordered a couple of men to take the lieutenant to the rear, and assumed command of the company himself.

But the battle wasn't over yet!

CHAPTER XXV.

THE REST OF ANTIETAM.

NOT much account of the time of day is kept during a battle, but everybody seems to agree that it was about 9 o'clock in the morning when Captain Irish was killed.

The battle of Antietam lasted all day on the 17th of September, 1862. So the fighting was not over yet, by any means. On the contrary it had just fairly begun.

People who are reading this story for the fun it contains will not find much that is very funny right here. They were certainly a good many amusing things in the army, but there were just as many that were horrible. All phases of war life will be given in the order in which they come, the object being to present all the different experiences of a soldier just as they are, and that these reminiscences are given faithfully and accurately I am sure every veteran will admit.

The battle of Antietam was not over yet, nor was the part the Thirteenth New Jersey played in it. From its position on the pike the regiment was ordered back into the woods, pretty nearly the same it had occupied before proceeding down to its baptism.

We had scarcely got there before the enemy made his appearance in full force on the other side of the turnpike. Then our artillery opened up on them in good shape. This attack of the Confederates had evidently been intended to capture that battery on the hill, which was giving them a good deal of trouble. But they didn't get that battery, not by a long shot. The enemy was given a hot dose of shot and shell and shrapnel and canister (packages of bullets and slugs which burst open and mow down the ranks of the victims like a scythe), and the enemy was promptly sent back to his shelter at the edge of the woods.

The Thirteenth Regiment, already demoralized by the volley down in the meadow, where Captain Irish had been killed and so many wounded, had not got over it and this second attack very much scattered them. It took some time for the officers to get them together in good shape again, but they finally succeeded in doing so.

Just then an order came for the regiment to report to General Green, over by the "Dunker church," where the enemy was massing in force and pressing the Union troops dangerously.

It is not often that I strike anything lucky, but I certainly did just then. It became necessary to detail some men to guard some ammunition wagons that were bringing supplies to the battery on the hill, and as my name was next on the roster, I was one of the men selected for this duty. It was dangerous, of course, but nothing to be compared with ordinary fighting, and I gladly welcomed the "assignment." Some of the other fellows greeted me enviously and offered to change places with me, but I did not see it in that light.

So for the rest of the day I viewed the battle from the hills, following the ammunition wagons around from one place to another on the heights as they visited the different batteries. I don't know what special use there was for a guard for the wagons, but I did not stop to inquire.

Any detail that will take a man out of the very front of a battle is always a welcome one. The cannon balls and shells came pretty close at times, but I had got somewhat used to them, and nothing after all was so bad as the insidious little bullets of the rifles.

The main portion of the regiment, however, was in it again for fair. They were marched down about a mile to the left, and up the hill back of the old Dunker church. This was a small brick structure, about the size of a country schoolhouse, and it was right in the thick of the battle of the afternoon. It was struck several times, and big holes were made through the walls by the shells.

And by the way the church and its surroundings look about as forlorn and uncivilized now as they did on the day of the battle thirty-two and over years ago. The name "Dunker" arose from the fact that the church was the worshipping place of a religious sect called the Dunkards.

Up back of this church the Thirteenth Regiment, led by General Green himself, came near being captured. The enemy advanced toward us with their guns held as if they were either out of ammunition or else wanted to surrender, and quietly marched down to the right as if going peaceably to the rear.

Adjutant Charles A. Hopkins (afterward captain of Company K), with another officer went out with a white handkerchief on a sword as a sort of truce to see what was meant by these mysterious movements. Hopkins had got out into the open field where he was exposed to every danger, when it became evident to everybody that the crafty enemy was trying to work the dodge of getting in our rear, and thus putting us between two fires, which would have annihilated the Thirteenth in a few moments.

The scheme was discovered by the Union troops, and the fact that it was seen through was discovered by the Confederates almost simultaneously, and the firing began at once on both sides in a very lively sort of a manner. Those who were there say that the horror of the fight that was commenced was almost offset by the sight of Adjutant Hopkins and his companion skedaddling over that field to get out of the way of the bullets that came from both directions at once. As if by a miracle, however, neither of them was struck.

This engagement lasted for an hour or so and there were a number of the Thirteenth killed and wounded. Some of those who are put down as being killed in the first volley may have been killed at this spot, as the records do not divide the encounters, the total loss being charged to the one engagement of "Antietam." The Thirteenth Regiment, however, stood its ground in a manner extremely creditable for new troops, but they were confronted by superior numbers, and were finally compelled to fall back to a safer position. Their place was taken, later, by fresher troops, who at least succeeded in holding the position.

In the meantime there was some very hard fighting in progress on the lower side of the Dunker church, where the memorable charge of the Sixth corps took place, a portion of which I observed from my elevated position on the hill with the artillery. Although I was personally in a state of fright for fear that something might happen to necessitate my being sent to the front again, yet I could not help admiring the magnificent exhibitions of bravery which I saw almost every minute.

Fortunately for me, however, I was kept guarding that blessed ammunition wagon for the balance of the day. Had a shell struck it and exploded, both the wagon and myself, including the driver and the mules, would have ascended skyward, but I never thought of that, even if I knew it. When an old soldier told me afterward that guarding an ammunition wagon under an artillery fire was one of the most dangerous things in a fight, I felt quite nervous over the risks I had run. But where ignorance is bliss 'tis folly to be wise, and I never knew anything about the likelihood of an ammunition wagon blowing up. I faithfully attended to the duty of seeing that no one stole anything out of the wagon, and I supposed that was what I was there for. Certainly I could see no other reason.

The Thirteenth Regiment after its retreat from the field near the Dunker church did not get into any more active fighting that day, although it was called upon several times to support other regiments and batteries. The fighting late in the afternoon was more severe further down in the direction of Sharpsburg, particularly around the old stone bridge over Antietam creek where General Burnside made his famous stand, and which has ever since been called "Burnside Bridge."

So far as I could judge the line of battle front extended a distance of eight or ten miles from one end to the other, and the Hagerstown pike was practically the dividing line between the two armies all day. It is needless to say that every soldier was completely tired out when night finally came.

Colonel Carman, the commandant of the Thirteenth, fell from his horse or was injured in some other way early in the engagement, and the command of the regiment fell to Lieutenant-Colonel Swords, and he acquitted himself with credit. General Mansfield was mortally wounded in the morning and the command of the corps fell on our division commander, General A. S. Williams. In the afternoon fighting Company K was commanded by Orderly Sergeant Wells, for there were no commissioned officers left, and so well did Sergeant Wells acquit himself that day, that just as soon as necessary preliminary red tape arrangements could be gone through with he wore the shoulder-straps of a second lieutenant, and his place as orderly sergeant was taken by Sergeant Hank Van Orden.

On the whole the Thirteenth, for the first time under fire, had acquitted itself with more than ordinary credit, and this was publicly accorded in subsequent "general orders," which is the only way the rank and file ever get any premium on having more than done their duty.

I am not trying to tell the whole story of the battle of Antietam. That is published in various volumes. I am only telling what I know of it. It is not much, to be sure, but it is as much as the ordinary private soldier knew about any battle in which he participated.

No one had stolen the ammunition wagon and I had done my part of the duties of the day. When evening came the wagon was turned in with a lot of others to a sort of extemporized quartermaster's department, and I naturally expected to be sent back to my company.

But my troubles were not yet over for that night. Something entirely out of the usual run occurred, which prevented me from getting the much-needed night's rest.

CHAPTER XXVI.

A "SLAUGHTER HOUSE" SURE.

INSTEAD of being ordered back to the regiment, I was, with some other men, sent down the road to guard some cattle that were to be killed in the morning for fresh beef. To my delight I found two other members of my company detailed on the same duty. They were Curtis Bowne and E. L. Allen, both old printing-office associates, too.

There were twelve cattle in the drove that we were to guard, under the charge of a corporal. We got them in a corner of a field, and divided ourselves up into three "reliefs," that is, one of us was to watch for two hours while the others slept, when our turns would be changed, so that each man would have "two hours on and four off," according to the regular custom.

We lighted a fire, cooked some coffee, and had a smoke before turning in for a rest. The conversation of course turned on the events of the day, and particularly on the death of Captain Irish. Then we began to talk about the wounded members of Company K.

"By the way," said Bowne, "I got a little dose of it myself. Look at this."

He took off his cap and turned his face toward the camp fire. In the middle of his forehead there was a small round bruise, as if it had been hit with a stone.

"What is it?" I asked.

"I don't know. I think I must have been hit by a spent ball that just bruised the skin without entering."

"You are sure that it did not go into your brains?" I remarked laughingly. I had no more of an idea of such a thing than Curt did.

"No!" he answered good-naturedly. "My brains are not as soft as that."

"Does it hurt?" I asked.

"Not a bit," was the answer. "It is nothing—not worth talking about."

And none of us thought at the time that it was. Yet at that very moment there was a one-ounce bullet imbedded in Curt Bowne's brain that afterward caused his death. He remained with the regiment for some days and then his head began to pain him so badly that he had to be sent to the hospital. He grew worse, but very slowly, and he actually lived until the following March, when he died from the effects of the wound which was at first supposed by all to be so trivial.

This certainly was a singular case. I am told that it was duplicated during the war, but there were few instances like it. For a man to live from September till the following March with a large bullet imbedded in the folds of his brain is certainly something wonderful. The theory of the doctors, if I remember rightly, was that the bullet had passed between the convolutions of the brain without lacerating their coverings, that there was consequently no immediate internal hemorrhage, and that death resulted at last from slow inflammation.

We couldn't get over the sad death of Captain Irish, and as two of my comrades of that night had worked with me under him in the *Guardian* office, we felt all the more keenly his loss. It seemed as if we had suffered the loss of a relative. I felt very moist about the eyes when I recalled how he had bathed my blistered feet with ointment only a few days before in the camp at Rockville.

"What is that strange noise?" remarked Bowne; "it sounds like some one humming."

We listened. There certainly was a queer noise coming from the direction of an old barn on the lower end of the field. But we didn't pay much attention to it then. We went on discussing the battle.

During the day, in the excitement, it had appeared like nothing but a gigantic excitement—a rushing mob, with deafening thunders of cannon and rattling volleys of musketry; of crowds of men rushing hither and thither; of men and horses falling around us; of bloody soldiers hastening frantically to some quiet and safe spot. It was a nightmare!

But now that it was over we began to realize what we had gone through. As each minute passed the horrors of the day seemed to stand out more and more vivid. With blanched faces each gave his version of the scene of the slaughter, and the merits and demerits of the individual members of Company K were discussed at length.

All through it all came that strange murmuring noise we had referred to. It was a low hum, like the sound of the insects on a summer's night, only less sharp. It formed a background of our whole talk. More than once we stopped to listen and wonder what it was.

"Did any one see John Ick during the fight?" I asked.

"Didn't you hear about him?" answered Curt.

"No."

"Why, he sneaked!"

"Sneaked!"

"That's what he did—sneaked out!"

"How was that?"

"Well, when the company was re-formed in the road after that sudden volley, you know," said Bowne, explaining, "some one asked what had become of John Ick and Reddy Mahar. Lem Smith said that he saw them going over toward the woods on a run. One of the sergeants, I think it was Hank Van Orden, was sent to see if he could find them and bring them back to the regiment, which was just then marching back to the place where it had been in the morning."

"Well," I asked, interrupting, "did he find them?"

"The sergeant didn't find Reddy. He turned up afterward from somewhere. But Hank found Ick, and where do you think he was?"

I answered that I was sure I could not tell.

"Up in the woods, behind a tree," said Curt. "He had got an old rubber overcoat somewhere, which he had put on, and then squatted behind the tree. The coat was covered with mud and looked like a big stone. In fact Hank said he thought it was a rock at first. But the stone coughed, and looking a little closer, Hank discovered Ick hiding under it. Hank gave him a kick and told him to come back to the company. Ick said that he had had enough of the slaughter-house business and was going home. But Hank made him come along."

"Did he take part in the fight in the afternoon?" I asked.

"Yes," answered Curt, "and he stood up to the rack like a major. He seemed to have got over his panic of the morning."

"Well, I declare," said I. "I imagined that with all his talk about slaughter houses that he would be all right when it came to a pinch. But where did Reddy come from?"

"I don't know," said Curt. "He arrived in the camp just as I left the company to come here."

"Did any of the other fellows of Company K sneak?" I asked.

"Not a single one of them, they all——"

"For the love of God, don't—Oh-h-h!"

This came over from the direction of the barn before referred to. It was not like a cry. It was a shriek. It was a loud-cracked voice, that seemed to come from the very depths of some human soul. I never heard such a tone of voice in my life again. It was like the shriek of a wounded horse.

We listened, breathless. Then we heard that mysterious, low moaning chorus that had attracted our attention so often.

"Suppose we go over to that barn and see what it is, Joe," suggested Liv. Allen.

I consented and went. I wished that I never had.

The old barn was being utilized as a field hospital. It was one of those big old-fashioned Southern barns, with a large open space in the middle of a row of stalls on the two sides. The floor was covered with wounded men, lying closely side by side.

On the bare floor, in a row, as thick as they could lie, were the maimed human beings that had just been operated upon. Some were conscious, but the most of them were moaning and groaning. These moans and groans arose in the night air like a chorus. It was this that we had heard from our place on the opposite side of the field where we were guarding the cattle.

I passed between the rows of wounded men, many of whom would never be removed from their hard couches, except as corpses. Liv. and I stopped to look more carefully at one poor fellow whose face seemed familiar.

This poor wretch—we didn't recognize him after all—had just suffered an amputation of the left arm at the shoulder joint.

He looked at me appealingly, as if he wished to say something. I knelt at his side and held down my ear.

He made an effort to speak, but not a sound came from his lips. On the contrary, he simply turned his head—and there ran from his mouth a stream of what looked like dark-green paint. His legs stiffened out, a convulsion passed over him, an ashen hue suffused his face. He was dead!

Horror-stricken I rushed through the barn and out of the rear side, closely followed by Liv. Allen.

We had better have gone the other way, for here were horrors a thousand times worse. The surgeons were at their ghoulish work on this side of the barn.

Upon a board, laid upon two barrels, was stretched a human form. Perhaps it was the same poor fellow whose yell of anguish had aroused and startled us. But he was silent now. A young medical cadet was holding a chloroform-saturated handkerchief to his nose. The doctors were about to amputate the shattered mass of flesh that was once a leg.

The surgeons were in their shirt sleeves. The aprons that some of them wore were as red with blood as if they had been butchers. Assistants held candles to light the operation. I saw the doctor give one cut into the fleshy part of the man's thigh—and fled!

But I ran straight into another amputating table—a board over two barrels. Here they were taking off an arm! Turning, I ran against another! In every direction that I might go, I would run against one of the horrid things.

Blinded with fright and terror, I tried to escape. I don't know what became of my companion. Seeing an apparently open way, I deliriously rushed in that direction, but meeting some obstruction, I stumbled and fell.

What had I fallen into? In grasping to steady myself, I caught hold of something wet and slimy! It was quite dark, but I could see! I could see all too plainly. Would to heaven I could not see!

I had fallen headlong into a heap of horrors—a pile of human legs and arms that had just been amputated. I shall not attempt to say how many there were. Were I to say there were a dozen wagon-loads of arms and legs, hands and feet, in that ghastly pile, I might not be believed!

And yet I do not believe that it would be an exaggeration.

As I lay there, scrambling for a foothold in that slimy, slippery, bloody, hideous mass of cold flesh—human flesh—there arose from one of the operating tables another wild shriek:

"Oh, doctor! Oh! O-h! Oh-h-h! O-o-o-o-h! . . kill me! Kill me and be done with it! Kill me, and put me out of my misery!"

My overwrought brain could stand no more! I fainted!

I dropped unconscious into the slimy, slippery, bloody mass of amputated legs and arms!

CHAPTER XXVII.

A WONDERFUL FREAK OF NATURE.

The incidents related in the preceding chapter are not exaggerations. There is not a soldier living who went through several battles, but that has seen great piles of dismembered arms and legs lying around the operating tables of the surgeons. A veteran who was at the battle of Gettysburg says that he was one of a detail to bury these horrible human remnants, and he counted no less than eight hundred in the pile around the operating table of one temporary hospital. And at that battle there were a hundred of such places where a similar thing was to be seen.

You pass middle-aged or old men on the streets even now, minus arms or legs. A large proportion of them were wounded in the army, and their lost limbs are mingled with the dust of some Southern battlefield. The sight of encountering such a hideous pile the first time is enough to overcome almost anybody. It overcame me, and when I fell headlong into the bloody, slimy mass, it made my stomach turn, my head swim, and I fainted.

I do not know how long I remained unconscious. When I recovered I was lying beside the rail-fence fire that had been started by my companions on the cattle guard. They revived me with a cup of hot coffee, which was the panacea for all the ills of the soldier, the same as whisky is for some people in civil life.

I was very much fatigued and fell asleep. So did the others. It was Curt Bowne's turn to keep awake and guard the cattle. Like the rest of us he was tired out, and perhaps the wound in his head made him the more drowsy. At all events he fell asleep too, when he should have remained awake, and some time during the night, Liv. Allen awoke to find that the cattle had disappeared. There was not a single steer to be seen.

Whatever became of those twelve cattle—whether they were driven off by some one when we were asleep, or whether they had some presentiment of the "slaughter house" that John Ick was always talking about—none of us ever knew. All that we did know was that there were twelve steers there when we were placed in charge and none when we awoke in the night from our sound sleep. Take twelve from twelve and nothing remains.

What should we do? Here we were confronted by an entirely new problem; we had a vague sort of an idea that it was a serious matter for a soldier to go to sleep on his post, but did not know what the penalty was—at least not then. We had no excuse to offer, for the offense was self-apparent. The cattle were not there. Any one could see that—or rather they could not see it —or them!

So we held a council of war.

"There is only one thing that I can see that we can do," said Liv. Allen. He wasn't a Methodist minister at that time and might perhaps make suggestions that he would not make in these days. "There is only one thing that we can do, and that is to see if we cannot find those cattle—or some others. If they are not the same ones, who can tell the difference?"

We caught on. Liv.'s proposition, stripped of all surplus verbiage, was to get twelve cattle somehow—honestly if we could, but get them anyhow. So we started out on a nocturnal hunt.

It has often struck me since as strange that we met no guards or pickets or other things to stop us that night and ask us where we were going, and if we had a pass. But we encountered nothing of the sort. We went right along without the least molestation.

We passed through thousands of sleeping soldiers along each side of the road (it was Hagerstown pike), and more than once passed droves of cattle, but their guards were more faithful than we had been. They were awake and watchful. There were no appropriating any of those herds.

"If we don't strike a fat barnyard, we're lost," said Curt Bowne. We all had arrived at the same conclusion.

"And there is no use following this main road," said Liv. Allen, wisely. "Let's strike off somewhere to one side."

I don't know how far we went, but we finally came to a large barn on a farm that seemed well stocked and prosperous, and carefully going around behind it we were delighted to find the yard back of the building filled with cattle. With as little noise as possible we picked out twelve (as we supposed) of the cows and corraled them.

None of us apparently remembered that we had been placed in charge of steers, and these were cows. In fact I don't think any one thought of that matter. In the darkness of the night it would perhaps have been somewhat difficult to distinguish anyhow.

The corporal who was in charge of the guard which we three printers from the Thirteenth composed, was an old soldier—one of the Third Wisconsin boys. He had gone through the mill and knew the ropes.

"This is a snap," said he, as he emerged from a small building alongside the barn, holding a big rooster by the legs. The fowl began to squawk, but that was soon stopped by seizing him by the neck.

Bowne and Allen followed suit, and each came out with a fine chicken. I was about to do the same thing, when the corporal interrupted:

"We have got about enough poultry," said he. "In that next shed you will find some fine suckin' pigs. Get one of them."

I reached over the fence and carefully grabbed one of the little pigs from its snug bed under its mother's side. The old sow grunted, but did not seem to appreciate the loss of one of her helpless offspring. But I had not gone far before that infernal young pig began the most outrageous squealing, and all that I could do I could not stop it.

"Drop it, d—n the critter," said the corporal. "Let's git. There is no time to fool around here now."

And we "got." The other fellows held on to their chickens but I was empty handed except for the stick I had picked up to facilitate the driving of the cattle.

"I'm afraid we will catch it for this in the morning,"

said I, when I began to appreciate the fact that we were nothing but a lot of cattle thieves.

"Nonsense, pard," said the corporal from the Wisconsin regiment. "These critters will be all cut up into mincemeat by the time the old codger who owns them finds out that they are gone. Besides this is nothing for these times. I have done this same thing many a time before. It's a darned sight better than getting hauled up for sleeping on our posts."

I thought perhaps this might be so, but my conscience troubled me a little still. I was a young soldier, and hadn't got hardened to such things. Many a time I helped do similar acts afterward and never once thought about it—unless caught at it!

It was nearly daylight when we got back to the place where we had been posted at sunset, and drove the cattle into the same corner and relighted the fire. And when the sun arose we sat and stood around with faces as innocent as if we had faithfully performed our duty and had not been away from the place at all.

We had a good breakfast of broiled chicken that morning. The broiling was done by sticking parts of the fowl on the end of sticks and holding them into the flames of the fire, and I can assure the reader that that is a good way to broil chicken all the same. We did not use the whole of it for breakfast, but put what was left in our haversacks for a future occasion.

At 9 o'clock the relief came along and a new guard took charge of the cattle.

"How's this?" asked the officer of the new guard, of our corporal. "This order says that you are to be relieved of the charge of twelve steers. And these are cows. And let me see—one, two, three, etc.—why, there are thirteen of them! How's that?"

We privates looked dismayed as we ran our eyes over the cattle and counted thirteen. In the darkness of the night we had stolen one too many. But no officer could throw that Wisconsin corporal off his guard.

"Don't know nothing about it, lufftenant," said he. "Them there's the critters we had turned over to us. I didn't count 'em. Guess the other fellows must have made a mistake."

"But they're cows, not steers," said the officer. "And you ought to know that the government never kills cows for beef."

None of us had noticed this wonderful freak of nature.

"Don't know nothing about that," replied the corporal. "If them was steers yesterday they must have changed during the night somehow, for they're cows now sure enough. It am a curious circumstance, I vow."

The lieutenant evidently thought there was no use arguing the point with the corporal any further, and said nothing more. We were relieved of our charge and ordered back to our brigade.

"Dash my buttons," said the corporal, when we had got out of hearing. "I wish some of you fellows would give me a good kick."

"What for, corporal?" I asked.

"Don't you see," he answered, "we had one critter too many, and we might ha' killed her and had fried brains for our breakfast. And then did you see them udders? We might ha' had milk in our coffee. Kick me for a fool!"

He was an old soldier. And to lose such an unusual opportunity to improve the menu of a soldier was not at all "in accordance with the regulations."

CHAPTER XXVIII.

SLEEPING WITH A DEAD REB.

We got back to the Thirteenth Regiment about 11 o'clock. We passed through what seemed to be many miles of soldiers, all resting. They were lying about, smoking and otherwise taking it easy. And they needed the rest, for it was the first time there had been a stop in many days, and everybody was played out from the previous day's big battle. There is nothing more fatiguing than a battle. One does not notice at the time how much marching and running about he has. When the excitement is over the reaction comes and nature demands a rest.

It was the first I had seen of my company since I had left them immediately after the murderous volley that killed Captain Irish. I found the boys downhearted over the loss of the captain. The particulars of the afternoon fighting were related to me, together with many other interesting and thrilling incidents that I had not personally noticed or participated in. Nothing was talked about but the previous day's experience. The boys had seen a battle. They did not care to see any more. All had had enough!

Lieutenant Scott had recovered from his sickness and was in command of the company, while Orderly Sergeant Wells, beside his legitimate duties, seemed to be acting in the capacity of lieutenant also.

What struck all the soldiers that day, and it has similarly impressed all the subsequent historians of the war, was why General McClellan did not follow up the enemy. The fight, as it stood, was what might be called a drawn battle. Neither party could claim a victory.

From the camp occupied by the Thirteenth Regiment

on September 18, 1862, we could see the camps of the enemy on the opposite hills. We could see their flags and their guards. We could see their cannons and their mounted officers. They seemed to manifest no disposition to renew the fight; neither did we.

All through that day we momentarily expected to hear a cannon shot that would be the signal for the renewal of hostilities, but it did not come. Everything was as quiet as a country convention, except for the drums and bugles that we could hear from the camps of the rebels as plainly as we could hear our own.

Toward night we could see the signal flags of the enemy wig-wagging from the hills, and we took it for granted that that was preliminary to a renewal of the fighting in the morning. When we went to sleep that night we fully believed that we would be aroused before daylight by the thunders of the artillery and that that would be another day of terrible carnage.

But the battle was over. In the morning when we looked in the direction of the enemy's camp there was nothing to be seen. The rebels had quietly sneaked away during the night and had crossed the Potomac in safety.

There was not one of us private soldiers but was glad that the fighting was over for the present, but at the same time there was not one who could understand why General McClellan had not followed up the advantage he had. He might have pursued the rebels that day, and, forcing them down to the banks of the river, simply annihilated them and ended the war then and there. General McClellan, in the opinion of the soldiers generally, was one of the best officers the army ever had, but his conduct on that occasion was never satisfactorily explained to them.

In the afternoon of the following day (the 19th) we were ordered to move, and we marched through a good part of the battlefield. Then for the first time we appreciated what an awful battle it had been. Blackened remains of soldiers lay scattered everywhere, gray and blue side by side, leveled in death. It was an impressive thing to see a dead Union soldier lying beside a dead Confederate. Both had been cut down in the act of trying to take each other's life. How futile it all was!

There lay the dead soldier in blue. By his side lay the dead soldier in gray. What was it to them now? Their life struggles were over, and what was the benefit? Perhaps both of them had families to support. I can tell the reader that this sight brought up many strange feelings. It touched the heart as nothing else could. Could the dispute have been left to the rank and file, how quickly would the war have been ended.

The Union loss in that battle was 11,420, and that of the Confederates, 10,000. But few of the bodies had been buried. In places—"Bloody Lane," for instance —the dead bodies had been piled up six and eight high, just where they had fallen upon each other in a hand-to-hand conflict. Many Union soldiers had been stripped of their uniforms by the half-clothed rebels, and lay there stark naked, stiff and dead, in most cases with their limbs drawn up as if they had died in agony. Many of the bodies had turned so black that at first they were mistaken for negroes.

Dead horses lay everywhere. Broken muskets, unlimbered cannon, wrecks of caissons and baggage wagons were scattered about. The ground seemed to be actually strewn with discarded cartridge boxes and belts, and you could pick up a vet's blanket every few feet.

There were a good many stragglers. Many fell out of the ranks from sheer fatigue. I was one of them. The excitement of the past two or three days, and the fact of having undergone so much fatigue were too much for me. During one of the stops I crawled up to the side of a fence, lay down and fell asleep.

The reader will perhaps begin to think that I was a confirmed "straggler." I can't well deny the allegation. But I had plenty of company, for there were many others just as bad.

I did not awake till some time late in the night. The last of the army had passed. I could hear the "tinkle, tinkle" of the thousands of tin cups in the far off distance. There was no use of my trying to catch up with the regiment. So I decided to make myself comfortable for the balance of the night.

There were plenty of other stragglers flying about. Some of them were not stragglers asleep, but dead men, although I did not know it at the time. We were still on a part of the battlefield. Although the days were warm, the nights were chilly, and I felt cold. The usual thing to do on such occasions is to seek some other soldier, lie beside him, and share blankets. The two blankets and the heat from each other's bodies keep the men warm.

I soon found a fellow alone and prepared to lie beside him. Nothing was thought of such a proceeding in the army. He was awake.

"Can I share your bed with you, pard?" I asked.

"Sartin," was the answer. "I am a little shivery, for I've shed a lot o' blood from this wound."

"Are you wounded?" I asked, in surprise.

"Yes," he answered, "right through my side here. But I guess it escaped by vitals, for it don't hurt much, although it has bled considerable. What regiment be you from?"

"The Thirteenth New Jersey."

"Why, that's Yanks!"

"Certainly, what did you think it was?" I asked.

"Nothin', only I'm a Johnnie," said my companion. I involuntarily pushed back a little. "Don't be scart, pard," said he. "I'm not going to harm ye. We're all the same. If we fellers had the settlin' o' this thing, I guess it wouldn't last long, would it, pard?"

"I don't think it would," I answered. "What regiment do you belong to?"

"I'm from Galveston. I belong to the —th Texas." (I have forgotten the number of his regiment.)

"How long have you been in the service?" I asked.

"I 'listed in '61," he answered. "How long you bin in?"

"Only about two weeks," I answered. "We got into a fight almost as soon as we got here, and lost our captain in the first round."

"Maybe I'm the fellow what killed him," said he. "Nobody knows. But that is all the better, isn't it, pard?"

I admitted that it was. And indeed such was the

fact. If any particular soldier on either side knew positively that he had killed any particular man he would feel a good deal worse over it.

I don't know how long we talked together, we men who had been deadly enemies the day before. It might strike the reader as a queer proceeding, but I can assure him that outside of the battles the men on each side were brothers and friends, as many an old soldier can testify. But we finally fell asleep.

It grew colder and colder toward morning. I snuggled closer to my companion, but that did not seem to increase the warmth as it usually does. I was too sleepy, however, to make investigations.

The sun was beginning to shine before I awoke the last time and threw off the blankets that covered myself and my bedfellow.

"Pard," said I. "It's time to get up. The breakfast bell will ring in a moment."

I shook my companion, but he did not stir. I looked closely into his face. It was ashen.

I put my hand on his face. It was as cold as ice.

My rebel bedfellow was dead!

CHAPTER XXIX.

"JEFF DAVIS" AND I.

To say that I was startled when I found that my bed fellow for the night was a corpse, would be putting it mild. I think it would startle anybody to wake up and find the person he had last spoken to at his side before going to sleep, cold and stiff in death. I sprang up in horror and involuntarily hurried from the scene.

Then a second thought struck me. As a matter of common decency was it not right that I should try to see who this poor fellow was, and send word to his family? He had said that he belonged to the —th Texas regiment, and that his home was in Galveston. That was all I knew. I decided to search his pockets.

Besides the usual miscellaneous assortment of strings, knives and other things to be found in a soldier's pocket, I came across two tintypes. One of them was of a middle-aged woman and the other was of a pretty little girl about ten or eleven years of age. These I at once surmised to be the dead rebel's wife and daughter. I also found two letters that he had received, which were addressed to "James H. Thompson, —th Regiment, Army of Northern Virginia."

This is the way envelopes were addressed by the Confederates. They called this particular branch of the army "the Army of Northern Virginia," while the Union soldiers always called it "Army of the Potomac." Letters to men in the army were thus addressed, giving the name, regiment and army, and in some mysterious way, after the lapse of two or three weeks maybe after they were written, the letters would reach the party to whom they were addressed—perhaps. The mail regulations in war times are anything but perfect!

It may also interest the reader of the present time to

know that a letter sent by a soldier to friends at home did not necessarily have a postage stamp on the envelope. It was for obvious reasons a practical impossibility for a soldier to go to the post office to buy stamps, and so the letters went through just as well without them.

Both of these letters to James H. Thompson were from his wife, and they were painfully pathetic and affectionate. I also found a half-written letter which was to be sent to the poor fellow's wife, which, so far as I can remember, read about as follows:

"MY DEAR WIFE: I will try to write you a few lines to let you know that I have been wounded in a fight in Maryland, but it does not seem to amount to much, although it prevents me from marching. They left me here on the field. I suppose they thought I was dead. Our army has marched on and the Yanks are coming this way and I expect that I will be taken prisoner. I cannot stir away from this place and they won't have much trouble in taking me, I guess. When you next hear from me it will likely be some time in a good while from some Yankee prison. But I don't care, for I am tired of fighting and marching and I hope this thing will soon be over, for I am sick of it. From the looks of things it will not last much longer, for Lee is driving the Yanks right up north and they will surely give it up. I expect to be home to see you soon. Tell Old Meigs that I will be back after my job in the shop before long. I wish you would see——"

Here the unfinished letter ended. Alas, how pathetically it read after what had happened. I was glad now that I came back to see what I could find in the poor fellow's pockets.

I tore a piece of paper off the blank side of the sheet and wrote on it the name and address, "James H. Thompson, —th Texas Regiment. This man lived somewhere in Galveston." This I put back in his pocket.

As soon as I got an opportunity, which was not for some days after, I wrote a letter explaining the circumstances, and inclosing the other letters I had found and the tintypes, and sent them all addressed to "Mrs. J. H. Thompson, Galveston." I never heard a word of the matter afterward, and so could not say whether they ever reached their destination. I intended to write again to Mrs. Thompson after the war was over, but the matter was forgotten entirely until I hunted over my memorandums for the materials for this story. It would have given me considerable satisfaction to have known if the information I sent to Texas had reached its destination.

I was not the only straggler from the Union army, by any means. As they say nowadays, the woods were full of them. From the worn roads, the demolished fences and other evidences, we knew what direction the army had taken, and we followed along the road in a go-as-you-please march. I here fell in with one of the most peculiar characters of the Thirteenth Regiment, and perhaps one of the most peculiar characters in the entire army.

His name was Davis. I don't remember what his first name was, but the boys always called him "Jeff." "Jeff Davis" became one of the noted characters of the brigade.

He never would keep up with the regiment on a march. He was a short, stout fellow, of the coarsest grain, physically, so stooped in the shoulders that he looked hump-backed. He was as strong as an ox, and about as bright intellectually as a mule. He also resembled the latter animal in stubbornness. He is the chap who has been already referred to as the man who would always insist on carrying two knapsacks and two haversacks, and if he had been asked to carry two guns he would not have minded it much.

Davis, at the battle of Antietam, when ordered to go into the fight, stepped out of the ranks and fired off his rifle into the air. He said that he wanted to see if it was all right before wasting any cartridges on the rebels. And all through the fight he had his gun swathed in an extra overcoat.

The quantity of stuff that this fellow carried was astonishing. He had enough equipments for the supply of an ordinary squad. He was a perfect miser so far as accumulating necessary articles was concerned, and it did not seem to make the slightest difference how heavy a weight he had on his shoulders.

As said, the officers could no more keep "Jeff Davis" in the ranks on a march than they could fly. He would take his time, walking along as he chose, and generally reaching camp two or three days after the regiment had arrived. It was always a great wonder how he escaped being gobbled up by the guerrillas.

Neither would he go into a tent with the company. He always insisted in making up a bed for himself on the ground immediately behind the colonel's tent. Neither would he drill or do any other of the ordinary duties of a soldier. He was too stupid to learn anything and it was not considered safe to intrust him to picket or guard duty, for the chances were ten to one that he would not remain on his post five minutes after the corporal left. He was punished in every imaginable way, but all that seemed to make no more impression upon him than pouring water on a duck's back.

After all sorts of trials, he was finally assigned to the duty of caring for one of Colonel Carman's horses, and that he did well, and he was retained as hostler for the balance of his term.

But old Jeff wasn't a bad companion during the time we were marching along with the stragglers, looking for the army that had left us behind. Jeff knew how to cook almost everything, and he managed to have a good supply of things in his larder (haversack) that were not included in the regular army menu. He also had two or three extra blankets, so that we were comfortable. Furthermore there was a quaintness and originality about the old fellow that made him interesting—at least for a while.

We stragglers were four or five days getting along alone before we reached the regiment in camp at Maryland Heights. In the meantime the regiment had reached Sandy Hook, a place some distance below Harper's Ferry, and was in camp there two or three days, but we could not find them. There were over one hundred thousand men scattered about, and it was no easy matter to find a particular regiment in that crowd.

When we got to Sandy Hook, we found that the regiment had moved down the river to Maryland Heights. It was the day after—that is, the 24th of September—before we finally found them, and rejoined our comrades of Company K.

Maryland Heights has already been previously described. It is located at the confluence of the Potomac and Shenandoah and immediately across the Potomac from Harper's Ferry.

There wasn't much to Harper's Ferry in those days, although so far as the village itself is concerned it really did not look much larger on the occasion of a visit there recently. It is a historic place, particularly in regard to matters relating to the civil war, for it was here that the first act of the preliminaries to the war was perpetuated—John Brown's raid. It also figured extensively in various movements during the war, for the reasons before described of its being such an important strategic point.

From our camp we could look down and take a bird's-eye view of Harper's Ferry. None of the immense railroad bridges now there were to be seen in those days. There had been a railroad bridge, but it had been destroyed and the only way to cross was on a pontoon bridge.

A pontoon bridge is made by taking a lot of small scows and anchoring them at regular intervals across the river. Then stout timbers are laid from one boat to the other, and across these timbers are laid heavy planks, which form the floor of the bridge. It is astonishing what a load these bridges will carry, even to quite large cannon and heavy baggage wagons. The boats are carried on the march on wheels and the timber and planking on wagons, and the shortness of the time required to make a bridge across the river is wonderful. These bridges are all right unless the anchors slip. Then there is trouble. The bridge goes to pieces in an instant, and whatever is upon it is precipitated into the water. I have seen this more than once.

Some of the things that occurred while we were in camp on Maryland Heights I shall defer till another chapter.

CHAPTER XXX.

THE "PUP TENT."

We had been in the service just four weeks. And what an exciting month it had been! We had gone through one of the hardest battles of the war up to that time, had participated in fatiguing marches, and had practically seen as much service in those respects as some regiments that had been enlisted five times as long.

And yet we had never had a rest, never been in a field camp, hardly ever had any drilling. We had set a pace and beaten a record, for there was not another regiment in the army that could equal this hasty, sudden precipitation into active warfare.

We were glad enough therefore when informed that we were likely to remain in Camp Maryland Heights for some time, and that we might proceed to make ourselves comfortable. As a matter of fact we remained there till the 27th of October, which is quite a long time for an army at a time of the year when the war might be prosecuted.

Of course we did not know how long or how short a time we were likely to remain there but we proceeded to make ourselves as comfortable as possible, and to do so was no easy task. We had no tents or anything else to shelter us. Our tents had been left at Rockville, together with our knapsacks, and we had nothing to protect us from the weather except such things as blankets, and a few overcoats, for we had been under light marching orders since we left Rockville. The old soldiers had "pup tents," but we had nothing. So we undertook to build some log huts.

It was a long distance to the nearest forest, and that made it a difficult job to get the necessary timber to the camp. Details were made from each company to fell trees and bring the logs to camp, but that was a slow process. In the meantime we were exposed to the weather.

For a wonder, ever since we had left home we had had clear weather. We never thought of its being anything else. The days were warm, and the nights cool, as they usually are in September, but it had remained clear. So when an old-fashioned rainstorm came along it introduced us to a new misery.

I can't imagine a more doleful state of affairs than a camp in a rainstorm. A more forlorn set than Company K it would be hard to imagine. We had erected the side walls of our little log cabins, and had plastered the chinks with mud, but they had no covering. Some of the boys had utilized their rubber blankets for this purpose, but the most of us had foolishly thrown away our "ponchos," as they were called.

So we had nothing to do but to mope around and answer to roll call and cook coffee in the drenching rain in the daytime, and sleep on the bare ground exposed to the deluge at night. Is it a wonder that many of the boys got sick? Is it a wonder that many of them never recovered from the effects of such exposure even after their return home when the war was over? I was "bunking" with Heber Wells, and it was at Maryland Heights that he received a box from home, filled with cakes, fresh homemade bread (fresh when it left home) and potatoes (something we did not get in the army very often); on the top of it all some fine smoking tobacco, which was a great improvement over the "dried chips" sold by the sutlers.

Heber and I used that box as a cover for our heads in the rain. To be sure the rest of our bodies was outdoors, drenched to the skin, but our heads and faces were protected and we pitied the other fellows who had no nice boxes to protect themselves with!

The rain lasted several days and I do not think there was ever more suffering and discomfort experienced by a body of soldiers during the whole course of the war. The consequences was that half the regiment was on the sick list from the exposure.

To add to the discomfort, everybody was affected by the water. There were altogether about six thousand troops in camp on Maryland Heights, and they all had to get their supply of water from a single spring. This spring was located at the bottom of a precipitous rock, and the water was as clear as crystal, and looked all right. It also tasted as good as it looked.

But it seems that the spring water was strongly impregnated with magnesia, or something of the sort, and the result was that every man in the whole camp was affected. The reader can well imagine what would be the result for a man to drink rochelle salts for breakfast, dinner and supper! Boiling it did not seem to make any difference. Some of the boys went half a mile or so down to the river for their water, but that was not till after the character of the spring had been discovered.

There was not a well man in the whole brigade, and the deaths were so numerous that it was scarcely a day that one did not see three or four funerals. Only one case in Company K resulted fatally, however—Martin V. B. Demarest. I was one of the pall bearers at his funeral.

The coffins in which soldiers in the army were buried were made of pieces of the boards from the cracker boxes, nailed together. These were carried by poles being tied at the sides. A dead soldier wears no shroud. He is simply dumped into the box in his everyday uniform, and nailed in. In the time of battle they don't even bother with the boxes.

The company is mustered, and the chaplain says a short service over the body. Then follows the parade to the grave, the lowest in rank marching first. The music is with the fife and drum, and the tune is always the same, the solemn Pleyal's hymn, or "Dead March," as it was called. At the grave six soldiers each fire three blank cartridges over the body, and it is buried. The remains are lowered and covered, and a piece of board from a cracker box or a barrel stave is marked with the name and regiment of the deceased. Then the mourners march back to camp while the "band" plays the liveliest tune in its limited repertoire.

As John Ick remarked, "Dey blays a solemn hym-tune by de zemmytery, un den ein dance tune back, all de times."

We buried Mart Demarest at the time in a shallow grave beside the camp, but his body was afterward removed to the National Cemetery at Antietam, where it lies in a long row in Section 11.

No one can tell the sufferings we endured at Maryland Heights, until the arrival of our "shelter" tents, or "pup" tents, as the boys more commonly called them. These reached the camp on the 17th of October, along with an extra supply of blankets and clothing.

Had the "pup" tents been given out to us at first, immediately after leaving home, we should have regarded them with scorn. But after the exposures we had suffered, they seemed veritable palaces. We immediately proceeded to make ourselves comparatively comfortable.

A "pup" tent consists of two pieces of canton flannel or thick muslin about six feet square. On one side is a row of buttonholes, and on the other side there are buttons. These things were made by contract, and it was seldom that the location of the buttons corresponded with the buttonholes, but as most of the boys were provided with needles and thread they soon overcame that difficulty. Each soldier carries one section of a tent. When they go into camp the two are buttoned together, making a piece about twelve by six feet square.

Two short poles, three or four feet high, are driven into the ground about six feet apart. The upright poles must have forks on the upper end. Across these is laid a horizontal pole. This forms the apex of the tent. The sides are fastened to the ground by pegs whittled from twigs. This makes a small tent the shape of an inverted "V" with nothing at either end. Generally the soldier carried in addition to the piece of shelter tent, a rubber blanket and a woolen one. One of the rubber blankets served as one end of the tent. The other was laid on the ground, and covered with one of the woolen blankets. This formed the bed. The other blanket formed the "bedclothes," which were added to by a spare overcoat, if it was too cold.

This tent was about the size of a dog house, which

perhaps gave it the name of "pup" tent. Of course there was not room enough in them to stand up, or hardly to sit up, but they kept off the rain and wind and that was enough. To get in one of them the soldier had to get down on his hands and knees and crawl in like a dog. There was no protection to the lower end of the tent unless one of the soldiers carried an extra piece, which was sometimes the case.

Don't laugh at the "pup" tent. It was one of the most useful things ever invented for the comfort of the soldiers. An old soldier would dispense with almost everything else before he threw away his piece of shelter tent, if it were in the inclement season of the year. In warm weather it did not matter so much. And the idea of two soldiers always bunking together probably begins to dawn on the mind of the reader.

These two soldiers were always called partners, or rather, for short, "pards." They were to each other as husband and wife, so far as a division of personal and "domestic" duties were concerned.

But I will defer a fuller description of my pard till the next chapter.

CHAPTER XXXI.

"MY PARD."

"My pard!"

What a host of recollections that expression brings to the mind of every old soldier!

Nearly every soldier in the army had his "pard." When the boys first enlisted the gathering into couples was a process of natural selection. It is innate in the human breast to have a chum. The Good Book says that it is not good for man to live alone. That of course referred to Adam in the Garden of Eden, and meant that our original grandfather should have a wife. It would have been extremely inconvenient for the soldiers to be accompanied by wives, so they did the next best thing—selected a "pard."

No one ever knows how this is done. There seems to be a natural affinity that draws men together. It cannot be said that it is generally on account of a similarity of tastes, for experience proves that men who are of the most radically opposite character get along best together. The selection of a "pard" came at the first as naturally as mating of birds in spring. The longer they were in the army the more did the soldiers appreciate the convenience, indeed the actual necessity of this arrangement.

It frequently happened that the original selection was not amicable, and there was a change. This in army parlance was called a "divorce." But these changes were not frequent after there had once been a satisfactory adjustment of relations. Only by death or the absence from sickness or wounds of one of the parties was the relationship broken.

The two soldiers constituted the "families" of the

army. They divided the numerous little duties of a personal nature, aside from the regular military duties. They pooled their rations, took turns at cooking and other things, and altogether made themselves more comfortable and happy.

On stopping for the night, one "pard" would hasten for the nearest rail fence or to the woods for twigs to make a fire, while the other would grab two canteens and go for water; sometimes this necessitated a trip of a mile, for the flanks of the army might be a long distance from the stream that had determined the camping place. One of the "pards" would then take a short trip out into the country to see if he couldn't "confisticate" a chicken or a stray pig, or even participate in the purloining of a calf. Not infrequently was a rabbit raised. If there was a granary or a potato mound handy, it afforded a valuable contribution to the larder.

More than once these foragers came back with bird shot in their epidermis, which came from the guns of the irate grangers. I have felt the sting of small bird shot on more than one occasion. But the soldier did not mind a little thing like that. No matter what happened he would not let go of his "rations," if he had been successful in getting anything. One of the cheekiest things I remember doing was to steal a chicken from a hen roost, and then go to the house and borrow an iron pot to cook the chicken in and make a fricasse.

And while one of the "pards" was putting up the "pup" tent the other would cook the supper. They before long become good cooks too, and could make a variety of dishes out of their limited supply that would surprise a professional chef.

Sometimes one of the "pards" was sick and tired out at the end of a day's march, while the other was comparatively fresh. Then the better one would care for his "pard" as if he were a brother, and do all the work. They stood by each other in sickness or trouble. They shared with each other the joys that came from surreptitious foraging, whether it be on some neighboring farm, or from the sutler's tent.

At night they shared each other's blankets. Thus they kept warm. Soldiers always slept, whether in a "bunk" in winter quarters, or alongside a fire on the march, in that peculiar shape called "spoon fashion." The reader will understand what that means. It was a convenient and practical arrangement except when one of the fellows desired to turn over on the other side. The other had to get around at the same time.

When in the stillness of the night you heard some one shout out:

"Attention—'bout—face!" you knew that it meant that the two "pards" were about to turn over on their other sides to ease their positions. To keep warm in cold weather they snuggled and hugged each other in the most affectionate manner, and it was only the direst necessity that induced them to change their position if they once got comfortable.

There were few men who did not have their "pards." If a soldier had a foghorn voice when he snored, it was considered a legitimate cause for "divorce." If one of the "pards" was less cleanly in his habits than the other, a bill of separation was in order. The "statutory grounds" from a soldier's point of view, was a chronic disposition to play off and shirk in the performance of a due share of duty. That was an unpardonable sin. If a soldier obtained the reputation of being a shirk in this respect, no matter how good he might be otherwise, he was doomed to live and sleep alone, with all its discomforts.

I was fortunate in the selection of my "pards." The first, as before stated, was Orderly Sergeant Heber Wells. He was the same dignified gentleman that he is now, a man of the highest instincts and most upright moral character, who never knew how to do a mean or dishonorable act. But Heber was the "orderly," and that meant no end of work. He had to attend to all the roll calls, make out the reports and be in constant communication with the captain or other commanding officer in regard to the different duty details. That kept him busy. By common consent the orderly sergeant is exempt from the ordinary menial service of camp life. So the most of the duties of a personal or domestic nature while he was "my pard" naturally fell upon me.

Heber, however, was not "my pard" very long, for

he was soon appointed to the position of second lieutenant of Company K. That meant his removal from the ranks to the officers' tent, and a separation between us socially. The social distinction between a soldier and a commissioned officer is very great. The man with the commission belongs to the four hundred of the army, while the private is the workingman. If it were otherwise it would be detrimental to discipline, for there is no greater truism than "familiarity breeds contempt." A servant or employee has comparatively little respect for the master or employer who makes himself familiar. The high-headedness of officers in the army is galling at times, but it is necessary for discipline, and no amount of philosophizing can change this fact.

My real "pard" was John Butterworth. John was an old employee of Daggers & Row, the bobbin turners. He told me all about wood turning, and I told him all about the printing business. He was married and worried a good deal about his wife, which was a pain that I had not to undergo. John was not an educated man, but he was possessed of an extraordinary degree of sound common sense. He knew how to cook everything that could be made of pork and beans and hardtack. The only thing in which John was lacking was in card-playing. I taught him how to play a fair game of High-Low-Jack with the greasy old pack of cards we had, but could never teach him the mysteries of poker. He conscientiously sent home every cent of his pay that had not been mortgaged to the sutler, while I had no one depending on me and so liked to indulge in the elusive pleasures of "draw." I found plenty of other fellows in the company, however, who could relieve me of my surplus cash, after a visit from the paymaster, with neatness and dispatch, and even go so far as to mortgage future months' income. When credit in that direction was exhausted, blankets, overcoats and other goods and chattels went the way of all flesh frequently in consequence of overconfidence in the security of three nines or a five high full house.

But other than in card-playing John Butterworth was an ideal "pard." I never heard him "kick" over the performance of a duty. I think I sometimes took advantage of his perennial good nature, now that I come to look back to those times. He would take the canteens and walk a mile for a supply of water, without a word of protest. He would gather twigs and branches for bedding, raid a rail fence afar off or do any other duty asked, without a word of complaint.

And he was always good natured. I never saw his temper ruffled. He was a good soldier in every respect, always ready to perform his duty with the minimum of "kicking," whether it were a battalion drill, a battle, a long march or a turn at picket. And when he had after a day's hard work succeeded in getting a few cedar boughs on a row of poles on the ground for a mattress, he would pull the blanket up to his chin and say:

"Oh, I tell you, Joe, but isn't this solid comfort? There's many a poor fellow in the world who hasn't such a nice comfortable bed as this, eh?"

I agreed, but I frequently did so with the mental reservation that no one but a veritable Mark Tapley could extract comfort and pleasure from such conditions.

I shall ever remember "my pard" John Butterworth with feelings of satisfaction and pleasure, for he was a good, true friend, and there were not many men in the army so well favored as I was in the selection of a "pard."

Some of the other fellows were not so fortunate. There were continual quarrelings and bickerings and even fights as to who should do this and who that. But I think the most comical thing of all was that John Ick and Reddy Mahar should have been thrown together as "pards."

Such, however, was the case. It would have been difficult to get two more incongruous characters together. One was German and the other Irish, and they were always quarreling. They were unlike in everything imaginable. Yet by some strange fate things happened so that they should bunk together.

I remember on the occasion of the first night we had our "pup" tents. My "tent" was next to theirs.

"Dot vas a devil uv a ting," said Ick. "How was a fellow to get dot ting on the outside, alretty?"

"Oh, shut your blarney trap," answered Reddy. "Wait awhile till we get the hang o' this consarn. You see here are some holes——"

"Und here be de buttonholes, by jimminey."

"We will button thim together, that we will, be gorra."

"We vill dot. ri-et away."

They buttoned the two sheets of the "pup" tent together and spread it out on the ground.

"That is the sheet, begorra," said Reddy. Whereupon he spread it out and rolled himself up into it.

After some altercation between the two as to the way to fix it, some of the other fellows showed them how to make a tent of the "sheet." When it was completed the two got on their hands and knees and crawled in. I never knew what started the trouble, but in a moment everybody in that part of the camp was attracted by the bellicose talking between Ick and Mahar, and pretty soon they became involved in a regular rough-and-tumble fight.

Now there isn't much room in a "pup" tent to carry on a fight according to the rules of the Marquis of Queensberry, or any other British nobleman. The fighters rolled over to the side of the little tent, and pulled it from its fastenings. The tent was on the side of a hill, and they naturally rolled downward. The further they rolled the closer were they wrapped in the folds of the "pup" tent, and they went down that hill as if they were done up in a muslin bundle, fighting and snarling as they went like a couple of cats in a bag.

It was one of the most comical sights I ever saw. The tent was torn to tatters. But John Ick and Reddy Mahar didn't want any tent that night. They slept in the guardhouse.

I also lost my tent that same night, but in an entirely different way, although fully as comical.

CHAPTER XXXII.

THE ARMY MULE.

Before I proceed to tell how I lost my "pup" tent that night, let me introduce the reader to the army mule.

There was nothing in the whole army that filled such an important and unique place in the prosecution of the war as the meek and docile mule. I use these adjectives with an unlimited degree of mental reservation. Appearances are often deceiving. There is nothing more plainly written in nature than the sign of meekness and docility embossed on the placid countenance of the mule.

But woe be to him who places faith in the meek and innocent appearances of the army mule. Somewhere in the interior of the mule there lurks a latent energy, a pent-up supply of total depravity that would do credit to the arch enemy of mankind. No doubt the original delineator of Satan had been a victim of misplaced confidence in the hind legs of a mule, for otherwise what would have suggested the adoption of hoofs as the orthodox representation of the devil's feet? If the aforesaid original artist had put a paint brush on the end of Satan's tail, instead of an arrow head, there would have been no room for doubt as to where he got his model.

Horses were never used in the army except by the mounted officers and soldiers. The motive power of all warlike rolling-stock was the mule. The teams consisted of from six to ten mules, according to the depth of the mud. They were driven by one line, the same as they are driven now through the South. The driver does not sit on the wagon, but in a saddle on the wheel mule on the near side.

I tried once to drive a mule team, but only succeeded in getting them into inextricable confusion. How a driver guides the team to the right or to the left as he desires, with only one rein, is a mystery in equestrian dynamics that I could never comprehend. The rein and the long-lashed whip had their uses to be sure, but they were insignificant factors in the art of driving a mule team.

The secret of this science lay entirely in the language used by the driver, or "teamster" as he was called in the army. In order to keep a mule team in motion it is necessary to carry a continual conversation. A man with a weak pair of lungs could never drive a team of army mules. Neither could a strict church member. The nature of the conversation is altogether inconsistent with orthodoxy. I have heard of men who were good and pious, and refined and discreet in their language, being appointed to the position of mule drivers. In such cases one of two things happens. Either the aforesaid teamster resigned his position, or else he fell from grace to a depth of hopeless depravity that completely ruined all hopes of future happiness.

I cannot describe the language a successful mule driver used to make his team start, and keep them going after they had once started. It would be entirely inconsistent with a work designed for general distribution. Besides, it would likely break down the press on which it was printed. Keeping within the confines of conservative respectability, I will merely remark that when the teamster wants to start the team, he grasps the blacksnake whip in his right hand and the single rein in his left, gives the former a snap and the latter a jerk and opens the conversation:

"Now, then, you—— —— ——! Git up there, you —— —— ——! You—— —— ——! —— —— ——, why don't you pull? —— —— ——! *******! —— ——! —— —— ——! —— ——! Gee——Haw——!"

Looking toward the noise you see a cloud of blue smoke arising and the air is filled with a suffocating odor of sulphur. Then you are conscious of a movement.

"She starts, she moves. She seems to feel
The thrill of life along her keel!"

The long mule team with its cumbersome, canvas-hooded baggage wagon has started. But don't let the innocent reader imagine that the torrent of vocal sounds ceases with the beginning of motion on the part of the team. No, indeed! The teamster must keep right on. The moment he stops the team stops. The yelling is a part of the mechanism of the motive power of the establishment. It is the supply of steam that actuates the valves and pistons of the long-eared, brush-tailed, four-footed locomotives. Thus it was that when night came, and the other soldiers were tired and fatigued in their limbs, the teamsters were played out in the muscles that move the vocal chords, the lips, and the bellows apparatus of the lungs.

When night came, the mule took up the refrain where it was dropped by the teamster and generally kept it up till daylight. The reader has probably heard the peculiar music rendered by the mule. It is hard to express it in type, but it is something like this:

"Onk-a! onk-a! onk-a! onk-a!"

The tone is a mezzo-soprano, alto, falsetto, basso combination, something like a bazoo. The exact intonation can only be given by a man in the last stages of diphtheria. I have heard some singers who could sing as well as a mule—but not many.

Such is the natural music of the individual mule. Now the average army mule never took much stock in solos. When one began his bazoo, another answered, and a third chimed in, till at last there was a chorus of mule music. Other mules in other parts of the army would join the refrain, till a cloud of discordant mule song arose to the ambient heavens and mingled with the twinkling stars. (That's pretty bad, but I'll let it go.)

The soldiers soon got used to imitating the music of the mule with marvelous accuracy. In fact at times it was almost impossible to distinguish between the genuine article and the counterfeit. A mule would begin with his indescribable "Onk-a, onk-a," and some camp wag would follow it up. Other mules (the four-legged ones, I mean) would join in the refrain, and so it would go, till the entire body, mules and men, would send forth a grand chorus that was limited only by the uttermost confines of the army.

The mule choruses were indescribably comical, and sometimes disastrous, as they would discover the whereabouts of the army to the enemy under circumstances that were unpleasant. I have known one man to start up the mule chorus on a quiet night till it involved every brigade, division and corps within twenty miles.

There was no accounting for the vagaries of the army mules. Sometimes they would be quietly crunching their fodder, when suddenly, without the least excuse or provocation, they would stampede. They did not care what direction they took. One would think after a hard day's work they would take advantage of the opportunity to get a little rest. But a mule is never really tired. At least no matter what may have been the work of the day there is a reserve force equal to any possible or impossible extra emergency. And when the mules got loose and stampeded there was nothing to stop them except their own sweet and angelic will.

I remember on one occasion in the middle of the night we were suddenly aroused from our sleep and ran for our lives under the idea that the enemy's cavalry had made a charge upon us, when it was nothing but the mules stampeding from a neighboring brigade. This same thing occurred many times, in different parts of the army, during the course of the war.

There is no dependence on the friendship of the hind-leg of a mule. It may rest in quiescence for months, but finally, like a long smouldering volcano, it will break forth without any preliminary rumbling. It is no respecter of persons or rank, that hind-leg of the mule. The man who had carefully and faithfully stood by the mule in sickness and distress, in hunger and thirst, in the camp and on the march, after having been left unmolested so long that a feeling of confidence had been created, was often made the victim of the irresponsible viciousness of the hind-leg. No, never put your trust in the hind-leg of a mule, no matter how innocent it may look.

In other respects is a mule deceptive. His eye is

gentle and bland, but don't trust it. The more gentle and bland, the more perfect the mask over the hidden stock of total depravity lurking within that silent but busy brain.

With a horse you can tell something about his intentions by the position of the ears. Ears slanted forward indicate alarm or extra watchfulness. Ears laid behind flat on the head indicate viciousness. A state of equine placidity is manifested by quiescent ears hanging loosely at the sides of his head. But not so with a mule. His ears generally hang senselessly beside his head. They are too heavy to move around to express emotion. So the driver cannot take warning of the feelings of the mule or his possible intentions for good or evil at any particular moment from his ears.

I doubt if the reader ever saw a dead mule. As many thousands as I ever saw alive, I can't remember more than half a dozen dead ones. They did not often get near enough to the front in the ordinary course of the war to be shot in battle, and they seemed impervious to all the usual influences of climate or condition. The only thing that ever kills a mule is not a physical ailment, but mental trouble.

I give this statement after full consideration of the gravity of the assertion, and reiterate that the main cause for fatality among mule folks is mental worriment—in other words, discouragement. When a mule for any cause becomes discouraged, his sphere of usefulness in this world has forever ended. He simply lies down, and without any unnecessary nonsense or fuss, quietly yields up the ghost. I never saw but one mule die. He tried in vain and faithfully to help pull a wagon out of the mire, but when he found that the task was impossible, he gently laid himself down and died.

Ask any old army teamster if he ever knew a mule to die from any other cause than sheer discouragement.

A word of sympathy and justice is due to the mule. All through his life he labors under the pain and disadvantage of a questionable ancestry. No matter how otherwise bright the surrounding circumstances may be, the mule always has within his breast the knowledge that he is an illegitimate offspring. While horses hold their heads high in the knowledge of a noble ancestry, the poor mule hangs his head in shame because his genealogical tree extends back only one generation; and in addition to that, the possibilities of future blood relations to honor his memory are so remote that it must forever be the source of carking care and mental pain. These things may possibly account for many of the vagaries of the mule that might otherwise be inexplicable.

The appetite of the mule is insatiable and omnivorous. His digestion is an object of envy on the part of many a two-legged dyspeptic. To the mule antediluvian hardtack crackers are but as mush. Like the Manhattanville goat he can digest anything short of coal scuttles. Old blankets, haversacks, newspapers, and leather belts form a sumptuous dessert for the mule; and instead of nuts at the end of a banquet, he would any day prefer the ridgepole of a tent.

And that brings me back to the introduction of this chapter.

Heber Wells had received a box from home, as before described. It looked like rain one night and he suggested that he keep the box under cover so that the rain would not spoil the remainder of the contents. I vacated, and bunked that night with Hank Van Orden. In the middle of the night I was awakened by the raindrops falling in my face, which I thought was strange, as I had gone to sleep fully protected by the "pup" tent.

Getting up I was surprised to find I was outdoors. The "pup" tent had entirely disappeared with the exception of a small end of one of the white sheets.

This was sticking out of the mouth of a mule!

The mule had eaten up our "pup" tent.

CHAPTER XXXIII.

GENERAL M'CLELLAN AND I.

YES, it was a fact. The mule had eaten up our tent.

This was not an infrequent occurrence, for as said before, an army mule liked a "pup" tent as well as a Harlem goat does a tomato can or a flesh-colored living picture on a three-sheet poster. But it was something entirely new to us, and we marveled greatly.

The worst of it all was, Hank Van Orden and I were out of a tent. We were outside in the cold, and the tent was inside the mule. It did not call for a moment's reflection to know that the further usefulness of that particular tent, so far as we were concerned, was at an end. What use it might have been to the digestive apparatus of the mule is another thing.

So we consulted Orderly Sergeant Wells, and he advised us to consult the captain, or rather the acting captain, Lieutenant Scott. The latter made out a requisition on the quartermaster for the respective two sections of "one shelter tent." We went to the quartermaster, but he had run out of a supply of tents, and he made a requisition on the brigade quartermaster and handed it to us. The brigade quartermaster sent us to the division quartermaster and the latter sent us to the corps quartermaster—all for one "pup" tent!

When we got to corps headquarters, we were kept waiting a long time for the convenience of the high and mighty official who had charge of the government clothing and tailorshop for that particular branch of the army. There were a lot of other fellows from other regiments waiting their turns for various articles for which requisitions had been made.

One of the men was a soldier from our own brigade,

a member of the Twenty-seventh Indiana. We got talking together and among other things we told him about the mule eating up the "pup" tent.

"Oh, that's nuthin'," said he. "Them air mewels are a curus critter, them are. Givvum a chance, 'n they'll eat a hull muskit, bayonet 'n all. But the funniest thing of 'em all is to see 'em shoot a cannon from atop a mewel's back."

"What!" I interrupted; "shoot a cannon from a mule's back? What are you giving us?"

"That are the dead shure fac'," was the Hoosier's reply. "I've seen it done many a time. They jis' strap the cannon—a howster (howitzer) is what they call 'em—on the mewel's back. They load the guns up, turns the head o' the mewel to the Johnny Rebs, and pulls the string."

"And shoot the cannon from the mule's back?" I asked increduously.

"Shure's you're livin'. The muzzle of the cannon are p'inted to'ards the head o' the mewel, and when the gunner gits ready for to shoot, the mewel he hangs down his head, ye know, and stretches out his four legs to the four p'ints o' the compiass, like the legs o' a sawbuck, ye know. That gives the mewel a solid footin', d'ye see, so that the shootin' o' the cannon can't knock the mewel over."

"How do they teach the mule to hold his legs that way?" I asked, "seeing the mule is such a stupid beast."

"They don't teach him nothin'. He hes sense enough to l'arn himself. The fust time the cannon are shot from the back o' the mewel, it jist knocks the mewel clean over. He luks around kind o' scared like, a wonderin' if that air cyclone struck any one else. Then he tries to shake off the cannon When the mewel finds that the cannon are a tight hold on his back, he gits up and kind o' concludes, d'ye know, that there have been some sort of a mistake like. The secon' time he reckons, d'ye know, that there ain't bin no mistake. And the third time, he squars off his four huffs."

"And don't get knocked over, eh?" I asked.

"That's whare ye're right, pard. And you oughter

see the 'spresshun on the mewel's eyes just then. He don't say nothin' but he jist looks as how he were saying to himself, 'Golly, but I fooled 'em that time for shure.' After that, every time the mewel hes sense enough for to stretch out his four legs and brace himself for the kick o' the gun. It are a queer sight I kin tell you, pard, but it air as true as the gospil, as you'll see for yourself, afore you are long in the sarvice. But come, here's a chance for to get our accuterments."

Strange as this may seem, the story given us by the veteran from the Twenty-seventh Indiana was literally true. Small cannon were strapped to the backs of the mules and actually fired therefrom, and the conduct of the mule on such occasions was just as described. These mule guns were called "mountain howitzers," and fired a shot of perhaps three pounds. Old soldiers have told me that the mules got so used to it that they did not stop nibbling at the twigs while the cannon was being shot from their backs!

Afterward I many a time saw a mule trudging along with a cannon strapped on his back, but I cannot say that I ever saw any of the shots fired. The cannon that I saw shot off were always on wheels. But these mule guns comprised quite an important adjunct to the army, and many a time, as said before, I have seen the animals clambering over the mountains thus equipped. It is a somewhat singular thing that I never saw any mention of this fact in any of the war books that I ever read, and doubtless the statement even now will be met with incredulity on the part of some readers. But nevertheless I can assure them that it is absolutely true.

After the usual delay and expenditure of red tape, Hank Van Orden and I got our new "pup" tents and made our way back to the regiment, arriving there just in time to be detailed to go on picket.

I had never been on picket. I had been on guard, both around the camp and to guard wagons and cattle, but this was the first time I had been assigned to the dignity of a picket.

The picket is "mounted" in about the same manner as the ordinary guards, and a guard mount was somewhat imperfectly described in one of the opening chapters of this story. In ordinary guard duty, the headquarters of the guard is a "guard house." In picket duty it is a little different.

The officer of the guard has charge of a certain number of men on picket duty. The men are divided up into squads under charge of sergeants. Each squad is composed of three times as many privates as there are posts to guard, and three corporals. The privates stand on their posts two hours, and then have four hours' rest. "Two on the four off," is the laconic way it was expressed in army parlance.

The "first relief" serve from 9 to 11, the second from 11 till 1, and the third from 1 till 3, when the first relief comes on again, and so it goes throughout the twenty-four hours of the day and night. The corporals serve the same way, although they are not on post. They hang around the camp fire, ready to respond to any call from any of the men on guard.

"Corporal of the guard, post No. 6," is a call frequently heard. It may mean anything. It may mean that the picket is confronted by the enemy, or it may mean that he wants a drink of water. It is the corporal's duty to wait upon him. For that reason although a corporal was of higher rank than the private, the former was frequently dubbed by the name of "waiter."

The sergeant stayed at the headquarters of the "picket post," which usually consisted of nothing more than a good fire in some convenient place along the line. The sergeant had the command of the pickets of that particular post, which might include a dozen or more places where the privates were stationed. The corporal reported to the sergeant, and if the problem presented was more than the sergeant could solve, he reported to the officer of the guard.

The difference between guards and pickets is this: Guards are merely men stationed around some internal part of the army. Pickets are the men stationed on the extreme outer edge. In other words there is nothing between the pickets and the enemy—that is if there is any enemy in that particular direction. Whether there is or not, there is always supposed to be.

I was on the second relief—that is, on duty from 11 to 1 o'clock, and my first post was on the road along the Potomac River, at the foot of Maryland Heights and about half a mile up the river from opposite Harper's Ferry.

It was a beautiful day. The rain had cleared off and the skies were bright. Any one who has been there knows that it is one of the most picturesque spots in the country. I felt good and for the first time since my enlistment seemed to enjoy the experience of being a soldier.

Here I was, I thought, on the outskirts of the Union army, with nothing between me and the Confederate army. I felt and enjoyed the responsibility of reflecting that so many men were under my watchful care. How faithful I would be. I imagined to myself how I would defend my post if any of the enemy's pickets should make their appearance. I would defend it with my last drop of blood, of course.

So I thought. If an enemy's picket had made his appearance I most likely would have suddenly decamped. But the enemy did not appear. As a matter of fact there was not a rebel within miles. How easy it is to be brave under such circumstances, although of course I did not know.

I had been very carefully cautioned not to let a living soul pass my post without the countersign. The countersign that day was "Manassas." I had of course heard of the tricks played on John Ick and the other greenies, but they couldn't come any such game as that over me. Not much!

Pretty soon I heard a clanking of swords, and a large number of brilliantly uniformed mounted officers approached. Who should the head one be but General George B. McClellan himself!

I had seen General McClellan several times, and knew him by sight perfectly. As he approached he came up to me and I brought my rifle to a "present arms."

"Do you know who I am?" he asked.

"Of course I do," I answered. "You are General McClellan."

"And these officers are members of my staff," said the general. "You must keep your musket at a 'present arms' while they all pass."

"All right, general," I responded, and I kept my rifle sticking out in front of me according to the way the tactics called for a "present arms."

I looked down to the next picket, another Thirteenth boy, and saw the same maneuver enacted there, and so on till the gay cavalcade had passed around the bend of the rocks.

I felt highly honored with the idea of having presented arms to General McClellan. What a story it would be to tell to the boys at camp.

What a story it was, indeed!

In less than half an hour after, the entire section of picket guarded by the Thirteenth's boys were relieved and marched back to camp and locked up in the log hut called the "guard house," or prison.

"What is this for?" we asked indignantly. "Who ordered that we should be locked up?"

"General McClellan," was the answer.

"What for?"

"For letting him and his whole staff pass you without the countersign!"

"Well, I'll be d—d!" said Lem Smith, one of my companions.

And so said we all of us.

CHAPTER XXXIV.

THE SUTLER.

WELL, wasn't this a nice predicament?

After all the instruction we had received! After all the fun we had poked at John Ick and the other fellows for being so green as to let officers pass them without giving the countersign, to think that we—we, who considered ourselves more than ordinarily well posted and on the alert, should be found guilty of the same stupidity, was too much altogether.

Of all the chagrined and ashamed lot in the guard house that day I do not think there was a single one who thought for a moment of making any excuse for himself. We had been found remiss in one of the simplest duties of a soldier, and had been caught in a trap that was considered only fit for greenhorns. And we had by this time begun to look upon ourselves as veterans, although in the service scarcely more than a month.

But we ought to have known better, that's sure enough. When a picket is given orders to allow no one to pass without the countersign, it means everybody, from the lowest private to the commanding general of the army, or even of the President of the United States.

As for myself I was blinded by the magnificence of General McClellan's staff. Or perhaps I imagined on the spur of the moment that of course the highest officer in the army could come and go as he chose, countersign or no countersign. Be it as it may, we all recognized the stupid blunder we had made the moment we were told why we had been arrested and by whose order.

Not only the comparatively green pickets of the Thirteenth New Jersey and some of the equally green New York regiment that was brigaded with us, had been caught in the trap, but also some of the members of the Twenty-seventh Indiana and Third Wisconsin, who certainly ought to have known more, had been hauled in for the same offense. It seems that on the retreat from the Peninsular discipline had become somewhat relaxed, and it was a common occurrence for the guards and pickets to let the high officers pass without question, and such a thing as demanding the countersign from them, in spite of the strict orders that had been given, had never entered the minds of these veterans. So it was that they fell into the same trap.

I cannot tell how many men were arrested that day for the same thing—there were a good many. It was only intended as a sort of object lesson to teach the men that orders were to be more strictly obeyed thereafter, particularly in regard to picket duty. So the punishment in this instance was nothing more than a reprimand, and a warning not to be caught in the same trap again. We were kept in the guard house, however, for several hours before we were thus disposed of, and during that time we were picturing all sorts of punishment for our remissness.

It was a good lesson to us all, for never again were we caught in the trap of letting any one pass without the countersign when on picket, no matter who it might be.

It was while we were at Maryland Heights that we were introduced to something new about army life—the "sutler."

If ever another war breaks out and I conclude to enter the service, I think I will be a sutler. At the first sign of a fight, the sutler mysteriously disappears and never turns up till the danger is over. Sutlers always got rich. They had a regular bonanza. Perhaps the majority of the readers of this do not know what the sutler was.

In the midst of camp one day some men began to put up a big, square tent. It was larger than the tent occupied by any of the officers. It was high and commodious. Wagons began to be unloaded of boxes and barrels and mysterious-looking crates. They were taken inside and the flaps of the tents drawn, while the actors inside got the properties arranged for the performance.

In the morning our eyes were dazzled with the layout. The upper part of two sides of the tent were rolled up, displaying on a sort of counter the most tempting assortment of articles. There were pipes and tobacco galore, boxes of sardines and tomatoes, butter in hermetically sealed glass jars, ginger snaps and cakes, apples, potatoes, fresh bread, herring and mackerel, dried apples, prunes and peaches, figs and dates, oranges, soda water and ginger pop, and a thousand other things that were likely to tempt the palates of soldiers.

And there were various articles of wearing apparel of a finer texture than that furnished by Uncle Sam, such as better stockings, finer shoes and long-legged boots, leggings, rubber overcoats, handkerchiefs, writing paper and envelopes, and in fact no end of articles in the fancy goods line.

Nearly every regiment in the army had its sutler. These things were sold to the officers and soldiers, and the trade was a good one, while the prices were something outrageous. You had to patronize the sutler of your own regiment or go without, and pay whatever was charged for the articles desired.

We were nearly all in need of tobacco, which was about the first thing sought for, and although it was villainous tobacco, half chips, it was better than smoking oak and laurel leaves, to which strait some of us had been reduced. The tobacco sold by the sutler was mostly known as the "Garibaldi" brand. It bore a gorgeous picture of the patriot in a red shirt and dark trousers, so he looked like a member of a volunteer fire department. Ask any old soldier if this description of the wrapper on the smoking tobacco used in the Army of the Potomac does not remind him of old times. The tobacco itself looked and tasted like pine sawdust, and had about as much flavor when smoked.

"I'd like to have some of that tobacco," said John Butterworth to me, "but I haven't a cent."

"I'm busted myself, Jack," said I, "but let's go and see if we can't stand him off for a paper of the tobacco."

Butterworth agreed to this proposition and we approached the tent of the sutler. "Say, Mr. Sutler," said I, "we fellows want some tobacco, and haven't a cent. Do you trust?"

"Oh, yes," was the reply. "You can have anything you want not exceeding the pay due you. You have been in the service for a month and consequently your credit is good for thirteen dollars."

"Say, Jack," said I to my comrade, "this is a snap. Let's lay in a stock. He'll have a time to collect it, won't he? There's no justice of the peace or constable around here to make a levy, you know."

"There's some trick about it," replied Jack, "or he wouldn't be so willing to trust. However, we will try it and see."

I chose a new briar pipe, price one dollar—anywhere else twenty-five cents. For a ten-cent paper of smoking tobacco the price was a quarter. Fifteen cents was charged for a plug of "niggerhead" chewing plug. I also paid fifty cents for about ten cents worth of paper and envelopes.

Total, one dollar and ninety cents.

The butter in the jars looked tempting. I hadn't tasted butter for over a month. The butter was done up in little muslin bags, and these were placed in a glass jar, which was hermetically sealed. Altogether the butter was supposed to weigh one pound.

"How much for the butter?" I asked, holding up the jar.

"Twenty shillings," I was informed.

"What?"

"Two dollars and a half."

"Two dollars and a half for a pound of butter?"

"That's the price," said the sutler. And he explained the difficulty of getting butter to the front and caring for it in such a convincing manner that I became satisfied that two dollars and a half a pound was not only reasonable, but, under the circumstances, very cheap indeed.

I invested, thus running up a bill of four dollars and ninety cents. It was the last pound of sutler butter that I ever bought, for it was a delusion and a snare. I guess it was nothing but colored lard—and very stale lard at that. We simply couldn't eat it—and when a thing is so bad that a soldier cannot eat it it must be bad indeed.

John Ick was disgusted with the sutler because he could not supply his demand for "ein glass lager." Reddy Mahar pleaded in vain for a little of "the old stuff," for in the rear end of the tent could be seen some bottles marked "Bourbon." The proper brand of whiskey in those days was "Bourbon." Such a thing as "Rye" was hardly ever heard of.

But the sutler could not sell intoxicating liquor to the enlisted men. It was against the regulations. These regulations did not apply to the commissioned officers, and some of them took advantage of the exceptional privilege. Lieutenant Scott was good to me in that respect, however. I did not take much to whisky, but enjoyed the opportunity to get it because it was "forbidden fruit."

Not infrequently, with all these precautions, one would see a drunken soldier. How he got his liquor was always more or less of a mystery, but generally on such occasions there would be found a bottle or so missing from the sutler's tent.

I thought the sutler was very generous in giving the soldiers so much trust, and often wondered how he could collect all his bills. But I found out at the first pay day. We were getting two months' pay—twenty-six dollars. When the paymaster called me up for my pay I signed my name at the edge of the big sheet of paper and the clerk handed me eight dollars.

"How's this?" I asked. "Here's only eight dollars, instead of twenty-six."

"That's right," answered the paymaster, with an imperious wave of the hand. "We have deducted your bill on the sutler, amounting to seventeen dollars and twenty-five cents."

Ah, I had discovered how the sutler collected his bills—why he was so willing to trust the soldiers. He had the bulge on us, sure enough. That was a nice arrangement, wasn't it?

"But hold on, major," said I, after making a hasty

mental calculation. "You say my bill at the sutler's was seventeen dollars and twenty-five cents, which amount, taken from twenty-six dollars, leaves eight dollars and seventy-five cents, and you have only given me eight dollars. That is seventy-five cents short."

"Haven't time for explanations," answered the autocrat. "Ask 'your captain. Campbell" (calling the next name on the roll).

"You see," said Lieutenant Scott, explaining the matter to me afterward, "the paymaster has no change and can only pay the even dollars. The seventy-five cents will go to your credit on the next pay roll."

That was the rule. The sutler came first, the odd change next, and the soldier got what was left. The cash I received for my first two months' service in the army was accordingly eight dollars, four dollars a month, a dollar a week—and found!

CHAPTER XXXV.

NEWS FROM HOME.

We all made up our minds that the sutler would not get such a large proportion of our pay the next time, but these good resolutions did not amount to much when the time came. And let me interpolate that a soldier's remuneration was never referred to as "wages" or "salary," or any other term than "pay." That was the only word ever used in connection with the compensation received from Uncle Sam for our services.

As said, the good resolution not to let such a large proportion of our "pay" fall into the hands of the sutlers was easier made than kept. Mild as it was, it was the only source of dissipation within our reach. The bill of fare provided by the government was very limited, and in a short time it became extremely monotonous. There was scarcely a day that there was not a demand for some little luxury or convenience from the sutler's tent.

With us young fellows this drain on our income did not amount to much, but married men, who had families at home who needed every cent that could be sent to them, had to be more economical. And the people at home probably never had the slightest comprehension of the privation and discomfort that their husbands and fathers went through in order to save every cent. That was patriotism from a domestic economy point of view.

There were some occurrences at Maryland Heights that filled us with indignation, in the shape of the resignations of several of the commissioned officers. A private soldier was enlisted and bound fast "for three years unless sooner discharged," but the commissioned officers had the privilege of resigning and going home whenever they saw fit, although it was generally regarded as arrant cowardice for one to resign on the eve of an impending battle. In such cases, however, as a general rule, the resignation would not be accepted.

But there were several resignations among the officers at Maryland Heights. They "knew when they had enough" and "wanted to go home." So did we privates, but we couldn't "go home." Of course all the resigning officers had "urgent business" or "sickness in the family" that required their immediate presence in the vicinity of the domestic hearthstones, but an altogether different interpretation was placed on these resignations by the average soldier.

Sometimes, under very extraordinary emergencies, a private could get a short leave of absence or "furlough," to go home, but one had to have a "pull" to obtain this inestimable privilege. It is easier for a camel to go through the eye of a sewing-machine needle than it is for a private soldier to get a furlough.

To their credit be it said, there were no resignations in Company K. We had at that time but one commissioned officer—Lieutenant Scott—and he stuck by us. He was daily expecting his commission as captain and that was another incentive for his remaining. But the members of Company K were not slow in expressing their opinions of those officers that did resign. Of course our friend John Ick bobbed up serenely on this occasion.

"Dey vas a lot of d—d cowyards," he said. "Dey gets us here by the front alretty, und den dey goes back by us all the times, by jimminey. Dey drives us likes ein lot o' sheeps by the schlaughter haus, und then dey runs avay. Dey was cowyards!"

The juxtaposition of "cowyards" and "slaughter houses" was a better pun than John had any idea of. But that is what he said, and he expressed the sentiments of a good many others. These adverse comments went to such a length that there was a warning that if the boys did not keep their mouths shut on the subject they would likely be disciplined for disrespect toward their superior officers—an unpardonable sin, by the way.

At Maryland Heights we began to get our first mail from home. It is impossible to describe the delight and satisfaction to a soldier to receive letters from home,

I received two. One was from my uncle, and another from—well, no matter.

I also received a copy of the *Guardian*—the paper on which I had worked—the one containing the particulars of the battle we had recently passed through. Then for the first time we learned the name of the battle—"Antietam." We had always imagined that it would be called "the battle of Sharpsburg," because it was near that village. But the Northern newspapers and historians named it after the creek—Antietam—and so it has been known ever since—throughout the North.

The Southern people named it by its natural and more proper appellation, it seems to me. They have in their histories no "battle of Antietam." With them it is "the battle of Sharpsburg." The theory adopted by the Northern historians was an old one. Cities and towns may be destroyed or otherwise disappear, running streams never. The name of the location of a great event is accordingly taken from some permanent landmark or watermark. Hence, "Antietam," from the creek, rather than "Sharpsburg," from the village.

I remember the articles about the battle in the *Guardian* distinctly. It had a lot of flaring headlines and a long list of the killed and wounded. I forget whether it was in this battle or some other one that I was reported among the killed. I had the pleasure (?) of reading my own obituary at least once in my life. I often wonder when the genuine article is published if it will be so complimentary!

It afforded an intense pleasure to read that paper from home. The local news was specially interesting. I saw that more of my old companions had subsequently enlisted in the army, in other regiments, and I began to wonder if there was anybody left at home at all. But I looked in vain among the list of those who had gone to the war for the names of those patriotic orators who had made the speeches from the steps of the old bank building on Main Street.

Nearly all the boys had received letters from home. Some of them contained bad news, telling of trouble or sickness, and these made the recipients very downhearted and unhappy. I was more than ever glad that

I had no one dependent upon me. The letter from my uncle told of the trouble he had to get out the *Guardian*, now that all his printers had gone to the war. He said that he had even to put one of the girls at work on making up the forms. I showed the letter to Davy Harris.

"Joe," said he, "do you remember how I kicked at being called up from the job room to make up the forms when Joe Mosley was sick? Well, I wouldn't kick at such an order now, you bet. What fools we were to leave that job and come here. But there's no use crying now. We are in for it, and that settles it. So Joe Mosley has enlisted too, has he?"

"So it seems," I replied. "Guess he will find it a little different from setting advertisements and making up the forms, eh?"

The conversation was interrupted by an order to fall in for drill.

And by the way, the drilling began to be incessant, and it was very tiresome. The boys were all more or less weakened from the effects of that magnesia spring, and the exposure of army life had begun to have other effects upon us. So far as I was concerned, this sort of life rather agreed with me. I had always had a rather indoor occupation—at least for some years before I enlisted—and the outdoor air was building me up. There is nothing like the fresh outdoor air for health, even with all its discomforts.

With drills and picket duties we were kept busy during the time we were at Maryland Heights. And so it ran on till the 26th of October, when we were informed that a new general had been assigned to the command of our corps—General Henry W. Slocum. He was to visit us the following day, and be formally "introduced." In other words, we were to have a "general review."

Later in the evening we were thrown into a state of still further excitement. We were told to have our uniforms neatly brushed, our guns cleaned to the highest pitch of perfection, and the brass work on our accouterments polished till we could see our faces in them.

"What's up? What does all this mean?" I asked Sergeant Wells.

"Why, don't you know?" he replied. "The president is coming."

"The president? What president?" I asked, not taking it in.

"The President of the United States, of course."

"You don't mean to say that President Lincoln is coming to see us?"

"Yes, he will be here to-morrow to review us."

I hastened down through the company to spread the news.

CHAPTER XXXVI.

I SALUTE THE PRESIDENT.

In the meantime Lieutenant James G. Scott had received his commission as captain, "vice Captain Irish, killed," as the rolls had it. William H. Miller, formerly a member of the Second New Jersey, had been appointed as first lieutenant in Scott's place, and soon after Heber Wells, the orderly sergeant, was appointed second lieutenant, while our old friend "Hank" (Henry Van Orden), was made orderly sergeant.

Similar changes had been made in the other companies. In fact so many changes had been made that the various companies were practically newly officered; but on the whole it was an improvement, for we were getting down to the practical hard pan only reached by service and experience. At the time mentioned in the preceding chapter therefore, the Thirteenth Regiment was getting down to a pretty good shape. The men had received considerable drill and knew the difference between "present arms" and "guard mount."

I appreciated the fact that I had even made some progress myself. I could shoot off a rifle without shutting my eyes, and in the marksmen's drill I had on at least one occasion succeeded in hitting the edge of a six-foot target. I felt if I continued to improve at this rate, it would soon be dangerous for a rebel to stand in front of my gun if it should go off, and that if I only got a chance at the enemy the war would soon be ended by the total annihilation of all the fellows on the other side.

I had also received a sort of a promotion. It was not a promotion in a strictly military sense, but it was a peg higher anyhow, and it involved certain enviable perquisites and privileges. In other words I had been dignified by the appointment of "company clerk."

The clerk of a company makes out the different and apparently never-ending rolls and reports connected with the company. He is practically the captain's private secretary. He is most of the time during the day in the captain's tent, and his associates are more the officers than the enlisted men. The advantages of being a company clerk consisted in being excused from squad, company and other drills, and from guard duty, police duty, and other menial service. It did not excuse him from regimental or brigade drill, nor from picket duty, inspections or reviews. There was no excuse from these except for those on absent assignments or detached service.

But the position of company clerk is altogether an enviable one, and much sought after. I received the appointment because I could write a good hand (those who see my writing now would never believe it) and because I was possessed of a certain degree of general intelligence that qualified me for the position. The place, by bringing the incumbent into close connection with the officers, gave him the advantage of certain important information ahead of the general rank and file, which sometimes was a good thing.

As said we had had a new general assigned to the command of our corps, General Henry W. Slocum. Our other general, Mansfield, had been killed at the battle of Antietam.

"What sort of a man is this Slocum?" I asked of a member of the Second Massachusetts whom I met that morning.

"He's a rip snorter," was the answer. "He is a fighting man from way back. I tell you we will catch it now when we get into a fight."

"Mine Gott und himmel," said John Ick, who stood near at the time. "Ish he a more by dot schlaughter haus yeneral by dot under feller? I no likes dot. Now we gets kilt sure enough, alretty."

And if it be true that General Slocum was a harder fighter than General Mansfield, it did not suit me either, not much. A man of peace would have been more to my liking. But we were in for it, and what was the use? The government did not consult the private soldiers as to who should be their commanding officers. Perhaps if it had we would have had better ones sometimes. This was not the case with General Slocum, of course, for a better general never lived.

As General Slocum died only a short time since, and his portraits were published by many papers in connection with that event, most people are familiar with his appearance. They will remember his white hair and white mustache, and a generally blond appearance. He was an entirely different-looking man in the army.

He was of course much younger then. His hair was a dark brown, and he wore a full beard, trimmed short. Most of the officers wore full beards in the war, not so much on account of appearance, but because it was supposed to be a protection against sore throats. But the principal reason was that the barber shops were not handy and the opportunity for regular shaving was not possible. I remember General Slocum as he looked then because I had a specially advantageous opportunity to see him close by.

It was my good fortune to be detailed for guard that day, and my still better fortune to be one of the men on guard at General McClellan's headquarters. It was a scene of great activity and magnificence. Extra tents, of a large size, had been set up, one of which was a sort of lunchroom, where a table was set that contained a marvelous collection, considering the situation. There were bottles galore, and numerous baskets of champagne. The idea of such a thing as champagne and glass goblets to drink it from, struck me with wonderment, out there "in the front."

Mounted orderlies and aids were galloping hither and thither with preparatory orders, and the number of handsomely uniformed officers wearing the stars of a general on their shoulder-straps was something wonderful. Many of the officers were from the ornamental detachment on duty at Washington, whose uniforms looked as if they had just come from the tailor's shop, and whose gold lace and bullion trappings were like those worn by the militia now. This was something oddly contrasting with the dull and dingy appearance of the uniforms and equipments of the officers who had been in active service in the front.

To a soldier who had just been through hard marches and battles, there was a feeling of intense disgust for these "play soldiers," as they were called. It is said that a man with a fur-lined overcoat is always tantalizing to a laborer in overalls. The same sort of a feeling seemed to overcome me and my companions at the sight of these gorgeously attired "West Pointers," with their clean and speckless uniforms, their bright golden trappings, and their airish eyeglasses.

Soon there began to arrive some coaches. How funny they looked—coaches in the army, where the only vehicles are mule-drawn baggage wagons and cavalry saddles. But funnier still was the sight of some handsomely dressed ladies getting out of the carriages.

Now it may seem strange, but with the exception of a *vivandiere* in one of the regiments of our corps, none of us had seen a woman since we passed through Washington. Every man seemed to straighten himself up with dignity at the unwonted sight. I really don't know whether those ladies were handsome or not, but to our eyes they resembled angels. The bright ribbons, the dainty, flower-decked hats, the pretty wraps, and above all the bright parasols, lent an addition of color to the surroundings such as we had not seen in many a long day.

These women were the wives and daughters of the distinguished officers and officials of the government. Harper's Ferry is not such a long distance from Washington and the visit for them was a nice little excursion trip. There were no rebels within miles, so that there was no earthly danger, but I imagined those women many a time after boasted about their having been "clear to the front" of the army during the war.

The last of all to arrive were the commanding generals of the different corps, and finally General McClellan himself with his brilliant staff.

With these was the President of the United States, and some members of the cabinet, all in citizens' clothes.

How plain and funereal those plain black suits looked

after having seen nothing but blue uniforms for so many weeks! It must be admitted that the contrast was rather in favor of the soldiers—or rather the officers. The president wore a silk hat, which looked woefully out of place.

With an imperious air some of the staff officers led the way into the collation tent, followed by the president and the other civilians. After them came some privileged army officers, and some of the ladies. If I remember rightly, however, the most of these remained outside, watching with interest the gathering army on the parade ground.

As President Lincoln passed me, on my post at the entrance of the tent, I brought my rifle to a "present arms" with a click and a snap. I purposely endeavored to attract his attention, but he never noticed me no more than if I had been a wooden Indian in front of a cigar store.

The distinguished party remained in the tent for some time. I could hear the popping of corks and clinking of glasses, the lively talk and the merry laughter. Ah, thought I, it's fun for them. Little do the most of them appreciate what real war is. I thought this way in my innocence. I did not appreciate then the worry, the anxiety and sleepless, troubled days and nights that were being passed by those who directed the war.

Others than soldiers fight. There are heroes who never shot a gun or wore a uniform.

In the meantime the vast army had got into position for the grand review. The different regiments and brigades, divisions and corps, were drawn up in line on the field, which from the elevated position we occupied we could see spread out like a cosmorama. It did present a beautiful sight, the straight lines, the thousands of soldiers, the glittering bayonets, the bright flags, all spread out there on the plain below us.

Then the generals commanding the different corps mounted their horses and, accompanied by their staffs, galloped to their respective commands and General McClellan and his staff, accompanied by the president and his associates, and followed by many of the ladies, went out to the place selected for them where they could have a good view of the maneuvers.

CHAPTER XXXVII.

A PRESIDENTIAL REVIEW.

"Attention! Present arms!" shouted General McClellan.

"Attention! Present arms!" repeated the various corps commanders.

"Attention! Present arms!" reiterated the commanders of divisions, and the commanders of the brigades, and the commanders of regiments, and the commanders of companies, until the order had gone down to the furthermost soldier in the army.

That is the way orders were given. It was manifestly impossible for one man's voice to reach the whole army, so that the command went down in sections, according to rank, like the signal corps wig-wagged their messages from hilltop to hilltop.

In an instant the entire army stood at a "present arms," and General McClellan turned, and with a graceful sweep of his sword, addressed the president:

"Your excellency, the parade is formed."

I don't know what the president said in reply, for it was in too low a tone. But he at once mounted a horse, as did those with him, and proceeded to move off. In the meantime the soldiers were ordered to bring their muskets from the uncomfortable position of a "present" to a "shoulder" arms. According to the tactics then in use a "shoulder" was a "carry."

President Lincoln, General McClellan and their brilliant cavalcade of staff officers then galloped down toward the vast army.

I will never forget the appearance of the president on that occasion. He was mounted on an enormous stallion, and sat in a Mexican saddle that was about four times too large for him. I think without exception he was the most awkward-looking man on horseback that I ever laid eyes upon. He was over six feet in height, slim as a rail, and naturally ungainly. On horseback he bobbed around in the saddle in the most uncomfortable sort of way.

His long black coat tails streamed behind comically, and his "plug hat" looked as if it would bob off with every jump the horse made. The officers rode like centaurs, as if they were a part of their steeds themselves, which made the contrast all the more startling. To tell the truth, I was in mortal terror that the president would tumble off his horse.

But he didn't. The bands played "Hail to the Chief," according to the orthodox rule, and the president, General McClellan and the big staff of gold tinseled officers cantered down the line and back on the rear, and along the front of the next line and around that, until the magnates had seen the front and rear of every line of troops in the vast army.

Then they returned to their starting point, called the "reviewing stand" and, still mounted, stood there for the second part of the performance, the "marching in review."

To the private soldier this is one of the most arduous and exasperating of all drills. The men march around the reviewing stand in what is called "company front." That is, they march by flank, and the idea is that when the different companies pass the reviewing stand, each one shall present a perfectly straight line.

On level ground and in single ranks this was comparatively easy. In the front, in two ranks, with the soldiers treading on each other's heels, and over uneven ground—perhaps an old plowed cornfield or something of that sort, with intercepting rocks and stumps, bushes, hillocks, and furrows—it became almost an impossibility.

But the army on this occasion did remarkably well. From the position I occupied, as one of the guards at headquarters, I could see the whole thing as plainly as the president himself. Then for the first time I got an idea of what a big army it was. I forget the exact number in that particular review. All that I remember is that it was something less than one hundred thousand.

What impressed me most was the number of cavalrymen and artillerymen, who came past after the infantry or foot soldiers. Then came the ambulance corps and the hospital brigade.

Ugh! This made the cold shivers run down my back. It reminded me of the unpleasant and grewsome experience I had that night after the battle of Antietam.

The grand spectacle was over at last, the assembled army broke up into its integral parts, and the president and general officers returned to the headquarters.

As the president passed me for the third time that day, I again brought my musket to a "present arms" with a more vigorous movement than ever, so much so, in fact, that it attracted Mr. Lincoln's attention, and he turned and looked at me.

Although I had really intended to attract his attention, in order to see if he would remember that morning in the capitol rotunda well enough to recognize me, yet when I had succeeded in getting him to look in my direction, I was so startled that I nearly dropped my rifle.

He paused and gazed at me intently, as if trying to remember something. I shook like a leaf in the wind. To say that I was embarrassed is no name for it. The incident was so marked as even to attract the attention of some of the officers, and they looked at me as if I was a culprit, for I suspect that they thought that I had been doing something wrong and had astonished the President of the United States.

I therefore felt considerably relieved when Mr. Lincoln renewed his steps and disappeared in the tent. He evidently did not recognize me, and yet my face had apparently awakened some recollection.

The corps commanders then came up and were formally introduced to the president and other dignitaries and to the ladies. The clinking of the glasses was renewed, and it was still in progress when the "second relief" came along and another soldier took my place.

The president did recognize me, but could not at the time place me. The proof of this will appear later. If I could have had recognition from him then and there it would have been of immense advantage to me. I had been in the army long enough already to appreciate the advantage of "a pull."

We had become quite familiar with some of the adjoining regiments of our brigade. Frequent calls and visits were interchanged between the men from different States at odd hours. That night I spent some time in the camp of the Third Wisconsin.

"Things look ticklish," said one of them. "That review by the president warn't for nothing."

"What do you mean by that?" I asked.

"Well, you see, pard," said the Wisconsin man, "whenever we are reviewed by the big guns, that means to see if the army is all right for a scrimmage. I never knowed there to be a review by the head general that we didn't have to git afore long. And when the president comes to see how things are, that means more than something ord'nary. I tell you there's goin' to be a scrimmage, and afore long at that."

"Why," I replied, probably in the effort to console myself, "there are no rebels anywhere around here. No enemy, no fight. We are not likely to have a battle with ourselves, are we?"

"Don't you fret yourself, pard," he replied; "the rebels may not be very near, and they may not be likely to come our way. But what's the matter with our going to hunt 'em up. That's what we'll likely do afore long. Mind what I say, pard, we won't be here long. You can bet your next month's pay on that."

That wasn't very consoling. We had scarcely recovered from the effects of one battle, and that ought to be enough for some time. In fact, I had had enough to last me for the remainder of the war.

It struck me as a very inconsiderate proposition on the part of the government that we should put ourselves to any trouble to hunt up the enemy so long as the enemy was not bothering us. What was the sense of seeking trouble? If the rebels came our way, all right. We would fight them. But so long as they did not molest us, what was the odds? Why should we go out of our way to get into trouble? So far as I was concerned I was perfectly willing to stay right there on

Maryland Heights for the whole "three years unless sooner discharged."

The readers will perhaps get the impression that I was no fighter. Well, maybe not. But I can say one thing. I was not the only one. There were lots of other fellows who thought and spoke the same way that I did.

Two days later we received orders to get ready to break camp.

It immediately struck me that the Wisconsin veteran was right. That review meant something. The army had been found in fine condition and ready for another engagement. We were going to hunt up the enemy and give him another tussle.

Some of the more restless men were glad of a change of some sort, but I would have preferred to have remained just then at Maryland Heights.

It was not thought that we would move for several days, but on the night of the 29th of October (this was in 1862, remember) at about 9 o'clock, an order was whispered around camp hurriedly to fill in for a march. It was also reported that the rebels had made their appearance at a spot a good deal nearer than any of us imagined.

Certainly there must be something important on hand or the start would not have been made at that late hour of the night.

But we were all surprised, after we had gone some distance, to find that we were retracing our steps, and were marching back over the same roads that we had come when we came from the battlefield of Antietam.

Was there going to be another fight on the same battle ground?

CHAPTER XXXVIII.

CAPTAIN IRISH'S BROTHER.

BEFORE leaving Maryland Heights, however, let me stop to relate one more incident that happened while we were in camp there.

Captain Irish's watch, sword, papers and other effects, taken from the body by Sergeant Heber Wells, were still in Wells' possession. Heber was with the regiment at Maryland Heights, and Lewis Irish, the captain's brother, had to make a journey thither to get them.

Visitors to camp could not come and leave as they chose in those days, but were obliged to wait for circumstances. Frequently they were compelled to wait in camp several days longer than they wanted to.

Lewis Irish was a nervous, timid sort of a man. The deadliest weapons he had ever handled were a needle and a pair of shears. He was a man of peace and had an inborn abhorrence and horror of everything appertaining to war.

As a result he was in a state of nervous trepidation all the time he was out at the front, although as a matter of fact there was really no more danger there than there was in the staid old village of Hackensack, where he resided.

Mr. Irish was in a constant fear that the rebels would pounce upon the camps at any moment. One member of the family had been killed. He was the only remaining brother. He didn't want the family name to become extinct!

At every unusual movement Mr. Irish would start. A stray shot from some soldier cleaning his gun would put him in a quiver. When the drum beat for reveille, guard mount or sick call, he would apparently imagine that it was the long roll for the whole army to fall in line of battle.

While there Lewis Irish "bunked" with Heber Wells, of course. It was before the "pup" tents had arrived, and the boys had rigged up all sorts of outlandish huts "to keep off the dew," as they expressed it.

Heber's hut, like many others, was made of poles and cedar boughs. A couple of poles with notches on the ends, like clothes poles, perhaps six or seven feet in length, were driven into the ground about ten or twelve feet apart. Across these was laid a ridgepole. From this, and slanting down to one side, the other end resting on the ground, were laid a lot of other poles, as close together as possible.

This formed the framework for a rude sort of shed. The roof was composed of cedar branches and boughs, and the ground was covered with the same thing for a bedding. This arrangement was of course perfectly useless in case of rain, but it sheltered the occupants from the wind and was more comfortable than sleeping out-of-doors entirely.

The occupants crawled in as far as possible when going to bed, so that their heads were near the side where the roof came down to the ground. There wasn't much space over the heads of the sleepers. When they wanted to get out they had to carefully back out before attempting to rise.

It was this peculiar characteristic of the improvised shed or hut that caused the mishap and scare that Mr. Irish sustained the last night he was in camp. It was quite a cool night, and he and Wells had snuggled themselves tightly under the blankets in the furthermost end of the shed to escape the cold wind that was sweeping through.

Either the lobscouse for supper or else perhaps some of the rich pound cake from home, had disagreed with Heber's internal department. Like Tit-Willow, maybe he "had a rather tough worm in his little inside." At all events, in the middle of the night he had a very bad attack of nightmare.

All who had taken part in the battle of Antietam were still thinking of the horrible sights during the day and dreaming of it at night. The visit of Mr. Irish and the conversation about the death of the captain had perhaps renewed the scene in Heber's mind, and probably he fell asleep while thinking about it. When he had the nightmare he thought that he was again in the battle.

Heber suddenly arose in his sleep, and throwing off the blankets, rushed to the company street and began yelling at the top of his voice:

"Hello, Hank, get the men out at once! Where's Dougherty? Get the men out quick, for the rebels are right on top of us! For heaven's sake, hurry, men, or we'll all be captured! Where's Hank Van Orden? Where's Sam Dougherty? Why don't they get out the men? Fall in, Company K!"

Wells yelled this out with such a loud voice that it aroused the entire company. Hank Van Orden ran half-dressed from his hut and grasped Wells around the waist, asking what was the matter. The other men were hastily buckling on their cartridge boxes and seizing their rifles. For a few moments there was a scene of the greatest excitement, and even the members of some of the other companies were aroused by the hullaballoo.

In the midst of all this Heber awakened, for he had been fast asleep all this time and did not have the slightest idea of what he was doing, and perhaps was as much astonished as any of the rest of them till an explanation was made.

But the funniest part of it all was the experience of Lewis Irish, the deceased captain's brother.

Hearing all the noise Mr. Irish sprang from his bed and attempted to jump to his feet. In doing so his head came in contact with the low roof of the shed, and gave him such a blow that it felled him. He was nearly knocked senseless.

Irish thought that we were surrounded by the enemy and that a rebel had hit him a blow over the head with the butt end of a rifle. He thought that his day had come sure. He rushed out of the hut, exclaiming:

"Oh, Heber, what shall I do? Where shall I go? Give me a pistol or a gun, so that I can defend myself! Which way is the enemy coming? Where's the one that hit me on the head?"

Wells had sufficiently recovered his senses to take in the situation, and undertook to pacify Mr. Irish. But he was too excited to be quieted at once.

"Quick, quick, Heber!" he exclaimed. "Tell me what to do! I can't stay here! I am not a combatant. I am a citizen. I've no place here. Where shall I go? What shall I do? What——"

"That's all right, Irish," said Heber, trying to reassure him. "There's no danger. There are no rebels round here. I only had an attack of nightmare or something of the sort. You'd better get back to bed again, for there are no rebels within miles of here."

"Yes, there is. Yes, there is," insisted Mr. Irish. "One of the scoundrels hit me on the head and almost killed me. I'm bleeding now from it."

Heber lighted a candle, and sure enough the blood was streaming from quite a serious wound on Mr. Irish's head. How it happened no one seemed able to guess at the time. A search was made around that part of the camp to see if there were any strangers lurking around, but nothing unusual could be discovered. The mystery remained unsolved until after Mr. Irish's head had been bandaged up and quiet restored, and Wells and his visitor proceeded to return to bed.

Then they found that immediately above the blankets where Irish had lain the poles of the low roof had been knocked out of place where Irish's head had come in contact with them. On one of the poles was a projecting knob where a small branch had been cut off, and this had some hair and a particle of blood on it. The color of the hair corresponded with that on Mr. Irish's head. That was the place where he had bumped his head as he sprang from his bed. It had been a hard knock, too, for the wound on Mr. Irish's head the next morning was large and painful.

But for the time being Mr. Irish thought sure that he had been hit in the head with a musket in the hands of a rebel. And no wonder. The startling yells and orders from Orderly Sergeant Wells in the middle of the night were enough to frighten almost anybody. Wells often laughed about the occurrence afterward.

As for Mr. Irish, he had had enough of war. He

made up his mind that he would not remain in the front another night if he had to walk all the way to Baltimore. But, fortunately, he managed to get transportation that day and left for home, and never so long as the war lasted did he again venture to the front.

Many a time afterward, before he died, a few years since, he laughingly referred to the adventure, and candidly admitted that for a little while he thought that his earthly career was at an end. He thought sure that the camp was surrounded by rebels and that one of them had hit him on the head with the butt end of a musket.

"But what's the difference?" he often asked. "What difference does it make whether a man has his brains knocked out by the butt end of a musket or the gable end of a house?"

CHAPTER XXXIX.

THE FIRST THING I KILLED.

The march on the night that we left Harper's Ferry was one of the hardest the Thirteenth ever experienced. I could never see the necessity for it. There was no need of any such hurry. We were not going to get into a fight, despite the predictions of my friend in the Wisconsin regiment. We were only going back to Sharpsburg to relieve the troops of General Fitz-John Porter, who were doing duty as pickets along the Potomac River opposite Sheperdstown.

The entire Army of the Potomac, with the exception of the Eleventh and Twelfth corps, had crossed the river and started over into Virginia, in pursuit of the enemy, while the two corps mentioned were left behind to guard "Harper's Ferry and the Potomac River." The Eleventh corps had taken our place at Harper's Ferry, and we—that is, the Twelfth corps—were sent further up the river. That there were some rebels in that neighborhood we soon found out.

But as said before there was no necessity, so far as we could ever see, for the impetuous and hasty character of that night's march. Many of the men fell out from sheer fatigue. While at Maryland Heights the most of us had got new knapsacks, and despite experience had again loaded ourselves down with various useful things in camp, but altogether too much to carry on the march.

The result of this was that the road was again strewn with all sorts of things which we would soon need very much. Had we marched a little more slowly we might have retained all these necessities. There were few who stuck to their loads. When we reached our camp, somewhere near morning, we were almost devoid of everything except our blankets and shelter or "pup" tents. And it must be remembered that the season was advancing and the nights were becoming uncomfortably chilly.

We went into camp near Sharpsburg, within but a short distance of the Antietam battlefield. Our duties consisted mainly of picket duty along the Potomac River. It was the first time we had ever been on picket immediately in front of the enemy.

The rebels were on one side of the river and we were on the other; we could see each other plainly. The river is narrow at that point, and when the water is low one can wade across, or step from stone to stone. At the time we were there the stones at the bottom could not be seen, but the river was shallow enough to wade across.

On one side of the river was the Chesapeake and Ohio canal. This was the side we were on. The towpath was between the canal and the river. Between the towpath and the river there was an embankment, and at various spots there were trees growing.

Our picket posts were supposed to be on the tow-path. Where there were trees we got behind them. In other places we got down on the water side of the canal and behind the protection afforded by the sloping banks. There was not much water in the canal at that time, for there were no boats running then.

These protections were very useful, for the rebels on the other side of the river kept popping away at us whenever they got a chance, and we fired back every time we saw an exposed head on the other side of the river. We had no change of pickets at night for a while, because of this danger. The sergeant and his squad of men would remain behind the protecting trees and embankment as long as it was daylight.

I remember one day while on picket with John Butterworth. We were both down in the ditch of the canal.

"I wonder if there are any Johnnies on the other side now, anyway," he said. The rebels were always referred to as the "Johnnies." The enemy invariably called us the "Yanks."

"You'd better look out, Jack," I replied. "Don't run any risks with that cocoanut of yours."

"I'm going to take a peep, anyhow," said John. And so saying he raised up his head so that his eyes were just over the level of the towpath.

"Z-z-z-z-ip!"

A bullet whistled by, uncomfortably close to Butterworth's head. You would have laughed to see him dodge. His head went down as if he had been shot!

"By jingo, Joe," said he. "I could feel the wind of that bullet in my hair. I guess there are some Johnnies over there after all."

"No doubt of that, Jack," said I. "But say, wait a minute and see some fun."

With that I took off my hat and placed it on the end of my rifle. Then I slowly lifted it up as if a soldier was taking another peep over the towpath.

"Zip!" came another bullet. It came near my cap, but did not touch it. I drew the hat down quickly, as if the wearer were dodging, and a moment later stuck the hat up again.

Another bullet, two, three, came whistling by, and one of them went plump through my cap.

"Pretty good shooters over there, Joe," said John. "It's a good thing your head was not in the hat then, or you would have been a goner, sure."

"If my head had been in that hat I wouldn't have held it there, you know. I merely wanted to see if there was any danger of those fellows hitting anybody. That settles it. I don't stick my head out there, in the daytime, you bet."

"Nor I, neither," said John.

I relate this to show the dangerous nature of the duty we were performing. In unguarded moments two or three of our men came near being shot, but the bullets missed their mark.

It was most nonsensical sort of business, but then a soldier in the war is generally like the Irishman at Donnybrook fair. Whenever he saw a head he struck at it.

In the night time one could walk along the tow path with comparative impunity. The rebels would fire random shots occasionally, but there wasn't much danger of their hitting anything in the dark. The grand rounds visited us and the officers of the guard very sensibly inspected the outer posts in the night time.

This desultory shooting at each other's pickets from the opposite sides of the river was kept up for some time, and it was a constant nuisance and bother, let alone the dangerous part of it. It was very uncomfortable to patrol a beat on the inside of a canal bank. It was exasperating to see the river so close and yet impossible to get down to it.

The first night I was on picket here I had an adventure.

It was after midnight and the night was very dark. For the reasons before stated there was no apparent danger then and I was walking along the tow path with my rifle carelessly hanging over my arm.

All of a sudden I heard something creeping through the bushes near me.

"Halt!" I cried, in the orthodox way. "Who comes there!"

But not a word came in answer. On the contrary the mysterious personage kept coming toward me. I felt my hair raise in terror.

"Halt!" I repeated, still more peremptorily, at the same time cocking my rifle in readiness to shoot.

But it didn't halt for a cent.

I imagined all sorts of things—spies, midnight assassins, guerrillas, rebels detailed to go around and kill individual soldiers, everything horrible. That it was anything else than a man I never for a moment imagined.

It became my plain duty to shoot. And yet then and there, under the extenuating circumstances that existed, I distinctly remember a horror at the idea of taking the life of a human being. It gave me the chills.

But something must be done, and done quickly. If I didn't shoot it, it would shoot or knife me, and so there was nothing to do but to take the best aim I could and blaze away.

How I managed to hit the mark in the darkness of

the night I don't know. But I did. It rolled over, struggled a moment and was still.

I was too much agitated to go and see who or what it was. I didn't want to gaze upon the creature whose death I had caused. So I yelled at the top of my voice:

"Corporal of the guard—post No. 10!"

"What's the matter?" asked the corporal, as he came running up, out of breath.

"I—I—I've shot a man," I stuttered. "He was sneaking up to me and would not stop when I hollered 'halt' three times, and so I shot him. See if he is dead."

The corporal proceeded to make an examination.

"Yes, he is dead. Dead as a door nail."

I thought I should faint. Dead! I had killed a fellow mortal. Horrible! In battle you shot, and didn't know whether your individual gun had killed anybody or not. There is a consoling uncertainty about it. But the thought that you, with your own gun, with your own hand, have been the cause of the death of anybody, is a terrible thing.

When the corporal came toward me pulling the dead body behind him, I wanted to run away, but of course could not.

"I'll share this with you in the morning, pard," said the corporal. "We will have a dandy dinner tomorrow."

Dinner to-morrow! What did the corporal mean? Eat a human being?

"Do you take me for a cannibal?" I asked, in astonishment.

"A cannibal? What do you mean by that?"

"I mean do you think I am going to eat the man I have killed?"

With that the corporal broke out in a fit of laughter that I thought very uncalled-for under the circumstances.

"A good joke, by thunder!" said he, as soon as he could recover his voice. "And did you really think you had shot a man?"

"Why, of course I did," I answered. "What else?"

"Take a look at the 'man' you have killed," said he, throwing the corpse toward me.

I leaned down and examined it. Then I felt of it. Then I lifted the body up, and broke out into laughter myself. I was a little hysterical, too. The sudden revulsion of feeling was the cause, for the body before me was not that of a man.

It was only a 'possum!

CHAPTER XL.

YANKS AND JOHNNIES.

Sure enough, we had 'possum for dinner the next day, in a savory stew. 'Possum tastes a little like very young pork, but has a much finer flavor. We relished it immensely, particularly as it was the first time the most of us had ever tasted 'possum.

The incident was duplicated many a time, for 'possum was very plentiful in that part of the country, and scarcely a night passed but that the men on picket saw one or more. They generally traveled at night. Of course the size of a 'possum was nothing to be compared with a man, but in the darkness I could not see what it was, and I was terribly frightened and overcome for the few moments that I really thought I had killed a human being.

Here let me tell the reader something strange. Experience afterward made us very suspicious of a calf or a large pig creeping past us at night. Spies and scouts used to take calf hides and complete pig skins, and getting inside of them, crawl past the picket lines. More than one supposed pig or calf has been shot and the body of a man found inside the hide.

Wolves travel in sheep's clothing, according to the Good Book. The little school geographies we had in the primary departments invariably had pictures of Indians in wolf's skin crawling toward the unsuspecting buffaloes. In war times all such devices are resorted to by the scouts to get past the picket lines.

About a week later I was on picket again, at pretty near the same place. The rebels had continued their popping at every Union soldier's head that they saw, and the Union soldiers had been keeping up their side in this nonsensical individual warfare. But one day we were astonished by an unusual sign on the other side of the river.

It was a white handkerchief—or rather a handkerchief that had once been white—held up on the end of a bayonet.

A white flag is a "flag of truce." It means a cessation of hostilities. If the other side agrees to the truce, an answering white signal is set. We had some trouble to find anything white enough to serve as a flag, and finally resorted to a small muslin bag that one of the boys had in his haversack to hold his sugar.

A very dirty-looking rebel then stepped out, and holding his hands to his mouth like a speaking-trumpet, yelled out:

"Hey, Yank!"

"Hey, Johnnie!" was our reply.

"Will you stop shootin' if we-uns do?"

"We will."

"All right. We-uns'll send you a message."

"How?"

"Wait'n you'll see."

We waited. We could see three or four of the dirty gray backs doing something down at the edge of the river, but could not see what it was, when something like a long, little boat started across.

It was a very ingenious arrangement.

A fence rail, one side of which was round and the other side flat, made something very much the shape of a boat. At intervals were stuck twigs, for masts. On the masts were sails made of paper. At the rear end of the rail was an improvised rudder.

The man who concocted this arrangement, and adjusted the sails and rudder must have been a sailor at some time in his life, for the gentle breeze that prevailed at the time brought it straight as if it had been manned by human sailors.

We went down to the side of the river and caught the queer little ferryboat as it landed.

On one of the masts was a sheet of paper folded up. Opening it, it was found to be the "message." It read, as nearly as I can remember it after so many years, about as follows:

"YANKS: If you fellers stop a-shootin we-uns will stop a shootin. Whats the sens of us a shootin at each uther? Lets be a little sochibul. Have you fellers any coffie what you'd like to swap for some tobaccy? We-uns has plenty tobaccy but no cofee, and we-uns knows what you fellers has lots of cofee and no tobaccy. Send anser by bote. Shift the sales and the ruder tother way, and she'll come over all right. Hoping these fu lines will find you enjying good helth, we subscrib oursels yours truly. JOHNNY."

Anything for a lark. Here was a chance seldom offered. It struck me very strangely.

All along I had regarded the rebels as something inhuman. I cannot exactly explain it, but all of a sudden it came to me that here were fellow human beings on the other side, who as individuals were no more concerned in the war than we were, who were willing to stop the practice of killing on sight, and anxious to strike a common-sense, everyday barter.

The impression such an event gave to the private soldiers was that the war was a useless and uncalled-for affair, and might as well be stopped then and there. It is impossible to convey to the reader the precise emotions aroused. Somehow everything that had passed slipped entirely from the memory, and awakened a dim, unaccountable, indefinable vision of the way things might be if peace were declared.

But we didn't stop to reflect or moralize. We had plenty of coffee, as the rebels had surmised, and were willing to share with the enemy, especially as it was always reported that the rebels had an unlimited supply of tobacco of a superior quality.

So we tied up in an old piece of paper as much coffee as it would hold, each man contributing his quota, and fastened it to the "boat." We also wrote a return "message," and stuck it on one of the tiny masts. As near as I can remember the message ran something like this:

"JOHNNIES: We send you some coffee; now send the tobacco. We will stop shooting at your hats if you will do the same. What is the use, as you say? If you fellows go back on your word, now, look out.

"YANKS."

I wrote the original of that letter, and so have a pretty clear remembrance of what was in it. I remember distinctly that I signed it "Yanks," the same as they had addressed us.

We adjusted the sails and rudder of the little craft as suggested and sent the comical ferryboat on its journey across the river. But somehow or other we did not fix the nautical tackle right, and instead of going across, as intended, the improvised boat suddenly turned down stream and started in the direction of Harper's Ferry in a lively manner.

If that message had got into the hands of some of the officers it might have caused us trouble, for to "hold communication with the enemy" was a grave offense —a good deal more grave than any of us appreciated at the moment.

But no such disaster happened. The rail boat had not gone far before one of the rebels jumped into the river and waded out to the little craft and carried it to the Virginia side of the river. The water was not very deep. It was hardly up to the "Johnny's" hips.

We could see them open the message and read it, and there was a scramble between them for a division of the coveted coffee. In a little while they sent the boat back again with some smoking tobacco that was excellent, and which we greatly appreciated. There was no message this time. One of the rebels shouted across the water that they had no more paper.

But it was not a great distance across the river and we could talk to each other in a somewhat loud voice. This sort of a conversation was not very satisfactory, however, but it ended in a somewhat startling proposition from "our friends, the enemy."

It was, if we would receive them in the same spirit in which they came, they would come over the river after dark and have a "chin" with us.

We counseled among ourselves about this. It was a rather risky proposition—not so much that we would be captured by the rebels or that they would take some other advantage of it, but that we might be caught by some of the officers, with disastrous results.

But we finally decided to take the risk, and the arrangement was that our visitors should come over immediately after the "first relief" went on their posts—that is at 9 o'clock.

And so the programme was carried out. The first relief had hardly taken the place of the third, when we heard the quiet splashing of the water from the little group of rebels wading over to us.

CHAPTER XLI.

OUR FRIENDS THE ENEMY.

For a picket post to hold communication with the pickets of the enemy is one of the things most emphatically forbidden by the articles of war. But that it was done many times during the course of the war is unmistakable. There is many an old soldier who can testify to the fact from his own personal experience.

If any of us thought of the magnitude of the offense he did not mention it. I know for myself, there was no idea of doing anything wrong. It was merely a little novelty that tended to relieve the terrible monotony of picket duty, and consequently simply regarded as a welcome diversion.

There were six in the party of rebels that came across the river. There were twelve or fifteen on our side, so that there was no danger of a capture or anything of that sort—at least so far as we were concerned. The greatest manifestation of trust and good faith had certainly been on the part of the "Johnnies," in the way they had put themselves in our power.

They had further shown their trust by leaving their guns behind them. They were completely in our power if we had wanted to be mean. But we never thought of such a thing as that.

"Hello, Yanks," said the spokesman, as he came up dripping from the water. "That was mighty good coffee you-uns sent we-uns."

That was a Southern provincialism that may strike the reader as funny, but it was used almost exclusively in conversation on the part of the majority of men in the rebel army. They always said "you-uns" for "you," and "we-uns" for "we" or "us."

"Hello, Johnnies," replied one of our boys, "and that was good tobacco you sent us in return. It was the best we have had in a long while."

"Yes, we know the kind of tobaccy you-uns have. It comes from Baltimore, don't it?"

We told them that they had guessed right.

"We-uns gets our tobaccy from Virginny crop, put up in Richmond—the best in the whole world. You-uns don't get much o' that nowadays. You-uns' tobaccy is from Maryland, I reckon."

We told the spokesman that we didn't know anything about it, except that it came from Baltimore.

"Where be you-uns from?" asked the rebel spokesman.

We told him. We represented several Northern States. In return they told us that they were from all the way from Virginia to Texas.

We sat down on the canal bank, and lighted our pipes. There was a fire on the canal side of the bank, which we had lighted for the first time after the agreement not to indulge in any more shooting. We boiled some coffee and proceeded to have a regular picnic.

Both sides were a little guarded in the conversation at first, so as not to give offense to each other. But on the general topic of the war we had a nice talk.

"How long do you-uns think this thing's agoin' to last?" asked one of the rebels.

"Till you fellows give up," replied I banteringly.

"If we-uns had our way," replied the Johnnie, "it wouldn't be long afore that happened. We'uns is good and sick of it. If it weren't for the officers and the polerticians, it would be settled mighty soon, I reckon."

"There is something in that," I answered. "But you all know we of the North are fighting for the Union, which you want to destroy."

"We don't want to destroy nothin'," answered the rebel. "We'uns don't want to destroy the Union."

"Then what are you fighting for?" I asked.

" 'Cause we have to," was the answer. "You-uns don't suppose we would be here if they didn't make us come, do you? Didn't they make you-uns come to fight the same way?"

"No, we didn't have to come," I replied. "We enlisted of our own accord. We volunteered, you know."

"What, went into the army and didn't have to?"

"That's as true as gospel."

"Well, I'll be derned," exclaimed the astonished rebel. "If we'uns didn't have to come I'll reckon there wouldn't be many of us in the front. Of course there's some of 'em what came at the first because they didn't want the Northern ablishionists to free our niggers. That's what the war's for, isn't it?"

Now I am willing to affirm that that is the first time I ever had any idea that the abolition of slavery had anything to do with the war. And from the exclamations and denials of my comrades I do not think any of them ever dreamed of such a thing. We vehemently protested against this view of the case and so told our strange guests. But they could not be shaken in their belief that the freedom of the slaves was one of the essential causes of the war.

"That's what we'uns believes, anyhow," said the spokesman of the party. "Now, see here. You-uns have factories and railroads and such like. Suppose we-uns went for to destroy all them, wouldn't you fight agin it?"

"I think we certainly should," I replied.

"Well, then," continued the rebel spokesman, "we-uns have no factories and few railroads. We have cotton fields and sugar-cane plantations. Our niggers do the work. We own 'em, the same as the plantations. You want to make our niggers free, and so take away all our property. Then we-uns fight agin it, see? You would do the same thing, I reckon."

The slavery part of the question had never entered my mind, and I was not prepared to argue it. But I said:

"I thought you said that you are fighting because they made you, and here you are saying that you are only defending your rights and what you call your property."

"I ain't talking for myself," said the rebel. "I was made to come. I don't own no niggers and never did. I worked in a grocery store in Montgomery. But I'm only telling you-uns what we-uns heard men say, what they are keeping up the war for. So far as we-uns here are consarned, none o' us have any niggers and we don't care how soon this thing stops."

"Nor which side comes out ahead," chimed in another of the "Johnnies."

This conversation, so odd and under such strange circumstances, was kept up for some time, and then branched off into other things more personal, mainly reminiscent of the war. They were all old soldiers and had seen some hard service, and their stories were very interesting.

" 'Sh-h-h! Hark!"

This came simultaneously from several mouths. We listened and heard voices further down the canal. It was at the next "post."

"Who comes there?" we heard.

"The grand rounds," was the answer we heard.

Then there was a quiet scattering. We were intensely surprised. We had gauged our time so as to keep on the lookout for the grand guards. Generally they do not come around till after midnight. And yet it was not yet 11 o'clock.

We hastily but quietly directed our rebel visitors to get behind the trees growing at the foot of the canal bank, at the edge of the river. They were thoroughly frightened.

"You-uns ain't agoin' to give us away?"

"Never fear of that," we assured them.

The sentry on the nearest post, the sergeant and corporal of the guard, went about their business, as if faithfully doing their duty, while the rest of us hastily pulled our blankets around us and pretended to be asleep, as we were supposed to be.

The grand rounds came along and were received in the customary fashion.

"Everything all right here?" asked the officer of the day, a captain.

"Everything quiet, sir," was the answer.

"I see some embers here. Have you been having a fire?"

"Y-y-yes, sir," stammered the sergeant.

"I thought the orders were not to light any fires on this line," said the officer. "It's rather dangerous. Put it out and don't light it again. It will draw the fire of the enemy."

"They've not been shooting at all to-day, captain," said the sergeant. "I guess there ain't any rebels on the other side now. We haven't seen any signs of them for some time."

The sergeant was a good deal more correct about there not being "any rebels over there" than the captain had any idea of. I saw through the subterfuge and could hardly keep from laughing outright.

"Well, keep a strict lookout, sergeant," said the captain, as he and the rest of the detail forming the grand rounds took their departure for the next post.

When the way was clear we gave the signal, and the concealed rebels emerged from their hiding-places.

"You-uns are a lot o' bricks," said the first one out. "You had us that time, if you wanted to go back on we-uns."

"Oh, we would never do a thing like that," was the reply, "after having given our words. But, all the same, you fellows had better get across again for——"

This advice was interrupted by a shot from a rifle, and the bullet came whistling past us and struck into one of the trees with a characteristic "zip!"

Instantly there was a scene of great excitement. Every one of our picket guards sprang to his feet and seized his rifle.

Our rebel visitors sprang into the river with a loud splash!

CHAPTER XLII.

AN ALL-AROUND SCARE.

Although alarming for the time being, the combination of occurrences that caused all the commotion prevailing at the conclusion of the preceding chapter was very comical.

It transpired that the man on the next post had fallen asleep, leaning against a tree, as frequently happened. It is wonderful with what ease a soldier would fall asleep, standing up, leaning against a tree, or even on the march. And he would suddenly awake at the first start, like a nodding deacon listening to the drowsy sermon from an old-fashioned minister of the "thirteenthly" sort.

The sleepy sentinel heard the approach of the grand rounds, and to his half-awake mind it probably seemed like the approach of the entire rebel army. So, in a dazed sort of a way, he raised his rifle and blazed away.

The startled grand rounds, hearing the bullet whistle past them, naturally imagined that they were being surrounded by a scouting party from the enemy, and they retreated hastily back to the next post, where we were, which was the headquarters of that particular section of the picket line.

The bullet zipping past us, and the footsteps of the running grand rounds coming toward us, made us also think that the rebels were making some sort of a flank movement around us.

The rebel visitors, hearing the shooting of the rifle and the whizzing bullet, perhaps thought that we had laid some trap for their capture despite our promises and pledge of immunity.

The splashing of the retreating visitors in the water

as they were scurrying across the river also added to the mystification of the officer of the day and his companions of the grand rounds, and thus it was that every one of the different characters in the farce was for the time being startled, because of his ignorance of all the circumstances.

"Halt!" our sentry called out, at the approach of the grand rounds on their backward movement. The usual exchanges were made and the countersign given. Then we began to speculate on the cause of that shot. Everything was quiet in that direction now.

"'Sh!" said the captain, who was serving as officer of the day. "I think it was a rebel scouting party trying to cross the river. I thought I heard them after the shot. Did you men hear anything?"

We all solemnly averred that we had not. But at the same time we knew well enough what had made that splashing in the water.

"Suppose I go up and see if there is anything the matter with the man on that post?" suggested our sergeant.

"That's a good plan," said the officer of the day. "But you'd better take a file of men with you to be on the safe side."

I happened to be one of three selected for this duty. We crept cautiously and with as little noise as possible, and when we got near enough we heard sounds that we recognized as those attendant on the loading of a musket.

"Hello, Jack," said the sergeant cautiously, abandoning the usual formula for approaching a sentry, "what's the matter?"

"Nothing," he replied. "Was that the grand rounds?"

"Yes."

"Well, they got on to me rather suddint, and I blazed away at 'em not thinkin'."

"And you nearly scared the life out of the whole of us," said the sergeant.

We returned to the post station and reported that everything was all right. The officer of the day was satisfied with that part of the explanation, but he was still dubious about that splashing in the water. He thought it strange that none of us had heard it, and it seemed to arouse his suspicions. Just then David Harris, who was with us, was smart enough to invent a story to get out of the dilemma.

"I guess I can explain it, captain," said he. "There's a big flock of ducks there feeding. I saw them before dark, and have heard them quacking several times. I guess that shot scared them, and their fluttering through the water was what we heard."

Davy Harris' stupendous audacity at this ingenious invention excited my most profound admiration.

"Ah," said the captain, "that must be it. But you boys must be careful for the enemy might make a feint at any time. Fall in, grand rounds." (This to his detail.)

The grand rounds then proceeded to the whilom sleepy sentry, who was wide enough awake by this time, and was received "according to the regulations." He gave the captain some cock-and-bull story about his gun going off accidentally, but that didn't work. Official dignity had been insulted. A high-toned commissioned officer could not be given such a scare as that with impunity. The sentinel was placed under arrest and another man put in his place.

The fellow told us afterward how he had got asleep for sure, and was thoroughly startled at the approach of the grand rounds at such an unexpected hour. But we never gave him away, and beyond a few hours in the guard house he escaped punishment.

In the morning we rigged up another rail ferryboat and sent a messenger over to our rebel friends on the other side, explaining the matter, as we did not want them to think that we had wilfully gone back on them.

We expected to see them again, but did not. I was on picket two or three times afterward, but always at some other post. But we told the men who relieved us of what had occurred, and the nightly visits were kept up for some time. There is more than one private soldier of the Thirteenth who could testify to these facts to-day, and it was a pleasant and enjoyable innovation on the usual monotony of picket duty.

I don't know if any of the officers ever "caught on" to it. I am inclined to believe that they knew nothing about it, at least at the time, or they might have put a stop to it. But then the officers did not know everything that was going on in those days—not much they didn't!

It was a frequent occurrence for the opposing picket posts to come together in this sociable manner, unless it was right before an expected battle, when the men were enemies in fact as well as in name. But by no means were the private soldiers thirsting for the blood of their brethren on the other side.

And I never heard of advantage being taken by either side of those who thus trusted the enemy's pickets and put them on their honor as men. Perhaps if it had been a war between two different nations there would not have been such a thing possible, for there would have been a natural enmity and antipathy that could not have been overcome. But this was a civil war, of brother against brother, and the circumstances were somewhat peculiar. At the same time it cannot be denied that it was "holding communication with the enemy," although never, to my knowledge, was an information given of each other's strength or movements. These intersectional calls and visits were always merely sociable and personal.

When we had been on picket we were excused from drill and other duties the next day. We were supposed to take it to rest, and we generally did, unless a march was ordered. But on other days we had no end of drilling and dress parades and other military maneuvers, so that we were kept pretty busy, and no one complained of the want of exercise.

CHAPTER XLIII.

AN INSPECTION.

AN inspection is one of the bugbears of the soldier. Not only is this so in an active campaign, but it is so with troops in barracks and forts, and as much so in the regular army, where a man makes it the business of his life, as it is in the volunteer service in time of war, when it is only an exigency.

We were always notified of the coming of the inspection officer. Of course we had an inspection by our regimental officers every Sunday morning while in camp, but the visit of the official inspector was another thing. It was a very useful thing, all must admit, but at the same time it was a perfect nuisance to the average soldier.

Upon receiving notification that the inspecting officer was coming every soldier proceeded to put himself in presentable shape. The first thing of all was to clean our rifles. They must be taken apart and cleaned to the acme of perfection. Not a particle of dust must be found anywhere upon them, and the polished parts must shine like silverware.

This, with the limited facilities at our disposal, was no easy task. There was a dearth of old rags and other material with which to clean the guns. Sapolio, silverine and other polishing materials were not furnished by the government, but a fairly good substitute was found in common dry clay, which gave a pretty good polish to the metal work of our weapons.

On the cartridge box at our side and on the belt around our waist there was a big brass plate, bearing the letters "U. S.," and on the cross over the breast there was another brass plate bearing what was supposed to represent the great American eagle, but which in reality more resembled a turkey buzzard. I think it was John Ick who originated the name of "buzzard" in our company, for he was always talking of the time when that bird would pick the flesh off his bones. That of course would be after he had passed through the ordeal of the "slaughter house."

These brass plates had to be polished to the highest notch of perfection. And then the belts and shoes had to be blackened or polished, although at times it was hard to get blackening, and the unfair part of it was that we had to provide ourselves with this, purchasing it out of our own pockets from the sutlers.

The clothes had to be neatly brushed and the entire toilet of the soldier made as respectable as possible. Not only that, but the knapsacks had to be packed in a certain manner, with each piece laid in a particular part of the pack, and the blanket rolled so that the edges came in just a certain position.

The whole object of this was to have everything in perfect uniform. The word "uniform" expresses the equipment of a body of troops exactly. Every man's apparel and equipment must be exactly like his fellow's. These things seem trivial, taken individually, but when it comes to a vast number of men the importance of the matter is obvious.

On assembling for inspection the regiment forms in line the same as in dress parade and then wheels into companies. Then at a shoulder arms the inspecting officer and his assistants, accompanied by the staff officers of the regiment, take a hasty trip down the front of each of the ten companies in succession and then around the back. Then he starts again at the company on the right and proceeds to inspect the arms of every individual soldier. This is the crucial test.

As the inspecting officer, who by the way was always a very airish and self-important official, with a strikingly arrogant manner, approaches each soldier, the latter holds up his gun in front of him in a certain prescribed manner, so that it is handy for the officer to take.

The inspector seizes the gun with a snap and jump,

something as a startled mother would grab a bottle of poison from the hand of a child. I don't know why they did it in this way, but the inspecting officers certainly always did so. Then the inspector takes the rifle, examines it carefully and tries the trigger, as if he were in a store examining a new gun which he proposed to buy.

The inspector invariably wore spotless white gloves to begin with. On the condition of those white gloves at the end of the inspection depended the percentage of perfection. The cleaner the gloves the higher the percentage. The more soiled they were the lower the rate of credit. The result of the inspection was accordingly decided automatically, as it were.

To begin with, the inspector would rub a finger under and around the hammer to see if he could find a speck of dirt there. But the next ordeal was the worst. I forgot to say that before handing the gun to the inspector the ramrod had to be drawn from its sheath and dropped into the barrel of the rifle. The inspector would give the gun a sort of upward throw that would send the ramrod up a ways and let it fall back into the barrel. If there was a bright, bell-like, musical result, it showed that the barrel was clean, for if there was dirt there there would be a dull sound instead of the bell-like result.

If there was any suspicion of dirt or dust the inspector would turn the ramrod around on the bottom of the barrel, and twist the end of it on the palm of his white glove. Woe to the soldier if there was any dirt on the end of the ramrod to soil that white glove.

When the inspector had finished examining the gun, he would throw it back with a force that would almost knock the soldier over in his efforts to catch it. The agility with which the soldier officiated in the catcher's box on such an occasion seemed to be an important factor in the inspector's opinion of that individual soldier.

As will be imagined this inspection of every individual in a regiment of seven or eight hundred men was a slow and tedious process and the fatigue of standing there in line so long was one of the reasons why the ceremony was so much dreaded. But this part of the inspection was finally concluded.

Then the soldiers had to open their percussion cap and cartridge boxes, while the inspector marched around and ascertained if they all contained the required complement of ammunition. After that each soldier had to unsling his knapsack and lay it carefully on the ground behind him, open, so that the inspector could see that every article was packed according to the regulations. Every article had to lie just so, even to the manner of its folding.

In times when the army was in camp, or otherwise so situated that the things discarded on the march could be replaced, every soldier had to have certain necessary articles and to show them to the officials on these periodical inspections. This fact got John Ick and Reddy Mahar into trouble.

The inspection near Sharpsburg was the first one wherein the inspector had pried into the interior of the knapsacks. On former occasions, only the outside of the "trunks" were examined. As a loaded knapsack is quite heavy, Mahar and Ick had invented an ingenious scheme to reduce the fatigue; they had done this so neatly that no one knew the difference. The knapsacks stood out firm and plump as if they contained all the articles called for.

Their ingenuity, however, on this occasion brought Ick and Mahar to grief. When the order came to "Open knapsacks," these two worthies looked at each other in a guilty fashion, and I could almost see them grow pale as they saw the nice and orderly manner in which their comrades had packed their knapsacks. Ick and Mahar held back. "Didn't you hear the order to open knapsacks," said Scott, who was in command of the company.

"Now, captain, you see—" Mahar began to say; but he was interrupted by the captain:

"Open your knapsacks, I said."

"Mister Scott," put in Ick, who always had a funny way of addressing the officer as "mister," "please excuse me. I don't vant to opens mine knapsack any more alretty this time. You see it vas—"

"Open those knapsacks!" roared the captain, getting angry.

The two men sheepishly proceeded to open the knapsacks, and then the entire company saw why they hesitated. Both were stuffed with straw!

The straight line that Company K had been maintaining was immediately broken up, for every man was nearly bent double with laughter. Captain Scott looked as if he would like to annihilate the two men on the spot, for it was a reflection on him. According to the rules he should have held a little inspection of the company himself before coming out on the field, to see that everything was all right, but this he had of course failed to do.

To make it all the worse, just at this moment along came the inspecting officer and his staff. That terrible autocrat seemed to take the whole thing as a personal insult and fairly roared. But even his roaring could not stop the laughter among the other members of Company K.

Poor Ick and Mahar rather got the worst of that scheme. They were sent to the guard house, and after the inspection were put through their punishment. The penalty prescribed by Captain Scott was appropriate.

For four solid and tedious hours John Ick and Reddy Mahar marched up and down the company street carrying knapsacks filled with stones. When they got through with the ordeal they were nearly dead with fatigue, and the straps holding up the heavy load had cut through the flesh of their shoulders seemingly almost to the bone.

CHAPTER XLIV.

WE BUILD A HOUSE.

"I AM always suspicious of those inspections," said John Stansfield to me, after the conclusion of the particular one described in the foregoing chapter.

"Why, John?" I asked.

"Because they are not held for nothing. They mean that there is something coming off pretty soon. These things are to see that the army is in good order and ready for a move of some sort. Do you remember what that Hoosier said just before we left Maryland Heights?"

"Yes," I replied. "But that did not amount to much after all. There was no fighting after that review. We were only given a little march."

"I don't exactly mean that we will get into a fight," answered Stansfield; "but there'll be something—either a march or a fight before long."

It really seemed as if Stansfield was right. There was generally some sort of a movement after a review or an inspection of more than ordinary formality, so that the soldiers had begun to regard the sign as unfailing. Every old soldier regarded these things as the first steps toward some important change or movement. But so far as this particular affair was concerned the rule did not hold good, inasmuch as we remained in the vicinity of Sharpsburg for some little time after that. This occasion, however, was unquestionably an exception to the general rule.

The rigors of army life and exposure, together with the approach of cold weather, began to play havoc with the soldiers of the Thirteenth New Jersey. A great many of them were taken sick, and the temporary hospital that had been improvised was full. Nearly two hundred were sick, and six of these cases resulted fatally. The hospital was an old two-story frame building about a mile from our camp, and about as comfortable as the pest house on the almshouse farm.

Although there were a number of the members of Company K on the sick list, yet there were no deaths among them. So far as I was concerned, my health was splendid.

While we were at Sharpsburg there were also a good many promotions and other changes among the officers. George M. Hard, a Newarker—now president of one of the leading national banks of New York City—was transferred to the position of first lieutenant of Company K. This made some grumbling, for the men argued that if there were any offices to fill the vacancies should be filled from among our own members. But Hard proved a good officer, and the grumbling did not last long. Furthermore he was soon afterward transferred to another company.

It is unnecessary in this story to refer to all the changes, but I will mention one case—that of Lieutenant Ambrose M. Matthews, who was promoted to the captaincy of Company I, a position he held to the end of the war, although he was entitled to a much higher position, for a better man never lived.

He is now a prosperous business man of Orange, N. J., and is fortunately so situated in life that he can devote a good deal of time to the interests of the veteran soldiers, and there is no man on the face of the earth who takes a livelier interest in these matters than he does. He was an excellent officer and is to-day one of the most esteemed citizens of Orange, holding many positions of trust and honor in the commercial world of that community.

It was getting very cold, for it was now November, and really the temperature in that part of Maryland is not much warmer than it is here. Every morning the ground was covered with a thick white frost, and when the company was called out for the reveille roll call, the breath came from the men's mouths like a jet of steam. We suffered considerably in consequence.

For a little while we were—that is a portion of Company K—quartered in an old school building on the main street of Sharpsburg. Out of curiosity I visited the same building a year or so ago. But we were glad not to stay there long, for it had been previously occupied by some of General Fitz-John Porter's troops, and the place was so infested with "*pendiculus investimenti*," that it was more than an offset for the protection the building afforded against the cold.

Somewhere about the middle of November the regiment was divided into two wings, and located a couple of miles or so apart to facilitate the work we were engaged in—picket duty. Lieutenant-Colonel Swords was in command of one of these wings and Major Chadwick of the other. The colonel moved his headquarters to a point about halfway between the two wings.

Then the story got out that we were going to remain there all winter and we proceeded to make ourselves more comfortable. Some of the officers even sent for their wives and friends to come and visit them. My pard, John Butterworth, and I proceeded to build a log house.

An army log house is worth a brief description. These houses were generally "built for two." In size they would perhaps not be larger than twelve feet long and about eight feet wide.

First of all, we dug a square hole, something like a cellar, the size of the cabin. Butterworth called it "the basement." That saved just so much timber, you know. Then we cut down some trees, which were split in half and cut the length and width of the house. These were notched near the ends, and then piled up after the manner of a "corncob house," such as the children used to make.

With considerable labor water was brought from the nearest stream and a sufficient quantity of mud made to fill up the chinks between the logs. The roof was composed of the pieces of our "pup" tents fastened together, and stretched over a ridge pole.

Then came the building of the chimney, the most important part. In one end of the "cellar" a hole was dug, like an oven, with a small round hole at the top, opening into the ground above. Above this was laid a lot of split sticks, two or three feet each in length, and covered with the peculiar red mud with which that part of this glorious country abounds.

Great care had to be taken to leave none of the sticks exposed, or the chimney would take fire. It was a very frequent occurrence to be awakened in the night by a small conflagration and destruction of the domicile of some comrade from this cause. I have gone through the interesting experience myself more than once, notwithstanding the fact that Butterworth was almost profligate in his use of mud.

The mud chimney would soon dry, and when completed it filled its purpose to perfection. Few of the most scientific chimneys of the present day would "draw" better than those stick-and-mud affairs that we had in the army.

On the other end of the hut was built the bunk. This was composed of poles about six or seven feet long, fastened across, and on top of these was laid a lot of evergreen or cedar boughs, which formed the mattress. The boughs were covered with a rubber blanket, and the result was a good bed that was a good deal more comfortable than would be imagined on reading this description.

A spare blanket or piece of shelter tent served the purpose of a door, and thus housed the soldier was quite comfortable, with a big fire burning in the "fireplace" even in the severest weather. Many a pleasant hour I have spent in such a primitive residence, cooking lobscouse or playing old sledge.

We began to receive our mail quite regularly too, and this was a source of great satisfaction and pleasure. The home papers came to me about a week after being printed and with more or less regularity—generally more less than more. The local news, such as there was, interested us greatly.

I say "such as there was" with all that it means. To tell the truth, there was not a great deal in the papers in those days beside war news. And we learned a good deal more about the war from these papers than we did otherwise. Even the very acts that we had participated in were presented to us plainer by the papers than we could see them for ourselves.

Many a movement that we could not understand simply because we were a part of it, was explained by the ubiquitous war correspondent. But the funniest part of all was the editorial columns. These were mainly devoted to telling how the war ought to be prosecuted. None of the generals were doing right. If they would do this or that it would be a good deal better than the way they were doing. I refer to no particular paper. All that reached us were about the same. We soon came to the conclusion that the government had made a big mistake and put the army in charge of the wrong men. Instead of the generals in command there seemed to be little doubt that the war might have been ended in half the time if the whole business had been placed in charge of the editorial and other critics at home.

We also received many interesting letters from home. It was while at Sharpsburg that I heard for the second time from "The girl I left behind me."

With one exception it was the last one I received from that source. The next one was not so interesting. To while away the time I had written a letter to Mabel Summers, the pretty little Frederick city girl. At the same time I wrote one to my Paterson girl.

The letter to the Frederick girl never brought an answer. She must have thought the writer crazy. The letter from the Paterson girl was a curt and dignified demand for the return of her picture. It was not till after the war was over and she had cast her lot with another and better looking man that I understood the reason for such a summary dismissal.

In directing those two letters, written at the same time, I had got them mixed up!

I can imagine the indignation and feelings of my Paterson girl, now that I know the reason she answered as she did, after having read the letter to the Frederick city girl, but I can't imagine how the latter received the letter that she got. And on such a brief acquaintance, too!

CHAPTER XLV.

THE FREDERICKSBURG CAMPAIGN.

But we didn't stay at Sharpsburg all winter, as we expected, after all. On the 10th of December, a bitterly cold day it was too, we were ordered to break camp. And from the rumors prevalent, notwithstanding the unusual time of the year, we were likely to get into another fight soon.

Some great changes had taken place during the past few days, of which we heard pretty soon. For some reason known best to the government at Washington, General McClellan had been relieved from the command of the Army of the Potomac, and General Burnside had been appointed in his place.

It should be understood, that, whereas the general in command in the field was popularly supposed to have charge of the operations, all the movements were directed from Washington, and these were mainly formulated by General Halleck. He, under the advice and direction of the president, was supposed to have command of all the armies in the field. The president had his hands full about that time, and of course he had to be invariably guided by the experience of General Halleck.

The soldiers always referred to Halleck as "Grandmother Halleck," and the name in my opinion was well placed. He was the greatest fogy imaginable. The records of the departments, the histories of the war, and the State papers of Abraham Lincoln, all of which I have carefully studied, go to show that Halleck did more to prolong the war in the first part of its existence than anything else. It was not till General Grant was given command that the ostensible commanding general of the army really had that control of it that he should.

Grant would take command under no other circumstances, and he was right.

The idea that a general in Washington could better direct the active movements of the army than the commander at the front in the presence of the troops, is absurd on the face of it. And yet that is the theory on which the first part of the war was prosecuted.

General McClellan was in this manner handicapped all the time he was ostensibly in command of the Army of the Potomac. Some writers may argue differently, but I am satisfied of these facts. General McClellan was the idol of the soldiers, and there was a very general feeling that he had not been fairly treated by the powers that be, but when he was relieved there was not so much of a commotion as there might have been. The feeling among the soldiers and many of the officers was: "Well, let them see if some other general can do any better than our Little Mack."

At the same time every soldier in the army had the most profound respect for General Burnside. He had been a corps commander and everybody knew that he was a good and fearless officer. The modest manner in which he accepted the command of the army was also calculated to create a favorable impression. He said that he would take the command and do the best he could, but at the same time he did not consider himself qualified to command such a large body and carry them successfull through an important campaign. The boys heard of this and manifested a disposition to stand by him every time.

General Burnside's very first move, however, ran against the political generals and others who were running the thing at Washington. Burnside proceeded to make some changes and transfers among the corps commanders, somewhat after the plan adopted by the late Superintendent Byrnes when he gave the precinct captains a "shaking up" in New York City.

The approval or disapproval of the powers that be was deferred till after the conclusion of the Fredericksburg campaigns, which were then in progress. Then when Burnside insisted on having his ideas carried out or being relieved from the command of the army, the influences brought to bear were too strong, and General Burnside was "relieved at his own request."

This is anticipating the story somewhat, but it is stated here to explain the state of mind and other adverse circumstances that prevailed during the brief time that General Burnside was in command of the Army of the Potomac.

The order which we received to march away from Sharpsburg was the beginning of the movements connected with the inauguration of the Fredericksburg campaign. General Burnside had taken a position with the main portion of the army at Falmouth, nearly opposite Fredericksburg, and on the day that the Thirteenth left Sharpsburg, the 10th of December, the Union forces were practically in a position to assault the lines of the rebels.

We were marched back to Harper's Ferry, and on the following day were in camp at Loudon Heights. The next day we started again and marched through the city or town of Leesburg. And before describing further progress, I want to tell something very sensational that happened at Leesburg.

Before that, however, I will explain that on the same day, or about the same time, the battle of Fredericksburg, one of the sharpest and bloodiest battles of the war, was fought. The Thirteenth, nor any part of the Twelfth Corps, did not get into that battle, but we were supposed to form a part of the movement somehow, in occupying a position that would cut off one possible line of retreat. At least that was the explanation given. The why and wherefore I cannot attempt to explain. I was only a private soldier then, and knew no more than the other private soldiers, perhaps not as much as some of them.

The battle of Fredericksburg was a peculiar one. Fredericksburg is a town on the southern side of the Rappahannock River, located on a hill. On the northern side of the river was the little village of Falmouth. The Union troops were on the Falmouth side while the rebels occupied the city of Fredericksburg, and were strongly intrenched behind breastworks. The enemy had destroyed all the bridges, and the only way to get across the river was on pontoon bridges.

The Union troops got across. They assaulted the town. They destroyed it, burned the houses and smashed the furniture, but—were driven back in confusion, as might naturally be expected under such circumstances. Result—nothing gained, much lost. The army that fell back across the river to Falmouth was 12,321 less in number than the army that went over the river. And the rebel loss was less than 5,300.

Burnside was right in the estimation he had placed upon himself. The soldiers liked him, and he was a good corps commander, but he was never intended to have command of a large army. At the same time, after this disastrous result he was left in command, although still handicapped by the powers at Washington in the refusal to make the changes he had recommended. Perhaps the powers at Washington might have been right in this particular instance.

I am getting a little "twisted" right here in trying to describe the movements of the two divisions of the army at the same time. I will return to the Thirteenth New Jersey once more. And this brings me back to what I was going to tell of what happened at Leesburg.

There had been a number of desertions from all the regiments at Sharpsburg. The cold weather had dampened the ardor of the troops. The position of the army was such that it made it a comparatively easy matter to get away from it. A good many took advantage of this opportunity.

I am sorry to say that there were some members of the Thirteenth New Jersey among the deserters. Some of these were recaptured and brought back by the provost guard. Others were never heard of till after the war.

Of those brought back, the most were punished in different ways. First it was by fining them several months' pay. Then it was by imprisonment in some military prison or fortress. But these penalties did not seem to have the desired effect. It was decided to make a horrible example of some of the deserters in order that it might possibly have a deterrent effect on the others who might be overcome with an overwhelming degree of homesickness.

A squad of deserters were captured, brought back, court martialed, and sentenced to be shot!

Now President Lincoln was the kindest hearted of men. There is no telling how many men he pardoned during the war after they had been sentenced to be shot for desertion. But advantage had apparently been taken of this leniency, and the time had come when the recalcitrant soldiers should be made to believe that the government meant business. Executive clemency was therefore withheld in the case of three of the deserters from our corps, and we were startled with the notification to fall in to witness the execution!

The entire division was marched out to witness the terrible scene of three comrades being shot to death by their associates. I don't believe there was a face in the division that was not pale, nor a pair of legs that were not more or less shaking at the knees.

The details of the execution will be given in the next chapter.

CHAPTER XLVI.

AN AWFUL SCENE.

THREE deserters were to be shot that morning and we were compelled to witness the execution! Fain would we all have escaped the ordeal, but it was impossible. No one was excused. Every soldier must have indelibly impressed upon his memory that it is a heinous offense to desert. Every soldier must be made to understand that this was hereafter to be the fate of deserters.

None who took part will ever forget that day. So far as the preliminary sensations and emotions were concerned it was a thousand times worse than any battle. The men were subdued and silent as if going to a funeral—and indeed they were. Poor John Ick's lugubrious expressions about a "slaughter house" met a response in all our minds, for like nothing else than a slaughter house did it appear to us.

It seemed as if the orderly sergeant was more quiet than usual in forming the company, and the tone of the captain as he ordered the company to march to the parade ground was low and sorrowful. When the regiment was formed there was an unusual lack of bustle and enthusiasm. A spirit of sadness, I might say of horror, pervaded the entire command.

It was a beautiful day. There was not a cloud in the sky and the sun shone down on the glittering bayonets till they looked like silver spikes. The men all wore sober countenances as we marched out to the place of execution.

There were three men to be shot. Two were from the Forty-sixth Pennsylvania, and the other, I regret to say, from the Thirteenth New Jersey. The latter was named Christopher Krubart, a member of Company B.

THE YOUNG VOLUNTEER.

These three men were to be killed!
And we were to kill them!

Fortunately for me and fortunately for the victims I was not one of the men detailed on the shooting squad. It was fortunate for me, because I would as like as not have shot myself in my excitement. It was fortunate for the victim, for I would probably have hit him, if I hit him at all, in some unimportant part of the body and only help to put him in agony, without killing him.

Before we started for the scene of the execution the order announcing the findings of the court martial and the approval of the sentence was read impressively to the regiment. That this had a moral effect on the men is beyond question. No one could describe the solemnity of that event, made all the more solemn from the impressive manner in which the order was read by Adjutant Hopkins.

At 12 o'clock precisely the different regiments of the brigade and division were marched out to the place selected for the execution and formed into a "hollow square." The officers gave their orders in subdued voices, and the men obeyed with impressive silence, as the rifles were dropped to the ground on the order to "shoulder arms."

Straight before us we could see the three graves that had been dug and into which were soon to be consigned the dead and mutilated bodies of three fellow beings who at that moment were as alive and full of health and vigor as we were. It seemed as if there was an unnecessary delay in the proceedings. Everything seemed to be done with painful deliberation. This was perhaps to lend additional impressiveness to the scene.

There was no use for that. The scene was sufficiently impressive as it was.

Then, moving so slowly that they scarcely moved, came in the wagons containing the three coffins which were soon to contain the bodies of the unfortunates. Behind the coffins came an ambulance surrounded by armed soldiers.

In the ambulance, securely manacled, were the three doomed victims of the tragedy. They were slowly, almost tenderly, assisted from the ambulance, and led to the coffins.

There was a coffin at the head of each of the three graves and the men were seated on the end of the coffins. Each man sat on the coffin he was to occupy!

Their eyes were blindfolded, their hands fastened to their backs, and their legs tied together. They could neither move nor see.

The firing party consisted of thirty-six men in all. Eight men were detailed to shoot each deserter, making twenty-four to fire at the first order, and the other twelve were held back in reserve, to finish the horrible work in case there was any sign of life after the first volley.

Not a man of that detail knew whether his gun was loaded. This was a merciful provision for such cases. In each squad there was one rifle loaded with only a blank cartridge. In firing a musket, one cannot tell whether there is a bullet in the cartridge or not. If the guns were all loaded every man would have it on his mind that he had shot a fellow being. With one blank in the squad no man knew for sure whether his gun had fired a fatal shot or not.

This left an uncertainty about it that was very consoling. Every man consoled himself with the idea that he had the blank cartridge. The guns had been loaded by the officers at the division headquarters and only one or two officers knew which of the rifles were really loaded. Even they did not know long, for the guns were mixed up indiscriminately in a pile, from which each member of the firing squad picked a rifle as he was marched past.

The firing squad marched to the place of execution with slow and measured tread, which served to still longer prolong the painful scene and add to the already almost unbearable impressiveness and awfulness of the event.

Then the death sentence was read again, in a solemn manner. Every face in the ranks was pale, and many of the men were trembling. In fact some of their knees were shaking so that they could hardly stand on their feet. I plead guilty to being one of this class.

At the same time everybody was curious enough to watch the condemned men. The handkerchiefs tied over their eyes obscured the upper parts, but the lower portions could be seen. They were ghastly—not white, but ashen and sickly in pallor.

From the furthermost parts of the "square" the men could see the unfortunate and terrified victims trembling. One of them was actually shivering, as if he had a severe chill. The lips of two could be seen to move slightly, as if in prayer. There is little doubt that it was really a prayer.

But not one of them undertook to speak a word aloud. They had all evidently made up their minds to die without a flinch, without a murmur or protest.

Such bravery and fortitude as this, displayed on the battlefield, would have won them a pair of shoulder straps. As it was, it was the ineffable disgrace of being shot as a deserter!

Chaplain Beck, of the Thirteenth Regiment, offered a short prayer for the salvation of the souls of the unfortunate men, and their lips seemed to move in response to every syllable of the supplication. Glancing around furtively among my companions, I noticed tears trickling down many a bronzed and weatherbeaten face.

The time has arrived!

The firing squad were placed in position, only a few feet in front of the condemned men—eight men to each deserter. There was a look of determination on the faces of the firing party, and yet they were all very pale. They all stood at a "shoulder arms."

It is usual in giving the order to shoot, to say, successively, "Ready! Aim! Fire!" But in this instance a somewhat original innovation had been made to the usual rule. One of the words was omitted. This was a merciful surprise, both to the condemned men and the soldiers who were compelled to witness the execution. The officer in command of the firing party and the members of the latter themselves were the only ones who had been informed of the change in the order. Consequently it came upon us as a big surprise, I might perhaps better say, a big shock.

"Ready!"

So commanded the officer of the firing party. Every nerve stretched to its utmost tension as the men in front of the condemned wretches brought their pieces up to their lips, the hammer at the same time being raised with the right hand.

I felt like shutting my eyes to escape seeing what was coming next, but a horrible fascination glued my gaze intensely to the scene. And I knew of course there was another command, "aim," before the shots were finally fired.

But no! With a quick, sharp command that gave us all a start, which came so unexpectedly that even the condemned deserters probably did not fully comprehend it, came the order:

"Fire!"

Like lightning twenty-four cocked muskets jumped up to twenty-four shoulders. The movement was made with marvelous rapidity. Before we could fully comprehend what had happened, there was a puff of smoke and the three deserters fell over backward on their coffins, or rather I should say, almost into them.

We saw the smoke from the guns before hearing the report, of course. It is always that way. The noise of the report was heard simultaneously with the sight of the dead deserters falling backward.

As the doomed men fell over they seemed to stiffen out convulsively, so that they did not go over bent in the sitting posture, but as if they had been standing up, and had fallen back like three felled trees. From the distance where I stood I could discern no signs of a struggle or even a convulsive tremor. Those who were close by failed to see even the twitch of a muscle.

Their deaths must have been instantaneous. It is doubtful if they even heard the reports of the rifles that shot them, for at that distance the speed of a bullet is greater than that of sound.

The effect of the tragedy on the silent witnesses was peculiar. Judging from my own sensations, it was one of intense relief that it was all over. The solemn and impressive preliminary preparations were emphatically the worst part of the whole transaction. As if a great weight had been lifted the sensation was one rather of exhilaration than of depression, for the time being.

But this was not permitted to last long. We still had another ordeal to pass through, perhaps still worse than anything that had preceded it.

We were marched slowly around and past the bloody bodies of the three executed deserters and compelled to gaze upon them as we went by. This was a shuddering ordeal, and all the more tended to impress the lesson the event had been intended to convey.

The marksmen had performed their duties well. Each one had aimed at a bit of paper pinned over the condemned men's hearts. It will be remembered that seven only out of each eight rifles were loaded with bullets. When we examined the body of Krubart, the Thirteenth Regiment deserter, it was found that the whole seven bullets had passed through his body in the immediate vicinity of his heart. Any one of them would have caused instant death.

The results in the cases of the others were the same. There was no need for the services of the reserves on this occasion.

The bodies were buried like those of dogs. Not a word of burial service was said over them. The bodies were hurried into the coffins while yet warm, the coffins were lowered into the graves, and in a few moments the ground was leveled over them.

No head board or other marker was placed over the grave of an executed deserter. He merely became a part and parcel of mother earth, and the precise whereabouts of his remains were never known afterward.

We marched back to the spot where we were to camp for the night without much talk, but everybody was doing a good deal of thinking. What was everybody thinking about? I think the answer can be best given in the laconic remark of the ever-ready John Ick:

"By jimminey, poys," said he, "des settles it. Ven you sees Yon Ick deserting some more alretty, he stays py de regiment all de times."

CHAPTER XLVII.

FLOODED OUT.

It must be admitted that the lesson had a salutary effect. There was not much deserting after the execution of the three men at Leesburg, and there had been a good deal before that time. It seemed hard to sacrifice even three lives for such a purpose, but it had become necessary, and it practically put a stop to the practice for a considerable time.

We resumed our tiresome march. Where we were going we did not know. It was nothing but getting up early in the morning, marching and halting all day long, and passing tired nights around sickly fires, half-frozen.

For the weather was getting cold now. This was adding another hardship to the boys' long list of troubles. During the daytime when we were on the move it was possible to keep comfortable. It was even uncomfortably warm in the middle of the day. But the nights were very cold.

Although the blankets and shelter tents and overcoats were just as heavy as ever, yet we stuck to them now, because they were absolutely necessary for comfort at night. I use the word "comfort" with some mental reservation, for I cannot say we were exactly comfortable at all during the night.

Some one suggested that the Indians slept with their feet to the fires and that if the feet were kept warm the rest of the body would be comfortable. There was a good deal in this, as we found out from experience, but at the same time it was not sufficient. The more ordinary practice was to sleep with one side turned toward the fires for a while, and then turn the other side, and so on. This alternate series of freezing and roasting became the universal rule, and as the boys were generally crowded so closely together that they had to lie spoon fashion, it became a sort of a drill. When one turned over, the other had to.

There are some men who are born to command, whether they hold rank or not. This soon became manifest in this "change side" order. By tacit consent, some one particular individual gave the word and it was obeyed. No attention was given to it if the suggestion came from any other source. This was a singular thing, but a fact. Some one soldier, regardless of rank, would always be accepted as the leader and commander of these petty duties, not in the strict line of military service.

Several times we had to ford creeks that were quite deep. This was not so bad when the weather was mild, but when it was cold it added suffering as well as discomfort. Then there was apparently a good deal of unnecessary marching. We would go for a distance along some road, and then turn and go another way, as if the leaders had lost their route. This made a good deal of grumbling.

We passed through Chantilly, which had once before been the scene of a battle, and through several other places that were big enough to be honored with a name and that is about all. Finally, about the 25th of December, we reached the Occoquan creek at a place called Wolf Run Shoals.

Here we had an experience worth describing.

During the night a tremendous storm arose. It was one of the worst I ever remember.

I plainly recall my own experience that night. John Butterworth (my pard) and myself had pitched our little "pup" tent on the side of a hill at the bottom of which was a good-sized creek or brook.

It was in a piece of woods that had evidently not been occupied by troops before, for the trees were standing, and the ground was covered with dry twigs and leaves. The skies were overcast and the air was damp and chilly, but we did not think that there was going to be a very big storm.

"I tell you, Joe," said Butterworth, "we're lucky to

get this good place to-night. See the leaves I have gathered for a bed. It beats a spring mattress. There's many a poor fellow at home that hasn't such a good place to sleep in as this."

"Yes," I replied, pulling the blanket up under my chin, "and this slope of the ground is just right. It brings our heads higher than our feet, which makes it more comfortable. I'm glad I didn't throw away my blanket in to-day's tramp, aren't you?"

"You bet I don't throw away mine while the cold weather remains," said Butterworth. "It is pretty tough sometimes during the day, but they come in mighty handy at night, I can tell you."

"Don't you think it is going to rain to-night?" I asked.

"Wouldn't be surprised," replied John. "But then what do we care? We have a good tent, plenty of blankets, a soft bed, and even a canteen full of spring water, for I filled the canteen fresh just before I turned in."

"Where is the canteen?" I asked. "I want to get a drink now."

"Hanging right over your head," said he, "on the tent pole."

I took a good drink of the refreshing draft, and John was right, for it was as fine a specimen of spring water as I ever tasted.

We talked a little while on commonplace subjects and soon fell soundly to sleep. Soldiers were too tired out on such occasions to indulge in much talking after they were in bed, and when they once got asleep they slept soundly. Only those who have had that experience can fully appreciate the soundness of the sleep of a tired soldier.

I was awakened during the night some time by the sound of the rain falling in torrents. The wind blew a gale and fairly howled through the branches of the trees over our heads. I felt uncomfortably chilly, and turning over to find what was the matter, found the blankets both under and over me soaking wet.

"What's the matter now, Joe?" asked Butterworth, waking up.

"I guess that confounded old canteen of yours has sprung a leak," said I, "for the blankets are all wet."

We made an examination and found the canteen all right, but as we sat up, there was a very uncomfortable sensation of water trickling down our backs.

"Phew!" said Butterworth, "here's a pretty mess. The tent has sprung a leak. The blankets are soaked and so am I. I am wet through."

"You're no wetter than I am, I guess," I replied. "Let's get up and see what is the matter."

We pulled the blankets from the ground and found a stream of water running through the tent. It was running through by the pailful. It will be remembered that we were in such a "nice place" on the side of the hill, and the water was running down through the tent like a brook.

We got outside. It was better to be standing out in the rain than it was to be lying there in a brook. We found the entire regiment up and standing under the trees, each man wrapped in his rubber blanket, to protect himself as well as he might from the pelting rainfall.

A more forlorn and unhappy lot of men it would be hard to conceive. There we were, in the middle of the night, in a desolate woods, with the rain falling in perfect torrents. And how it did rain! It came down by the bucketful!

"I haf change my mind alretty," said John Ick. "I beliof I will desert alretty, so soon by I got chances."

"What's the matter now, John?" I asked.

"Dot's vot I said alretty," he answered. "Dose fellers vat vas deserted was died und don'd haf to go through by dot rain-storm all the times. Dey vash happy, und ve vas——"

"That's true, John," I said. "They are dead and maybe they are happy. I can't tell about that. And we are not very happy. There's no denying that. But at the same time wouldn't you rather be a live soldier than a dead soldier? And maybe perhaps those dead fellows are not happy after all. Maybe they went to the other place, where the people are not so happy, according to general belief."

"I don'd care, neider," said John. "Dose fellers vas warm if dey goes by dot under places vat you says don'd was so happy be. Dey vas warm and dry und ve vas wet und cold alretty. Ya, I wish I vas dead all the times. I change my minds. I vas goin' to desert so soon by the storm vas over."

There was no getting over this argument. The executed deserters might be in purgatory, as Ick said, but if they were, it was a good dry place. And a dry place, in our present frame of mind, comprised all the essential elements of complete happiness.

But John didn't desert, then or afterward. He was, as a rule, a good soldier, despite all his talk.

We tried many times to light a fire, but were unable to do so Everything was so water-soaked that nothing would burn. We passed through a miserable night, and when it came daylight, although the storm let up a little, we were a miserable lot, soaked to the skin, shivering, uncomfortable and hungry, for it was even impossible to get enough of a fire to boil coffee for breakfast.

But, sleep or no sleep, wet or dry, hungry or surfeited, the operations of the army must proceed. The relentless march must go on. Whatever spot we were aiming for must be reached.

And so, wet and tired, hungry, listless, depressed and enervated, we mechanically obeyed the order to—

"Fall in, Thirteenth!"

CHAPTER XLVIII.

RATHER MUDDY.

BUT we didn't march very far that day. When night came again we were not more than two miles from where we started in the morning.

And now for the first time we encountered what was a genuine specimen of "Virginia mud." We thought we had seen Virginia mud before, but all previous experiences were a farce in comparison.

The storm had cleared off. That is, the rain had stopped falling, although the skies were still overcast. It was but a short distance from where we had camped for the night to the ford at Wolf Run Shoals, over the Occoquan creek.

It was called a ford, because in ordinary seasons the water is only a foot or so deep, and the place was used for a crossing for wagons. The economical Virginia grangers never wasted county appropriations in building bridges when they could find a place shallow enough to wade across. And they would go miles out of their way to reach the ford.

The spot was called Wolf Run on account of a tradition that in former days it used to be a favorite haunt for the wild ancestors of the domestic dog. But we saw no wolves. Neither did we see any ford.

On the contrary we encountered a raging creek. Usually it was but a foot or so deep. Now it was several feet deep, and the water was rushing through with the speed of a tail race.

The mounted officers rode across, although the water was high enough to have wet their feet if they had not held them up. But the main portion of the vast army was not mounted. It was not a big enough stream to use pontoon bridges, and there was not time to construct a regular army truss bridge, for we were in a hurry. It was a part of the movement somehow or other connected with the Fredericksburg campaign.

As things turned out it would have saved time for the officers to have stopped the entire army for a day or so and built substantial bridges. But then everybody's foresight isn't as good as his hindsight, not even an army officer's.

There were plenty of large trees growing along the edge of the creek and some bright genius suggested that these trees be felled in such a way as to fall across the stream and let the troops go over these logs.

I was not a general. I was not even a commissioned officer. I was "only a private."

But if even with my ignorance I could not have devised something better than that I think I would have been ashamed of myself. The idea of marching an army of several thousand soldiers across a log over a stream of water, and in a hurry at that, was simply ridiculous.

And yet that is just what was attempted. I forget how many of these primitive bridges were thrown across the creek. Perhaps eight or ten. They were big trees, eighteen inches or two feet in diameter.

I saw the first two or three men cross. With their heavy rifles, their knapsacks and various accouterments, they had about all they could do to walk along a country road, let alone balance themselves on something only a trifle better than a tight rope. It took perhaps a minute for a man to get over.

The first three or four went across with comparative ease. Then the dripping clothes and the muddy shoes of the men began to besmear the round top of the logs, and they became perilously slippery. From that moment it became something like a man trying to walk along the top of a rail fence with a pair of roller skates on his feet.

About every third man slipped off into the water and of course that was not a very pleasant thing. As I said before, the stream was deep and the current was swift. The first two or three unfortunates were nearly drowned, hampered as they were with their cumbersome accouterments. So, below each of the log bridges, they established a cordon of cavalry, to catch and fish out the men as they slipped off. Fully one-half the men consequently got on the other side drenched to the skin.

It was very tedious. We had to wait for an hour or so after reaching the stream to get a chance to cross, for it could only be done one by one, as may be imagined. And after getting to the other side we had to wait for the rest of our companions. I think of all the experience I ever had in the marching line this took the premium.

I felt sure that I would be one of the fellows to slip off the log and go into the water, but I didn't. Although I slipped and scrambled and twisted myself into all imaginable shapes in keeping my balance, I managed to get over somehow, and took my place with those waiting for the others to come over.

Then and there we indulged in the customary kicking, and the army, the war and everything connected with it was cursed uphill and down. If Jeff Davis had come around just then he would have met with a warm reception from a disgusted army. The loudest in their imprecations were of course those who had tumbled into the creek and were wet to the skin and shivering with the cold, as they tried to dry themselves by the sickly fires that had been kindled.

In the meantime the wagons were coming across by fording. Each wagon and team naturally brought up out of the creek its quota of water, which dropped off on the banks as they emerged from the creek. This was a little thing at first, but wagon after wagon and team after team soon had the ground saturated, not only close by the creek, but for some distance up the side of the bank.

The wheels of the heavy baggage wagons, wearing into this, mixed it over and over again, till the mud got deeper and deeper. First it was a few inches deep. Then it worked down till it was a foot deep. Soon it was up to the hubs of wheels. It did not take long to work the mass till it came up to the bellies of the mules and the bodies of the baggage wagons.

The mud grew thinner and thinner till it was of the consistency of paste. Its color was a bright red, as Virginia mud usually is. Not only did it grow deeper and deeper, but the slough extended further and further until it was fully a quarter of a mile in length, if not more.

It was muddy all over that part of the country at that particular time. In the wet season the normal constituent of the State was mud. But I am now talking of more than ordinary mud. The sort I am trying to describe is the regular old army mud, such as was only seen by the soldiers on the march.

It was not long before the mud was too deep for an ordinary six-mule team to drag the wagons through. Teams from other wagons would be unhitched to help those still in the sloughs. I have seen not only twelve, but frequently twenty-four, mules, attached to a baggage wagon to pull it out of a mud hole, and on the particular day I am talking about I saw thirty-six mules attached to one wagon, and yet unable to budge it.

It was in such a place as this that the mule would become discouraged and lay himself down and die, as I have described in a previous chapter.

It was in this place and on this occasion, that originated the following incident, which perhaps some of my readers have heard before:

Out in the middle of the road, resting apparently in a mud puddle where it had been left, lay a brand new army hat of the "slouch" pattern. A soldier whose hat was somewhat the worse for wear caught sight of this, and decided to secure it. The mud was too deep for him to wade out for the hat and so he got a long pole from the woods and reached out for the hat with the pole, as if he were fishing.

As he lifted the hat on the end of the pole the soldier was astonished to see that he had exposed a human head. And not only a head, but a very much alive one at that, with the mouth in good working order.

"Here you," shouted the head, "what are you about there? Put that hat right back where you got it!"

"I didn't know you were there," replied the soldier

who had just fished off the hat, as he tried to wiggle the pole around so that it would fall back on the head.

"I didn't know there was anything under that hat. Don't you want some one to help you out of the mud?"

"N-no, I g-guess not," said the man in the mud nonchalantly, "I have a good horse under me, and I guess he will bring me out all right after awhile!"

CHAPTER XLIX.

AN UNCOMFORTABLE NIGHT.

I DON'T know if that man's good horse ever brought him safely out of the mud, but I do know that the story is not so much of an exaggeration as it might appear at first glance. No amount of extravagant description could greatly exaggerate the depth, diabolical character and general cussedness of Virginia mud.

A soldier cannot march in boots. Experience soon proved that the only proper footgear was a broad, low-cut shoe. This was of course no protection to the mud. The usual custom was to pull the woolen stocking up on the outside of the trousers, forming a sort of legging. That protected the bottom of the pantaloons, and made marching easier. But as may be imagined the shoes were soon full of mud and water and one's feet were constantly in soak.

In civil life it is supposed to be a dangerous thing to go long with wet feet, but some kind Providence must have inured the soldier to this. None seemed to be much the worse for it. Of all the ailments of life ordinary colds were the least troublesome to the soldier after he had become once hardened to the service.

But that it must have had an effect on the health is evident from the large numbers of veterans to-day who are suffering from rheumatism and kindred ailments, all unquestionably the result of the exposure suffered while in the army.

That day, with the mud and wet and the cold, was one of the hardest we ever experienced. In ordinary times we would have thought little of a twenty-mile march in a day, but on that particular day we did not make more than two miles, and when night came we were completely exhausted with the fatigue of the day.

We went into camp that night within a mile of the crossing at Wolf Run Shoals, and not two miles from where we had slept the night before on the hillside, where the rain poured down our backs. It wasn't a jolly crowd that night. Everything was wet through. It was almost impossible to find a piece of wood dry enough to burn. Butterworth and I, however, managed to discover and cut down a couple of good-sized sassafras trees. These, no matter how wet, will burn like pine, although they make a terrific smoke.

Of all the trees that grow in the woods, none will burn as readily when green as sassafras, a fact which the rising generation should remember, as it might be of use to them in case there is ever another war—which God forbid.

Poor, clumsy John Ick was of course one of the fellows who had fallen off the slippery log into the creek and got wet through. This nearly led to a fatal disruption between him and his "pard," Reddy Mahar.

"Ye clumsy blackguard," said Reddy, "couldn't ye kape on ye're feet loike a sober man. How d'ye suppose Oi'me a-goin' to sleep wid ye this night?"

"I don't care, needer," said Ick, "you can schleeps where you likes. You don't have some tents to schleep mit, under you don'd schleep by me, all the times."

"The divil I don't. Half uf that tint is moin, and Oi'll roll meself up inside uf it, and no thanks to ye for a favor, ye spalpeen."

"No, you don't, needer. Both pieces by dot tents vas mine. Don'd you remember dot you loose your tents de under night, Reddy?"

"Oi didn't lose my tent at all at all, you old slaughter house. Half uf that tint is moin and ye know it."

"Nein. You vas mistooken, Reddy. You know you lose your halluf de under day, und you don'd draw some more from the quartermaster alretty."

"Ye can't come that over me, ye spalpeen," answered Reddy, as he proceeded to seize half the "pup" tent from Ick. John grabbed the other end, and they began to pull on the two sides of the piece of canton flannel.

The language that ensued between the two during the scramble that took place for the possession of that piece of tent was altogether unparliamentary. It was a funny conglomeration of Celtic and Teutonic, and beat any character dialect acting that was ever placed on the variety stage.

You have perhaps seen the picture of the pug dog and the baby tugging at the two legs of the rag doll, and if you have you, no doubt remember the fate of the doll. Well, that was the fate of the piece of "pup" tent. It came in two and was torn to pieces in the struggle.

Then a grab was made for the other half of the tent, and before long it met the same fate. That was torn to pieces also.

After the mischief had been done, the two belligerents gazed upon the ruin, and then looked each other in the face for a moment as a curious expression came over their countenances.

"John," said Reddy, whose sense of the ludicrous always overcame his animosity on such occasions, "we're a pair of fools, that's phwat's we are."

"And I vas anudder, Reddy," replied Ick.

That settled the difficulty then and there. The two worthies shook hands cordially, and were extravagantly profuse in offering each other the use of their blankets for the night. Reddy and John had no tent at all that night, nor for a number of nights afterward, in consequence of that disastrous quarrel, but they were closer friends than ever. Although Ick was wet through, and must have been a very uncomfortable bedfellow, they slept that night as close as brothers, and not a word of complaint was heard on either side, although they must have been anything but comfortable.

This is only one of the many examples of the peculiar incompatibility of these strange "pards." They were always quarreling and there was scarcely a day that they did not have a fight. They did not seem to be able to agree upon anything. And yet, if any one abused one of them, the other always took it up, and behind the uncouth, incongruous exterior there was a depth of friendship that was astonishing.

There was many another soldier that night that had a wet "pard," although there was not the same way adopted for the settlement of the matter as in the case of Mahar and Ick. But if there was anybody comfortable and happy in camp that night I did not hear of it. In the course of my war experience I do not think that patriotism was ever at a lower ebb than it was that night.

We were glad enough when it was morning. Then we learned that not half the army had been got across the creek, and it had been decided during the night by the officers in command to retrace our steps and take some other route.

This was one of the things that always disgusted the soldier—to spend a whole day getting somewhere and then immediately go back again. We could not understand the why and wherefore of such things of course, although there must have been some reason. But the why and wherefore was not explained to the private soldiers.

"Their's not to reason why,
Their's but to do and die."

It did not take so long to get back, for the weather was still colder and the mud had partially dried and partially frozen, so that it was not near as deep as it was the previous day. The water in the creek had also gone down so that it could be forded, and many crossed that way, although I stuck to the log and again managed to get across without tumbling off. We marched some distance further back that day, and before night reached Fairfax Station, a place where we were to remain for awhile, it was said, as the weather was getting too cold for army movements.

And as we marched into camp that night it began to snow. It was a tradition that it did not snow very often in that part of the country; it did that afternoon, and it snowed as hard as I ever saw it snow in the North.

Here was another new experience. We had suffered from the intense heat of the sun and we had gone through some pretty cold nights already We had been drenched to the skin in the rain and half-drowned from fording creeks. But this was the first time we had ever encountered a snowstorm.

Although it might not be thought to be a fact, yet it is not nearly as cold to be outdoors in an ordinary snow storm as when it is a clear cold. The principal inconvenience was in the fact that the snow covered up the twigs and little sticks in the woods which were so useful in kindling and maintaining fires in camp.

But the ever willing Butterworth, "my pard," hustled through under the trees, pushing the snow from the ground with his feet, and gathered a big armful of small branches and brushes while I went to the nearest stream and filled the canteens. We put up the "pup" tent and had everything fixed nicely for the night, and were preparing to cook some lobscouse for supper, when to my intense disgust I heard my named called to go on picket.

So, donning my haversack and equipments, and deferring my supper till later, I fell in line, with my companions, and started for—no soldier knows where he starts for!

CHAPTER L.

A LESSON IN GUERRILLAS.

On the way to the picket headquarters we were cautioned to be careful, as although the main portion of the rebel army was some distance from that spot, yet there had been some evidences of guerrillas around and they might make a raid upon us at any moment.

"What are guerrillas?" I imagine I hear the reader ask.

Guerrillas were isolated detachments of the cavalry of the enemy. They did not seem to be connected with any main branch of the Confederate army, but conducted the war on a sort of a go-as-you-please principle. They rode in detachments of from fifty to five hundred men.

The guerrillas particularly infesting the Virginia campaign were Moseby's, Morgan's, Stuart's, and Wheeler's. They were generally called "men," that is, "Moseby's men," "Stuart's men," etc. A rumor that any of these bushwackers were in the neighborhood always put the soldiers on the alert.

The particular province of the guerrillas was to harass the Northern army. I suppose there were similar guerrillas on the Northern side, but we did not come across them, of course. In the Union army, if there were such things, they were given the more dignified appellation of "skirmishing parties."

The guerrillas also perhaps made it a part of their business to take hasty surveys of the Union forces, positions and strength. They would suddenly dash down upon our camps, generally in the night time, and galloping through the lines would cut and slash and shoot after the manner of a lot of Western cowboys on a round-up through some small, out-of-the-way settlement.

Their appearance was generally so sudden and unexpected that it found the Union soldiers unprepared for it. They would dash through the picket lines, rush through the camps, and then as suddenly disappear, before our lines could be formed to drive them off. Cavalry has no chance to fight against infantry when the latter is once formed into a "hollow square," but that takes some time to form, and the guerrillas would nave disappeared before the boys had received the orders to fall in.

There was one good thing about the guerrillas. Their proximity always served to make the soldiers more on the alert. The report that guerrillas had been seen around always kept the pickets and everybody else on the *qui vive*.

Our picket post was a very lonesome spot at the edge of a woods. It continued to snow quite hard and the ground was covered to the depth of several inches. We managed to start a fire, however, and made ourselves as comfortable as possible under the circumstances.

I was on the second relief and did not have to go on post till 11 o'clock. We thought it was no use trying to get any sleep before starting out, we fellows on the second relief, and consequently sat around the fire, after cooking some coffee, and indulged in talk.

"Those guerrillas," said one of the Third Wisconsin boys to me, as we sat there smoking our pipes, "are a derned nuisance. I remember once before the Second Bull Run they made a raid through our camp and gave us the derndest scare you ever saw. We were a sittin' around the fire just like this, when all of a suddint there was a whoop and a hurrah, and a lot of shootin'. Then the guerrillas dashed through us, firing and slashing and yelling like Injuns. None of us was shot, but one of the Twenty-seventh Infantry boys got a slash on the arm with a saber. They was right through us afore we could do anything. Then they dashed down through camp, clear through, mind you, with their yelling and racket, and went out of the other side, and all so suddint that not a single one of them was shot."

"What is the sense of it all?" I asked. "What object have they in making these rushes through camp?"

"Derned if I know," replied the veteran. "Pure cussedness, I guess. If they find there's only a small force they will grab up everything they can carry. If there is a big army lying around they simply dash through. I guess it is simply to find out how many there are on our side and perhaps to give us a little scare."

"Do they ever attack the picket posts?" I asked somewhat nervously.

"Oh, yes, that's their main hold. One time down on the Peninsula they raided the post I was on, wounding the sergeant and one of the men, and they grabbed our blankets and haversacks and guns and skedaddled before we could say beans. Say, I'd rather go into a good-sized battle than be raided by guerrillas. Not that there is so much danger, but it gives a fellow such a scare, you know, and you don't get over it for some time. Somenow after you have once been raided by guerrillas you have no confidence in yourself for a long time. especially when you are out on some lonesome post on a dark night."

"Do you think we are likely to have any guerrillas around to-night?" I asked. I was beginning to feel a very lively personal interest in the matter, considering the fact that I would have to go on post in a short time.

"I wouldn't be much surprised," was the reply. "I heard the officers say as how guerrillas had been seen near by some of the skirmishers, and it kind o' looked as if they might be along this way afore mornin'. But then we will keep on the lookout for them."

"Isn't it rather dangerous to have a fire burning like this, so that they can see where we are?" I asked.

"Well, I don't think as how that makes much difference They would come anyhow, fire or no fire. And say, if a fellow was going to go without a fire simply because there might be guerrillas around, he would freeze to death before the winter was over. We have to take chances on that."

"But then a man is in more danger when he is out alone on post, isn't he?" I asked.

"To be sure, pard," was the encouraging reply.

"You have to keep your eyes open. But then you can hear the tramp of the horses long before they are near, unless they have the hoofs muffled, which they sometimes do. Then you can hardly hear them till they are close on top of you."

"What do you mean by having their hoofs muffled?" I asked wonderingly.

"Why, they sometimes have sort o' cushions or pads on the feet of their horses, and they go along softly, like a man wearing gum shoes. They don't do this very often, you know, but they do sometimes, and then they make scarcely any noise at all. An old soldier, however, soon gets to know the guerrillas are coming even with the horses' hoofs muffled, if they only learn how and keep a close watch."

"How do they do that?" I asked. I was getting interested.

"The weight of the horse as he comes down when on the gallop, makes a sort of thud, you see, and although it is little, it jars the ground just enough to feel it. You hear them through your feet. If you suspect that there is something of the sort going on, just plant yourself solid on the ground, both heels down. Don't raise on your toes, but put your whole weight on your heels. Then the sound of the cavalry a-comin' will go up through your legs."

"It's just the same if they are galloping toward you through the mud or over soft ground?" I suggested.

"No, it isn't, either. When galloping through soft ground there is a sort of a kerchuck and a suckin' as the hoofs come out of the muck, that you can hear quite a distance on a still night. And then with the ground muddy and soft you can't hear them coming by the sound passing through your legs, as I have said. It is only on solid ground with the hoofs muffled that you can hear the rumble through your legs when you can't hear them with your ears."

"But can't you hear the rattle of the sabres and other things? I have noticed that there is aways a considerable lot of jingling with a company of cavalry."

"Oh, they have them things muffled too," was the reply. "When they muffle the hoofs, they muffle everything else and come along like a lot o' spooks. As I said afore, the only way you can hear them is through your legs, with your feet firmly planted on the ground."

"Do you think it likely that we will be visited by any of these fellows to-night?" I asked, as unconcernedly as I could.

"Shouldn't be surprised, pard," was the answer; "I heard the officers say as they thought we would likely have a scrimmage with them before long, and the way we have moved about lately is another sign that there are some rebs not very far off. But you and I have to go on the second relief and then we'll find out. Better be careful to-night and keep a close watch, and remember what I've been telling you about listening with your feet as well as with your ears."

"I will that," I replied. "And I am much obliged for the information you have given me to-night, for it is something I never heard of before, and I might have been caught napping, for I never heard of horses having their hoofs muffled."

"It's a fact, all the same, and——"

"Fall in, second relief!"

This interrupted the conversation, and we strapped on our cartridge belts and picked up our rifles to go on picket, perhaps to be attacked by the hated guerrillas.

CHAPTER LI.

"I'M NOT AFRAID."

It was an awfully lonesome place where I was posted on picket at 11 o'clock that night. It struck me that it was the furthermost post of the entire picket line. At all events I was the last man of our detail to be posted and I could neither see nor hear any one further out.

The snow was falling, but not so hard as it had been. It was not as dark as it would have been had there been no snow on the ground, but there were obstacles in the way of my seeing very far.

My post was alongside a clump of small trees, scarcely more than bushes. About fifty yards behind me was the woods, but I did not anticipate attack from that direction, as there lay the Union army. About a quarter of a mile in front there was another wood, and about halfway between there was a stone fence, perhaps four or five feet in height.

After the snow had stopped falling so thickly, I could see quite plainly as far as the stone fence, and that particular thing was the object of my most earnest solicitude. I could not help thinking that there might be some rebels concealed behind that excellent breastwork.

Then I remembered what the old veteran of the Third Wisconsin had been saying to me. It struck me that a horse with muffled hoofs would make very little noise galloping over ground covered with three or four inches of snow, and that made me all the more watchful.

I commenced to practice the art of hearing through my legs as I had been instructed. I shuffled a clear place in the snow and stood on my heels with legs stiffened out till they became lame. I paced up and down my beat and at each end and about the middle, stopped to listen, first with ears, and then by standing still, resting the weight on my stiffened legs, and straining every sense of observation and conception to see if I could distinguish any unusual noise, or any abnormal trembling of the ground.

But everything remained as still as a graveyard. Everybody knows how snow muffles all sounds, even in a big city. There out in the country, at midnight, alone, in a dismal corner, the stillness was oppressive. It was almost supernatural. The sense of the loneliness was intense.

Now and then, as we simultaneously reached the ends of our respective beats, I could catch a glance of my next companion on the picket line, and we would exchange a few words. We had been cautioned to keep very quiet and listen intently all night, but this became unbearable, and finally when I came up, after several turns, and again met my neighboring picket, I was glad to hear him suggest that we stop and have a talk.

He was a member of the Second Massachusetts. This regiment was composed almost entirely of college boys. Nine-tenths of the members left college with Colonel Gordon to go to the war. Consequently in intelligence and general information that regiment probably had no equal in the entire army.

My companion was a young fellow, not over nineteen years of age, only a little older than myself. He was a delicate-looking, refined young fellow, and had an entertaining manner of talking, strikingly different from the language of the uncouth Western men belonging to the Wisconsin and Indiana regiments of our brigade.

"It seems to be very quiet out here to-night, partner," said he. He didn't even use the ordinary abbreviation and say "pard."

"It is," I replied. "And I have been listening with all my ears and legs for the guerrillas they said might be around to-night."

"So have I. They said that there were guerrillas in this vicinity during the afternoon and I was told to be very careful, but so far I have never seen a quieter night. I haven't even heard or seen any signs of a 'coon or 'possum. How do you like this sort of life, anyhow?"

"I can't say that I like it at all," I replied, honestly. "Especially on such a night as this."

"It isn't such a bad night," said my companion. "I would a good deal rather have this sort of weather than a hard rain."

"I don't know but I would, too," I answered, "but I was speaking generally. I don't like picket duty anyhow. A fellow never knows what is going to happen and has to keep on the alert."

"That's so, but then there really isn't as much danger as one would suppose. I have been on picket a good deal, and never yet had any trouble but once, and that was just before the Second Bull Run, when the rebel guerrillas made a skirmish upon us and drove us back. That is the only time I ever had the least trouble, or even a scare."

"Did you ever hear of the guerrillas coming down upon you in the night with their horses' hoofs muffled?" I asked. And I explained what the Wisconsin soldier had told me.

"Yes, I've often heard of that," he answered, "but to tell the truth I never met a fellow who actually saw it. I don't see how— Hark! What is that?"

I was much startled at the sudden manner in which he had interrupted his own conversation. We both listened intently.

It was the sound of galloping horses, and not muffled at that. We also heard the unmistakable clanking of the sword scabbards as they jingled around against the stirrups of the saddles.

The clanking of cavalry sabers is an unmistakable sound. No one who had once heard it could be misled as to what it was.

My companion hurried down a little further on his own post while I sneaked back to the little clump of trees referred to. The sound of the clanking swords sounded louder and louder as the cavalry, whatever it was, came nearer.

Whatever it was it apparently made no attempt to be quiet. There was no muffled hoof business about this, that was sure.

I was not a little startled, however, when the approaching horsemen made their sudden appearance around a bend in the woods. It did not strike me at the moment that they were coming from the Union side of the line, or I might have inferred what it was.

I cocked my rifle, however, to be ready for any emergency, and determined to put on as brave a front as possible, although to tell the truth I was shaking.

I remember that it struck me then that there was something wrong about the tactics and regulations for a man on picket. Instead of first crying "Who comes there?" and then shooting in case the answer was not satisfactory, I thought the operation ought to be reversed —in other words, the shooting to come first and the inquiry after. It would have given a fellow a good deal better chance for his life, at times.

But I waited until the party, ten or fifteen horsemen, came within hailing distance, and then cried out:

"Who comes there?"

"The grand rounds."

This answer almost took me off my feet. In the first place it was rather an unusual thing for the grand rounds to be mounted, and then I had become so worked up on the subject of guerrillas that such a thing as grand rounds had entirely slipped from my mind.

The unexpectedness of the reply to my challenge, as well as the sudden relief from the tension when I found that it was friends and not enemies that were confronting me, as I said before, almost threw me off my feet with astonishment. I imagined that my voice was a litth shaky when I gave the next salutation:

"Officer of the grand rounds, dismount, and give the countersign."

It was the rule, at that time at least, when the grand rounds came on horseback, for the officer in charge or whoever else was delegated to "take up the password," to approach the picket on foot. Otherwise it would give the person approaching the picket an undue advantage had he been other than friendly.

The officer dismounted, shambled through the snow, and said, "Trenton" over my musket at a half-charge bayonet, and I continued with the usual permission for the remainder of the grand rounds to approach.

"Everything quiet out here?" asked the officer of the grand rounds.

"Everything quiet, sir," I answered. "I haven't seen or heard of anything unusual whatever."

"All right, then; but keep a close lookout, for there are unquestionably guerrillas about. There have been some suspicious movements in front of one of the posts further down. You can't be too careful, my man."

"All right, sir," I replied bravely; "I'll keep a close look out for them. I'm not afraid!"

I am rather inclined to think that I lied a little when I said that.

CHAPTER LII.

CHRISTMAS EVE.

Despite the repeated warnings of the officers, we saw nothing in the shape of guerrillas or anything else unusual that night. It was more than ordinarily quiet. Shortly after the departure of the grand rounds it began to snow hard again, and it was so supernaturally still and quiet that I almost imagined that I felt the flakes strike as they fell. The rustle of a twig breaking from a tree with the weight of the accumulating snow upon it could be heard some distance, so still was the air.

It would have been a bad night for an attack of guerrillas under such circumstances, although that did not strike me at the time.

My feet were becoming painfully cold and I was getting chilled through and generally disgusted when the approach of the third relief gave me the welcome signal that my turn was over and that it was 1 o'clock.

The picket post headquarters, when I returned to it, did not present a very inviting appearance. The fire had gone down till it was little more than a pile of smouldering embers, and all the good places had been pre-empted by others. They lay in a circle with their feet to the fire, and some of them were snoring with a noise that would have made a Silsby steam fire engine envious.

The sleeping men stretched around the fire presented a curious aspect. While the heat from the fire had melted the snow from their feet and the lower part of their legs, their heads and shoulders were completely covered. In fact they looked like piles of snow, with human legs sticking out of the sides.

Then I noticed for the first time another curious circumstance.

Each soldier as he lay down to sleep had pulled the cape of his blue overcoat over his head, which protected that part of the body from the falling snow. When covered it resembled a small snowdrift.

But right in the middle of the top of each of these miniature mountains there was a small round hole which gave it the appearance of a baby volcano. Had it been daylight it would have all the more resembled a volcano, for steam would have been seen issuing from the "crater."

"What are those holes for?" I asked my friend of the Third Wisconsin, who, being an old soldier, was supposed to know all about everything.

"Those are breathing holes," he answered. "They let the air in."

"But," I asked, "how is a fellow to keep those holes open after he is asleep. Won't he smother if somebody don't attend to it?"

My companion laughed heartily at my ignorance.

"Why, you goose," said he, "those holes make themselves. The breath coming out of your mouth keeps them open. No matter how fast it snows, the warm breath melts it away above the mouth and keeps the air hole open."

"Then how is it that men die when buried under the snow, as they do out in your part of the country, as I have often heard?" I asked.

"Never heard of anybody smothering to death under the snow," was the reply. "People get asleep and freeze to death, but they don't ever smother for want of air. There's no danger of freezing to death here, so long as your feet are near the fire. Besides, it isn't cold enough for that. Out our way, where we have it below zero half the time through the winter and a fellow gets asleep on a cold night he never wakes up. But there isn't any such danger here, I guess."

Still, those curious little air holes over the mouth of each sleeping soldier interested me very much. I had never heard of such a thing before. But I saw it several times afterward. I cannot say that I saw it a great many times, for to tell the truth we did not often have snow in Virginia.

I think the one I am describing was about the deepest of my experience there.

I warmed my feet as best I could at the smouldering embers of the fire and then curled myself down on the snow-covered ground to sleep, covering my head with the cape of my overcoat as I saw the others had done.

For a few moments I was very cold and shivered as if I had a chill. But before long I grew more comfortable and in a little while became deliciously warm. I could feel the weight of the snow on my overcoat cape over my head, but there was no sense of suffocation or even discomfort for the want of air. In fact I was soon so comfortable and contented that I fell into a sound sleep and slept on until aroused by the unwelcome cry:

"Fall in, second relief!"

Could it be possible that it was nearly 5 o'clock in the morning! But such was the fact. I had had nearly four hours' good sleep and must once again go out and relieve the fellow who was patrolling the post I had left at 1 o'clock.

"It isn't quite 5," said the sergeant; "but I thought as how you might want to make a can of coffee to warm you up before you went out."

Thoughtful, considerate sergeant! I don't know that I was ever more grateful to a human being. Although warm and comfortable while lying there asleep, yet I was shiveringly cold on arising, and anybody knows that it makes a fellow cold under the best of circumstances to jump out of bed and hasten to work without anything in his stomach.

It did not take many minutes to boil my tomato can of coffee and drink it, while I ate a hard-tack, and I was in first class condition for another round on the lonesome post.

From 5 to 7 o'clock in the morning is one of the most dismal turns on picket. The slow process of night turning into day makes it appear twice as long as any other time during the twenty-four hours. Then a fellow is tired and sleepy, and there is a nervous strain unknown to any other time of the day.

Anybody who works for a living ten hours a day, during the usual laboring hours, knows that the longest time of the day is between 4 and 6 o'clock in the afternoon. So it is with the last two reliefs of a soldier on picket.

For this reason these hours just before dawn were regarded by old army officers as the most dangerous, for the alert enemy, knowing the condition of the men on picket, frequently adopted those times for raids and surprises. Many a battle has been commenced unexpectedly just before daylight and with disastrous results to the army attacked.

But nothing occurred to disturb the monotony of those two long hours, and daylight at last began to make its appearance. Better yet, the rising sun commenced to dissipate the snow clouds and the prospects were that we would have a clearer and milder day.

This turned out to be the case. We had to remain about the picket headquarters after going off duty at 7 o'clock till 9 o'clock, when the new picket came on. The sun came out bright and strong, and the snow began to melt, till it soon became a disagreeable mass of slush.

While cooking another can of coffee my Massachusetts friend said to me:

"You didn't have much of a chance to hang up your stocking last night, did you?"

"Hang up my stocking?" I answered, wondering what he meant. "I should think not. The best place for a fellow's stockings last night was on his feet, I think."

"Why, don't you know what night it was?" asked my Massachusetts comrade.

"What night? Really I hadn't thought. To tell the truth I have lost the hang of the almanac."

"It was Christmas Eve," he replied. "To-day is Christmas."

Sure enough. It was Christmas. And last night was Christmas Eve.

What a Christmas Eve!

Those were the times that made a fellow homesick. He was all the more impressed with the great contrast between "the is and the was."

Christmas Eve! I wondered what was going on at

home. The hanging of stockings, the exchange of presents, the merry-making? Were all these things going on as usual?

Were the streets filled with women and children carrying mysterious packages? Were the men sneaking home with the ends of half-covered sleds and hobby-horses and little express wagons sticking out from the bundles under their arms?

In fact, was the world—the gay, happy world, going on just as usual? Were people laughing and singing, and pianos playing Christmas carols as of yore?

Were the girls——?

The girls!

What in the world did a girl look like, anyhow? Was there such a thing? Was it reality or a dream that I once danced with my arm around a pretty Paterson girl at a Christmas Eve hop?

Confound it! Could it be possible that this was the same world that I lived in last Christmas, one short year ago?

Was it all a dream?

Or is the present all a dream?

Poor boy! Poor soldier boy!

CHAPTER LIII.

A MERRY CHRISTMAS.

CHRISTMAS, 1862. The snow storm had cleared off and the sun came out strong and bright. The snow was turned into slush in a remarkably short time, and the slush soon turned into water. The water mixed with the red Virginia clay, and the result was—mud!

And such mud!

In a previous chapter I told about the mud at Wolf Run Shoals, where it was of the consistency of thin paste, and so deep that it came up to the bodies of the baggage wagons till they resembled boats. But this mud was different.

It was of the consistency of bread dough that has been rising in front of the fire all night and is ready for kneading in the morning. It was tough, sticky, stringy. One could not go many steps before his shoes were covered, first so that they resembled red arctics, and soon they bore resemblance to pillows. It would be no exaggeration to say that the clump of mud stuck fast to every soldier's foot was as big as a real pillow—of the Pullman car size.

This sort of walking we had that Christmas morning, even through the company streets of the camp. The men moved about slowly and laboriously, and there is no slang in the statement that at every step he got his leg pulled.

Such surroundings and the fact that it was a holiday, put the boys in anything but a pleasant frame of mind, but their attention was drawn from it by the introduction of a novelty. This was something new in the line of rations.

When the order came to "fall in for rations," I asked John Butterworth, my pard, to go and draw mine with his, as I was tired with the night's picket duty. John came back presently in a state of pleasant excitement.

"They've given us something new this time, Joe," said he.

"What is it, Jack?" I asked.

"I don't exactly know what it is," he replied; "but I think they called it dissected vegetables."

"Dissected vegetables?"

"Yes, that's what they called it."

"Let's see it."

John pulled out two cakes of the "dissected vegetables." They were supposed to be three days' rations each. Each cake was about twice the size of a stick of patent kindling wood. It looked like a mass of compressed sawdust and hops.

"What do you do with the stuff?" I asked.

"They say it is vegetables," replied John. "You put it in the kettle or tomato can with a piece of pork and some water, boil it and make soup."

"Sawdust soup?" I asked.

"Don't know," answered John. "I only know that's what they told us to do with it."

We concluded to try it at once. We put one of the cakes into a tomato can, together with a little piece of pork, and filled it with water and went to the camp fire. It will be remembered that in the front every man was his own cook. It is only when in a camp that is somewhat permanent that he had a regular cook for the whole company.

Pretty soon the water began to boil and then the cake of "dissected vegetables" began to swell. It swelled till it not only filled the can, but ran over. I never saw anything swell so in my life. It was worse than a piece of plug tobacco. It was a common expression in the army when borrowing a chew of tobacco from a comrade to hear the remark:

"Don't take too big a bite, for it swells in your mouth."

So it was with the "dissected vegetables." They swell, not in the mouth, but in the kettle. The result of it was that about half was wasted before the stuff was fairly cooked through.

This was supposed to make vegetable soup. The theory was that the vegetables were preserve by pressure, the same as they preserved fodder for cattle in kilos. It was supposed that there were potatoes, turnips, cabbage, carrots, onions and other succulent vegetables in the mass, but as a matter of fact there was nothing but cabbage and carrots, and a very poor article at that. At first trial the soup was utterly tasteless, but with the addition of plenty of salt and pepper, and a little more grease from the pork it became somewhat more palatable.

It was the only thing in the shape of vegetables ever served to the soldiers in the army and insipid as it was, it was a pleasing addition to our bill of fare The first lot we received was tolerably good, but the quality degenerated till it became nothing more than a lot of rags, apparently, and the time soon came when the soldiers would not take the trouble of putting it in their haversacks. In the course of time it was entirely dropped from the list of rations.

But we got something more that day. In addition to the usual coffee and pork and beans we got some rice, and this was most acceptable. Rice boiled with pork really makes a palatable dish. I think that of all the things served to the soldiers rice and beans were the most acceptable, next of course to the indispensable pork and coffee.

It may here be of interest to the reader to know what allowance of food was made for the soldiers "according to the regulations." I will give it.

Twelve ounces of pork or bacon or twenty ounces of salt or fresh beef; twenty-two ounces of soft bread or flour, or one pound of hard-tack; (twenty ounces of corn meal was sometimes given in lieu of either of these). The above was for each man. Then, for every one hundred men, fifteen pounds of beans or peas, ten pounds of rice or hominy, eight pounds of roasted coffee or twenty-four ounces of tea, fifteen pounds of sugar, four quarts of vinegar, twenty ounces of candles, four pounds of soap, four pounds of salt, four ounces of pepper, thirty pounds of potatoes and one quart of molasses.

The potatoes did not materialize. The only tubers, that we got were procured by foraging. I remember seeing molasses two or three times. Tea wasn't a popular beverage, and the soldier never took it unless he could not get his beloved coffee. One of the items on the allowance was never seen—fresh bread.

It will be seen that there was plenty of the substantials of life to keep body and soul together provided we got them all. But there was always something short. There was always something "out." We simply had to take what we could get or do without. Of course we grumbled.

Kicking was one of the inestimable privileges of a soldier that was never interfered with.

Everything was furnished the army by contract. And every government contractor got rich. They took the contracts at ridiculously low prices and then got square by swindling the soldiers. The food was frequently of inferior quality, while the shoddy clothing that was furnished was at times so bad that it would almost fall apart of its own weight. To the soldier, who judged the thing simply by experience and observation, the terms "contractor" and "robber" were synonymous.

Then another discomfort was discovered on that day —that merry Christmas Day!

The place where we were stopping had been used as a camp ground before, and there was the usual result. It was not long before the pesky *pendiculus investimenti* began to show himself in great numbers.

"Why isn't this a good time to get rid of these graybacks for awhile?" asked John Butterworth.

"How'll we do it, Jack?" I asked.

"I heard Jake Engle say he wasn't going to use the kettles to-day," was the reply. "We can get them and give our shirts a good boiling."

"Agreed," said I, "although it isn't a very pleasant day for such work."

"That's so, but we must do it when we can get the kettles. Jake may be making bean soup to-morrow."

The indiscriminate use of the camp kettles for boiling lousy shirts and making bean soup may probably strike the reader as not being quite as nice as it might be. But then these are facts as every soldier can testify. "Everything went" in the army. We had to make the best of such things as were at our command.

So we got the kettle and made our way down to the brook. It was the same brook that we got our water from for culinary purposes; but what of that? I must admit, however, that this made me a little "feasty." The brook was lined I don't know how far up with other soldiers performing both personal ablutions and engaged in laundry work, and the surface of the little stream was covered with soap suds that floated by us.

We built a fire, filled the kettle with water and before long the water was boiling.

Then we pulled off our coats, cardigan jackets and shirts.

I can tell you that it isn't pleasant to stand outdoors in one's bare pelt in the winter time, even though it be in Virginia. We quickly put on the cardigan jackets and coats, minus a shirt, but still shivered with the cold.

Why didn't the men have two shirts? I hear the reader ask.

What was the use of two shirts when one would do? Furthermore every ounce counted on the march and that was of more importance than the temporary discomfort of going without while washing the one shirt.

"Say, Joe," said Butterworth sarcastically, as he gave the boiling shirts a poke with a stick he had picked up somewhere, "this is a merry Christmas, isn't it?"

"A Merry Christmas" it was indeed!

CHAPTER LV.

OUR SHIRTS " SWIPED."

Boiling shirts was one thing. Drying them was another. The brook where we were engaged in the laundry work ran through a woods, in the shade. Although the sun was melting the snow in the clearing, it seemed to be about at the freezing point there in the woods. This fact we didn't notice as we carefully spread the wet garments over some bushes to dry.

We went out into the sunshine where it was a little warmer, and indulged in a game of tag and a running race to keep from being chilled. When we thought the shirts might be a little dry we went for an examination.

Instead of being dry they were frozen stiff. When we bent them they cracked like a printing office towel that hasn't been washed in six months.

"I think we are a pair of fools," said Butterworth. "We might ha' known that the shirts wouldn't have dried there in the shade on this cold day."

"Well, to tell the truth, Jack," said I. "I have not had much experience washing shirts and I didn't know anything about it. But I guess it will be all right if we hang them out in the sun."

So we hung the shirts in the sun, and as it was getting toward noon we thought we would kill two birds with one stone and keep comfortable around the camp fire while cooking some coffee. That warmed us up.

"The shirts must be pretty dry by this time," said John. "I will go and see."

Butterworth went to look after the laundry while I put away the coffee pots. In a few moments my pard returned with the most lugubrious expression on his face that I ever saw.

"What's the matter, Jack?" I asked. "Aren't the shirts dry yet?"

"I don't know," he answered, with a quizzical look.

"Don't know? What's the matter now?"

"Well, the fact is, Joe, somebody has stolen those shirts!"

"Stolen the shirts?"

"Yes, they're gone."

It was true. Somebody had "swiped" the shirts. Some bright comrade had come to the conclusion that it was easier to get a couple of clean shirts that way than it was to wash them. There was no use trying to discover the thief in such a case as this. The different things furnished to the army were as alike as peas, and could not be identified. Some of the boys put private marks on their articles, but we had never bothered with that.

All through the army there were a thievish lot of fellows in every regiment who seemed to delight in taking other's property. I don't think it was considered a sin. It was a perfectly natural operation, and legitimately within the ordinary degree of normal turpitude of a certain class. Blankets, muskets, canteens, everything, were indiscriminately "swiped."

Of course no one suspected a member of his own company! It was always laid to some wicked fellow who had sneaked into camp from one of the adjoining companies. In such cases, frequently, if the loser was a big fellow and a bully, he would coolly go to some smaller soldier and calmly demand his blanket or whatever it might be, claiming it as his own and charging the little fellow with having stolen it! A pretended private mark, some peculiarity suddenly observed at the moment, would be utilized to back up the claim of ownership.

That reminds me of a story which may be old to many of my readers, but which will serve to illustrate the fact stated.

A soldier went to another who was lying on the ground covered with his blanket. The first man coolly pulled off the blanket and proceeded to walk off with it.

"Here, here, what are you doing there?" asked the

man who owned the blanket. "What are you taking my blanket away for?"

"That's my blanket, you spalpeen, and I have a right to take it."

"Your blanket! How do you make that out?"

"Sure'n there's my name on it."

"Where?"

"There. Don't you see the letters, 'U. S.' on it."

"What's that to do with it? What's your name?"

"Pat Murphy. There's the U. for Patrick and the S. for Murphy—Patrick Murphy. That's my blanket and ye can't deny it."

History doesn't tell us the termination of this story, but it is only an exaggerated illustration of the cheeky claims for ownership that were sometimes made in the army.

But there we were shivering in the cold for the want of a shirt. What should we do? We consulted Heber Wells.

"The quartermaster has just received a lot of clothing and perhaps he has some shirts," said Heber. "I will give you a requisition."

Heber made out the requisition for "two shirts" on the blanks provided for that purpose and we went to the quartermaster's and after the usual delay and red tape managed to procure the desired garments, which we put on then and there. They were neither of the right size, but we had learned not to mind a little thing like that.

"Joe," said Butterworth, "I have an idea."

"If you have, Jack," I replied, banteringly, "keep hold of it for fear it will get away from you."

"No, but it's a good idea. What's the use of bothering with washing our shirts when we can draw new ones?"

"True enough," I replied. "That is a good idea. I don't think I will do any more washing."

And I think that this was the usual practice with old soldiers, whenever it was possible. The government allowed a certain amount of clothing, and so long as the account was not overdrawn a soldier could always obtain a supply. Of course it was not always possible, for the quartermaster was one of those fellows who was not with the camp when there were signs of a conflict; but the allowance was liberal, and the practice of drawing new underclothing became more general with the old soldiers than washing out the old ones.

It was on the next day after this, if I remember rightly, that General Williams woke up and decided that the army under his command had not had quite enough work to do, and that it would also add to his glory and renown to have a division review.

Now a review or inspection was always obnoxious under the most favorable circumstances, but at that particular time, with the ground so thickly covered with mud, we came to the conclusion that the officers all had gone mad. "Kicking" doesn't fairly express the conduct of the boys on that occasion.

But what was the use of kicking? The generals and others gave the orders and all that we had to do was to obey them. We wallowed through the mud and went through the various evolutions connected with a review as well as we could, and it must have been pretty good after all, for we were subsequently complimented by "general orders."

"Something on hand, pard," said my friend of the Third Wisconsin, who had got in the habit of making friendly visits. "As I told you often before, there's always something coming when we have these reviews and inspections. We won't stay here long."

It really did seem so, and I remembered these words when the very next day we were ordered to fall in for a march.

That was the most ridiculous day's march we ever had. We had only fairly got started, and in fact had not gone more than a mile, when we were formed into companies, ordered to stack arms and go into camp again.

What could this mean? We soon found out that the doctor had pronounced the water in the other camp impure and had advised a change. I guess the doctor must have examined the brook immediately after we had washed our shirts. If so, no wonder he found it impure!

But the change was a good one. The brook alongside of which we camped this time was as clear and pure as crystal—although there was no telling how long it would remain so. The ground was higher and dryer, the wood was plentiful, and altogether it was an improvement that pleased us much. We were also delighted to hear that we would likely remain there for some time.

Early next morning, however, we were hustled out and ordered to put all our knapsacks in a big pile, with a layer of light wood between them, so that the whole lot could be set afire and burned up at a moment's notice!

What under the sun did this mean?

Had the officers all gone crazy?

CHAPTER LVI.

REDDY AND ICK AGAIN.

To us private soldiers the scene in which we had just participated was incomprehensible. Why the officers piled our knapsacks in a great heap, mixed with light wood and small branches, ready to form a gigantic fire, was something that we could not understand.

Equally incomprehensible to us was the fact that we were ordered to fall in for a march in "light marching order."

Here it was, as one might say, in dead of winter, and we were ordered off with nothing but our overcoats and blankets, in addition to our accouterments, at a time when we needed every article that we could possible carry to make ourselves comfortable.

It was a hard march that the officers gave us that day. We hurried along the muddy roads, and across lots through muddy fields, hither and thither, till tired out and completely disgusted, we once more came to a creek, that we immediately recognized as that forlorn place, Wolf Run Shoals.

Here we halted for the first time, and despite the condition of the ground, we were so tired that we lay right down in the mud to get some rest, being absolutely too much played out to cook the coffee that we were all in need of.

When we halted we imagined of course that we were going into camp then and there, and there were loud and deep imprecations over the orders that had deprived us of our knapsacks, and other things so much needed at that time of the year.

"Dat vas ein shames, don'd it," said John Ick lugubriously. "Vat you tinks, Reddy?"

"Be jabers and Oi think they are a set of lu-nat-ticks," replied Reddy. "Do they suppose we're a lot of Eskimoxis to be able to slape in the snow and ate taller candles? A grease-eatin' Dutchman like ye, shouldn't moind, but for respectable men the loikes o' me, be jabers, it isn't roight, that's phwat it isn't."

"Who vas dot grease-eatin' Dutchman, you ninperpoop," replied Ick, somewhat angrily; "don'd you call me by some names like dot, Reddy."

"That's phwat ye are," replied Reddy. "Don't Oi know? You Dutchmen do nothing but ate sourkrout and blood puddin', and fat sausages and duck livers win at yer home, and that's next door to atin' taller candles, don'd it?"

"Der Deutschmens lives better as by the Irishes, Reddy, und don'd you forgot dot. You Irishes eats gooses, und dot's worser by taller candles, don'd it?"

"Oi wish Oi had a good fat goose now," said Reddy, smacking his lips.

"Vas you hungry, alretty, Reddy?"

"Oi am that. Oi could ate a whole soide o' sole lither."

"I vas so hungry mine own selluf, Reddy. You gets some woods und I vill der coffee cooken."

"No, ye get the wood, and Oi'll cook the coffee."

"Nein, I will dot coffee cooken. Dot vas your turns to get some woods."

"Phwat d'ye mean, ye spalpeen? I got the last wood."

"No, you don'd, Reddy. It vas me by dot last woods begotten."

"John, ye are the worrust loyer Oi iver saw. You know that's your turn to get the wood."

"Don'd you calls my dot name some more, Reddy, oder I'll smash your face all over your nose."

"Let's see you do that, ye spalpeen," said Reddy, getting angry and jumping to his feet. "Oi have had enough o' this palaver from the loikes o' ye."

Ick thought Reddy meant business, and squared himself for the encounter. Reddy thought that Ick was going to carry out his threat to "smash his face all over his nose."

The discomforts of the situation and the fatigue from

that day's march through the sticky mud had put everybody in a bad humor. Reddy Mahar and John Ick, whose respective characteristics were more animal than intellectual, had created a safety valve for their outraged feelings. They were both in a humor to fight. They would have fought anybody. It made no difference whom. But the conflict had naturally arisen between these two strange companions.

They both struck out simultaneously. I never saw a prettier rough-and-tumble. The first blow given by Ick looked as if he really would carry out his face smashing threat. He landed a right hander square on Reddy's proboscis, which set the claret flowing. Reddy retaliated with a blow that would have been declared foul in the prize ring because of its being below the belt. To this day I can hear the grunt that came out of Ick's body involuntarily.

Then they withdrew a few steps from each other, and after looking into each other's eyes for a moment like wild beasts at bay, they once more came together with a clash and crash.

The result of this collision simply involved a problem in momentum. Ick was the heavier of the two, and to use a slang phrase, he walked right over Mahar. The latter went down, with Ick on top of him.

Reddy was the slimmer of the two and more supple in his movements. Ick was a big, clumsy fellow, and although on top, the under dog in this fight had decidedly the best of it. They punched and scratched, gouged and bit, rolling first one way and the other, through the thick mud on the ground, till they were both besmeared from head to foot.

I guess the fight lasted fifteen minutes. The officers of the company, with the others, were holding a consultation at regimental headquarters, so that there was no interference from that score. The privates and non-commissioned officers had learned never to interfere with these periodical conflicts between Reddy Mahar and John Ick, for we all knew that they would again be the warmest of friends when it was over.

Besides, it was rather a diversion to the rest of us. It was a sort of relief to our feelings. We all felt in the humor to fight something or somebody. Even I, who had never fought anything in my life, felt as if I could whip anything that came along. There is a certain time when man's endurance has been about exhausted that this feeling is natural and involuntary.

Exactly how the fight ended I can't tell. I remember that both the belligerents got up simultaneously, wiped the blood and mud out of their eyes with their coat sleeves, and then Ick said:

"I told you vat we does, Reddy; we'll both go after some wood and then both dot coffee cooken, don'd it?"

"Thin why didn't ye say that before, ye spalpeen, and act like a gintlemen?" replied Reddy.

The two dromios thereupon shook hands in the most cordial manner imaginable, and they were friends once more. The comical termination of the fight, although it was the way all their fights terminated, set us all to laughing for the first time that day, and I must confess that it put us in better humor.

The rest of us had been aroused from the depression we had fallen into, and by mutual consent we concluded to follow their example, get some wood and cook some coffee, for we were all in need of it.

But we had wasted our valuable time. We had been watching a pugilistic encounter instead of attending to very necessary culinary duties. It was too late now. The officers just at that moment returned to the company and gave the order to "fall in."

There was more kicking, of course, but it did not amount to anything. All that we had to do was to obey orders. The duty of a soldier is to "say nothing and saw wood."

They say that the work that drives convicts to insanity quicker than anything else is the apparently nonsensical labor of carrying a pile of stone one by one from one end of the prison yard to the other, and when that is done, carrying them back again one by one. This is kept up incessantly day after day, and the monotonous labor eventually drives the unhappy victim to the lunatic asylum.

It was for a somewhat similar reason that the soldiers were frequently driven to the verge of insanity. There seemed to be no end to the practice of marching the troops back and forth, hither and thither, without any apparent cause or reason. The object of all this probably was known to the officers, but the privates were kept in ignorance. I often thought that the enlisted men would have a good deal less mental worriment and fatigue if they had some of these things explained to them. But that wouldn't be "according to the regulations."

Imagine our disgust, therefore, to be marched back right over the ground we had taken in the fore part of the day. We followed the same course so accurately that we almost stepped into the same tracks that we had made in the forenoon.

We reached the old camping grounds toward night, tired out, hungry, discouraged and utterly disgusted.

Some such experience as this must have inspired the author of the old Mother Goose story about the famous king who, with his forty thousand men, marched them up the hill and then marched them down again.

CHAPTER LVII.

THE PAYMASTER.

There lay our knapsacks and other things in the great pile, with the light wood mixed with them, ready to set fire. They hadn't been burned up after all. This made it look more mysterious than before.

They had been left in charge of a detail of men under command of Major Chadwick. He had taken good care of them. No one had stolen any of the knapsacks.

It seems that the movement that we had made that day is what they called a "reconnaissance." It was reported that there were some rebels in the neighborhood of Wolf Run Shoals, and we had gone to see if it was so. Had there been any we would naturally have got into a fight. This going out of the way to get into a muss was one of the things that never met my approval. Why not leave well enough alone?

But we met no enemy at Wolf Run Shoals, for the reason that there was no enemy there, and we consequently all came back on foot instead of on stretchers or in ambulances.

It also seems that the officers feared a raid by the rebel guerrillas while we were on the reconnaissance, and so the knapsacks had been arranged in a pile ready to set fire and destroy on the first appearance of the enemy. Rather destroy government property at any time than permit it to fall into the hands of the enemy. That is war!

When the ranks were broken the men were directed to find their own knapsacks.

Well! Here was a job!

There were six or seven hundred knapsacks in that pile, and they were as much alike as so many peas in a pod. Not half a dozen in the entire lot had any particular mark to identify them.

There had been no arrangement or system in piling them up. They were thrown in the pile promiscuously, indiscriminately. For each man to pick out his own was consequently a tedious task. Nearly every one had to be opened to see what was inside, so that it might be recognized by the owner. That took a good deal of time. It was late in the night before they were all claimed, and even as it was, some mistakes had to be rectified the next morning.

Butterworth knew my knapsack, and while he was looking for his and mine, I cooked some coffee, so that we did not crawl under our blankets hungry. But many another soldier did. I have heard kicking many a time on the part of the Thirteenth Regiment, but I cannot recall any occasion when the kicking equalled that which was indulged in that night.

We remained in camp at this place about ten days. We had become convinced that we would make it our winter quarters, and had spent some time and gone to no little trouble in fitting up log houses, "with all modern improvements." But alas! there's no rest for the wicked—nor for the soldier.

On the 4th of January we were once more ordered to break camp, and once more started on the march. It was not in light marching order this time, however. We carried our knapsacks and everything we could pack in them.

Once more we went over that too familiar road toward Wolf Run Shoals. It was not so bad this time, however, for the mud had either dried away or the ground was frozen, I've forgotten which. Anyhow, the walking was not nearly as bad as it was on the previous occasion, nor did we seem to be in a like feverish haste.

We were halted and directed to form camp almost on the same identical ground where John Butterworth and I had got such a soaking that night when the rain rushed through our "pup" tents, going into the backs of our necks and coming out at the bottom of our trousers' legs.

It was a good place for a camp. There was plenty of

timber to cut down and make into log houses, and there was an ample supply of good water. We were more than pleased to hear that we had at last reached our "winter quarters," and that we might proceed to make ourselves comfortable with some degree of certainty of remaining there for a while.

Butterworth and I spent a busy day making another log house, after the style of architecture described in a previous chapter. It was the most cozy place we had yet had, for experience had taught us how to make things comfortable with the limited means at our disposal.

It was a wonderful thing how quickly the dense woods disappeared. In twenty-four hours the ground around the camp, for a space covering several acres, was entirely cleared, and where there had stood large trees there was nothing left but a lot of stumps. These stumps came in useful for a number of purposes.

I was detailed a day or so afterward with some other fellows to smooth off the top of a big stump in front of Colonel Carman's tent. We did not know what it was for, the only instructions we received being "to make it smooth enough to write upon." Inasmuch as the only tools we had for this purpose were some axes (and not over sharp at that) and our jackknives, it may be imagined that it was no easy task, and the result was not quite as satisfactory as the green baize top of a roll-top desk of modern times. When we had done the best we could, the colonel said: "Let it go at that," and that settled it.

Then Captain Scott called me to his tent and set me to work making out the pay rolls. This showed what the stump was to be used for. The paymaster was coming

The pay rolls, as well as all the other rolls of the army, were enormous affairs. There is hardly a desk made in these days that would accommodate one of them. With the limited facilities at our command at the front it was a difficult thing to make them out at the best. The "desk" that I wrote upon was the top of an old cracker box, which took in about one-quarter of the big sheet of paper, and so it had to be made out in sections, as it were.

Three copies of these rolls had to be made out. They contained the name of the soldier, the date of his enlistment and muster, and lots of other things, beside the time he had served since his last payment. When completed they had to be certified to by the commandant of the company.

In the army enlisted men had to swear to all legal proceedings. The commissioned officers only had to "certify" on their word of honor. The "word of honor" and "certification" of a commissioned officer was considered as binding as the oath of a private or "non-commish." The former were a higher grade of mortals, and were governed by a different code of morals.

That may be all right in theory, but—well, never mind!

A day or so later the paymaster arrived. His high and mighty giblets was of the usual arbitrary and arrogant character, an autocrat of the autocrats. His clerk spread the rolls out on the stump we had cleared off, and an assistant carried the grip that contained the boodle.

The officers were paid off first, of course, and we envied them as they stuffed the thick wad of crisp greenbacks, never before used, fresh from the press, into their pockets. Then came the non-commissioned officers and then the "men."

The amount given to each diminished in size as the process continued. The omnipresent sutler was there for his grab, as usual. What was left for each private wasn't much. He might have stuck it into his ear, and it wouldn't have impaired his hearing at that!

There were two months to be paid for. There was a good deal more than that coming, but the paymasters were always several months behind in their payments for some reason or other. If we were paid to within six months of the time due, we were lucky.

When I had signed my name to the three rolls—and signing one's name with a scraggly pen on the rough top of the stump was no soft snap at that—and the paymaster had deducted the amount due to the sutler, I had fourteen dollars left. I hadn't spent so much with the sutler this time, probably because the sutler had been separated from the regiment so much of the time.

A large proportion of the men sent their money home, through the medium of messengers sent to the front for the purpose by Governor Marcus L. Ward. This was a good and safe arrangement. It was also touching to witness the devotion of the men to their families at home. Some of them sent every cent when a little change would have provided them with many a luxury.

I didn't send mine home. I had no one to depend on me, and I was glad of it. On the contrary I soon got rid of the bulk of mine in another way. I am sorry to tell how, but the truth must be told, even though it be not very creditable.

Sam Dougherty, one of the sergeants, came up to me and asked:

"How much did you get?"

"Fourteen dollars," I replied.

"What are you going to do with it?"

"I don't know. Keep it, I suppose."

"Suppose we have a little draw?" he said.

CHAPTER LVIII.

A LITTLE GAME OF DRAW.

"WHAT do you mean by draw?" I innocently asked Sergeant Dougherty.

"Poker," he replied. "Draw poker."

"I'd make a pretty fist at that," said I; "I never played a game of poker in my life. I can go you on High-Low or euchre, but I don't know anything about poker."

"That makes no difference," said he insinuatingly; "it is the easiest game to learn you ever saw, and I can show you in five minutes."

I was innocent, and imagined that it must be a simple game that can be learned in five minutes. Sam Dougherty was perhaps the first man that ever lived that had the assurance to make such an assertion.

We went to Sam's log house, and with a greasy old deck of cards spread out on the lid of a cracker box, he began to initiate me into the mysteries and intricacies of the great game of "draw."

He fired at me a perfectly bewildering lot of straights, full houses, bob-tail flushes, royal flushes, ace and king highs, and all that. The more he explained the more I got mixed up. One thing particularly struck me, however, and that was the "bluff." He carefully impressed this on me, and told me how a man with a poor hand could frequently win if he kept the right sort of an expression of confidence and didn't lose his nerve.

I concluded that I'd let the other things go and confine myself to the bluff. I would make that "the feature" of my game.

The quartette indulging in that wonderful game comprised Sam Dougherty, Lew Van Orden, Charles Ruestow and myself. Van Orden was a good player already, having had considerable experience in the game. Ruestow, like myself, was a novice. We always called him "Rooster." Nearly all the soldiers had some sort of a nickname.

We used little pieces of twigs for "chips," and each was supposed to represent five cents.

"We'll make it five cents ante with a dollar limit," said Sam. I didn't know an ante from an uncle, but didn't want to display my ignorance before the others.

Sam dealt the cards. I got two deuces, a tray, a jack and queen. I had caught on to the fact that three of a kind was better than two of a kind, and so discarded the jack and queen. Then I drew two cards.

They were two jacks.

What a fool I was, I thought to myself. If I had only kept that other Jack I would have had three of them. As it was I had two jacks and deuces. I thought that was a pretty good hand.

All the other fellows "went five better." Neither Reustow nor myself had the slightest idea of what this was, but when we saw the others lay down another twig we did the same thing. This thing went around twice and then some one "called."

We threw down our hands, and strange to say I had won. The next highest hand was a pair of ten spots. My jacks had beaten that. The man with the ten spots had also a pair of nines. It struck me that twice ten and twice nine counted more than twice two and two jacks, but I entered no protest when they said I was the winner, and I raked in the chips representing about sixty or seventy cents, I've forgotten exactly how much.

I was elated at this victory. It swelled my head and I began to imagine that I saw through the whole thing. Sam was right when he said this was an easy game!

In the next hand I made a phenomenal draw. I held four aces. By intuition I recognized that as good, and I could not help looking pleased.

Sam thought I was profiting by his advice on the question of bluff, and he apparently made up his mind to push me to the wall. The other fellows seemed to have good hands also, for the betting went round and round.

I won again. My four aces was "good."

"Are you sure you never played this game before?" asked Sam incredulously.

I solemnly assured him that this was the first time I had ever played draw poker. But from the look on his face I don't think that he believed me.

Lew Van Orden said nothing, but I noticed that he exchanged glances with Sam Dougherty. I didn't understand what it meant at the time. Charley Roustow was also silent. But he was a bright little fellow, and I felt that he was closely studying the game. As for myself I began to think that I was a boss player.

My next hand positively had nothing in it. I gave myself away by drawing five cards. Then I found that my hand was just as bad if not worse than before. But I decided to try the bluff game this time. I didn't know that bluffing doesn't generally "go" after a five card draw, but I tried it all the same.

Singular to say it worked all right. The others had grown suspicious of my good luck, and Sam apparently didn't think that I would bluff after drawing five cards, and imagined of course that I had struck another phenomenal hand.

When I had scooped in the third pot, Sam asked me to let him see my hand. I didn't know any better and showed it to him. When he saw that there was nothing in it he made a remark that I didn't fully understand. It was something like "being taken for a sucker." I wasn't yet sufficiently acquainted with the technical terms of the game to understand what this meant. Again I noticed Lew winking at Sam in a somewhat suggestive manner.

Another hand being dealt and getting another poor lot of cards, I again tried the bluff game and laid down my chips with an expression supposed to represent a man who has a good thing and knows it. But it didn't work this time. I was "called" and Van Orden grabbed the pot, after exhibiting three nines and two trays. "A full house," he called it.

I began to lose faith in the bluffing business, but

thought that maybe after all my losing the hand was only an accident.

The next hand I drew was " 'way up in G." It contained four queens and a jack. I chipped in with the greatest confidence and could not conceal the certainty I felt of winning. When somebody had "called," I threw down my four queens and jack with a wave of triumph, and made a motion to grab the stakes.

"Hold on there," said Sam, seizing my hand. "Don't be quite so fast, my young man. I think I'll take that pile."

"What have you got?" I asked.

He threw down his hand. It didn't look to me as if it was anything very wonderful.

"Well, what of that?" I asked. "That lot of stuff don't beat four queens, does it?"

"Of course it does. That's a royal flush."

"What is a royal flush?" I asked.

"It is a hand," replied Sam, "where you have the cards in regular order, like one, two, three, etc., and all of the same color."

"Well, what of that?"

"What of that!" said Sam, with a face as sober as a judge; "that's the highest hand you can hold, and takes anything."

"I thought a royal flush must be all the same suit," interrupted Ruestow. "I don't see how you make it out of a mixture of diamonds and hearts."

"That don't make any difference," said Sam, "so long as they are of the same color. Isn't that so, Lew?" turning to Van Orden.

"Yes, that's so," replied the latter gravely. "All that is necessary is that the sequence should be of the same color."

"I know that it isn't so," interrupted Ruestow. "They must be of the same suit." Sam looked angrily at this interference, and demanded:

"I thought this was the first game of poker that you ever played?"

"So it is," replied Ruestow; "but I've read a great deal about the game and know that I'm right."

A very black look came over the faces of Sam and

Lew. Ruestow noticed this, and throwing down his cards he got up and said he would not play any more.

I remained, and at the suggestion of the others made it a three-handed game. From that moment my luck seemed to forsake me. I couldn't understand half the decisions that were made, but I supposed they were all right. They were experienced poker players and this was my first game.

Under such circumstances the result was inevitable.

When I walked out an hour afterward my fourteen dollars were gone!

I can't say that I regretted the experience. It had taught me a good lesson. I played many a time after that, while in the army, but never again for real money. Plain, everyday chips having only a supposititious value were good enough for me after that.

But in all my subsequent playing I never ran across anybody who had the same interpretation of a "royal flush" as the two gentlemen who initiated me into the mysteries of the game of draw.

CHAPTER LIX.

A PRIVATE'S PHILOSOPHY.

The camp we occupied was "Near Fairfax Station," and so our letters were dated and our mail addressed. We occasionally, when we had the chance, went out to see the "station." That was all there was of the place, by the way. It was a big storehouse, built of rough boards, alongside the track, with the platform on the railroad side, so that it was simply and purely a freight house. It was the depot of supplies for the army in that part of Virginia.

Such a thing as a passenger car was never seen. Everybody who rode, even the officers, sat in the freight cars. The officers seemed to have a good deal of business to call them back and forth, but there were not many privates to be seen on the cars—at least not outward going. Occasionally some lucky fellow would get a furlough. But the most were new recruits, arriving from home.

The quantity of goods and provisions that continually kept coming was immense, and for the first time we began to get an idea of the tremendous quantities needed to supply an army. And we constituted only a very small portion of the army at that.

There was a strange sensation at the first sight of a railroad train, primitive and rough though it was, after not having had that pleasure for so long a time. We had become impressed with the feeling that we were in another sort of a world and that such things as steam cars and carriages, houses and stores, were but the memories of some half-forgotten dream. But the sight of the locomotive and car seemed to open a new link with the outer world.

Particularly striking was it to me to see on the locomotive the familliar name of "Rogers." Oh, you delightful old thing from Paterson! I could almost have hugged it—that is if I could have got my arms around something small enough to hug.

I sat there on the rough platform and gazed at the name "Rogers" as if fascinated. I forgot the surroundings of the place and was carried back to glorious old Paterson! Then my thoughts wandered down to the corner of Broadway and Main Street, to the old *Guardian* building, and for a few moments I was back there again, wearing a long apron and "kicking" the Ruggles press. I forgot for the moment that kicking a Ruggles press is likened to nothing under the sun beside a treadmill or a slave galley, but it seemed a delightful occupation just then by contrast.

But I was suddenly awakened from the dream by a sergeant.

"Let me see your pass," said he.

I had no pass. I had simply wandered over from the camp to "take a look at things."

"Then get back to your camp," said the sergeant harshly. He was a member of the provost guard or something. They always had something of this sort hanging around the depots. The powers that be knew that the cars awakened just such memories as they had awakened in me, and that it was one of the greatest known incentives to desertion.

I never thought of desertion. But it may be imagined what would be the tendency of such a train of thought on the part of a soldier who ever dreamed of "skedaddling." So I went back to camp—thinking.

There perhaps was never a soldier in the army who did not have such moments as these, when some outward conditions or situation would arouse a terribly strong feeling of homesickness. With some it was a good deal stronger than in others. With some it was irresistible.

'Twas not always cowardice that made soldiers desert. Something stronger than fear caused some to forget their oaths. Not even the hardships of the winter at the front, not even the horrors of the forced march was it that made men forget their oaths and disgrace themselves in the eyes of their country. It was pure and unadulterated homesickness.

Had there been a more liberal policy in regard to the granting of furloughs this might have been offset. The officers refused furloughs as much as possible for fear that the soldiers might desert. In my opinion exactly the opposite would have been the result.

I knew of one poor fellow who deserted because he had received word that his wife was on her deathbed. He asked for a furlough but could not get it. There was no reason for the refusal at the time. So he obeyed the stronger instinct and deserted. When his wife died and was buried, he started to return, but was captured by the provost guard, tried, convicted, and sentenced to one year in a military prison. Of what use was that?

I am not going to defend the deserter. There is nothing in the world more despicable. But there were deserters and deserters, and in dealing with them there was a lamentable lack of common sense and humanity.

Another thing that made us disgusted just about this time was the way the officers were resigning. They were going home by the score and new men were taking their places. Our captain, Scott, sent in his resignation, and it was accepted in a few days, and the first we privates knew about it was when he came around and bade us good-by.

Captain Scott was not the most noted officer in the war, as officers are regarded, but he was kind to the men. He was a boy with the boys. At the close of a weary day's march he would gather the company around him and start up a song in which we would all join, and the hour or so thus spent relieved many a heavy heart. The other officers criticized this severely, saying that it was unmanly, and that it was not conducive to discipline to have a captain mingling so familiarly with his men. But there was no airishness on the part of Captain Scott and his men liked him for it.

At the same time I cannot commend this sort of business as a general rule. The more an officer holds himself aloof from his men the more will they respect him in the end, and the better will be the discipline.

This was made manifest by the character of **the officer**

who succeeded Captain Scott. It was the late adjutant, Charles H. Hopkins. He was a man of high breeding, finely educated, refined, and what might be called a member of the four hundred, had there been such a thing in those times.

He was the exact opposite of Captain Scott. At first he would have been considered a martinet and an utterly heartless officer. But he understood military matters better than his predecessors, and brought into the officers' tent a degree of dignity and manliness theretofore unknown, with the exception of Lieutenant Heber Wells.

With the men Captain Hopkins was rather austere. Everybody soon recognized the fact that he was way above him in more than his finer clothes and his shoulder straps. It is rather a hard task to take a rough stone and make a finished diamond out of it, but that is just what Captain Hopkins did with Company K.

We first feared, then respected, then admired. We recognized in him a man of superior intelligence and ability—one who could not only command, but one whom every man considered it an honor to obey. The result of it was that Company K soon obtained the reputation of being one of the best companies of the Thirteenth Regiment, both in discipline and drill, and even those who liked the free-and-easy familiarity of Captain Scott soon began to appreciate that it is better to have a captain who preserves his dignity on all occasions, and proves by his conduct his superiority and his fitness to be the commanding officer.

So, therefore, not only does this sort of conduct make a better officer in the opinion of officers, but the fact is very soon appreciated among the privates. The old army officers are right. The general rule is good, that the less contact and less familiarity, in a strictly personal way, there is between officer and private, the better the discipline and the greater the efficiency of the organization.

I think this rule holds good in civil life as well as military. It is human nature for men to hold those over them in higher respect if they keep themselves behind a breastwork of dignity that is not carried to such an extent that it is offensive.

There were changes in all the other companies, so many had been the resignations and consequent promotions. Many of the sergeants stepped one grade higher, and discarded the government uniforms of "enlisted men," for the finer cloth of "commissioned officers."

And let me say right here, that of all the martinets, the rough, tyrannizing officers of the army, there were none so bad as a man who had just been promoted from the ranks to the shoulder straps. For a little while the sudden transition from subserviency to power made the new officer a petty tyrant. But fortunately this soon passed over, as soon as he became familiar with the privileges and novelties of power.

Some of the promotions from the ranks were obtained from what in these days would be called a "pull." Political influence, friendly connections or relationships with those in authority, and similar causes, frequently resulted, for instance, in a private being promoted right over the heads of a lot of corporals and sergeants whose turn would have come next. This always made a great deal of dissatisfaction and grumbling. But it couldn't be helped. All that the disappointed ones could do was to kick—like a mule.

While all this comes in quite properly and consecutively, yet it is somewhat of a digression from my story, to which I will now return.

CHAPTER LX.

"THE MUD MARCH."

"Joe," said my pard, "if you want to see a queer sort of a bridge, just come down to the creek."

"What is it, John?" I asked. "What is there so very queer about it?"

"Come down and see. It's only a little ways."

We went down to the little creek that we had already crossed over several times. There was still a considerable quantity of water in the stream and it was running almost with the swiftness of a mill race.

The bridge was really worth going to see. One had been constructed already and the "sappers and miners," as the military engineers were called by the soldiers, were at work upon a second one near by.

The distance between the sides or banks of the stream must have been forty or fifty feet. The bridges that were being constructed were made of trunks of small trees perhaps five or six inches in diameter, and not one of them more than ten feet long. It is not such a hard task to erect a bridge fifty feet in length out of timber ten feet long, providing one has plenty of spikes or bolts or something of that sort to fasten the pieces together, and there are piers in the stream to lay the ends, so as to divide the bridge into spans.

But these bridges were being built in a single arch, and there was not a pier in the middle. Furthermore the short pieces of timber were not nailed or spiked together. They were simply interlocked in a curious manner hardly possible to describe without a diagram. The ends passed each other, and there were two cross pieces at each end of the poles—they were nothing more than thick poles—all arranged in such a manner that they bound against each other and made a very solid structure. The greater the weight placed upon them the stronger they were, while a comparatively slight pressure upward from underneath would have knocked the structure apart as if it had been of cardboard.

This was a curiosity to me and the many others who watched the erection of the bridges. To make a bridge with a forty or fifty foot span out of pieces not more than ten feet long, without a piece of metal or a rope to fasten it together, is really a feat in engineering wonderful to contemplate.

I have since that time made little bridges on this principle out of matches or toothpicks, with a span of nearly a yard, to the great wonder of all who saw it. We saw the same sort of bridge many a time after, as well as many other curious things that were done by the sappers and miners. But when we saw the first of these structures, and presently saw heavy baggage wagons crossing them, it really did seem as if all the rules of mechanics had been upset.

"I think the building of these bridges is rather suspicious," said Butterworth.

"What do you mean by that?" I asked.

"I think that this army is getting ready for a move."

"Why," I replied, "they said that this was to be our winter quarters and that we would remain in camp here till the weather got better. I don't think we are likely to make a move for some time yet."

"You remember what a time they had getting the wagons and artillery through that mud before," said Butterworth. "Well, they are making better arrangements this time. Those bridges are so that the wagons can be got across better. I tell you they would never have built them if they did not intend to make a start. If we were to remain here some time longer they would wait till the water went down and then ford the creek."

"That looks reasonable," I replied. "But what is the sense of changing our position now? We have got as good a place to camp in for the winter as we could find anywhere. They certainly would not be so foolish as to start a campaign with the roads in their present condition, would they?"

"I shouldn't think so," replied Butterworth. "I

don't see what they could do if they did make a start, for they couldn't get far anyhow. But there is no telling what they won't do. And I tell you I believe those bridges are not being built for nothing. If we are not ordered to pack up our knapsacks and get out of here very soon, I'm greatly mistaken in my guess."

John Butterworth was a pretty good guesser. He had a habit of putting this and that together and coming, by a sort of intuition he possessed, pretty near the truth. In less than twenty-four hours we received orders to pack knapsacks and get ready for a march.

I don't think we ever received this order less joyfully. We had the most comfortable log house we had ever occupied. There was plenty of wood and an abundant supply of excellent water. It was an ideal spot for winter quarters, and we had come to the happy conclusion that we were sure of having a comfortable place to remain till the spring weather made going better.

But there's no rest for the soldier. No sooner does he think that he is settled for a while and proceed to make himself as comfortable as possible under the circumstances than along comes that relentless order to "Fall in for march."

We started early in the morning of the 19th of January, 1863. We bade adieu to our comfortable house and our cozy camp with genuine regret. We were off for no one knew where. "Anudder schlaughter haus," John Ick said.

We had not gone a great distance before the skies became overcast, and the gathering clouds in the east betokened the approach of a great storm. But soldiers do not stop for storms.

Under ordinary circumstances I might not have mentioned the fact of the approaching storm here, for I have already described several storms in the front. But this storm was one that has gone into history. It has ever since been referred to as one of the events of the day.

It didn't rain right away, however. Great bodies move slowly. Great storms usually come up deliberately. In fact the length of time a storm takes in making preliminary operations, as a general rule, is indicative of its duration and severity. We marched through

Dumphries, a place that had just been occupied by General Siegel's corps, and went into camp on the further side of the town, near a little stream called Quantico creek.

In the night the threatened storm broke loose. And such a storm! The rain came down literally in torrents. The "pup" tents were of no more use than so many sieves. They were called "shelter tents," but they were anything else than a shelter on that occasion. We spent the night standing up or walking around, on the principle that a man erect affords less surface to be exposed to the rain than a man lying down. Besides the water was apparently two or three inches deep on the ground, so that we might as well have undertaken to go to bed in a bath tub.

There was not a man who was not drenched to the skin. If we had been thrown into the river we could not have been more thoroughly soaked. The wood was so saturated that it was impossible to build a fire in the morning, and we consequently had to go without our much-needed hot coffee. The wet clothes, saturated knapsacks and other things almost doubled the load we had to carry. But all this made no difference. The relentless march was ordered to proceed.

We had not gone far before we were compelled to throw away our woolen blankets and other things, which were so saturated with water as to be useless, and the weight was more than we could carry. And here it was in the dead of winter at that! The loss of the blankets unquestionably meant suffering for us when night came, but we could not help that. There was no alternative.

The mud had become deeper than ever, and the tramp of so many thousand feet made it sticky and mushy. We floundered around, seemingly aimlessly, for awhile and finally came to the banks of another creek, which we were expected to cross to get to where we were going, wherever that might be.

Here another obstacle was encountered. The rain had swollen the creek several times its usual height, so that it could not be forded. Fortunately some big trees were growing in the neighborhood and these were felled and dragged to the creek and thrown across. This involved no end of labor and consumed a good deal of time.

It took five or six hours to get the infantry across on the rough bridge that had been completed, but then it was found that it was impossible to get the artillery and baggage wagons over. So there was another delay. The bridge had to be made more perfect for the wheeled vehicles.

A row of logs was laid across the timbers of the bridge and the tops hewed off, till it formed a sort of corduroy road. The artillery was then brought across on this structure, but here another trouble was experienced. The wheels of the heavy cannons only mixed up the mud on the other side of the creek, till it became impossible to pull the artillery through, no matter how many horses and mules there might be harnessed up.

It is no exaggeration to state that the mud was above the hubs of both the cannon wheels and those of the wagons and ambulances. But a small portion had got across when everything came to a dead halt. Not a wheel could be moved. The army of the Potomac was stuck in the mud!

For four days we labored there trying to get out of the mire. Every soldier had to take his turn at the wheels of the wagons and cannons, trying to help push them through, but in those four days not more than two miles were made.

Then the infantry, of which we were a part, were ordered to cut loose, and we were marched off in another direction, and after a long and tedious tramp, or rather I should say "wallow," we finally reached Stafford Court House, completely exhausted. It was several days later before the artillery got out of their mud hole. They were stuck fast in the mire when they should have been shooting the big guns at the enemy.

Of course we did not appreciate at the time what all this movement meant, but we found out afterward that General Burnside had commenced a second attack on Fredericksburg, and this was just what that was. One would think that after the first terrible repulse Burnside had received at Fredericksburg he would have hesitated before trying it again, or at least waited till the weather was suitable. But he didn't. He tried it at a time when it was not fit for an army to march, let alone engage in a battle with a fortified enemy, and the result was another disaster.

This was the affair that has gone into history as the "second Fredericksburg campaign." Not a shot was fired. Instead of engaging the enemy we were stuck fast in the mud, not far from Dumphries. As said, history calls it "the second Fredericksburg campaign."

The boys forever after called it "the mud march."

To this day you never hear an old soldier speak of that affair without calling it by its natural and appropriate title of "Mud March."

That event settled the career of General Burnside. Immediately after that he was relieved from the command of the Army of the Potomac.

CHAPTER LXI.

THE CORPS BADGES.

GENERAL BURNSIDE was right when he said, on somewhat reluctantly assuming command of the Army of the Potomac, that he did not consider himself qualified for the position. He had been one of the best corps commanders in the army. When ordered by the commanding general to perform a certain duty he always did it, and did it well. But when it came to commanding a big army himself, and originating the movements as well as executing them, he was an utter failure.

The historian therefore must not blame General Burnside for what he did not do. He was not qualified for the position of commander and knew it, and he should never have been appointed. But his service in other respects in the army and his subsequent brilliant career in congress more than offset all his shortcomings as a commanding general.

General Hooker, who succeeded Burnside, was an entirely different sort of a man. Among the soldiers he always went by the sobriquet of "Fighting Joe." He was a dashing, courageous man, one born to command. The soldiers liked him and had the most implicit confidence in his ability and judgment. The only fault with General Hooker was that he was not exactly a representative of the total abstinence party. Not to mince words, he used to get gloriously drunk.

Truth compels the statement, I regret to say, that if this were a disqualification, there would not have been many men left in the army to command it. General Howard on the Union side and General Stonewall Jackson on the part of the Confederates, are the only ones credited with having gone through the war without touching intoxicating liquors. There may have been others, and probably were, but these are the only ones I ever heard of. I am merely mentioning it as about the only thing that could be raised against General Hooker as being a proper general to be placed in command of the Army of the Potomac.

The common soldiers did not care for that, however. They all liked General Hooker, and the result of his appointment was immediately noticeable. The men had become discouraged and downhearted with the repeated failures and defeats, the senseless marches and seemingly meaningless maneuvers and they hailed with delight the advent of a commander who, they believed, would put an end to this sort of work.

The effects of the improvements resulting from the orders given by the new commander were apparent throughout the army. Desertions, which had again become alarmingly frequent, the executions at Leesburg having become by this time almost forgotten, were at once stopped, and the discipline of the army generally was otherwise improved in a thousand different ways.

General Hooker began to manifest a hitherto unknown regard for the individual comfort of the troops. He issued orders that did away with many of the existing abuses and in some way managed to infuse a degree of life and vigor among them such as had never been known before. The cavalry had hitherto been a sort of go-as-you-please attachment of the army, confined to squadrons or regiments, and attached to no regular branch or department more extensive. He organized them into brigades and divisions, the same as the infantry, and soon made them a most important branch of the service.

It is perfectly safe to make the statement that before the advent of General Hooker none of the commanders had much of an idea of the use of the cavalry anyhow. They were used without system or order, and seemed merely to exist because it had been the custom from time immemorial to have such a thing as cavalry in an army. General Hooker, however, changed all this, and from that time on the cavalry were made to understand that they constituted a most important department of the army.

The gallant General Phil Kearny, whose death at Chantilly has been before referred to, was a great friend and associate of Hooker before the former's death. One of Kearny's pet schemes was the idea of adopting corps badges, after the French idea. He had something of the kind for his own corps, but never lived to see it adopted by the army generally. It is generally supposed that General McClellan was the originator of the corps badge idea, but as a matter of fact it was General Kearny who originated it, and General Hooker who carried it into effect.

Remembering the pet idea of his old friend Kearny and being impressed with its utility, General Hooker decided to adopt it for the entire army immediately after his assumption of command. The corps badges from that time on became a distinguishing mark and their usefulness was proven on more than one occasion.

The badges for the officers were generally made of velvet with a border of gold braid, like the shoulder straps. Those of the men were cut out of a piece of cloth or flannel. The shape of the badges designated the corps, and the color the division of the corps. This designation was not subdivided down so low as brigades. All these badges were worn on the top of the forage caps, or in the front of the hat, if it were of slouch pattern.

Take the Twelfth corps for instance. Its badge was a five-pointed star. If red, it indicated the First Division. If white, it meant the Second Division, and blue was the color indicative of the Third Division. There were seldom more than three divisions in a corps, nor more than three brigades in a division.

No matter where an officer or soldier might be, the badge not only indicated what corps he belonged to, but even the division. The officers could therefore see the command of any man, and the men could the more readily discover friends and associates, for it must not be imagined that every soldier knew every other soldier, even of his own corps or division, by his face. These corps badges were, so to speak, the signboards for both officers and privates in the army, and they were one of the most useful things ever concocted. That this is so, may be inferred from the fact that ever since the war of the rebellion in this country the corps badge has been regularly adopted in the army of every civilized country on the face of the globe.

For further information of the unmilitary reader I will give a list of the corps badges of the army, viz.:

First corps, a lozenge, or "full moon," as the boys called it.

Second corps, a trefoil, but more commonly designated as the ace of clubs or the clover leaf.

Third corps, a diamond, the badge of Kearny's old command.

Fourth corps, a triangle.

Fifth corps, a Maltese cross.

Sixth corps, a Greek cross.

Seventh corps, a star and crescent.

Eighth corps, a six-pointed star.

Ninth corps, a shield, anchor and cannon.

Tenth corps, a sort of diamond cross.

Eleventh corps, a crescent, or more commonly called by the boys, "new moon."

Twelfth (and afterward Twentieth) corps, a five-cornered star.

Thirteenth corps (there was never a Thirteenth corps).

Fourteenth corps, an acorn.

Fifteenth corps, a cartridge box in a square.

Sixteenth corps, a circular cross, made by taking a First corps badge and cutting four small wedges out of it, from which some of the soldiers called it "pie."

Seventeenth corps, an arrow.

Eighteenth corps, a sort of scolloped-edged diamond.

Nineteenth corps, an ornamentally shaped Maltese cross.

Twentieth corps, same as the Twelfth. The Twentieth corps was composed of the consolidation of the Eleventh and Twelfth when they were transferred to General Sherman's Army of the Cumberland, and the Twelfth corps badge was adopted, the "new moon" of the Eleventh being discarded.

Twenty-first corps. This corps was disbanded before the badges were adopted.

Twenty-second corps, a five-armed cross.

Twenty-third corps, a shield.

Twenty-fourth corps, a heart.

Twenty-fifth corps, a diamond inside of a square.

Potomac cavalry corps, crossed swords, surrounded by lines representing the rays of the sun.

Wilson's cavalry, a badge containing crossed swords and suspended from a miniature carbine.

Engineering corps, a rather elaborate badge, consisting of a scroll, surmounted with a castle, underneath which was an anchor and pair of oars.

Signal corps, a torch, flanked with a couple of "wig-wag" flags. In the army this corps was always referred to as the "wig-waggers," as they are in the New York militia to-day.

I have given all the corps badges here as a matter of information, not only for the readers of this generally, but for the old soldiers as well. I do not believe that there are ten per cent. of the men who served in the army who ever saw a complete list of these badges before this. They were only acquainted with those of their immediate army. The Army of the Potomac comprised the First, Second, Third, Fifth, Sixth, Eleventh and Twelfth Corps and these badges are perhaps very familiar to the veterans living hereabout. Those residing in the West will be more familiar with some of the others.

Of course General Hooker had nothing to do with any of the soldiers except those in the Army of the Potomac, but the other generals, hearing of it, thought well of it and so adopted the badge system also, until it spread over the entire army of the Union.

It is singular that there never was a Thirteenth corps in the army, and consequently no badge for that number. It is said that this was on account of there being a superstition against the number thirteen. This rule did not apply to regiments, however, and it is a noteworthy fact that those bearing the alleged unlucky number turned out pretty lucky after all, comparatively speaking. Take the Thirteenth New Jersey, for instance.

There was a Twenty-first corps once, but it was consolidated with the Fourth and some others before the badges were adopted, and never rehabilitated.

I might mention the fact right here that there was never a Company J in the infantry of our army, and this rule holds good to the present day, not only in the armies of the United States, but of other countries of the world. One reason for this, it is said, is that a J is so like an I that the two get mixed in making out the reports. But the better and more probable reason is in the fact that at the time, centuries ago, when they began to enumerate companies by letters, there was no letter J in the alphabet.

Regiments of infantry seldom if ever have more than ten companies, which only runs down to the letter K. In the cavalry and artillery, however, I have seen companies way down to L and M.

But to return to the story.

CHAPTER LXII.

CAPTAIN AND PRIVATE.

Some of the boys kicked at the adoption of the corps badges. It was to have been expected. They would have kicked at anything under the sun. Had an officer come along with an honorable discharge for every one of them, I really believe that two-thirds would have kicked because they had been discharged without having asked for it.

As before stated somewhere, a soldier's efficiency was indicated to a large degree by the vigor of his strength in kicking. And with this as a standard of excellence, it can never be gainsaid that the Thirteenth Regiment of New Jersey Volunteers was one of the very best regiments in the army of the Union.

"Well, what is your objection to the badge, John?" I asked Ick, who was one of the most vigorous objectors to the new insignia. "Isn't that pretty red star an addition to your make-up?"

"I don't want some make-ups, what you callem," he answered. "I don't like dot alretty. Dot vas nottings else under ein bull's-eyes. Dot vas for dose rebbels to shoot mit, ain't it."

"Shut ye'r blarney," interrupted Reddy Mahar. "D'ye ivver s'pose ye will venture close enough to the innemy for 'em to see that little sthar on yer cap? How's the rebels ter see the sthar wid yer head forninst a rubber blanket, Oid loike to know?"

"Who vas dot hides his head alretty under dot rubber blankets, Reddy?" demanded Ick, getting angry.

"Ye did, ye spalpeen," replied Reddy.

"Ven do I dot?"

"At An-tee-tam."

"Who did?"

"Ye did."

"Who told you dot?"

"Ivverybody. And faith, an' didn't Oi see ye meself?"

"Den vot vas you doing there your own selluf, alretty, eh?"

It wasn't often that Ick got the better of the ready witted Irishman on a repartee, but he did this time. As will be remembered, Ick was discovered at the battle of Antietam hiding under a rubber blanket, where he was found and dragged out by Sergeants Wells and Van Orden. Reddy started to taunt Ick about this, but Ick had turned the tables on Mahar by demanding to know what he was doing there to see it.

While Reddy was always ready to make a joke at the expense of John Ick, he didn't like to have it turned on himself, and this turn of the tables made him hopping mad, and he completely forgot himself.

"I didn't say Oi was there meself," said Reddy unblushingly. "I said that everybody said that you hid ye'rself forninst the rubber blanket while the foightin' was goin' on, and ye can't deny it, that's phwat ye can't."

"You just said you vas there und see me under dot blanket, under you vas notting but ein liars all the times. Don'd he vas said so, fellers?" (addressing the crowd.)

We had to corroborate John in this instance. He had Reddy foul and no mistake. Now when Mahar was cornered he always wanted to settle the matter with a fight, and he quickly came to the conclusion then and there that the only way he could retrieve his mistake was to give John Ick a trouncing.

Off went his coat and hat, and he spat on his hands ready for the fray. Ick was in a good humor over the way it had turned out, and made no attempt at self-defense. Mahar began berating him for being a coward, and the words were becoming loud and angry when suddenly Captain Hopkins put in an appearance.

Now Captain Hopkins was a man who never lost his dignity, and he had the respect of every member of

Company K to that extent that every one was on his good behavior when he was around. The incipient fracas was therefore ended as if by magic. Mahar slowly put on his coat and hat again, and Ick went to his tent a moment afterward.

Captain Hopkins stood there like a statue, looking at the crowd without saying a word. But everybody knew what sort of a man he was, and soon the crowd was dispersed quietly and orderly as if it was a handful of snow melting under the rays of the sun. I was one of the last to remain.

"Come up to my tent, Joe," said the captain. "I have some writing for you to do."

I went. But there was no writing of importance, only a letter or so, the order having been given me simply to get me to the captain's headquarters.

"What was the trouble down there?" asked Captain Hopkins.

"Oh, nothing to speak about," I replied. "Only a few words between Ick and Mahar. It didn't amount to anything."

"Those fellows are always quarreling and fighting, are they not?" asked the captain.

"It doesn't amount to anything, captain," I replied. "They are the best friends in the world."

"They certainly have a strange way of showing it," said the captain. "But then they are both pretty good soldiers. I don't suppose we can repress the exuberance of such fellows."

"Not unless you kill them," I replied laughingly.

"Then I guess we will have to stand it," replied Captain Hopkins, "at least for a while. The Lord knows they may get killed soon enough."

"Why, do you think we are likely to get into another fight soon?" I asked, somewhat nervously.

"Not right away," was the reply. "But when we do make a start I think it will be something big. We have got "Fighting Joe" over us now, and you probably know what that means. From what I hear I don't think there will be any more fighting till spring opens, but when it does happen it will be a big battle, and I think a decisive one. I think General Hooker intends that the next fight shall settle the whole thing."

"But you don't think this will happen soon?" I asked again. I did not like to hear this matter-of-fact talk about a tremendous battle that was going to "settle the whole thing." There was altogether too much suggestiveness about its settling me at the same time.

"No," replied the captain. "As I said before, I think we will remain somewhere about this neighborhood till the winter weather is over. We have had two campaigns this winter and both have resulted disastrously, and I don't think that anything more of that sort will be attempted. But General Hooker is making preparations and trying to improve the army in a manner that was never tried before, and I think his idea is to have it in readiness for a supreme effort."

"I suppose that you, being an officer, have a chance to hear all about these things, captain. You know that everything is blind to us men. We don't know what anything is for, but merely obey orders and follow like so many sheep wherever ordered."

"There could be no discipline if it were otherwise," replied the captain. "If the men always knew where they were going, they would sometimes weaken. It is a part of the science of war to make the rank and file as much of a machine as possible. I cannot see how there could be a successful army otherwise."

"But I think it would be better if the men did know some of these things sometimes," I replied. "I believe that the result would be better and that the men would act more willingly and do more to carry out the movement if they were treated more as intelligent men instead of, as you say, part of a mere machine."

"That is a common idea," said the captain. "But it would not work. When you get older and have more experience you will understand this matter better than you do now. I can see very plainly why it is better to keep the rank and file in as much ignorance as possible."

"I think it is cruel—at least from my standpoint," said I. When together in the privacy of the captain's tent we were quite friendly, and our difference in rank was forgotten. The captain went further in this respect than he probably would, because I never took advantage of it. I knew my station. When I was outside of the tent, or when there was any one else present, I was as quiet and humble as the lowest soldier in the company. This was a trait that the captain liked and appreciated and he thought more of me for it. When we had these little conversations we were only two American citizens on a level footing. When we were outside, I was a private, he a captain.

"So you think it is cruel?" said the captain, half-musingly. "Well, perhaps it is. But tell me, Joe, if you can, what there is about war that is not cruelty?"

This was a poser. War and cruelty are synonymous.

"But you are mistaken," added the captain, "about my knowing much more about what is going on than you do. Captains are kept in nearly as much ignorance of general movements as the men. Even the colonel does not know what is going on till he is ordered to do something, and all that he has to do is to obey the order without asking any questions. The commanding general and his corps commanders perhaps are the only ones who really know the why and wherefore of everything. But then some things do leak out, nevertheless. We hear little things here and there, and put them together and form our own conclusions, and sometimes they turn out right—sometimes not."

"Then you are only inferring from what you see that General Hooker's intentions are something like you have said?"

"That's all, Joe," replied he. "But I guess you will find out that it will come out about that way. The next battle we get into will be one of the hardest ever fought, but it will not take place till the winter is entirely over. You may depend upon that."

For this respite I felt grateful, but I did not give the captain any intimation of my feelings just then.

"Don't say anything to any of the men of what I have said to you," said the captain, as I turned to leave.

"I will not," I said. "I think you understand me well enough."

"I do," was his answer. "Otherwise I would not be so free with you, only a private."

"Only a private," I repeated with a touch of irony.

"I never thought of it before," said Captain Hopkins. "You deserve something better. Would you like to be a corporal?"

A corporal? A non-commissioned officer? I hesitated at the temptation over the possible promotion.

"Would it deprive me of my place as company clerk?" I asked.

"Yes, I am not allowed to detail a non-commissioned officer for that purpose. I can only use a private for that. And I don't know whom else I could take that would suit me as well, after all."

"How about Jimmy Post?" I asked.

"Post? He's a good man, but—but I'd rather have you, for several reasons."

"That settles it, captain," said I. "I would rather be your secretary than wear the two stripes of a corporal."

"Thank you," said the captain. "That's complimentary, and I'll not forget it."

"When I go for anything, captain," said I, "it will be for something higher than a corporal." I had certain ambitions, and I threw this out as a feeler.

"All right," replied Captain Hopkins. "When the time comes, you can depend on me for anything you want."

I left the captain's tent in more than a good humor, and I remembered the captain's kind promise and months afterward took advantage of it. He faithfully kept his word.

But of that later. I will say, however, that the time did come when I did wear a shoulder strap and carry a commission signed by the President of the United States, and Captain Hopkins was largely influential in the achievement of that much desired result.

CHAPTER LXIII.

WHEREIN GLADSTONE AND I DIFFER.

It was on the 24th of January when the Thirteenth Regiment went into camp at Fairfax Court House, if my memorandum of the date is correct. A thickly wooded pine forest was selected as the site for the camp, and there was an abundant supply of water. It was in every respect as good a place for the camp as the one we had left before the "mud march."

"Well, John," said I to my pard, "here we are again, and I suppose the best thing we can do is to build another house."

"I don't see much sense in it, Joe," replied he; "we seem to be doing nothing but building houses and moving out of them again. As soon as we get nicely settled then along comes that confounded order to fall in for a march. What's the use of it? Why not make ourselves as comfortable as possible without going to all the trouble?"

"But we are likely to stay here now till the winter is over," I replied, "and we might as well make ourselves comfortable."

"What makes you think we will remain here any time?" asked John.

"Well, I just think so," I replied. I did not want to tell him what Captain Hopkins had told me confidentially, but I gave him to understand that I had good reason to believe that we would remain in that camp for a while.

"You do seem to find out things somehow," said John, "and if you say we are likely to stay here for a while I will take some stock in it. If you say so we will begin on the new house at once."

"I think we had better," was my only response.

Butterworth fell in with my suggestion. Somehow I was always the dominant spirit of our partnership—the "head of the house," so to speak. We got axes and saws and started out into the woods, where we found nearly all the other members of the regiment engaged in gathering material for the construction of their primitive residences.

It took a couple of days to complete our log house, and when done it was the largest and best that we had ever had. It was fortunate that we took so much pains with it, for, as prophesied, it was our abode for a considerable time to come, and we passed many pleasant hours in it.

We had plenty to do while in that camp in a military sense. There was no end to the drilling and other maneuvering. I was excused from company drill by reason of being the company clerk, but there was no end of regimental and brigade drilling. The constant fear of being raided by the enemy's cavalry made the officers pay especial attention to a peculiar formation specially intended as a defense against attacks from that branch of the opposing army.

This was technically called "forming into a hollow square." The title indicates the character of the formation. The regiment was formed in a square, four deep, which made it look like a human fence around a vacant lot. I said "vacant," but that is hardly correct, for there was something always inside the square —the officers. The enlisted men formed the fence or wall inside of which the commissioned officers were comparatively secure.

All the rifles were equipped with bayonets. The outer edge of men knelt on one knee and held the rifle with the bayonet sticking out at an angle of about forty-five degrees. Behind them, stood another row of men at a charge bayonet. This made a double row of glistening bayonets sticking toward the suppositious enemy, like a *chevaux de frise*. The two inner rows of men were there ready to shoot their guns over the heads of the men in front.

These hollow squares were supposed to be invincible. And so far as an attack of cavalry was concerned they were practically so. No troop of horses could stand or run against that array of bayonets if the men only stood to their posts. But the trouble was that it took some time to get the men to understand this. When they saw a whole company of horsemen galloping toward them, the natural instinct was to get out of the way, and even in the practice attacks that we had it was seldom that the men all stood their ground.

Useful as this precautionary drill was, however, we never had occasion to use it in actual warfare. The Thirteenth Regiment, so far as I ever heard, never was attacked by cavalry at a time when they were in a hollow square.

Another drill that we had was called "bayonet drill." This was a pet scheme of Major Grimes, who seemed to always imagine that the regiment would some time get into a hand-to-hand conflict with the enemy, and that it would be a good thing to know just exactly how to stick the sharp end of the bayonet through the enemy's intestines, give it a sort of corkscrew twist, and then be able to complacently contemplate the sight of a rebel writhing in death agony on the ground.

With that, the "guard," and "tierce," and "parry," and other things, and the jumping sideways and forwards and backwards, it would be hard to imagine any more vigorous sort of exercise than the bayonet drill. We were put through it day after day, till every man became a sort of an athlete of the high jumping variety.

This was only a silly waste of time. Perhaps every regiment in the army had to go through the experiment at one time or another, but it was finally dropped as useless. It is unnecessary to state that very seldom did the two armies come close enough together to indulge in the interesting pastime of making holes in each other's anatomy. And even if they had, under the exciting circumstances it is not likely that any man would ever have remembered the first thing about the scientific instructions he had received in the best way of doing it.

The worst experience I ever had while at this place was to be detailed one day to go out and build a corduroy road. A corduroy road is made by placing felled trees side by side along the road, like the planking on a bridge. This made a pretty rough sort of a thoroughfare, and the wagons went bumping over it at a fearful rate, while as for marching over it, it was something terrible. But it was better than deep mud at that.

Now I had never cut down a tree in my life. When we were building log houses John Butterworth did the felling and I helped in other ways. But this day I was given an ax and set to work cutting down trees.

The first two or three went all right, although I was always in a quandary as to which way the confounded thing was going to fall. All that I could do was to wait till it began to move and then scamper out of the way. Some of the fellows knew how to make the tree fall in any direction they desired, but that was a mystery utterly beyond my comprehension. My trees fell whither they wisted, and they generally wisted to fall in a manner that threatened the life of some of the other fellows who did not see the thing coming in their direction.

The first two or three were small trees, not over six or seven inches in diameter.

But then the confounded officer in command of the work took it into his head that larger trees were indispensable, and he set me to work on one at least three feet thick, a tremendous fellow. It was a tall pine, and the wood seemed to be extraordinarily hard and tough, while my ax appeared to be as dull as a hoe.

I contemplated the job with discouragement, but went to work with a will. I never could see what fun Gladstone could find in cutting down trees. There isn't much to amuse a man in England if he calls that fun.

I hacked and hacked. I cut on one side and a while on the other, trying to see which side of the tree was the softest. My hands, unaccustomed to such work, became covered with blisters, my arms and legs ached, and the sweat poured from me in a stream, notwithstanding the fact of its being midwinter. At the end of two hours I had not succeeded in making more than a shallow ridge in the tree, hardly enough to have set the sap running.

Then I gave up in disgust. I called the sergeant and

told him there was no use of my trying to cut down that tree. I never did such a thing before, and told him that it would take six months for me to get that tree down, and I felt sure that when it did come down it would kill somebody, for I had no idea as to which way it would fall.

The sergeant took pity on me and told me to take a rest. He called another man, a tall fellow from the Wisconsin regiment, a backwoodsman who had been accustomed to that sort of work.

"Which way do you want this tree to fall, sergeant?" he asked.

"Right about here," said the non-commissioned officer, marking the place in the ground with his foot.

I was filled with admiration. Here was a man who could not only cut down a tree but who could make it fall just where he wanted it to fall. And he did so. It seemed but a few moments, with a remarkably few dexterous blows with the ax, that the tree was nearly cut through. The wood seemed a good deal softer and the ax much sharper for that man than it had been for me, somehow.

Finally the tree wavered, moved and fell. It came down almost exactly where the sergeant had marked the place for it to fall. This was the difference between a man used to the work of cutitng down a tree and one who had never had any experience in that sort of thing. But I was willing to bet a day's rations of hard-tack that I could beat that man setting type.

I didn't have to cut any more trees. They set me to work helping to carry them and at other things, till night came, and I went back to camp probably more tired out and generally used up than I had ever been before. I begged the captain that he would never let me be detailed for such a service again, as I was never calculated for that kind of work. Captain Hopkins did not know that I had been sent to do that sort of labor, and he laughed at my description of the ordeal. But he saw to it that I never had anything like it again, and truth compels me to state that Company K escaped the most of that sort of menial labor.

Of course there came times, in the face of a battle,

when every man, and sometimes some of the officers, had to come to the rescue and assist in the hurried construction of breastworks. On such occasions, however, a sort of feeling that it was necessary for personal safety overcame the repugnance to such labor.

These things are described because they are legitimately a part of the life of a soldier. The men in the army had something else to do besides shooting at the enemy and reducing the number of Confederate soldiers.

The paymaster was long a-coming in those days. We were months behind with our pay. The most of us had gone to the fullest extent in running credit at the sutler's, and we missed the little luxuries that we had been accustomed to get there. One day there was a good deal of mysterious consultation and whispering around camp, which for some time I could not get the hang of. But after a while the other fellows took me into their confidence and let me into the scheme.

The sutler had just laid in a new stock. His counters were piled high with all sorts of tempting dainties. In the rear part of the tent we even saw many bottles of whiskey and other things that made the boys' mouths water, for "it had been a long time between drinks." Perhaps had there been plenty of it within reach I would never have thought of such a thing, but now that it was practically impossible to get, the more I thought of it the more it seemed as if a good horn of the real old stuff would be just about the thing.

The scheme was nothing more or less than to make a midnight raid on the sutler's tent and help ourselves to the first things within reach.

Butterworth, my pard, did not altogether approve of the idea, but he was overruled, and there were enough of us without him to carry the thing through. The plan was for about twenty of us to wait for a signal, and simultaneously sneak out in the middle of the night, and then raid the tent of the sutler. I'll admit that I was one of the twenty midnight prowlers, and burglars, if you will. The others were all in it in a secondary sense. That is, they were to keep watch, give whatever alarm might be necessary, and afterward partake of the booty.

Midnight came, and I quietly sneaked out and walked softly to the sutler's tent. I found the others there and ready for the depredation.

The leader of the gang gave the signal, and the attack began.

CHAPTER LXIV.

THE SUTLER RAIDED.

The plan had been to cut the ropes that braced up the tent, on all sides at once, so that the whole business would come down together and then make the raid on the good things there concealed.

Usually the sutler and his assistants slept in the back part of the tent and we supposed that they were there this time. Our plan had been to grab the things and hide them somewhere before the sutlers could extricate themselves from the folds of the tent and get after us. We had the places all ready to hide the articles, and we were to feign sleep and profess ignorance of the whole thing if any officers came around afterward to make inquiries.

We were destined to have better luck than this, however. For some reasons none of the sutlers were asleep in the tent that night. The cords were cut simultaneously on all sides and the tent came down with a flop in a heap, just as expected. It is hardly necessary to state that what we were after was the whiskey, or "commissary," as it was called then. We each grabbed a bottle of the supposed whiskey and hastened back to our log houses, hid the liquor, and fell asleep with a suddenness that would have surprised a hypnotist.

We waited patiently for the expected alarm, but none came. Everything was as quiet as usual. Directly some one poked his head in the door of our house and said that there was not a sign of life around the sutler's tent, and that we might go and help ourselves to whatever else we wanted. We did so, and could scarcely find room to hide the purloined goods.

Then we proceeded to sample the liquor. I didn't know exactly at the time what was in the bottle Butterworth and I had, nor did we care, so long as it was liquor, but it tasted just like the juice off the mince prepared for a mince pie. It was nectar!

But the confounded thing flew to my head, and that was the last I remembered till morning, when Orderly Sergeant Van Orden stuck in his head and asked how it was that we did not turn out for the morning roll call. I got up as best I could, for my head was spinning around like a top. Butterworth had evidently taken less, for he was not so badly affected. When we got out to the line there were only seven men there. There should have been some seventy. Most of the rest were really sick. And no wonder, when it is explained that the liquor on which we had got boozed was Hostetter's bitters!

By some bad luck the captain had taken a notion that morning to turn out to see the reveille roll call, and he asked how it was that the other men had not turned out.

"I don't know, captain," replied Hank Van Orden, the orderly sergeant. "I can't wake them up this morning. I don't know what is the matter with them."

Captain Hopkins stuck his head in one log hut and then another. From both he brought an empty bottle.

"I guess this accounts for it," said he. "What does this mean, anyhow?"

Sergeant Van Orden hadn't been let into the racket, and he was in ignorance of what it did mean. He told the captain so.

"The whole company's drunk," said the captain. "Where did they get the liquor, I would like to know."

Just at this moment the adjutant came down.

"Captain, are any of your men in this?" he asked.

"In what?" asked Captain Hopkins.

"In this robbery of the sutler's tent. Don't you see that it is down? That isn't the worst of it. There has been a robbery. Nearly all the liquor there was in the tent has been stolen, as well as some other things."

The captain pointed to the two bottles that he had thrown on the ground.

"That looks somewhat suspicious, doesn't it?" he said.

"The colonel will be furious when he hears of this,"

said the adjutant. "There's trouble ahead for all who were concerned in it. Try and find out which of your men are implicated."

I began to shake in my boots, but said not a word. I think that I was the last man in the company the captain would have suspected, for I was there all right in the line for roll call, and the captain knew that I wasn't much of a hand for liquor anyway.

Well, the captain and orderly sergeant made a search, and a partially emptied bottle was found in nearly every tent or hut in the company. The sutler must have had a big stock on hand, for not only was Company K concerned, but several of the other companies had been in the scheme, and a similar discovery was made there also.

Now I never knew how it came out the way it did, but as a matter of fact not a single man was punished for that night's escapade. In the first place it was against the rule for the sutlers to have more liquor or "bitters" on hand than just sufficient to be used for medical purposes, or perhaps an occasional little "blow out" on the part of the officers. Then the sutler we had at that time was a mean sort of a fellow, a regular Shylock, who took advantage not only of the men, but of the officers as well, whenever the opportunity offered. So he did not have much sympathy as far as that was concerned. But be it as it may, none of us were ever punished, and not much was said about the matter beyond a little "general order" on dress parade that the men should remember that they should act as law abiding citizens in the army the same as if they were at home, and that it was as much of a crime to break into a store there and steal as it was in a city. This was the only hint, in an official way, that we ever had about the matter and it was the nearest that we ever had to a punishment.

Indeed the result was the other way, for the next day orders came that the credit at the sutler's would be extended, and the door was opened so that we were able to get whatever we liked on the strength of the credit of future months' pay. So as a matter of fact, instead of being punished, we were practically rewarded for the part we had taken in the robbery of the sutler's tent.

They say that there are some kinds of liquor that will keep a fellow drunk several days. This must have been the sort that we had on that occasion, for it was several days before I fully recovered from that debauch. I felt heartily ashamed of myself, not only for that, but because it was the first time I had ever been concerned in what might be called a burglary at night. And it was the last time I was ever guilty of such a crime. But then we were soldiers, and there are few men who served in the army that cannot relate some such experience.

We didn't often get the chance to obtain liquor while in the front. Occasionally after great exposure it would be dealt out sparingly to the men. I remember one occasion.

It was while we were stationed at Fairfax that we went out on one of those mysterious raids or reconnaissances, and we had to ford a creek. The water was up to our waists and it was very cold.

It so happened that we had been much troubled with the pestiferous *pendiculus investimenti* and the surgeon had said that anguinum, or blue ointment, was a good thing to kill the nits. We had saturated the seams of our clothing with this salve, which is largely composed of mercury.

There is danger in getting wet after using any sort of a mercurial ointment, for the result is salivation. This, judging from my own personal experience, is one of the most horrible sensations. The saliva runs from the mouth, the eyes water and the whole body aches terribly.

When we laid ourselves down that night on the wet ground, soaked to the skin as we were, the flesh seemed too soft to bear the weight of one's bones, and one could feel his skeleton from the top of his head to the soles of his feet. The sensation is simply horrible. One felt as if he were nothing but a skeleton, and every individual bone appeared to sink into the soft flesh with a sickening pain.

It was then that the surgeon ordered to be dispensed a good ration of "commissary," and if liquor ever did a man good it was then and there.

After being at Fairfax Station for a while the Thirteenth Regiment was ordered to change camp and we marched to Stafford Court House, a place that enters very largely into the history of the regiment, for it was from that place that we went into the greatest engagement in which the Thirteenth ever participated.

CHAPTER LXV.

AN UNEXPECTED INVITATION.

We were stationed at Stafford Court House from the early part of March till near the end of April, and taking it altogether it was the quietest time we ever had while in the army. It was officially given out that there would be no more fighting or marching till the spring fairly opened; and we were in fact in training for the arduous campaign of 1863, which, as all will remember, was the turning year of the war. It may be truthfully stated that till the middle of 1863 it was a grave question which would win, the North or the South. England and other foreign countries had manifested a strong sympathy for the Confederacy. Peace commissioners were endeavoring to settle the contest in a manner that would have left the South the winner. The Confederacy appeared to be more desperate and determined than ever, and throughout the North there was a feeling of despair and a sentiment that the best thing to do would be to give up the struggle before more lives were sacrificed.

But the fact that the North meant business was evident from the Emancipation Proclamation of President Lincoln. That settled all questions of peace. It was from that moment "a fight to the finish," with equal determination on both sides. No one could foretell the result. It was an even contest till Gettysburg, and then the tide turned in favor of the North, although it took nearly two years after that to finally suppress the rebellion.

Many of the men about this time succeeded in obtaining furloughs. I had the opportunity to go home for ten days, but did not. Only so many were allowed to each company, and I gave up my chance in favor of one of the men, who had a sick wife at home.

I was rather glad that I did so, for all the men came back discouraged, downhearted and despairing. They had become imbued with the feeling of discouragement that prevailed at home, and it was worse coming back than the original enlistment, for every soldier, when leaving home from his furlough, bade good-by to his family with the impression that it was the last time he would ever see them. For some of them indeed it was the last time!

We had not been long at Stafford when several of the companies of the Thirteenth were ordered on detached service at White House Landing, on Aquia creek. There was nothing but a small dock there, where curious little stern wheel steamboats landed provisions from Washington. Our duties there were to be 'longshoremen or stevedores, but Butterworth and I did not go on duty the first day.

We spent the entire day building a log house, and by night had a fine one. But we slept in it only one night. The next morning we were ordered back to camp and another company took our place. I never knew why Company K had been returned in this manner. But I was not sorry for it for one, for the work of unloading provisions from the boat and placing them in the baggage wagons was laborious.

Many of the men received boxes from home containing quantities of good things, and many of them also contained whiskey. This made some of the men drunk, and after that all the boxes were inspected by the officers before being turned over to the men. Three of the boxes contained nothing but whiskey!

The officers took charge of all this. What they did with the liquor history does not tell, but one might guess!

Another discovery was made by the inspection of those boxes. Fully one-third of them contained citizen's clothes. It looked as if one-third of the recipients of favors from home were making preparations to desert. In fact there had been a good many desertions before this, and the officers wondered how the men had succeeded in getting away without detection. This explained the business. After the wholesale confiscation of citizens' clothes the desertions were materially lessened.

We had considerable fun in the sporting line while at Stafford. Several times we obtained permission to go to Aquia creek, where the fishing was good, and we caught many shad with the most primitive sort of nets. The greatest fun, however, was in shooting ducks.

I never saw so many wild ducks in my life. The river seemed to literally swarm with them. We had no shot guns, nor even shot, for that matter, but we got around this very nicely by cutting bullets into small bits called "slugs," and shooting them from the rifles. Indeed we became quite expert, shooting the ducks with the full sized bullets, although naturally this tore the birds to pieces so that they were practically useless.

The greatest difficulty was in getting the ducks after we had shot them out on the river. There were no dogs of course, and only one small boat, a sort of dug-out, which had to be utilized in turn by the men. A large proportion of the ducks consequently were not recovered, but we got enough for our own use, and we had duck cooked in every possible and impossible style.

One of our duties at Stafford Court House was to erect a gigantic stockade. What this was for I don't know. There was no enemy anywhere around at the time, and there seemed to be no possibility of there ever being an engagement in that neighborhood. But I presume that the theory was that if we were kept busy we would not get into mischief.

One day while at Stafford Court House, Captain Hopkins came to me and asked me if I didn't want a day off?

"A day off? What do you mean, captain?" asked I, wonderingly.

"Well, if you do," he replied, "you are at liberty to go. Come to my tent and I will give you a pass. You will also find a horse there for you."

A horse for me! What could the captain mean?

However, I went up to the captain's tent and sure enough there was a horse—two of them, in fact. Both were saddled and held by a tall cavalryman with yellow trimmed riding jacket and boots.

"This is Crowell, orderly," said Captain Hopkins by way of introduction. The big cavalryman looked at me, I imagined not with a very high degree of admiration. And I didn't look very pretty. I had not had my hair cut in some time, and looked like a foot ball player. I had been sleeping in the dirt so much that I presented anything but a tidy appearance. But then I was as well fixed as the average soldier.

"General Stagg presents his compliments," said the orderly, "and invites you to come and take dinner with him."

General Stagg? For a moment I could not recall who that could be. Then I remembered. It was Peter Stagg, the brother of my old companion in the *Guardian* office, John Stagg, who had enlisted in the Eleventh New Jersey—the same John Stagg who is to-day the chief of the Paterson Fire Department.

I remembered that Peter, who was also a Paterson boy, had moved to Michigan when he was married, and knew that he had entered the service as a captain in the First Michigan Cavalry, but I had not heard that he had become a general.

"Do you mean Peter Stagg, of the First Michigan Cavalry?" I asked the orderly.

"Yes," was the reply. "He was our colonel. He has been promoted to brigadier-general. He sent me over to bring you to our camp and have dinner with him."

"Well, well," said I, in amazement, "and so Peter Stagg's a general. And he wants me to come to take dinner with him. Well, well!" I couldn't get over the surprise.

"Yes," said the orderly, "and he sent his horse over for you to ride. This is the critter."

I looked at the horse. I hadn't particularly noticed the animal before, for I was so astonished that Peter Stagg had become a general (and by the way he was the only Paterson boy that ever did become a general), that I hadn't noticed anything. But when I saw that horse I was struck with terror.

I never had much experience riding horseback. Taking my father's docile old nag to water was about the extent of my experience in that direction. But here before me was a big black stallion, that looked as if he could only be ridden by a Buffalo Bill or a cowboy. I confess that I weakened. But I didn't want to let the cavalryman think I was afraid.

"Say, pard," said I familiarly—and my familiar tone at once put me on good terms with my to-be-escort—"I am a pretty looking fellow to take dinner with a general of cavalry, am I not? I look as if I ought to go to the barber's and tailor's before I tackle anything like that. I think I had better send my regrets."

"Oh, that's all right," said the orderly. "You're all right. Besides, the general said that I must insist on your coming if you could get away, and the captain here says that's all right. So come along. Here's your horse."

Again I looked at the skittish looking stallion. Then I looked at the tamer looking animal of the orderly, which I could distinguish was a private soldier's steed from the comparative plainness of its trappings.

"Hadn't I better ride your horse, orderly?" I asked. "He looks less frisky. This stallion here will break my neck."

"No," replied the orderly, "you take the general's critter. He is as gentle as a kitten. You couldn't ride mine. He is a bucker and would throw you off before you got half a mile on the way."

"How far is General Stagg's camp from here?" I asked.

"About twelve miles. It is straight across the country. We don't follow the road, but cut across lots. It's a good route and a pleasant ride. You will enjoy it, I'm sure."

"I will if that horse doesn't break my neck," said I, "but I suppose I will have to tackle it."

The boys had begun to gather around, wondering what was going on. Some of them envied me the chance of the trip. Others I thought regarded me with admiration on account of having been honored with an invitation to dine with a general. But Stansfield took the starch out of me with the remark he made.

"Say, Joe," said he, "if you get back alive from your ride on that horse you're a lucky cuss. I wouldn't get on that stallion's back for a farm."

"Oh, I'm not afraid," I replied, jauntily. But I lied; I was scared to death. I nearly fell off with trembling.

We started on our ride, and to tell the truth I never expected to survive the journey.

CHAPTER LXVI.

I DINE WITH THE GENERAL.

I HADN'T ridden far, however, on General Stagg's stallion before I began to feel perfect confidence. A nicer saddle horse no man ever strode. But I had to take some instructions before I knew how to guide the animal.

When I pulled the right hand rein he turned to the left, and *vice versâ*. Either the horse or I had lost the compass.

"That horse is trained for the cavalry service," said the orderly, "and you have to handle him a little different from what you would a farm horse. Just hold the reins together in the left hand. When you want to turn to the right, hold your hand over to the right. That presses the bridle reins against the left side of the horse and makes him go to the right. When you want to go to the left you hold the hand over to the left, so that the rein presses on the right side."

"Then," said I, "you really pull the left side of his bit to make him go to the right, and the right side of his bit to turn to the left. Is that it?"

"I s'pose it is," replied my escort. "But cavalrymen don't pay any attention to the bit. They drive by the rein. The right hand is supposed to be busy with carbine or saber, and only the left is used in guiding the critter. Now if you want him to lope, give a couple of quick jerks upward, and if he is loping and you want a gallop, jab in the spurs."

I hadn't put on the spurs, however. Nothing could induce me to do that, or I would have had the horse running away in short order. Loping was rapid enough for me.

"If you want to bring him to a walk again," continued the orderly, going on with his equestrian instructions, "just pull gently on the reins, and a good hard pull will bring him to a standstill. That's the way to drive the critter with the bridle. But generally we do it with our knees."

"With your knees?" I asked.

"Yes, we don't bother much with the bridle, for often we have both hands busy in a scrimmage. When you want to start, give a 'cluck.' When you want the horse to lope, press the two knees against his withers two or three times, sharply. Do it again if you want him to gallop. If you want him to turn to the right, press the left knee only. If to the left, press the right knee. If you want to stop, press both knees hard."

I went through all these things and the noble animal obeyed like a child—a good deal better than some children, by the way. I never rode, before nor since, such a well trained animal. Riding him was like sitting in a rocking-chair. I was delighted with the experience, for it was not long before I had perfect confidence restored, and felt as self-possessed as if I had been riding horseback all my life.

But I was not altogether self possessed for another reason. I was overcome with the idea of being the guest of a general officer. Only those who have been in the army can appreciate the vast gulf that exists between a private and a brigadier-general.

And a brigadier-general of cavalry was more than a brigadier-general of infantry. In army etiquette and precedence the cavalry general comes ahead of the infantry general. And then a brigade of cavalry is as big, so far as the ground it covers is concerned and its military importance and pomp, as a whole corps of infantry. There was a peculiar dash and show about a high cavalry officer that no infantry commander ever attained. And yet, all the way, I couldn't help repeating to myself, "Pete Stagg a brigadier-general! Pete Stagg a general?" And the last time I saw him he was working at his trade in the locomotive works, if I remembered correctly.

After a pleasant ride of twelve or fifteen miles, the

camp of the cavalry brigade commanded by General Peter Stagg loomed into sight.

General Stagg's headquarters were quite pretentious. Instead of a tent it was a good sized barrack made of rough boards, the cracks between which were slatted so that it afforded perfect protection from the weather. The general's brigade was in winter quarters and it was the most comfortable and complete thing of the sort I ever saw in the front.

The general came to the doorway of his house as I rode up, and greeted me cordially. Had I also been a brigadier-general there could not have been a warmer or more friendly welcome. I must confess that I felt a little ashamed. I was only a private, with all that implied, and my clothing was not very creditable for even a private.

On the other hand, the general, who had just been superintending some maneuver, was in full uniform, as bright and spick as a militia officer, and there was a dash and vivacity about his manner that was altogether different from the plain mechanic I had remembered in Paterson. He was surrounded by a glittering staff of colonels and majors and captains, and the scene was so dazzling that I felt extremely abashed, to say the least.

But the cordiality manifested from him of the star to the stripeless private was so hearty, and the consequent attitude of the officers around him so condescending, as I was introduced as "My old friend, Crowell," by the general, that I soon felt at home, and for the time being forgot altogether the difference between our ranks.

I do not altogether remember the details of that day's visit. I do remember, however, that we had a good dinner—wonderfully good considering the place and circumstances—and I was filled with wonder as to where they had got all the provisions and delicacies that made up the *menu*. The wind-up of the dinner was a sort of punch that was very palatable, but which for a few moments made my head swim. That dinner impressed me strongly as to the difference between the lobscouse of the high privates and the tempting lay-out of the general officers. All the while I felt my subordinate position keenly, although I tried my best to put my brightest and most nonchalant side forward.

We lingered long at the table, which, by the way, was spread in a large barrack back of the general's headquarters, and in which all the officers participated. And many were the stories and experiences related, which gave an interesting insight to the exciting and dangerous life of a cavalryman. Of the stories told, I particularly remember one. It was by the general himself:

"It was down on the retreat from the Peninsula," said he, "when we were halting as if uncertain whether we should continue toward Washington, or go back toward Richmond, that we stopped on the way for a few days. I met an old friend of mine from another Michigan regiment, of which he was the colonel, and invited him to dinner. Now it happened that we were rather short of rations just then, and it was hard to get anything out of the usual line of provisions. The worst of it all was that we had run out of pork entirely.

"But," continued the general, "my cook had somehow managed to get hold of a couple of good cabbages. This was something so unusual that I thought a cabbage and pork dinner would be an acceptable novelty to my guest. When it was served there were only three or four thin slices of pork, which were spread around the sides of the dish of cabbage, as a sort of garnishment. It made it look very tempting. I wondered where Nick had got that pork, but said nothing.

"There were half a dozen or so officers at the mess that day; when each one was asked if he would have a piece of pork, he saw what a small supply there was and politely answered no. So there was not a mouthful of the pork eaten. The party seemed so delighted with the cabbage that they were satisfied. The dinner was a success, and all expressed themselves as pleased with having had the opportunity of partaking of a dish which they had not seen for many a day.

"I saw the cook remove the pork from the table with some satisfaction, for I thought that would come in good for breakfast in the morning. But when breakfast came, I looked in vain for the pork. I asked the cook what he had done with it.

" 'Say, Nick,' said I, 'where is that pork that was

left over from dinner? I might as well have it for breakfast. We have not had meat for so long that I am hungry for some.'

"The darkey hesitated in making reply, and seemed strangely nonplussed. But I insisted on an answer. I began to suspect that the confounded nigger had eaten the pork himself.

"'Ex-ex-excuse me, massa, I done gone take dat po'k back again.'

"'Took the pork back again?' I asked, 'what do you mean by that?'

"'Well, you know, massa, dat dere was no po'k in de com'sarry, an' I done gone an' borrid et.'

"'Borrowed it?'

"'Yes, massa, I borrid dot po'k from Cap'n Wilkins, ob de Fust Ill'noy, an' when you'ns were through I done tuk et back again. Dis nigger only done borrid et. I tole de cap'n so when I done got it.'

"'That was a risky thing to do, Nick,' I told him. 'Now suppose we had eaten that pork, where would you have been? You couldn't have taken it back then?'

"'Yous cawn't fool dis nigger, gen'ral,' replied the confounded darkey. 'I done know'd better. I know'd that when gen'lmens dine, an' dar's only a little bit ob ennythin', dey nebber teches et. I done know'd et. I done know'd it wouldn't be teched. I know'd I cud took dat po'k all back ag'in, widout a brack in de skin.'

"And so it was. The shrewd darkey had waited on tables long enough to know that when there is very little of anything on a dish at dinner none of the guests is likely to touch it, out of politeness. But it struck me that it was a mighty big risk to run, under the circumstances."

After dinner we sat and smoked and talked about Paterson and things at home till the time for the afternoon dress parade. Here I was given a horse and accompanied the general as an orderly, and as there were two or three other privates mounted in that capacity, I did not feel much abashed. But they had given me another horse, which was not as good a one as the general's, and when the staff galloped along the line with me following them, I had a difficult job to hang fast to the saddle.

Escorted by the orderly who had come for me in the morning, I rode back to the camp of the Thirteenth late in the afternoon, after having had a most enjoyable day, and passed through an experience not often allotted to a private soldier. The distinction of having been invited to dinner with a general also set me up a peg or so in the opinion of my companions. No civilian can fully appreciate the influence of little things like this.

En passant, speaking of General Stagg, reminds me that his brother John, who originally enlisted in the Eleventh New Jersey Infantry, was later in the war promoted to a lieutenancy in the First Michigan Cavalry and served as an aid-de-camp on General Stagg's staff. As before said, John is now a sort of general himself, being in command of the Paterson Fire Department.

From that time on, till the end of the war, I always remembered Peter Stagg as the dashing cavalry general surrounded by a brilliant array of staff officers. The picture was, as it were, photographed on my memory.

Great was the shock, therefore, when I next visited him. I had remained in the service for a year or so after the war was ended on special service in the Freedmen's Bureau. But the main portion of the army had returned to their homes and settled down to the routine of citizens' lives.

Great was my surprise, I say, when I saw Peter Stagg. He had opened a little grocery store on Main Street, and there I called.

"Is the general in?" I asked.

"The what?" inquired the half-grown lad I had addressed.

"The general," I repeated. "General Stagg?"

"Oh, it's Pete, you mean. Yes, he's in the back part of the store, waiting on a customer."

And there I found General Stagg, wearing a long grocer's apron, and measuring out a quart of kerosene for a woman!

The transformation from the picture in mind to the reality before me, nearly knocked me over. But it was the same welcome, the same hearty manner. Peter Stagg was the same whether in a general's uniform or in a grocer's apron.

> "Rank is but the guinea's stamp,
> A man's a man for a' that,"

said Robby Burns; but still, I fain would repeat, the change was startling.

And when I went down the street, whom did I meet but Captain Scott, my old company commander, standing on the corner of Broadway, yelling at the top of his voice, peddling whips!

As for myself, I went back to the *Guardian* office to set type!

But there were many exciting scenes to pass through between the time I took that dinner with General Stagg and the time I next had a composing stick in my hand. The most terrible scenes and experiences were yet to come. And I am getting close upon them!

CHAPTER LXVII.

AGAIN WE START.

It was the purpose of the author in writing this story to present some idea of the daily life and experience of a private soldier. It was to give an inside history of real army life in war times, rather than follow the stilted route of maneuvers, movements, engagements and statistics. As said earlier in the story, the experiences and services of the Thirteenth New Jersey merely formed the thread on which the incidents were strung.

And yet the truth as to dates and names has been adhered to, so that to the extent to which this is carried, it is practically a history of the regiment to which the writer belonged. The further history of the detailed incidents of the campaign and individual experiences, however, would be largely repetitive of what has already been described, and henceforth only new experiences will be detailed, those similar to what have already been described being cursorily referred to.

There still remain, however, some novel incidents and adventures to be described, and some scenes more terrible than anything yet presented to the reader, and it will consequently be to the advantage and interest of the latter to patiently pursue the story to the end.

I interpolate these remarks here, because it is an appropriate place. The Thirteenth Regiment at this particular time was going through the most inactive period of its entire experience. Never before and never afterward did it have such a long rest as at Stafford Court House.

Yet we were not entirely idle, for the ordinary duties of a soldier do not leave much time, whether it be in camp or on the march. The term "idleness" is only comparative, when mentioned in connection with a soldier.

I remember one incident of a personal nature. I heard that my Uncle David, a lieutenant in the Thirty-fifth New Jersey, was at Aquia creek, and obtained a pass to go and see him. It involved a walk of five or six miles through the thickest and deepest mud. When I reached his camp, my trousers were besmeared to the knees and my shoes were filled with the red pigment. My uncle went to the sutler's and presented me with a nine dollar pair of boots, coming to the knees. They were admirable for the purpose of keeping out the mud, and I was heartily pleased with the present.

My uncle probably never knew what became of those boots. On the next march they hurt my feet so that I temporarily traded them with Cornelius Mersereau, one of my companions, for a pair of English shoes that had been captured from a blockade runner, bound for the Confederacy. There is no use talking, nothing is as good as low, flat, broad soled shoes for marching.

But I only intended the exchange to be temporary, till after we had concluded the march. Alas, Mersereau was killed in the next battle, and his feet swelled so that I could not pull off the boots, and they were buried with him at Chancellorsville. Of that, later. Mersereau's name is carved on the base of the soldiers' monument at the falls in Paterson. The boots are absorbed by the soil of Virignia, somewhere.

It was just about this time that there were numerous changes among the officers in consequence of the resignations and consequent promotions. Lieutenant Colonel Swords, who, despite his name, was a peaceably disposed man, resigned. Captain John Grimes was promoted from captain to major. But the greatest sensation was caused by the promotion of Priva'e Franklin Murphy, of Company D, to the position of second lieutenant. As said before somewhere the promotion of a private over the heads of the sergeants and others in the direct line of promotion, always created a sensation and not a little indignation over what was esteemed a sense of injustice. As a general rule, it indicated a "pull" somewhere that was not popular among those concerned.

There was consequently not a little kicking at first

when Murphy made his first appearance on parade ground in a brand new uniform of a commissioned officer. But he proved such a kind-hearted officer, and seemed disposed to put on so few airs, that this feeling soon wore off, and Frank Murphy became one of the most popular officers of the regiment.

I refer to him particularly, because this Frank Murphy has become one of the most prominent men in the State of New Jersey. His name was mentioned recently in connection with the office of United States Senator, and he was also spoken of as a candidate for Governor of New Jersey in 1895. This is the same Franklin Murphy.

Along about the middle of April (this was in 1863, remember), we received word that the army was about to be honored with another visit from President Lincoln. The other parts of the Army of the Potomac had been reviewed, and this demonstration included the Twelfth Corps, under command of General Slocum, only. The review was a grand success and a magnificent sight.

The corps included about twenty thousand men, comprising all branches of the service. It marched to a large field about four miles from camp, and there went through all the evolutions incident to such an occasion.

The army was never in better condition than at the present time. The men had had a good rest, for some time the rations had been plenty and good, and all the regiments had been perfected in their drill. In fact the army was recuperated, fresh, and in magnificent shape for the beginning of the campaign which we all anticipated as soon as the spring fairly opened. The long rest had put everybody in good condition bodily, and every man's spirits were proportionately buoyant.

While we all knew that there was arduous marching and hard fighting in store for us, yet no one felt downcast or discouraged. In fact, I might almost say that every man was eager for the fray. The desire to get into something active and less monotonous was universal.

Even our old, and for sometime forgotten, friend John Ick, prated not of "slaughter houses" and manifested such a desire to get started at something that he actually excited the admiration of Reddy Mahar. Without exception, I think I am safe in saying, the entire army was desirous of being "on the move."

It was not my luck at this last review in which President Lincoln participated to get anywhere near him. I was in the ranks while he rode down and around the line, and afterward marched past him in the review, but only got a somewhat distant glimpse of one I had almost come to regard as a personal friend.

I imagined, from what I saw of him, that he looked more gaunt and careworn than ever. It may have been imagination, but every succeeding time that I saw President Lincoln the more did he appear to me to be aging. And now that we can more fully appreciate what he had to go through, how could it have been otherwise?

Just about this time, the surgeon of the Thirteenth, Dr. J. J. H. Love, was promoted to the position of brigade surgeon-in-chief. This took him away from our immediate vicinity, greatly to our regret, for every soldier revered Dr. Love. He was, until his recent death, a highly respected citizen of Montclair, and held in great esteem far beyond the limits of that picturesque New Jersey town.

But at last the expected order to move was received. We were suppled with sixty rounds of ammunition per man.

That meant business!

The usual quantity carried by the soldier was about forty rounds. Sixty was never given out except on the eve of an expected battle of more than ordinary dimensions and importance. We were also directed to dispose of every superfluous article, and place ourselves in marching order in the fullest meaning of the word. We were "in it" now for fair.

On the 14th of April came the order, "Fall in, Thirteenth," and after the usual preliminary preparations, bustle and excitement, we started off—many never to return.

Little did we know then—and perhaps it is better that we did not—that in a short time the Thirteenth Regiment would be back in that very camp, with decimated numbers, torn and shattered, after having passed through one of the bloodiest conflicts, one of the most disastrous repulses of the whole war—the engagement that has gone into history as "The Battle of Chancellorsville!"

CHAPTER LXVII.

"MEN THAT AIN'T AFRAID OF HELL."

On to Chancellorsville!

Now for a battle that was doubtless one of the bloodiest and most disastrous of the war. And yet the Union army never started into a campaign more confident of success. Little did anybody apprehend that it was to be the most terrible repulse ever sustained by the armies of the North!

The army was in magnificent shape. The discipline was perfect. General Hooker had won the confidence and esteem of every man under his command, from the highest to the lowest. The spirit of his dash and vigor had permeated rank and file, line and staff, and the soldiers believed themselves part of an army that was invincible, under a commander who was unconquerable.

Colonel T. H. Ruger, the fighting commander of the Third Wisconsin, had been promoted to brigadier general, and was in consequence our immediate commanding general. We had as much faith in him as a brigade commander as the army had in Hooker as the grand commander. The men had had a good rest, they were in fine condition physically and full of fight and spirit.

The sentiment was universal that the rebellion was about to be quenched, and that the coming battle would be the settler.

That it was going to be a terrible conflict was evident to everybody from the extensive and complete character of the preparations. It is unnecessary to go into all of the details in this respect. But it is significant to remark that soldiers were served with one hundred pounds of ammunition and eight days' rations just before starting on that fateful campaign, on April 27, 1863.

"'The plan of the campaign was that the Fifth, Eleventh and Twelfth (our) corps, should rapidly move up the Rappahannock and get into position in the extreme rear of the enemy at Fredericksburg, rendezvousing at Chancellorsville (of course we privates knew nothing about these plans at the time; I am here quoting from 'Toombs' Reminiscences,' Swinton, and other authorities). General Couch, with two divisions of the Second Corps, was to follow as far as United States Ford, and cross there as soon as the success of the first movement was apparent by the driving away of the enemy guarding that point. Reynolds, Sickles and Sedgwick, with the First, Third and Sixth Corps were to cross the Rappahannock below Fredericksburg and make a vigorous demonstration at that point."

Such the authorities say was the programme for the campaign, and it was really well planned, for it involved a simultaneous attack on the enemy from three sides, and a series of those flank movements which in battle are supposed to be invincible.

Nothing unusual from an ordinary march occurred for two days. There were no signs of the enemy and everything was as quiet and peaceful as a militia parade on the Fouth of July.

The only thing that specially attracted my attention was the ascension of a military balloon. It was a good sized balloon inflated with gas from a generator carried on wheels for the purpose. It ascended several hundred feet and from it we could see the two occupants scanning the enemy's country through their field glasses. The balloon was attached to the ground with a long rope, on a windlass, and at a given signal, the men below would wind up the windlass and haul the aeronauts down. I distinctly remember wondering what would happen if some rebel sent a bullet hole through the balloon while it was in the air.

On the afternoon of the same day I saw the first military telegraph. It was just being introduced and the men were drilling as we marched along, in preparation for its use in the coming battle. The men ran along like skirmishers, carrying poles about ten feet long, sharpened at one end, while the other had a sort of double fork, like the hook on the end of a cistern pole. Another lot of men would come along with wire on reels on a wagon, and this was strung on the poles about as fast as the horses could run. Three or four miles of telegraph line could be put up in an hour in this way, and removed in less time.

At each end of the line was an operator. The idea was a good one, but the movements of an army in battle are too rapid to use the telegraph much. I remember seeing the lines in the first part of the battle of Chancellorsville, but before long they were lying useless, scattered along the ground.

On the third day of our uneventful march, I think it was, we crossed the Rappahannock River on pontoon bridges, and were once more in what might be called the enemy's country. On the afternoon of the same day we approached the Rapidan River, and were about to cross it at Germania Ford, when we were suddenly interrupted and startled by a volley of musketry from the boys in the Third Wisconsin and Second Massachusetts, immediately in front of us.

We had suddenly pounced down upon a lot of rebels busily engaged in building a bridge over the river, and we captured nearly the entire party. They were a jolly lot of Johnnies, and wanted to know why we had not waited till they finished the bridge, so that we could cross the river easier!

There was one thing at this point that filled me with horror. As we approached the bank at the edge of the narrow river, we saw on the other side a rebel who had escaped capture and who was running over the open field. A big Wisconsin man alongside me lifted his rifle and aimed at the fleeing rebel.

"Don't shoot him," I cried. "Tell him to surrender!"

"To —— with him," replied the bloodthirsty Wisconsinian. "Dead rebs tell no tales!"

"But—" I started to say something more, but my voice was drowned by the report of the rifle, and the fleeing rebel dropped dead.

I did not relish that sort of warfare a bit. It looked to me like murder, this shooting down in cold blood one poor man. But when I ventured to express my sentiments to the slayer, he gruffly turned upon me and said:

"Say, young feller, when you know the devilishness of those varmints as well as I do, you won't be so chickenhearted. I never let pass a chance to kill every —— —— one of them I can. So just hold your wind, young feller."

I said nothing more, but I had my opinions about it just the same. It is one thing to stand in a line and shoot at a body of troops collectively shooting at you. It is quite another thing to shoot down a single human being in cold blood without giving him a chance for his life.

The bridge, as before stated, was not completed. The pontoon trains were some distance behind. It was necessary to cross at once, and we were ordered to do so. There was no alternative except to ford the stream.

The water was at least four feet deep. The current was very strong. We had to put our bayonets on our guns and hang our knapsacks, haversacks and cartridge boxes upon them, so as to carry them high over our shoulders to keep them from getting wet. Cavalry pickets were stationed a little further down the stream to catch those who were carried from their feet by the swift current, which, by the way, were not few.

We were wet to the skin and it was growing quite cold, as night was approaching. Fires were lighted to dry our clothing, and we were just gathering around to make ourselves comfortable, when Major Grimes dashed suddenly into our midst and yelled out:

"I want seven men that ain't afraid of hell!"

I don't know what impulse struck me. I, one of the biggest cowards in the army at that moment, volunteered as one of the seven men who had no fears for the future abode of the wicked.

It was a sudden impulse of some sort for which I could never account. I did not know of course what it meant. I did know that it meant some dangerous duty to perform. My comrades naturally looked surprised when I volunteered for this unknown horror.

I, of course, repented at once and felt like kicking myself for being so fresh. I wondered why I had answered as I did. But I wouldn't back out now. I would have been a laughing stock forever afterward. Indeed, after going that far, I would have stuck to it if I had positively known that I was to be killed in half an hour. But although I tried to look brave on the outside, everything inside of me was quaking with terror, and the cold chills were chasing each other down my back.

With my fellow volunteers I was marched to brigade headquarters, the party was duly formed, and, under the command of a captain, we started out for the unknown place that Major Grimes had described so calorically.

CHAPTER LXVIII.

JO-SI-ER AND HIS OLD' OMAN.

IF there was reliable proof that the real old-fashioned, orthodox, red-hot, fire and brimstone hell were of no longer duration than the Tophet described by the excited Major Grimes, I fear that there would be a good deal more wickedness in this world.

We were marched up the hill, and, like the famous forty thousand men of old, we were marched down again, and back into the camp of the Thirteenth Regiment. We were received with all sorts of jeers as to how we liked it, whether it was hot, and if we had returned for our linen dusters and fans! We assured our comrades that his Satanic Majesty was enjoying good health and was as active as ever, but he wanted more company, and we had come back for the rest of them.

We were justified in saying this, for we learned that it had been decided to send the entire Thirteenth Regiment out on picket that night, instead of only a smaller detachment. The enemy had been discovered, it was said, just in front and it was thought best to send out a very strong picket line. So the other fellows had to go through the same service as we few who had been so very fresh in volunteering.

I shall never forget that night. Remember, we were drenched to the skin from fording the Rapidan River, and the night was cold, as it is usually during the latter part of April, even in Virignia. There really isn't very much difference between the climate of Virginia and New Jersey, except perhaps in midsummer and midwinter. The spring and fall are about the same in both States.

We had advanced into the enemy's country, and the scouts had reported the rebels immediately in front of us. So quietly had the movement of this wing of the Union army been that the enemy evidently had no idea that we were so close upon them, and there was a likelihood of a collision at any time.

As said before, we were sent on picket on the very outposts. There was nothing between us and the rebels, and there wasn't supposed to be much space between us at that. No one was permitted to speak above a whisper for fear of its attracting attention. When I was placed on my post, which was in a thick woods, under a big tree, where it was as dark as Egypt, the officer of the guard instructed me in a low whisper, and I was advised to be unusually quiet. I was not even to march up and down the usual proverbial "beat." The noise of the footsteps might attract attention. Under no circumstances was a match to be struck for lighting a pipe or any other purpose.

Now this made it worse than ever. Being wet through it might have afforded considerable comfort to be able to keep moving to and fro. But to stand still, drenched as we were, made us shiver with the cold, and pretty soon my teeth were chattering a tattoo that made more noise than my footsteps would have made had I been patroling a beat.

But orders were orders and there was nothing to do but to do nothing—except shiver. I never suffered worse. Inside of half an hour I was almost paralyzed.

The night was very still. The slightest noise seemed to penetrate a long distance. Way out in front somewhere there was a subdued hum, as from distant voices, and they were supposed to be from the camps of the rebels. Every nerve seemed to be strung to the utmost tension, and one's ears, under such circumstances, were phonographic with their supernatural keenness.

The inactivity of the position finally made me drowsy, and I feared it was the drowsiness that preceded the act of freezing to death. I shook myself to arouse my senses, and was wondering if I could stand it for another hour or so, when suddenly my acute ears caught the sound of breaking twigs. Instantly I was all attention. I at once brought my rifle into position and raised the hammer.

Nearer and nearer came the sound of the crackling twigs, till it seemed to be within ten feet of me, when, in a subdued voice, I said:

"Halt! Who comes there?"

"Fo' de Lo'd's sake! What's dat?"

That was the answer that came to my military salutation. It was so unexpected, so different from what I expected, and withal so comical, that I came near laughing aloud. But I was suspicious. It was the voice of a negro, but it might be the assumed tone of a rebel scout. So I again said:

"Who comes there, I say? Answer, or I will shoot!"

"Fo' de Lo'd's sake, massa, don't shoot dis poor nigger. I'se doin' nothing. I done gone done nothin'. Doan' shoot! Oh, Lo'd! Oh, Lo'd!"

"Come here and let me see what you look like," I said.

There was a rush that frightened me, and before I could fully realize it, there kneeled at my feet the worst scared darky ever seen. My eyes had become somewhat accustomed to the darkness, and I could see him kneeling at my feet with his hands clasped in the attitude of supplication.

"Oh, doan' kill dis poor nigger!" he cried. "Doan' shoot me. I doan' know'd dere was any so'gers about here. I tho't dey was all on the udder side of de crick. Say, boss," he added, interrupting himself, as he drew a little nearer and straightened himself up: "be you-uns a Yank?"

"Yes," I replied, "I am a Northern soldier. I am not a rebel. And there's thousands more right behind me."

"Thank de Lo'd!" he cried devoutly "Praise de Lamb! Salvation am come at last! Glory Halleluyer!"

I didn't know what the confounded darkey meant. I thought I had struck an escaped lunatic.

"Praise de Lamb!" continued the excited negro. "Am it true we niggers is free? Be you-uns one ob Massa Lincoln's men?"

I assured him that I had the honor of being one of the humble members of the army fighting for the government presided over by Lincoln—although of course in not exactly those words. Then I asked the poor darky what he meant by all this rigmarole.

He told me that the colored people there were waiting for the arrival of the Northern army that was to set them free and take them "Up North," where they were to spend the rest of their lives in the midst of plenteous milk and honey—and whiskey. He announced his willingness to accompany me at once.

"I'se ready to go 'long straight away now," said he, gladly. "Only wait a min'it till I gits de old 'oman and de pickaninnies. We-uns 'll have our bund'l ready in a min-it. Praise de Lamb! We'se free at last! Glory halleluyer!"

The excited darky fairly yelled this out, and I feared that it would attract the attention of the rebels supposed to be a short distance in front. So I told him to stop his noise. The corporal of the guard did hear it and came running up to see what was the matter. He thought of course that it came from one of the men on picket.

The matter was explained to the corporal, who told the darky that it would be his duty to take him back to headquarters. This was done in spite of the protests of the darky, who wanted to go back after "the old 'oman and de pickaninnies."

He had not been gone long before another sound in the darkness ahead of me nearly frightened the wits out of me. It was a female voice, and a lusty one at that:

"Jo-si-er!"

Now the front syllable of this appellation fitted me exactly, but I concluded to remain quiet and see what it all meant. I recognized the voice as that of a negro woman, but the presence of a woman out there in the woods at night was something strange. Presently the call was repeated:

"Jo-si-er! Jo-si-er! Whar you is, Jo-si-er?"

The voice didn't seem to be twenty-five feet distant, and I thought I would venture forward and investigate. The crackling of the twigs was heard by the old woman, and she said:

"Oh, dar you is, Jo-si-er. What for you go out jist as de hoe cake am done bake? Come, it am ready, you good for nothin' lazy nigger. Seems to your ol' mammy you'se allers hungry."

To my astonishment I found myself at the threshold of a typical negro's log cabin. On the hearth blazed a roaring fire that was temptingly warm. From a crane of the old-fashioned sort hung a big broad spider, upon which was a thick hoecake, done to a turn, while on a little table at the side of the room stood a steaming pot of coffee. Goodness, didn't it look tempting!

I had no idea that there was a human habitation within miles, and I was thunderstruck to come across the cabin occupied by this negro family. I stood at the open doorway contemplating the scene with curiosity and interest.

The fat old negro woman was standing with her back to me and did not see me. She was busily engaged in the intricate operation of getting the flap-jack off the griddle upon a huge platter of wood, ready to remove to the table.

"Here, you hungry nigger," she said, "here's yo' hoecake. De nex' time yo' gits yure old mammy to bake a cake for yo' in de middl' of de night, yo'll——"

Here she turned and saw me. Instead of "Jo-si-er" she unexpectedly contemplated the apparition of a very wet, very tired and very dirty-looking soldier, armed with a bayoneted rifle, standing there like a wandering ghost.

She gave one yell, and tottered backward, upsetting the table, spilling the steaming coffee on the floor, and dropping the platter with the hoecake back into the fire.

CHAPTER LXIX.

A MASKED BATTERY.

The first thing I did was to make a grab for that hoe cake before it got burned up in the fire. While I was doing this, I was startled by a series of unearthly yells from the opposite side of the cabin.

Looking over toward that direction I saw three young negro babies, ranging in age from two to five years. They had been asleep on the floor in the corner, and had hastily arisen in terror when aroused by the noise of the old woman's yelling. The "kids" were as naked as the day they were born. The colored people in those parts never put on such frills as dressing their children in nightgowns when they put them to bed.

My attention was then directed to the old woman herself. She had got upon her knees, and with her hands clasped devoutly was praying with a vigor that would have done justice to a Methodist deacon in the amen corner of a church.

"Oh, Lo'd! Oh, Lo'd!" she exclaimed. "Hab mercy on dis ere mis'ble sinner. Oh, Massa Debb'l, doan' take dis poor nigger! Doan' take me war de fire burn and is not done squelched! Oh, Lo'd sabe me from de debb'l afore he take me down below! Massa Debb'l, please, kind Massa Debb'l, good Debb'l, doan' tote dis ere poor nigger off to der——"

"What in thunder are you getting off?" I interrupted. "What's the matter with you anyhow? I am not the devil. I am not going to 'tote' you off to the fire and brimstone. What I want is some of that flapjack. And put the coffee on again. The best you can do if you don't want to be carried off is to get that supper ready again. Those things make me hungry. The devil don't eat. I will soon show you that I am no devil if I once get my teeth on the edge of that flapjack."

I remember to this day how the whites of the old woman's startled eyeballs bulged out as she stood there looking at me, not even yet satisfied whether I was real flesh and blood or his Satanic Majesty.

And no wonder. It was the first time she had ever seen a Union soldier in full uniform. The rebel uniforms, originally gray, had become dirt color, and if you took a lot of prisoners from the Passaic county jail and armed them with old guns, and hung a dirty blanket around their necks, it would make a good representation of a Confederate private.

Untidy and soiled as my uniform was, it looked imposing to the old woman, with the brass belt plates, glittering bayonet and other accouterments, and altogether it looked unlike anything she had seen on the earth or in the waters under the earth. It was only natural that she took me for a devil. But I can't say that I felt much complimented!

Shivering and shaking, the old woman hastened to comply with my orders. Presently she managed to muster up courage to ask me if I was one of "Massa Lincum's sogers." I assured her that I was and then followed another scene of thankfulness over freedom similar to that of the man I had encountered on the picket post.

Then she thought of the man herself.

"Whar's dat Jo-si-er?" she asked. "Did you see a lazy, good-for-nothin' nigger out yar? He done gone so long dat I'se afeared he am gobbled up."

"Oh, he's all right," I answered. "He is out there talking with some of the other soldiers." I did not want to alarm her by telling her that he had been captured and taken back to headquarters.

Just then I heard some sort of a commotion outside. I had forgotten all about my duties as a soldier on picket. The sight of that toothsome hoecake and steaming coffee had driven everything else from my mind. The noise outside, however, brought me to my senses again and I started to go out.

"Here, what's going on here?" asked the sergeant

of the guard, whom I met at the door. "What are you doing off your post? Don't you know this is disobedience of orders?"

"I suppose it is, sergeant," I answered; "but just look at that flapjack there on the table."

"Halt, second relief," said the sergeant, turning to the men outside. He was coming around with the second relief. It was 11 o'clock.

Human nature is human nature. The sight of that hot supper there on that cold and cheerless night had the same effect on the sergeant and the half-dozen men with him that it did on me, and they one and all leaned their guns against the door of the cabin and came in.

The old woman had the coffee ready again by this time, and it is needless to say that we made quick work of that hoecake. Some pork gravy was served as butter and I don't think that I ever tasted a meal that I relished more than I did that lonely and singular repast there in the wilderness.

We learned some of the facts from the old woman, too. The rebels had been there during the afternoon, but had marched off toward Chancellorsville. They did not know that there were any Union troops anywhere in the vicinity. The old woman had heard them say that they were going away for good, and that she would not see them again.

This settled us that there were no rebels in that immediate vicinity at least, and we felt that there was not so much need of being quiet and careful to watch for attack. Of course it was a gross violation of duty for any of us to be there in that hut, even for a few moments, but I don't think there was a soldier in the army who would not have taken advantage of the occasion.

I was relieved from my post by the second relief, and went back to the picket headquarters for a little sleep, as I did not have to go on duty again till 3 o'clock in the morning. I slept soundly, despite the racket going on around me.

This racket was caused by the arrival of the remaining portion of the army. The Thirteenth Regiment, being needed for picket duty, was the one that forded the Rapidan. The others crossed on pontoon bridges that had been placed in position, and they came over between midnight and morning and went into camp around us. But despite all the noise incident to this, we men who had been on picket slept the sleep only known to tired soldiers.

And well was it that we could sleep. Had we known what was in store for us on the two or three days following, none of us would have felt much like sleeping.

I was on picket again from 3 to 5 o'clock, and a more lonesome two hours I never experienced. The old negro woman's cabin was silent, showing that she and the pickaninnies had gone to bed, regardless of the absence of "Jo-si-er," and with the exception of the occasional hoot of an owl, the woods were as quiet and dismal as a cemetery.

I leaned against a tree, and I believe that I fell asleep standing there. This was often the case. It did not take much for a soldier on picket to fall asleep on the relief just before daylight. But on such occasions the picket would be aroused by the slightest noise. The noise that aroused me was the approach of the second relief again at 5 o'clock. If I was asleep I was wide awake enough when the relief took my place, and I gladly returned to camp, completely tired out. But there was no more sleep that night. Already the army was making preparation for a move.

It was on Thursday morning, April 30, 1863. It was the day previous to the commencement of the great battle of Chancellorsville. We knew that we were engaged in some important movement, of course, but did not know when the fighting would begin or where. All the signs, however, with which we had become so familiar, indicated that we were close upon a serious conflict with the enemy.

It was a beautiful sunny forenoon. The weather was simply delightful. We were marching along comfortably, leisurely and contentedly. It seemed like a spring excursion party, so peaceful was everything. There was not a sign of anything like an enemy, and the only sound that greeted our ears, beside the joking and laughter of the soldiers, was the chirping of the birds in the trees which we passed. Now and then a chipmunk would dash across the road, and occasionally the cotton tail of a fleeing rabbit would be seen scurrying through the brush.

All was peace. Nothing could seem further than anything like war, when—

"Boom!"

Simultaneously came the familiar "Ker-chew, ker-chew, ker-chew" of a flying shell.

Then a great crash! Then yells of agony and moans of pain, for the shell had fallen and burst in our ranks, right in front of us.

Involuntarily we all turned our eyes toward the place from which the report came, which was plainly indicated by the still hovering cloud of smoke. A moment later we saw a small battery of artillery hurrying away from the spot on a gallop. It was hidden behind a clump of bushes on the hill. It was what was called a "masked battery." It could not be seen from the road, and no one knew that it was there.

A company of cavalry made a dash after the fleeing artillery of the enemy. I don't know if they were captured or not.

Our column halted its march, and everybody made a rush to the place where the soldiers were crowding around the wounded men. I rushed forward with the rest.

CHAPTER LXX.

BEGINS TO LOOK LIKE BUSINESS.

I RUSHED forward with others to see what damage had been done by the shell that had exploded in our ranks.

And I was immediately sorry that I had done so. I received a shock that made me feel sick all over.

Two men had been literally torn to pieces. Their remains was strewn over the roadway from one side to the other. One man's heart was still throbbing. Pieces of skull and human brains lay here and there!

One poor fellow had lost a leg, and his writhing was terrifying. Others were less seriously wounded. Altogether there were two men killed, one fatally, and six others severely wounded by the explosion of that single shell. I turned from the scene sick at heart and sick at stomach.

Nearly every man's face was pallid. It was the suddenness, the unexpectedness of it. Had we been in the midst of a battle, when such things are expected and looked for, it would not have been so startling. But everything had been so quiet and peaceful, and everybody's thoughts were so far away from anything like carnage and death, that it was just like such a tragedy would be in the quiet and peaceful streets at home.

John Ick came in with his customary remark about "slaughter houses," but no one disputed him. It looked more like a slaughter house than anything else. And it seemed more like cold-blooded murder than warfare. But then what is warfare but murder, at the best?

For some time after we resumed our march there was an unnatural quiet in the ranks. The incident through which we had just passed seemed to have an effect on every one. It perhaps impressed each one with the fact that we were likely to soon meet the same fate as the poor wretches we had seen writhing there in the dusty road.

But the spirits of soldiers do not remain depressed. Pretty soon we came to a small farmhouse along the road, and in the barnyard behind the dwelling we caught sight of an old sow with a lot of sucking pigs.

There was no orders to "break ranks," but immediately there was a grand rush for those porkers. The squealing captives were carried back into the line despite the indignant protest of the woman in a very shabby dress who came out and futilely ordered the return of "them 'ere shoats."

As we marched along we passed quite a number of farmhouses and each one was denuded of everything in the shape of live stock. Soon there was a remarkable chorus of squealing pigs, squawking chickens and quacking ducks all along the line. The boys were assured of a change in their *menu* for once, that was sure.

We marched on and on and on. Detouring the woods and fields on each side of us was a lot of cavalry, on the lookout that we might not be again surprised by a shot from a masked battery. But nothing of the sort occurred during the remainder of the day, and we did not stop till night, when we went into camp in line of battle in a fine large open field between two clumps of woods, in the immediate vicinity of Chancellorsville.

That night we had a banquet with the fresh meat and poultry we had captured during the day. We had no duty to perform that night, except to be called out in line to hear the reading of some orders.

It was an order from General Hooker complimenting the Fifth, Eleventh and Twelfth corps for the commendably successful manner in which they had achieved the movement, whatever it was. We did not know what it was. It did not seem anything more than an ordinary day's march, with the exception of the interruption from that deadly shell from the masked battery.

But General Hooker said it was, and that settled it. There was a good deal of braggadocio about that order, by the way. In fact General Hooker was entirely too previous. The order said:

"It is with heartfelt satisfaction that the commanding general announces to the army that the operations of the last three days have determined that our enemy must ingloriously fly, or come out from behind his intrenchments and give us battle on our own ground, where certain destruction awaits him."

We all cheered, of course. It was the proper thing for us to do under the circumstances. It wasn't a bad idea either, that order. It filled the troops with encouragement and fight, and impressed them with the idea that this really was to be the deciding battle of the war.

It is said that General Hooker took a drink—perhaps several of them—after the issuance of that order, and made the remark that "God Almighty himself couldn't get the rebels out of the hole he had put them in." There is good reason for the statement that the general did make some such remark as this.

And although irreverent, there was good reason for felicitation over the successful preparations for the contest. It is admitted by all military authorities that it was one of the best planned campaigns in history, and up to the time of the issuing of that order by General Hooker it was perfect as a military movement.

But the very power that General Hooker had so irreverently referred to was the power that got the enemy out of the hole, and turned a glorious victory into one of the most disastrous defeats of the civil war. Heaven literally interfered and upset the calculations of an able general.

Man proposes, God disposes. Never was this truer than in the Chancellorsville campaign. But of that soon.

We slept quietly, peacefully and unmolested that night. Nothing seemed further off than a battle, except for the sanguinary orders that had been read, and the fact that when we lay down that night the regiment was formed in line of battle, and every man had his musket at his side. As for any sign of any enemy there was no more right there than there is here where I am writing at the present moment. Little does a soldier know what the morrow may bring forth.

Early on Friday morning, May 1, after my companions had been hammering me to their heart's content because it was my birthday—a boy of nineteen years—we fell in line and resumed the march.

Soon things "began to look like business."

We had scarcely gone more than a mile, when we were turned into a line of woods and formed a line of battle. We were ordered to throw off our knapsacks and leave them there—temporarily. But we never saw those knapsacks again. I suppose mine is lying there yet! I never had a knapsack on my shoulders after that morning!

Slowly and cautiously we moved forward through the woods. The very atmosphere seemed ominous. Pretty soon we emerged from the woods and reached an open field where we were ordered to lie down—lie flat to the ground. I think that I occupied the space of a flounder!

In a few minutes we were ordered up, and we sneaked —that is the word—sneaked forward, slowly, cautiously, till we reached a post and rail fence along another piece of woods. Into this we marched.

In getting over the fence, our regimental commander, Colonel Carman, fell and was wounded! He retired to the rear! When I saw him go, I wished heartily that I might fall off the fence too!

Lieutenant-Colonel Chadwick was happily—for him —home on a furlough, and the command of the regiment fell on Major Jack Grimes.

Company D was sent forward as skirmishers, supported by Company C. This was to discover the whereabouts of the enemy, supposed to be hiding somewhere in the front—to go forward and rake up the muss, as it were!

We cautiously moved forward some five or six hundred feet, momentarily expecting to unearth the enemy. Our ears were constantly on the alert for the first sound of the ominous minie bullet. But none came.

Just as we had got in a good position and things looked as if the impending conflict could not be long deferred, we were surprised to receive orders to retreat, and we went into camp again not very far from the camp we had left in the morning. Every man felt as if this was a retrograde movement and a mistake, and all wondered what it meant.

But soldiers must ask no questions. They have nothing to do but obey orders, and the next order we received was to begin cutting down the trees in front of us to build up a breastworks to guard against surprise from the enemy during the night.

While we were engaged in this work, we were startled by the discharge of a cannon, not in front of us, where it had been expected, but immediately in our rear!

CHAPTER LXXI.

CAPTURED BY THE ENEMY.

The discharge of the cannon was immediately followed by the usual swish of the flying shell. We were greatly surprised that there should be such an apparent attack from the rear, instead of the front, where we had been expecting it. I dropped to the ground and wallowed in the leaves like a pig, to escape the flying missiles from the exploding shell.

But there was no exploding shell, at least near us. The shot was fired from our own side, from Battery M, of the First New York artillery, and it was followed by two or three others of the same sort.

I thought it was the beginning of the fight, of course, but it seems that it was only intended as a "feeler," to see if the rebels would take it up. It elicited no response whatever and everything was as quiet as a graveyard in the direction where the enemy was supposed to be.

This quietness made us all the more apprehensive of an attack. It was suspicious and we became impressed with the idea that there was some sort of a surprise in store for us. We went to work all the more vigorously in the completion of the breastworks.

Well do I remember that day's work. We had been served with a ration of fresh meat, which seemed for some reason to be always the case immediately before a battle. Whether this was to arouse the animal nature within us and make us ready for a fight, I cannot say, but it was always a fact that there was a service of fresh meat immediately before a premeditated engagement.

The cattle had been killed near us, and there lay around on the ground great numbers of heads. These we placed on top of the breastworks, with the horns pointing toward where the enemy was supposed to be. This gave the breastworks a terribly ferocious appearance, but as a matter of fact it was about as useful as the bearskin hat of a drum major.

When I afterward read how the Chinese soldiers went to battle with umbrellas, and making hideous noises to frighten the Japs before shooting at them, it involuntarily took me back to those cows' horns on top of the breastworks at Chancellorsville. We are not so very far advanced over the heathen when it comes to the details of war, after all our boasted civilization. But I forgot. War is not civilization. When the time of perfect civilization arrives there will be no such thing as war.

We had just about finished the breastworks that afternoon when General Ruger ordered us to move forward in light marching order. This, bear in mind, was Saturday, May 2, 1863, a date that has gone down in history for more than one reason as being one of the most important in the history of the war.

As I said, we were ordered out in light marching order. We had already lost our knapsacks, but this meant to leave even our haversacks, canteens and blankets. A detachment was left behind to guard these things, which we left with considerable reluctance, for whatever else a soldier may cheerfully do he hates to leave behind his "grub-bag" and "watering can."

We were conducted to a position far in advance of the one we had occupied, and there were ordered to lie down. "Lie low and be quiet" was the order. I lay as low as "B'rer Rabbit" and wallowed in the leaves of the woods like a hog. We all remained quiet, speaking not above a whisper. These things were most disagreeably ominous.

The rest of our brigade, with General Pleasanton's cavalry and brigade of the Eleventh corps, had been sent out to reinforce General Sickles. The latter had been ordered to go forward and reconnoiter the position of the enemy, and had come across them sooner than they expected. General Sickles had struck the rear guard of Jackson's rebel troops and had taken quite a number of prisoners.

Word came back that the enemy was retreating and we all felt delighted at the easy way the thing was going. We felt a degree of security that we had not entertained in some days. But alas! It was false security.

One brigade of the Eleventh corps, and our brigade of the Twelfth, were guarding the extreme right of the line of battle, while General Sickles and his associates were chasing what was then supposed to be the main body of a rebel army.

But here is where the rebels fooled us. The supposed retreat which Sickles was following was only a comparatively small detachment of the enemy. The main body was flanking us, and the scene of the flank attack was immediately where we stood.

The Eleventh corps brigade was a little to the right of us. My company was just then on the top of a hill, in front of which was a ledge of rocks. On the right was the edge of a piece of sparse woods. On the left and behind us, were the sloping, rocky sides of the hill on which we stood.

In front was a low, level space, like a plain. From my elevated position I could see General Sickles' troops corraling the rebel prisoners and bringing them toward us. A forlorn lot they were, in their dirty gray uniforms, shapeless slouch hats, and generally disreputable appearance. I felt pity for the poor fellows, on many of whose faces I imagined I could see traces of satisfaction over having been taken prisoners.

It was just before dusk. The sun had set in a scene of glory behind the western hills. The sky was cloudless, golden in hue. It was the approach of a beautiful night. It was so beautiful that I even remember having remarked it, there in that exciting scene.

Exciting scene, did I say? The excitement was just to commence.

Suddenly there were yells, cries, shouts, and the whiz of flying bullets on every side.

Immediately I was surrounded by thousands of flying men.

The first that came were hundreds of Eleventh corps officers and men. I immediately recognized them by the half-moons on their hats.

Their eyes fairly bulged from their heads in their terror and excitement. Many of them were hatless, and their hair streamed behind from the breeze caused by their rapid flight. Hundreds were unarmed, having thrown away their guns in their panic.

Then, mixed up with the blue, was the gray. The rebels, right there in our midst, all running, all shouting and yelling, were as numerous as the fleeing boys in blue.

Then there came horses, some riderless, pack mules, artillery caissons, ambulances and what not, in inextricable confusion, a perfect mob, demoralized, disorganized, utterly beyond control—for it was a panic!

The Union troops were fleeing as they supposed for their lives. The rebels were chasing them to take them prisoners. There was nothing like order or discipline. It was simply a crazy mob, a rout, a flight of panic-stricken men, rushing with about the same judgment and sense as a big audience would rush from a burning theater.

They came like an avalanche—like a whirlwind. Union and Confederate, blue and gray, were inextricably mixed together, all rushing, screaming, yelling, shouting!

Nothing could withstand that rush. For an instant I stood petrified, and was then swept from my feet as if I had been a wisp. What became of my comrades I knew not. They had disappeared, been swallowed up in the tidal wave of humanity. I was knocked down and rolled, fortunately, behind an overhanging ledge of rock.

I did not attempt to rise. If I had I would have been trampled to death in an instant. Instead, I crowded as closely as possible under the protecting rock, while over me there poured a steady stream of human beings, friends and foe alike. They went over that rock, jumping over to the further side, like the endless roll of Erie's waters over the precipice at Niagara.

This was the scene that has gone into history as "The break of the Eleventh corps at Chancellorsville." I was right in it. In fact I was altogether too much in it for comfort's sake.

What was it all? What did it mean?

History calmly tells us that the Eleventh corps had been surprised by Jackson, and the latter, by a flank movement, had charged upon the former, compelling them to fly. This is what history says. And history is right when it says that the Eleventh corps did fly. No other word could justly describe the movement.

After a little while the main portion of the grand rush subsided and I thought it was safe to emerge from my place behind the rock and start to hunt for the Thirteenth Regiment of New Jersey Volunteers.

I straightened myself up, and was about to pick up my rifle from the ground, when a rough hand was placed on my shoulder and a gruff voice met my astonished, and I might say, very much startled ears.

"You are my prisoner, you —— Yank!"

I turned, and found myself in the firm grasp of a stalwart rebel sergeant!

CHAPTER LXXII.

A SECOND BALAKLAVA.

I WAS a prisoner!

A more terrible situation it would be hard to conceive. The approaching darkness of the ending day was made the more gruesome by the smoke that arose from the desultory firing of many rifles, and the intermittent boom of artillery posted on every elevated position.

Demoralized soldiers were rushing hither and thither, apparently without system or order, separated from their regiments, without commanders. Cavalry horses, some riderless, galloped to and fro, apparently not knowing where they were going. The whole battlefield was a scene of indescribable confusion, noise and smoke.

I turned to look at the Confederate soldier who had taken me his prisoner. He was a tall, gaunt specimen of a rebel, with protruding cheek bones, little, glistening eyes, hair long and unkempt. On his head was a broad-brimmed, gray slouch hat, much the worse for wear and dirt. His uniform, if uniform it may be called, looked like the clothing of a man who had just come from a trench where he had been mending a bursted water main.

The rifle he carried, as well as the blanket slung over his shoulder, his canteen and haversack, I immediately recognized as having been recently taken from some Union soldier. Half the Confederate army were provided with these equipments from the Northern side, although where they obtained them was a mystery.

I must confess that my captor presented a rather picturesque appearance. He looked like a cowboy on the plains—or in a circus. Although he was so tall and gaunt, there was a kindly expression in his eye, and I was not the least frightened, for some reason or other.

"Well, now that you've got me, what are you going to do with me?" I asked.

"Wall, Yank," replied he, "I reckon as how we-uns 'll have to take you-uns back to the coop."

"I've a good mind to take you prisoner," said I, impudently.

This made the rebel laugh outright. And it was rather funny. I had no rifle or other arms, and my captor was not only well provided in that respect, but he was almost twice my size. He could easily have picked me up and carried me off. The idea struck me as being comical. It wasn't a very cheerful place for mirth, but we both laughed in concert at the idea I had suggested.

"The trouble 'pears to be, jist neow," said he, with that peculiar twang noticeable alike way "down East" and in the South, "the trouble 'pears to be, that we-uns can't tell which way to go. Things seem to be all mixed up. We-uns men and you-uns men be a running all ways ter onct, an' if we-uns don't look out, we-uns 'll take you back to your own camp, an' we-uns 'll be taken prisoners by you-uns a'ter all!"

It seemed very likely. Union and Confederate soldiers appeared to be inextricably mixed in the wild, panicky rush that still continued, although it was subsiding. So we just stood there, hardly knowing what to do. A moment later, however, something occurred that riveted both our attention, the contemplation of which so absorbed us that we both forgot our respective conditions.

A Union general, accompanied by several members of his staff, rode up to near where we stood. I heard subsequently that it was General Pleasanton. The latter called to him another officer, a major of cavalry.

"Where is your command, major?" asked General Pleasanton.

"Right over there under the edge of that woods," replied the major, saluting.

"How many men have you?"

"About six hundred, general. But there's Captain

Bassett's cavalry immediately beyond, and I can get them if necessary. That would make twelve hundred, about."

"How comes it that Captain Bassett is in command? Where is the colonel?"

"He is wounded, general. He was shot from his horse only a few minutes ago."

"Very well, major. We have not a moment to lose. I want you to hold back that corps coming over at the edge of the woods at the foot of the hill, and hold them till I place my battery here. Do you understand?"

I saw the face of the major first flush and then turn pale. And no wonder!

From the position where we stood, we could see the rebel corps referred to approaching. It was General Jackson's Confederate troops—the same that had flanked the Eleventh corps and driven them back, causing the panic-stricken stampede which we had just gone through. In that corps, approaching us to give battle on a part of the Union army where all was demoralization, where there was not a gun in position for action, there were from fifteen to twenty thousand men!

And yet that vast body was to be kept back by a comparatively insignificant body of twelve hundred cavalrymen!

The major saw what was meant, and turned pale. But I will never forget his answer: "General, I understand your order and will do my duty."

Now here was the theory of that murderous movement. General Pleasanton wanted to bring some of his artillery to that hill, place them in position, and be ready to repel the attack of the rapidly approaching corps under General Jackson. It would take ten or fifteen minutes at the very least to post the artillery. That time must be secured at whatever sacrifice.

It was simply a question of occupying the enemy's attention for that ten or fifteen minutes. In projecting a body of twelve hundred men against a corps of some twenty thousand, there was but one result possible. That was the practical annihilation of the smaller number.

.. It was this principle on which General Grant later on

prosecuted the war. He argued that war was but a question of attrition. That, other things being equal, the larger army would succeed. By just so many men as the larger army exceeded the smaller, just so many men would be left on the larger and victorious side when the battle was over.

In the present instance it was merely a question of the number of minutes that would be consumed by the approaching rebel corps to annihilate the interposing Union cavalry. Would it take ten or fifteen minutes? If so, then there would be time for the posting of the artillery. If not, then the movement would be a failure.

It was a ride to death, but unflinchingly did that major and his twelve hundred men throw themselves into the jaws of almost certain destruction.

And I saw that movement—an achievement that has gone down into history in prose and in poetry as one of the most marvelous examples of bravery seen in the civil war. It was an achievement that rivalled that at Balaklava, made immortal by Tennyson's famous "Charge of the Light Brigade."

Yes, I was an eyewitness of that terrible cavalry charge of twelve hundred against fifteen or twenty thousand. I and my rebel companion stood there petrified with amazement, as we watched the scene. We saw the cavalry charge into the rebel corps, only to be cut down in rows. It was an indescribably awful conflict while it lasted.

Men were shot from their horses. Horses were shot under the men, and the latter in many instances fell under the steeds struggling in their death agony. Soon the smoke rising from the firearms arose and obscured the view from our vision.

In the meantime General Pleasanton was getting his artillery into position on the hill near us. For some reason we—my captor and I—stood there, comparatively isolated from the rest. Near us were a number of Union men in charge of detachments, men who had been taken prisoners by the enemy the same as I had been. It was rather a strange situation.

The trouble was that things had got so much mixed that the rebels did not know which way to take us.

Union and Confederate soldiers seemed to be everywhere alike. This perhaps was never known before or after during the entire war, but all who were in the midst of the Eleventh corps rout at Chancellorsville will testify that it was as here described.

The movement of the handful of cavalry was a success. It took the rebel corps fully twenty minutes to disperse, I might almost say annihilate, for of that gallant twelve hundred, if the records are right, but thirty-eight survived the charge! Among the first killed was the gallant major to whom General Pleasanton had given the fateful order.

But the posting of the cannon soon changed the aspect of affairs. In a few minutes shrapnel and shell were plowing down the ranks of the approaching troops, and they were driven back.

A moment later a division of infantry attacked General Jackson's corps on their left, and they were driven off in confusion, and as history puts it, "with great loss."

My rebel captor still stood there standing guard over me nominally, but so absorbed in what he had just witnessed that he said not a word nor made any attempt to conduct me further.

Just then a sudden inspiration seized me, and acting upon it, in less time than it takes to tell it I had made my escape. There was probably never anything like it during the war. I have to smile every time I think of it even to this day.

But I will wait till the next chapter to tell just what did happen.

CHAPTER LXXIII.

A QUEER ESCAPE.

Now the usual weapons of warfare are rifles, pistols and swords. I don't think it is customary to use one's fists in battle. It is not often that the two opposing sides get near enough together to use swords, let alone knuckles

But this is an exception. I did use my fists. I knocked my rebel captor down, and made my escape. I believe it is the only time in my life, at least since schoolboy days, that I ever knocked a person down with a blow from my fist.

As stated in the preceding chapter, my rebel captor and I were simply petrified with amazement at the scene we had just witnessed, and we still stood there after it was practically over. As before stated, we were on a rocky ledge or hill, one side of which, that toward the enemy, was precipitous, while the other side was sloping.

My tall companion stood a little lower than I, so that our heads were about even. Glancing down I noticed that he was standing right on the edge of a rock, from which there was a step of four or five feet.

Visions of the horrors of Libby prison, about which I had heard so much, flashed through my mind with the rapidity of lightning. Why should I go there without a struggle, at least? Was it possible that I might make my escape?

Then I noticed the advantage of my position. That settled it! My thoughts, which were working with electric swiftness, were hardly more rapid than my action.

An inspiration seized me, and I suddenly let out, with my full force, with my right fist, and gave that big rebel a blow under his ear that must have astonished him greatly, even if it did not hurt him much.

I saw him reel, lose his balance, and fall headlong from the edge of the rock where he had been standing. As he fell his gun flew from his hands, and he went sprawling down the steep side of the elevation.

I went the other way!

Talk about sprinting! Talk about bicycle scorching and breaking records on the Blank Company's patent light-weight, non-puncturable tires!

None of them could hold a candle to the gait I maintained as I rushed down the other side of the hill. I ran, I knew not whither, neither did I care, so long as I was escaping. I went through a brook without as much as wetting my feet, jumped little precipices, vaulted over deserted breastworks, dodged under the shells flying from the cannon's mouths, and never stopped till I at last fell, almost senseless, with palpitating heart and panting breath, alongside a little brook in the midst of a thicket!

But I was safe, and that was all that I cared about.

I never knew what became of my rebel captor. While I was running I felt the buzz of a bullet swish past my head, which I imagine came from his rifle, although of course there was no telling who fired the bullets that were flying around so recklessly just about then and there!

But I was left quiet only for a moment. There was a mighty cry and yell, a wild rush, and the first thing I knew I was knocked headlong into the brook by a team of runaway horses—a six-horse team at that!

It may sound queer to the reader who has not been in the war to hear one talking about horses running away in the midst of a battle. That sounds too much like an everyday street incident. But nevertheless such was the fact. It was a very frequent occurrence, and many men were injured by runaway horses during the war. Horses are horses, whether at home or in the army, and they will run away just the same and from similar causes.

It is a wonderful thing how a horse becomes acquainted with his surroundings. Here at home, no matter how much he may be frightened at first, he soon becomes accustomed to the electric cars and the steam road roller. In the army the horse becomes accustomed to the moving of large bodies, the racket of the bands, and even the intolerable noises of a battle. But some little thing, insignificant in itself, but out of the usual order, will startle a horse and set him to running away.

I don't know what started the team that ran over me. They were attached to the limber—the front wheels and ammunition box—of a cannon, and they came dashing down the hill, striking me, and knocking me into the brook, and passing over me.

The soft mud in the bottom of the brook probably saved my life. I was pressed deep into the slimy ooze, and covered from head to foot—a veritable "mud bath."

I pulled myself out with difficulty, quite badly hurt, having received a severe bruise on the hip. I did not think much of it at the time, but it began to hurt badly afterward, and has bothered me ever since more or less, particularly in cold and damp weather.

But I was young then, and comparatively tough, and although I was still stiff and sore, yet I scrambled out, and scraping off some of the mud with a stick, proceeded to discover "where I was at."

Just then I heard a moan in the bushes near me, and a cry for help. I went to the spot and found an officer lying there with the blood flowing from a wound in the fleshy part of his leg. A closer inspection discovered, to my astonishment, that it was none other than Major Grimes.

"Why, major," said I, "what's the matter? Are you hurt?"

"Yes," he replied. "I'm shot through the leg, I guess. Can't you help me to get somewhere?"

The major was a big man, and it was about all I could do to support him on his feet, but I managed to do so, and led him back a ways, where there was a fire and a little yellow flag stuck in the ground. This indicated the headquarters of some surgical detachment. The doctors were there engaged in their customary butchering work. I turned the major over to their tender mercies.

Perhaps Major Grimes never knew till now who was the private that led him out of the thickets where he was shot, on that eventful Saturday evening, May 2, 1863. Major Grimes was not seriously hurt, however. It was only a flesh wound, and not dangerous, although, doubtless, painful enough.

I then started out to see if I could find the Thirteenth Regiment of New Jersey Volunteers. But it was like finding a needle in a haystack. It was simply a disorganized mob.

It had become dark, and only for the faint lights of campfires here and there was there any guiding beacon for the homeless wanderers who were looking for their respective commands.

In a case like this, the regimental flag is the designating emblem of the position of the command. I looked for a long while for the colors of the Thirteenth in vain. I passed flag after flag, but they were all of some other regiment.

Non-commissioned officers were calling out "This way for the One Hundred and Seventh New York," "Here is the Twenty-seventh Indiana," "Fall in, Third Wisconsin," and such cries, which facilitated matters considerably, and knowing these to be regiments of my own brigade I felt that I must be getting pretty close "at home."

And I was. In a few moments more I heard the welcome cry, "Thirteenth New Jersey," and proceeded there.

Was this the Thirteenth New Jersey?

There were the well-known colors, sure enough. And there was Corneil Mersereau, poor fellow, holding the flag—his last day on earth, for early the next morning he was killed.

"Hello, Corneil," said I, "how's my boots? All right?"

"Yes, the boots are all right," he replied. "But you can have them in the morning. I wouldn't have them for a gift. My feet are covered with blisters."

"All right," I answered. "I will take them back in the morning, for my feet seem to have got a rest."

But I never wore those boots again. Mersereau was killed with them on in the morning, as I said before.

The Thirteenth New Jersey Volunteers never presented a more forlorn aspect than they did that night. When they arrived there were not a hundred men there. They had all become scattered in the wild rush of the evening, and had not come together again. But one by one the boys came straggling in, so that by 9 o'clock there were three or four hundred of them. The most of the remainder came back during the night.

Some never came back. What became of them is not known. Whether they were killed, and buried as "unknown," or whether they went to some rebel prison to die the most lingering and horrible of all deaths, is something that perhaps will never be known. They are down on the matter of fact army rolls as "missing."

Everything went crosswise that day and night. By some strange fate we occupied the same breastworks we had built earlier in the day, and there were the steers' horns just as we had placed them, looking as ferocious as ever.

But we were on the other side of the breastworks. The rebels had got around on the side we had occupied in the forenoon, and we had got around to their position. Everything seemed to have been turned topsy-turvy. That 'rout of the Eleventh corps" was one of the worst panics the Army of the Potomac ever experienced.

There was no chance for rest that night, however. We had not been long in that position behind the breastworks before we were again ordered to move forward.

Scarcely had we started when there began a rattle of musketry in front of us, and a roar of artillery in the rear!

CHAPTER LXXIV.

SHOOTING OUR OWN MEN.

It was right here that General Stonewall Jackson was killed.

General Jackson was one of the ablest officers on the Confederate side. His only superior, either in rank or ability, on the side of the rebels was General Robert E. Lee.

It seems that General Jackson, flushed with the success of his early evening maneuver, which resulted in the disastrous repulse of the Eleventh corps, undertook to follow up his advantage.

He ordered General Hill's division to the front, and it was the firing from these troops that we had just heard. General Jackson, accompanied by his staff, rode forward to examine the position of things personally. The Union pickets, under General Berry's command, heard him coming and fired.

Jackson fell back toward his own line, but in a different place from where he had started. Hill's (Confederate) troops, mistaking Jackson and his staff for the Union troops, fired upon them, killing and wounding half the escort, and fatally wounding General Jackson.

So Stonewall Jackson was killed by his own men, and not by the troops of the Northern army.

Suddenly the firing ceased. The rattle of the musketry in front and the booming of the cannon in our rear stopped almost simultaneously, as if from a preconcerted signal.

The command of the Thirteenth Regiment had fallen on Captain Beardsley, the senior line officer, all the members of the field and staff being either absent or wounded. I remember how he walked up and down the line behind us, urging us to be calm and cool, and advising us to lie close to the ground. We did not need a second admonition of the latter kind. As for myself I fairly scooped a hole in the ground, so that I could snuggle closer and be out of the way of any stray bullets that might come along.

About midnight, Burney's division of Sickles' corps made an attack on the enemy. The moon had come out and it was quite light in the open, although dark enough in the woods. The ground that we occupied was composed of alternate open spaces and dense patches of woods.

The moonlight charge on the enemy aroused them like a broken hive of angry hornets, and immediately there came a perfect shower of bullets whistling over our heads. We lay only a short distance in the rear of the attacking column.

Then the Union artillery behind us began their cannonading of the woods in which the rebels were massed. In a moment or so there commenced the worst racket that I had ever heard.

Upon the raised ground, some quarter or half a mile in our rear, the guns of the artillery were stationed. We occupied lower ground, but the mouths of the cannon were pointed right toward us, although of course with elevated aim. Anybody who knows anything about it is aware that the most noise and most concussion from the discharge of a cannon is experienced by those in front of the guns. The noise was simply terrific. A hundred summer thunderstorms combined could not come anywhere near it.

The murderous shot and shell passed directly over our heads. In the night the burning fuses left behind a train of fire like a sky rocket. This made, as it were, a perfect arch of fire over us. The rebel artillery replied. They accepted the challenge and the long range duel began.

No pen could describe an artillery duel. It is as if all the demons of hell were let loose at once. The shrieking shell, the deafening thunder of the cannons, the fiery arch over us, the shouts of the men, combined to make a scene the like of which is indescribable.

Occasionally a shell would prematurely explode in the air, and the fragments would scatter in every direction, a perfect rain of broken iron, dealing death and destruction where the missiles might fall. Fortunately none was hurt in our regiment, although there were a number wounded in this manner in other commands.

Once or twice the shells from the opposite sides collided in midair. They burst simultaneously with a terrific crash.

The old soldiers could distinguish the kind of a cannon from which the shell was fired from the character of the noise they made while passing through the air. Some went through with a prolonged shriek. They were Armstrongs. Others went with a "chew-chew-chew," like a train of cars. These were the Whitworths. Then again there was a peculiar sort of a shell, such as came from Best's and Hexamer's batteries, that seemed almost human. Their noise could be best interpreted as:

"Where-is-he—where-is-he—where-is-he!"

And when the shell struck and exploded, some of the boys would answer:

"There he is!"

For an hour, maybe more, this infernal artillery duel continued, till we were almost deafened. Startling as it was at first, the men finally became accustomed to it. They talked of other things as calmly as if they had been at home. Many even went to sleep and perhaps dreamed—perhaps dreamed of their peaceful homes!

It is wonderful how quickly human nature can adapt itself to circumstances. It is marvelous under what conditions a soldier can sleep.

After a long while, after the apparent waste of a good many tons of iron and steel, the duel came to an end. It did not stop suddenly, but gradually died down, till, after a desultory explosion now and then, everything became as quiet as the country, and so far as any noises were concerned, there was nothing warlike to be thought of.

This silence was so intense as to be ominous. Old soldiers do not like anything mysterious. Anything that they cannot understand they regard with suspicion. A silence like this, under such circumstances, meant that something was up.

There was!

It must have been along about 2 or 3 o'clock in the morning when suddenly, from the woods in front of us, there began the most exciting sort of a racket. There were yells and cheers and discharges of musketry. The line of Union troops immediately in front of us had apparently become engaged with the enemy.

A singular thing struck us, however. The yell that the rebels were indulging in was not the regular "rebel yell."

When the Union troops cheered their cry was a succession of "Hurrahs," generally repeated three times. The rebel war-cry was more continuous and unbroken, a sort of "Hi-yi-yi-yi-yi!"

It was not the rebel "Hi-yi-yi" that came from the troops in front of us, and which were shooting in our direction. It was, on the contrary, the regular "hurrah" of the North!

What could this mean?

"Oh, that's plain enough to understand," said Lieutenant Wells. "The rebels have adopted our hurrah to deceive us. They are using it as a surprise or a decoy. It is an old trick of the Johnnies."

We all thought that this was a good explanation, for there was no doubt entertained that the opposing forces in our front were those of the enemy.

The fight continued for some little time. We were just beginning to think it was about time for the Thirteenth to take the place of the line actively engaged in front, when suddenly an unexpected, a startling thing occurred.

Our side had made a little charge and captured a number of prisoners. The fighting had been in the woods, where it was quite dark. Neither side could see the other. The muskets had been aimed and fired from the sound rather than at any body of troops, for it was too dark to distinguish the troops.

But when the prisoners were brought in, and taken out in the open field where the moonlight was brighter, a terrible discovery was made.

We had been fighting Union soldiers! We had been shooting our own men!

CHAPTER LXXV.

NOW FOR THE GREAT FIGHT.

At this moment General Ruger rode up.

"For God's sake," he shouted, "stop this! Cease firing! Send some one out to tell them that these are our men."

To send some one on this errand was rather dangerous work. It was like flying in the face of death to go forth and inform the opposing army they were making a mistake.

But there were brave men in those famous days of the war. Volunteers there were in plenty. These messengers of peace started on their dangerous journey, and some of them succeeded, by making a detour, in getting around to the commander and explaining the fact that they were fighting their own men.

The shooting stopped, and we advanced and mingled with the men we had just been trying to kill. Then the mistake was verified. We men in blue had been really fighting other men in blue, shooting them down like dogs.

I don't think anything ever happened during the war more heartrending. The idea that we had been shooting at our own men was something terrible. The feeling we experienced was indescribable.

And there on the ground they lay, brave boys in blue, some already still in death, some writhing and struggling in their last agony, many grievously wounded. Shot by their own fellows!

It was horrible!

We had fallen into precisely the same sort of a mistake as happened when General Stonewall Jackson was killed.

Some of the Union soldiers further in the advance

had been ordered to change position. In making the movement they passed to the front of what had previously been the advance guard. The latter, not being able to distinguish blue from gray in the dark, naturally took them to be the enemy.

The Union troops changing position, being thus assaulted, of course imagined that the rebels had got in the rear, and turned upon them. Each thought the other the enemy, and thus the nocturnal battle began.

The discovery of the terrible mistake nearly threw the Union soldiers on both sides of the engagement in a panic. For some time they were completely demoralized. The criticism the officers received for the blunder was unlimited. It was also unjust, for it could not well have been avoided. But the men were so indignant at the occurrence that they were altogether unreasonable. Under the sad circumstances of the case it was only natural.

There was a disposition on the part of both officers and men that this night fighting, when friend could not be distinguished from foe, ought to be stopped. And it was stopped. No orders were given, but it appeared to be a tacit understanding that whatever further fighting there was to be done would be deferred till after daylight.

We remained lying on the ground for the remainder of the night. We hugged our rifles as our bedfellows, for there was no telling when there might be another attack from some source. There was not much sleep after that. The men were all too much excited. The episodes of the night had been too enervating to permit of slumber even on the part of the most calloused.

Everybody instinctively knew now that the great battle was on. Everybody appreciated the fact that the morrow would be the decisive day. It was felt that the fighting would begin at daylight.

But it did not.

It was as beautiful a morning as the Lord ever made. It was Sunday—the first Sunday in May. I distinctly remember what a beautiful morning it was, how all nature seemed to smile, how peaceful it all appeared.

There was not the first sound of battle anywhere,

The birds were singing in the branches of the trees, that were soon to be torn asunder with shrieking shot and shell. The men were standing or lying around, talking quietly and wondering what was going to happen next. In the distance could be heard an occasional bugle call or some drum signal, and mounted aids and orderlies galloped about as if delivering orders, but otherwise everything was remarkably quiet.

Before daylight along came that ominous ration of fresh beef—so indicative of approaching carnage. We were being fed for the battle.

"There's a schlaughter-haus somewhere by here alretty," said John Ick, who had been remarkably quiet during the past day and night.

"It's quite evident, John," I replied, "for here is some of the beef that has been slaughtered."

"We vill be schlaughtered dot way our own sellefs, I tinks so mit," replied John Ick in his broken English. "We vas goin' to haf some bad fights before much longer, ain't it?"

"Oh, don't get the blues, John," I said.

Those were the last words I ever addressed to John Ick. That was the last time I ever heard his voice. The next time I saw him he was dead.

Even while we were talking there came the sound of a cannon.

It was but a single shot. A moment later it was answered by another, further down the line. Then another and another, gradually becoming so distant that it could scarcely be heard.

Well enough did we know what that meant. It was the signal!

It was the signal for the great battle to begin.

And thus, on that quiet, beautiful Sunday morning, May 3, 1863, began the battle of Chancellorsville proper. Of course all the occurrences of the two preceding days were a part of the battle. They were the preliminaries.

But now the great conflict itself was to commence.

The battlefield extended from where we were, on the extreme right at Chancellorsville, to far beyond Fredericksburg, sixteen miles or so below.

All along the river we had advanced across to the

enemy's side and challenged him on his own soil. The rebels had a clear space of country to fall back upon. We were backed by the river. We felt that we could not retreat if we desired. But no one thought of retreating on the Northern side that day. We expected to "drive the enemy ignominiously from his lair," as General Hooker had put it in his famous order only two days previous.

The Union cannon signals were at once repeated on the rebel side, summoning that army to battle array. It sounded like the acceptance of a challenge. The gauntlet which we had thrown down had been picked up by our antagonists!

Immediately there was a commotion all over. Corps commanders, surrounded by their staffs, could be seen galloping from the vicinity of General Hooker's headquarters at the old Chancellorsville house to the different parts of the field where their commands were located.

Orderlies and messengers dashed hither and thither. Flying artillery earned its name by flying to advantageously elevated positions further in the advance. Great bodies of cavalry galloped off somewhere.

Here and there, in the rear, we could see the staffs stuck in the ground from the tops of which waved a yellow flag. Arranged in rows near these ominous yellow flags of the surgical and hospital departments, we could see the ambulances, all in waiting for their horrible freight, for soon their passengers would be dismembered and mutilated human beings.

The surgeons took off their coats, rolled up their shirt sleeves, and placed their glittering array of knives and saws handy within reach on trays. Attendants superintended the placing of splints and bandages and piles of lint.

They were getting ready to mend the men soon to be broken.

I think this affected me more than anything else. Would I be one of those soon to fall into the surgeon's hands? Or would some cruel and relentless bullet do its work so effectively that no surgeon would be needed?

They say that in the navy the worst moment is when

the sailors sprinkle sand on the decks to absorb the blood of the men to be killed and wounded, so that the living will not slip while in the performance of their grewsome work! In the army, I imagine that the supreme moment of mental torture is when one contemplates the systematic preparations of the surgeons, as just feebly described.

But something else very soon took our attention from the surgeons and everything else rearward.

A sudden commotion in front of us. A crash!

And the bullets began to whizz past and over us like hail, literally like hail!

CHAPTER LXXVI.

SURROUNDED BY DEATH.

Literally like hail flew the wicked minie bullets over and around us!

When bullets come along singly, or in twos or threes, they come with a buzz and a zip, very similar to a big bumble bee flying past you and striking against a fence or a barn. But imagine, if you can, the sudden capsizing of a thousand hives of big bees and the simultaneous release of the insects.

The single buzz would become one continuous hum or whirr. And so became the noise of the thousands of bullets that now whistled around and above us!

I say "above" because we were just then lying flat upon the ground, waiting for our turn to become actively engaged in the battle that was raging in all its fury. The Second Massachusetts and Third Wisconsin had been ordered in first. The Thirteenth New Jersey, Twenty-seventh Indiana and One Hundred and Seventh New York were waiting there to relieve the first two mentioned reigments when they should have exhausted their ammunition or have been driven back or annihiliated!

I heard a voice, low, cool, calm, behind me. I turned my head and saw Captain Beardsley, who, as before said, was in command of our regiment just then. The rest of us, officers and men alike, were hugging the earth for all we were worth, so as to expose as little of our bodies as possible to the storm of missiles flying about us. But there stood Captain Beardsley, erect, courageous, unexcited, as cool and collected as if he were in the peaceful street of a city, utterly regardless of the bullets whistling around him, and of the shells that now and then exploded close by! I was struck with amazement at such an exhibition of bravery.

"Keep cool, men," said he, in that calm, low voice of his, "keep perfectly cool, lie low, and don't get excited. Be calm. Keep cool now!"

Keep cool! I couldn't have kept cool to save my life. I was fairly burning up with the fever of terror and apprehension. My tongue was hard and dry, and I could hardly have spoken if I had tried. And yet, although thus hot, I was shivering, not from cold, of course, but from very fear.

Some men pretend not to have been afraid in the beginning of a battle. It is my opinion that such men deliberately lie. I think every man there was frightened. Captain Beardsley was outwardly calm, but he was as white as a corpse, and I doubt not that he was fully as terrified as the rest of us, but he was too much of a man to show it.

I think the inaction of the moment, coupled with the knowledge that it was "our turn next," was a thousand times worse than it was for those actively engaged a hundred yards or so ahead of us. In times of danger there is nothing like activity to keep the mind from constantly thinking, dreading, apprehending. Great calamities are magnified by apprehension, the same as pleasures are enhanced in the anticipation.

As I turned my head still close to the ground, to look at Captain Beardsley, a staff officer rode up to the captain to give him some order. Perhaps it might have been the order for the Thirteenth to advance! It was Adjutant-General Williams, of our division. As he leaned over the neck of his horse to speak the word to Captain Beardsley, I saw a terrible sight.

Suddenly the chin and lower jaw of the adjutant-general disappeared entirely! In its place was a mass of blood, raw flesh and gore! A piece of shell had come along and torn away the entire lower portion of his face. One could not see pieces of shell in their flight, so rapidly did they go, but the effect could be seen, which made it seem as mysterious as it was horrifying.

The adjutant-general sat still on his horse for an instant, with the blood gushing from his neck in a great stream. Then he reeled and fell. He soon bled to death where he lay.

I involuntarily shrieked! A man lying almost alongside of me, a member of Company I (for I was the last man in Company K's line), raised his head to see what was the matter.

It was his death! Even while I looked at him, I saw a little red spot appear on the side of his forehead, the head fell back, the man gave a convulsive stretch, and was dead!

If I had been hugging the ground closely before, I fairly wallowed in the dirt after that!

From where I lay I could see some distance down the side of the slope where we were located. The field presented a scene of devastation. The bodies of horses and men could be seen lying everywhere. Some were silent in death; others were writhing in their last agony. Broken ammunition wagons, dismounted cannons, accouterments, rifles and other *débris* were scattered all over the field. A dense smoke hovered over the scene, giving the atmosphere a lurid glow. Everything seemed on fire! Everything appeared to be red—the color of blood.

I saw a mounted orderly galloping across the field. Suddenly, as if by magic, the head of the horse flew off! It literally disappeared! An exploding shell had decapitated the animal while on a gallop.

And yet, strange to relate, that horse actually gave two more leaps before it fell! The muscular action of the gallop had continued two jumps before the nerves could telegraph the word that the horse had received its death stroke.

Then the animal fell, in a somersault, throwing the rider some distance, and apparently stunning him, for I did not see him move again. Aghast, I turned my head to the ground!

But only for a minute, for then came the order which we had been awaiting, yet dreading.

"Fall in, Thirteenth!"

It was Captain Beardsley who spoke, cool and calm as ever.

"Steady now," he said. "Don't get excited! Keep cool!"

We were ordered forward, and I thought our time had

come. I couldn't conceive how any man could stand erect in that storm of flying missiles, and live a second.

We arose to our feet and were ordered forward!

I can hardly say that I arose to my feet. I distinctly remember crouching down as much as possible, so that I almost crept as we moved forward, perhaps a hundred feet. Here we were again halted, and every man dropped prostrate, as if shot, and once more we hugged the ground.

Here a new danger confronted us. We had before been just outside the woods. Now were lying a short distance in the forest. The cannon balls and shells were crashing through the branches of the trees over our heads, and there was a continual fall of the limbs as they were cut off. It did not take long to transform those trees into telegraph poles, but the rain of the branches while it lasted was almost as dangerous as the duly recognized ammunition of the ordnance department. Several of the men were so severely hurt thereby that they had to be removed to the rear.

The cannonading by this time had become incessant, uproarious, deafening! The bullets were whistling past us more wickedly than ever. The tree limbs were dropping among us. There was death staring us in the face, apparently from every direction.

In our new position we could see the enemy just beyond the Second Massachusetts and Third Wisconsin regiments ahead of us. The union side had slightly the advantage of the position, for the ground was gently declining and the rebels were somewhat lower than their opponents. But the rebels had reached an old stone fence, which they were utilizing as a breastwork, and this made chances about even.

As the Confederate host loaded and fired their guns, they looked like a lot of devils in a war-dance. The upward movement of the arms in manipulating the long, old-fashioned ramrods, made them look for all the world as if they were dancing.

We could hear the battle cries of the opposing armies—the continuous "Hi-yi-yi" of the rebels, and the well-known three cheers of the union men. These were given alternately as each side wavered or advanced.

The two battle lines appeared to advance and recede, like the waves at the seashore, so that it looked at one moment as if the Confederates were retreating and the next as if the Union side had been driven back. Each side would then cheer when it advanced.

There is something inborn in human nature to like a contest of power. The staidest citizen becomes excited and interested in a sparring match, a wrestling bout, a horse race, or any sort of a competition. Even in the terrible surroundings of that battle, I distinctly remember the arrival of a new interest in the desperate fight that was taking place.

It is when this moment arrives that the feeling of fear over personal safety in a more or less degree leaves the participant. As for myself I will not say that I was not still frightened—terribly frightened; but I felt the fear not altogether disappearing, but being overshadowed by the interest in the contest.

CHAPTER LXXVII.

"LOAD AND FIRE AT WILL."

THE excitement of the battle had effected us all to a great extent, as related in the previous chapter. At the same time I cannot say that I felt any very intense desire to get up and rush forward to be an active participant.

Not so with William Lambert, one of our Company K members. He had become more interested and excited than the rest of us. Suddenly jumping to his feet, and waving his gun high over his head, he yelled out, in a voice that could be plainly heard even in that tremendous din:

"Come on, boys! Come on! They're running! The cowardly —— are running! Come on! If you're not all cowards, come on!"

And with that Lambert rushed ahead and was soon in the ranks of one of the regiments ahead of us.

In less than two minutes Lambert came back!

This time he did not have his rifle with him. On the contrary he was carrying something else in one of his hands! It was the broken remnants of one of his arms! It had been struck by something and literally torn to shreds. A strip of skin and the cloth of his coat sleeve prevented its falling off altogether, but what there was left of it was being carried in the other hand. That was the last of brave William Lambert's fighting. He went to the rear, had his arm amputated, went to the hospital, and was discharged when he got well.

I have just told how Lambert was holding his wounded arm in his well hand as he came back from the battle line. That was typical of all wounded soldiers. There is an involuntary and irresistible desire or inclination to take hold of the part that is wounded, as if to carry it, and this habit became so recognized by the "boys" that they invariably referred to the wounded member as "the baby." The fact that wounded men carried their injured hands and arms and heads so carefully and tenderly, naturally created the term, "baby."

It was recognized by all of us that we would in a very short time be precipitated to the very front and become actively engaged with the enemy. I involuntarily looked around and glanced at such of my companions as were near enough to be seen.

Every countenance bore a peculiar expression. Every face was pale, ashen in its pallor, and yet bore a striking expression of determination.

It is said that there is no other place in the world where a man gets that expression. It is known as "the frenzy of battle."

It seems as if a man under these circumstances concentrates all his energies, all his power, mental and physical, into one thing, and that is to be brave! He becomes an animal. His eyes have the same glare you see in the eyes of dogs as they stand ready to spring at each others' throats. It is seen in the eyes of a bull in the fighting ring. It is the glassy expressions of death without the concomitant of despair. It is the look that means death—death to one or the other. I imagine you might see that same expression in the faces of two men who are about to fight with bowie knives, "till one or both are dead."

In poetry and history it is called the look of "the frenzy of battle."

I turned to the man beside me. It was David Harris.

"How do you feel, Davy?" I asked. I found that my tongue was so hard and dry that I could scarcely articulate.

"I wish I was feeding the press in the *Guardian* office," replied he with a sickly smile—such a smile as one might expect from a corpse.

I glanced in the direction of John Ick and Reddy Mahar. Both were pale, which was an unusual thing for Mahar, for his complexion was like his name—reddy.

Down on the end of the line I saw Corneil Mersereau,

and wondered if my boots hurt his feet as they did mine. But such a thing as blistered feet didn't worry one at that moment, I guess.

I noticed John Stansfield and Henry Speer, lying quietly, saying nothing, pale, like the rest, and having a worried expression. On the other side of me lay Butterworth, my faithful "pard."

"How do you like this, Jack?" I asked him.

"I guess we're done for, Joe," he answered, quietly and solemnly.

"I think I am going to be one of the first one killed," I replied. And I really felt so.

"I would rather be killed outright than wounded like some of these fellows," said Butterworth.

And the way some of "these fellows" were wounded was frightful. There was passing through our line a perfectly endless stream of reddened, mangled human beings, shot in every imaginable part of the body. There seemed to be no end of them. It made me wonder how it was that there were any of them left at the front to fight.

Some of our men had been detailed to carry the worst wounded to the rear. One of these was Jimmy Post. As we were talking, Post and another man came along with a helplessly wounded man in a blanket, which they were carrying with the ends over their shoulders. The wounded man sank the blanket down till it looked like a bag.

"Whom have you got there?" I asked.

"Some poor devil," replied Jimmy. "I don't know whether he is dead or alive. But I am going to take him back to the doctor anyhow."

I plainly remember how Jimmy Post looked on that occasion. He was naturally very ruddy, with a face covered with freckles; but he was then so pale that it seemed as if nothing but the freckles could be seen.

Perhaps the terrific noises of the battle prevented one from hearing little things, and maybe that is the reason why I failed to hear much from the wounded men. The soldiers had so nerved themselves up, as it were, that they were in a condition to stand terrible pain without complaining. Horribly wounded men made no sign whatever of being in agony. Those who were comparatively slightly wounded seemed to be actually laughing. The more seriously hurt perhaps moaned and groaned, but the outcry then and there was not what would have been expected.

When a man was shot through the abdomen, it seemed to be excruciatingly painful, and he would shriek, as he writhed and rolled on the ground, like a decapitated chicken. But I am inclined to think that in other cases the victim was stunned, so that there was comparatively little pain at the start, and consequently none of those demonstrations of agony that might be expected. It is unquestionably the fact that in civil life, perhaps because it is less expected, an injured person makes considerably more of a demonstration than does a soldier in battle.

I don't know how long we remained there in our advanced position, waiting for our turn to take the places of those actively engaged in the fight. It might have been hours, it might have been seconds, so far as our sensations were concerned, for there was no thought of time. As a matter of fact it could not have been many minutes. Then came the long-awaited order:

"Fall in, Thirteenth! Forward, march!"

We marched forward, in battle array. The line was wavering and unsteady, but as good as could have been expected under the circumstances. As before, I fairly crouched on the ground as I walked along, as if desiring to present a less surface for a target to be shot at.

It was the very worst possible thing for me to have done. If a bullet passes through a man (interesting thing to talk about, isn't it?) while he is standing in a natural position, the same as through he were lying in his bed, it makes it the easier for the surgeon to probe the wound and remove the ball. If he is twisted out of shape, the course of the bullet is erratic, and to trace the ball the wounded man would have to put himself in precisely the same shape he was at the moment he was wounded, and this of course would be a difficult thing to do.

But I must confess that I "scrouged" a good deal, and tried to contract my body into the smallest possible compass. And no wonder, for we were getting into the thick of the fray, and the bullets were whistling past us more wickedly than ever.

We had, in obedience to orders, removed the bayonets from our rifles, so that they could be loaded the more handily, and opened the lids of the boxes containing our cartridges and percussion caps. We were ready for the fight.

A strange feeling began to come over me. The feeling of fear was vanishing. As if by magic the strength appeared to come to my legs again, and they no longer shook and trembled. I suddenly became utterly oblivious to personal safety, and I straightened myself up as stiffly as if I were on dress parade.

For an instant, the briefest sort of an instant, there flashed through my mind the leading events of my past life, and they as suddenly disappeared. Everything was forgotten in the excitement—the fighting excitement of the moment. I was possessed by a sudden and bloodthirsty desire to kill every gray-backed rebel that I saw dancing not the distance of a city block in front of me.

I have often heard old soldiers tell of this feeling. While all honest men will declare that at the commencement of a battle, or while waiting for their turn to become engaged, they are frightened out of their five senses, yet when they actually get into the fight all this disappears. I never believed it, but it turned out to be true in my case as in others. Every trace of fear and apprehension disappeared, and for the time being I was utterly oblivious to any feeling of danger.

Slowly, steadily we moved forward.

"Don't shoot till you receive the order," said Captain Beardsley, behind us, in that calm voice of his—a voice that seemed to inspire us all with confidence and fearlessness.

This made me wonder. We were close enough to the enemy to shoot. We could almost "see the whites of their eyes," to use a revolutionary simile. Every shot would perhaps have taken effect, but still the order was not to shoot till we received the order. A few more excited soldiers could not restrain themselves and a shot was heard here and there, but as a general rule the men faithfully obeyed their instructions about firing.

The men in our ranks began to fall. I remember plainly the case of Silas Abbott, who was immediately beside me. He was shot through the abdomen. He fell on the ground before me, rolled in the dry leaves of the forest, twisted and turned, and contorted his convulsed body in a manner that showed he was suffering exquisite torture. Poor fellow! He died a few days later from the effects of that wound.

But it did not seem to affect me very much then and there. My sensibilities and feelings appeared to have become blunted. I cared for nothing.

I felt a sting in the calf of my leg, and glancing down saw the blood coming from the bottom of my trousers. But it didn't hurt. In fact the only inconvenience was in having my leg wet, and it was warm. The warmth of my blood appeared to have no more effect than if it had been a cup of warm coffee that had been spilled on the inside of my pantaloons.

I was too much excited to care for that. I had made up my mind to stick to my place until I was disabled.

Another bullet scraped along my side. I plainly felt that and it hurt a little, but still I had no intention of retiring from the field—as some of them perhaps would have done under the circumstances.

Still the men kept falling around me. And still the order was repeated not to fire till we had received the order.

I felt something trickling down my face.

"Joe, are you wounded?" asked little William J. Post, who stood at my side.

I lifted my cap and brushed my hand over the top of my head. When I looked at my hand it was covered with blood. But I never would have known that I was hurt had it not been for the blood. There was not the slightest pain. It turned out only to be a scalp wound.

The reader will perhaps think that the author was getting peppered pretty well about this time, and it is the truth. The writer was wounded in six different places in that battle, and some of the wounds subsequently turned out to be quite painful. Two of the wounds, however, hurt so little at the start that they were actually not discovered till the victim had an opportunity to undress. That was in the hospital. But at last the order came to fire.

We were close upon the enemy. We could almost distinguish their countenances. Perhaps the distance was between one and two hundred yards.

Then came Captain Beardsley's order—

"Attention, Thirteenth! Load and fire at will!"

CHAPTER LXXVIII.

WOUNDED.

The order to "Load and fire at will!" meant for us to load and shoot our guns as fast as we could, and pepper away at the enemy continuously, without further orders.

My rifle was already loaded, as were most of the others, and the first salute the rebels received from the Thirteenth might appropriately be called a volley. As soon as possible after firing I looked in the direction of the enemy, and it seemed to me as if the number was smaller already! Of course this might have been mere imagination.

I continued to load and shoot as fast as I could. I remember Lieutenant Wells, who was in command of Company K, and who was stationed immediately behind me, cried out:

"Don't shoot too high. Aim low. Aim at their knees and you will hit them."

This was a common order. In the act of aiming and firing, the pull on the trigger or something else would raise the muzzle of the gun, so that the bullet would pass over the heads of the men aimed at. It is estimated that this peculiarity is the reason that such a comparatively small number of men were killed in battle. The bullets aimed at them went over their heads.

But by aiming at the knees of the enemy, the bullet would go about right to hit them somewhere in the upper part of the body. Of course there was more or less lateral variation in the course of the bullets, but that made less difference, for as the soldiers on the other side stood in a row, if one of them was not hit, the next one to him might not escape.

As said, I continued to pepper away. I loaded and fired my rifle at fast as I could do it. It took some time to load the old-fashioned muzzle-loading muskets, for there was the cartridge to tear open with the teeth, and it had to be rammed down home with the ramrod, the percussion cap had to be placed on the nipple, and lots of other things attended to, taking perhaps altogether a minute, maybe two minutes, for each shot. How different nowadays with the breech-loading, ready-made cartridge guns, with which all that is necessary is to raise and lower a lever.

Phew, but it was hot work! The perspiration streamed from every pore. The saltpeter in the powder of the cartridges got into one's mouth, making him terribly thirsty. The men wiped the sweat from their foreheads with their powder-stained hands, which they smeared over their faces till they looked like the begrimed stokers of an Atlantic liner.

Pretty soon my gun began to get very hot. It was so hot that I could hardly handle it, and I had to take hold of the wooden part of the stock under the barrel. Then it began to expand so that the bullets would hardly go into the bore. One would naturally think that when the barrel of a gun expands from the heat, it would make the hole bigger, but the contrary is the case. The metal expands on the inside of the bore and makes the hole smaller. I followed the example of some of the other fellows and jammed the bullet in by putting the end of the ramrod against a tree—for be it remembered we were fighting now in a thick woods.

The fact that the men were falling on all sides of me seemed to make no difference what happened. All that possessed me was an ardent desire to do my part in killing the rebels in front of me, and there is not the slightest doubt that some of them were laid low by the bullets that came from my gun, for I took deliberate aim every time.

The Thirteenth, and other regiments in the same line of battle, seemed to waver forward and backward. The rebels would apparently retreat, when we would advance. Then the enemy would appear to come nearer and we would fall back again. And so it went, back and forth, so that the effect was to preserve about the same distance between the two contending sides throughout.

As the men fell out of the ranks, either from being killed or wounded, we were ordered to "close in on the colors." That meant for the line to be closed in and the gaps filled up as fast as the men fell out. When the battle began I was somewhere about two hundred men from the flags. The last that I remember looking at them, there were not over fifteen or twenty men between where I stood and the colors. That shows the way the Thirteenth was being mowed down!

Several times I saw the colors drop as the color bearers were disabled, only to be immediately picked up by some survivor. Several times the right and left general guides were felled, and the little flags they carried were seen to fall, but they immediately reappeared. Once when the left general guide colors fell they were being borne by my comrade, Cornelius Mersereau, the man who wore my new boots. He was fatally wounded.

The first man I saw hit in Company K was Llewellyn J. T. Probert, who was shot dead. Directly Corporal Henry Speer dropped out. Then in turn followed Isaac Clark, William Freeland, Alexander Kidd, Francis More, John J. Nield, William J. Post, James W. Vanderbeck, Stephen Carlough and others. These were only members of Company K. The other companies were suffering equally, if not even worse.

Altogether that morning the Thirteenth Regiment lost eighteen killed, and eighty-nine wounded, including seven commissioned officers.

I had fired perhaps twenty or twenty-five shots, when suddenly—

"Bing!"

I thought that somebody had hit me in the hand with a stone. It felt exactly as if it was a blow from a small stone thrown from the other side of the street.

I did not think much of it, for the moment, but when I tried to lift my gun to fire another shot, I found that my hand was disabled, and looking at it, saw that it was covered with blood.

The little finger was torn to pieces and the side of my

hand shot away. What was left of the little finger was pulled over the back of the hand by the tendons. I could not move a single finger. I was disabled!

I remember carefully leaning my gun against a tree. That was the last I ever saw of the old rifle that I had carried so far, that I had so often cleaned and polished, and that, on the march, at times seemed to weigh at least a ton.

I turned to leave the ranks, as was the right thing for a wounded soldier to do, when Lieutenant Wells gave me a whack on the back with the flat side of his sword.

"Get back into the ranks," he cried. He thought that I was skulking or had been seized with one of those panics that frequently attack soldiers under such conditions.

"But I'm wounded, Heber," holding up my bloody hand.

"Oh, all right then," he said. "Get back to a doctor as soon as you can."

Just then Lieutenant Wells raised his sword aloft with a sort of hurrah, and while I looked I saw that sword fly from his grasp and go spinning through the air perhaps fifteen or twenty feet. It had been struck by a bullet or something and knocked out of the lieutenant's hand.

And the same bullet took Wells' first finger along with the sword.

Heber looked at his hand a moment, went calmly over and got his sword, and then joined me in the retreat for the rear, on our mutual search for a surgeon to attend to our respective hurts.

On going back to the rear we had to pass down the side of one hill and up another, and as we ascended the latter we went through what might be termed a veritable shower of lead. Bullets fairly rained around us. We could see them strike the sod and tear up the dirt, causing a puff of dust to arise. It seemed even hotter here than it was in the midst of the battle itself. I have since thought that it was here that I received one of those minor wounds which I did not discover till later, although of course that is only conjecture. At all events I had no consciousness of being hit by anything at that time.

We finally got back to a place where we found a yellow flag sticking in the ground, which we recognized as the stand of some field surgeon. Here were a lot of other wounded men and we had to wait for our turn at the "slaughter house," as John Ick would have called it had he been there.

While waiting I saw something that I never saw before nor afterward. It was a *vivandière*. She was rather a pretty girl, only for the fact that she was tanned and sunburned like a farmer in haying time. She wore a costume which was very much like the latest make-up of the female bicyclists—a sort of zouave dress, with bloomers and leather leggings.

"Will you have a drink?" she asked; and then I noticed that she had a little wooden keg hanging at her waist, and carried a tin cup in her hand.

Would I have a drink? Would a duck swim?

Of course I answered in the affirmative, and she turned a little spiggot in the end of the keg, and poured me out a cup full of—

It was brandy, and good brandy at that. Never before nor afterward did a drink of brandy taste so good. I didn't ask for any "chaser," for I didn't want any in the first place and there was none to be had if I wanted it!

That drink of brandy nerved me up considerably, and I was ready for almost any sort of a surgical or other operation.

Heber Wells was by this time having his wound attended to. The doctor was a young fellow, a mere boy, apparently some medical student. Everything was pressed into the service in those times that could handle a carving knife.

I watched the operation on Heber with some trepidation. He winced a little but did not complain.

"Does it hurt much?" I asked, very much interested.

"No," he replied. "It's nothing more than a snip of the scissors." When Heber got finished up, he bade me good-by, saying that he would not wait, and the young doctor turned to me.

"Come, it's your turn," said he.

I held my hand, and he examined it curiously. Then he stooped down and picked a stout twig.

"Here," said he, "hold this between your teeth."

"What's that for?" I asked.

"Something for you to bite on," he replied coolly. "This is going to hurt you a little and you don't want to break your teeth, do you?"

Then he took my hand in one of his hands, and a blood-stained knife in the other!

CHAPTER LXXIX.

"FOR THE LOVE OF GOD, SHOOT ME."

THE man who undertook to amputate my finger and patch up my mangled hand, was a butcher, if there ever was one in the world. He did not know any more about surgery than a three year old child. There were so many wounded men to be attended to there, however, that they had pressed into the service everybody who knew enough to handle a penknife, and the fellow who got hold of me must have been either a medical cadet or a hostler.

He went at me as if he was going to carve a piece of mutton chop—perhaps a pork chop might make a more appropriate simile, eh? He cut and sliced and mutilated my hand in the most horrible manner, and when he got to the bone he produced a pair of nippers similar to those used by the electricians of the present day to cut small wires, and with that he nipped off the broken bones of my finger and hand that protruded from the flesh.

It was well that he had given me the twig to bite upon, or I should certainly have broken my teeth, for I chewed that thick stick into mince. The recommendation to hold that twig between my teeth was about the only degree of intelligence manifested by that amateur human butcher.

When he had got through with having all the fun he wanted out of me, he turned me over to a still less experienced young man to bandage up the wound, and that was done in a bundle so large that it looked as if I had on a big white boxing-glove. I cannot describe how much that little operation pained me. I did not make any outward demonstration, but it was all that I could do to keep from crying out loud. I took satisfaction out of the stick between my teeth.

While I was there the wounded were being taken past in a perpetual string, some being carried by the arms and legs, others on stretchers, and still more being supported between two comrades. Among these were many of the members of the Thirteenth Regiment, and some of them were terribly wounded.

I remember seeing Adjutant Thomas B. Smith, who was badly hurt somewhere about the body. Then they brought along Lieutenant George G. Whitfield, of Company A, who was horribly wounded on the head. He was on a stretcher, and his head seemed one mass of gore, and he writhed around on the stretcher in a way that made one's blood run cold. Poor fellow, he died a couple of days later.

Pretty soon I saw some men assisting from the field a man from Company C, whom I recognized as George H. Comer. His arm had been so badly wounded that it had to be cut off. Then I saw many other acquaintances come along, wounded in one way or another.

Among these I remember George Baitzel, Freeborn Garrison, Charles B. Burris, David Burris, Amzi Brown, John C. Crawford, Andrew Loise, R. B. Manning, Jacob Mickler, William Parker, Gilbert Smith, and others. Some of these are still living, but others have answered their last roll call.

It would be impossible to state the exact loss of the Thirteenth in killed and wounded at the battle of Chancellorsville. The official number has been given in a previous chapter, but it is known that it was considerably larger. After every battle there was always a number put under the head of "Missing," and it was never known what became of them, and these should perhaps be placed in the list of killed.

On the other hand some of these that were "missing" after a battle turned up after many years, with a more or less accurate account of their doings. There have been many Enoch Arden cases of this nature.

The "missing" department of the rolls of a regiment after a battle is one of the most wonderful and mysterious features of a war.

After having had my wounded hand dressed I started to go to the rear. To the rear is a term universally used as going in the other direction than the front. It is also always supposed that there is a haven of refuge and retreat somewhere in the rear, and that is the objective point of all wounded soldiers. There was a perfect procession of more or less severely wounded men strolling rearward and I joined this parade.

I passed the old Chancellorsville house, which was General Hooker's headquarters, and was an eye-witness of the accident that occurred to General Hooker on that morning. There have been many versions of the manner in which he was wounded, but I can give the facts, for I was not far distant from him when it happened. I had stopped to look at the old fighting general, whom I recognized, standing on the porch of the ancient hotel, half-leaning against one of the posts or pillars that held up the shed over the porch.

The cannon balls and shells were flying around very lively, and one of them struck the post against which the general was leaning and broke it into splinters. The general naturally fell over and appeared to be stunned. It was reported afterward that he was struck by the shell, or whatever it was, but this was not the case. When it was found that there were no external marks upon him and that he did not appear to be dangerously hurt, it was reported that he was knocked over by the concussion from the passage of the shell. But this is not true either. He simply lost his support and fell over and was injured by the fall from the porch.

Report has it that the general soon revived after the application of a dose of good old commissary, and that it made him feel so good that he took another and another dose, until pretty soon—but this may be a base libel. Like Grant, the president perhaps inquired what sort of whisky he drank, so that he might get some of the same sort for some of the other generals!

Not far from the Chancellorsville house was an immense barn, which had been turned into a hospital. My first idea was to repair to this hospital, which I knew to be such from the large yellow flag floating over it.

Now in civilized warfare—as if any warfare could be called civilized—the hospital flag is presumed to protect the building or tent from the fire of the enemy. It is an unwritten law, in the interests of common humanity, that hospitals shall be exempt from being shot at. But imagine my horror to see that the enemy had trained their guns on this hospital.

It could not have been accidentally done. Shell after shell poured into the building, almost tearing it to pieces in the course of a few moments. The wounded men came streaming out, some helping themselves, others on stretchers. They were suffering untold agonies from their wounds, and many of them were horribly stained with their own blood. As they came streaming from the hospital, the upper part of which had taken fire, it presented one of the most horrible scenes that I ever witnessed, and never before did I feel so thoroughly mad at the inhumanity of the gunners who would do such a thing.

But the shells and the bullets came flying still faster and it was getting too hot for me. I concluded to get further back, where it was safer.

Just about this time a remarkable revulsion of feeling came over me. From the time I had become actively engaged in the conflict of the battle, as previously described, I had not experienced the slightest emotion of apprehension or fear. But suddenly I began to be frightened. In fact I was almost panic-stricken, and my sole desire was to reach a place of safety. Now that there was a possibility of saving my life, the desire of doing so was all the more intensified. I started to run at full speed, and for a little distance made good time, till I began to feel some strange pain in my legs.

Upon the top of a hill I saw what looked like a comparatively safe place behind some ammunition wagons, caissons and limbers, to which the horses were attached, as if ready to move on a minute's notice.

Getting down behind these, I pulled off my trousers and began to examine my nether extremities. I found my legs streaming with blood, and then found the two bullet wounds that I had never before suspected. I must have received these in the midst of the fight a little while before, when I was too much excited to notice "a little thing like that."

While I was at this, there was a tremendous crash and explosion, followed by yells and curses, and a dense cloud of smoke arose to the skies.

Looking upward, I was amazed to see the air filled with flying *débris*, and among the lot I was horrified to see human beings and horses mixed with the broken pieces of the wagons and timbers.

Before I could recover my senses there dropped right alongside me a human being—or what was left of him!

Such a sight! I nearly dropped senseless. It makes me shudder to this day when thinking of it.

Could it be a human being? Could there be any life left in that—that thing?

But it was alive! It spoke!

"For the love of God," it said, "for the love of God, shoot me! Put me out of my misery!"

CHAPTER LXXX.

RETREAT FROM CHANCELLORSVILLE.

"IF there is any one near me," moaned the poor man, "if any one can hear me, let him shoot me!"

This the poor wretch repeated time and time again. His voice was thick and his words could hardly be comprehended, but I understood them. And I confess right here that if I had had a gun or pistol I would have done as he wished and put him out of his misery.

A shell had struck one of the caissons and it had exploded. That one shot had, as afterward ascertained, killed sixteen horses and twelve men, beside wounding nearly as many more. One-half of these had been blown high into the air, amid a mass of scorching flames from the exploding powder.

The poor fellow before me had gone up in the midst of the flame, and the fire had not only burned off every stitch of clothing, but had roasted his flesh to a crisp. His hair was gone. His eyes were burned out and his ears had entirely disappeared. The ends of his fingers were roasted off to the very bone. Through one of his knees protruded the end of the bone. Such a sickening sight was never seen.

And yet the thing was alive, and not only alive, but conscious, and able to pray that some one might put a merciful bullet through his heart. I have always regretted that I was not able to answer that prayer. I do not think it would have been wrong to kill a man under such circumstances.

What became of that man I don't know. I could not stand the sight, and ran away as fast as I could, not even taking time to put on my trousers, which I had taken off to examine my own wounds. With these hanging over my arm I scurried down the other side of the hill as fast as my legs would carry me, and when I got to a safe place I redressed myself. It was many a day before I got the horrible sight from my eyes.

Once more I joined the procession of wounded men, and pretty soon came to the river again and crossed on a pontoon bridge.

An army was moving in opposite directions. One was the army of wounded men with which I was moving. The other was composed of the fresh troops that were going forward to relieve those actively engaged in fighting.

Right glad was I that I was going the way I was instead of in the opposite direction. And when I thought of the difference I began to feel exhilarated and joyous.

Gradually a sense of the situation came over me, and it grew stronger and stronger as I walked along.

I began to appreciate what a glorious thing it would be to see my name in the papers among the list of wounded. Here was unanswerable proof that I had been actively engaged in a battle. For a time at least there would be no more fighting for me. Only an old soldier can appreciate what that sensation means.

Perhaps—and the idea struck me like a flash—perhaps I might get a furlough to go home. A furlough! Could it be possible?

Would I again see Paterson? Was it possible that I might go home with my arm in a sling, bearing the honorable wounds of a soldier who had bravely done his duty?

These sensations are the ecstacy of a soldier's happiness, and then I experienced them for the first time. What were all the hardships and terrors I had gone through now? They all sank into insignificance. All that I knew was that there was a chance of my seeing home once more, and that for a time I would go into civilization and be free!

Free! Yes, that is the word. Service in the army is a sort of slavery in one sense, a nightmare, an ever-present sense of not being your own master. And the feeling that one may be exempt from this slavery, this trammel, or whatever it may be called, is a pleasure that can only be comprehended by those who have gone through it.

I had a long walk that day, and it was a tiresome walk for me, for the wounds in my legs pained and weakened me. But the mental sensations of getting away from the active and horrible front, kept me going and gave me strength.

Somehow or other it got out that the wounded soldiers were to repair to Aquia creek, where the general field hospitals were located. How far was Aquia creek? "About ten miles," was the answer. Ten miles—in Virginia! We knew what that meant, and made up our minds that it was at least twenty.

But what is twenty miles to a soldier, especially when not hampered with the weight of a heavy musket and knapsack and accouterments? It was nothing. As a matter of fact, however, it was not twenty miles. Sixteen was nearer it.

While we were walking along one side of the river, we could see the rising smoke and hear the rattling musketry and booming cannon on the other side of the river all the way from Chancellorsville to Fredericksburg and below.

I reached Aquia creek somewhere about dusk, and reporting to an officer was assigned to a straw bed on the ground in an immense hospital tent. The conditions were not very favorable for sleeping, for the tent, as well as many others like it scattered around, was filled with wounded men. The wounds, at first comparatively painless, had by this time begun to inflame, and the men were growing restless under the agony. There was a perfect chorus of moans and groans, prayers and curses.

But I was too fatigued from the day's excitement to stay awake and soon fell sound asleep. During the night some time I was awakened by the water running through the straw on which I lay. I listened and heard the rain pattering on the outside of the tent and the wind was blowing the canvass in a way that threatened to turn the whole hospital upside down.

A terrible rainstorm had come up during the night.

It is a singular thing that a heavy rain always follows a big battle. It is supposed to be the result of the cannonading. It is upon this theory that the "rainmakers" recently made such an ado. I haven't the slightest doubt that if as much powder were spent in these scientific tests as there is consumed in a big battle, there would be a heavy rain afterward. At all events I think that history will prove that there never yet was a heavy battle that was not followed by a big rainstorm.

That rain-storm, by the way, was one of the causes of the failure of the Union troops at Chancellorsville. General Hooker, in his braggadocio order, had said in effect that he had got the enemy in such a position that even the Almighty could not save them. That was where he made a mistake. He had arranged the details for the battle all right and all had been done that human skill could do. But the very power that General Hooker had derided frustrated the whole scheme, and turned into a defeat what might, but for the storm that heaven brought up, have been a glorious victory.

After I had been wounded the Thirteenth Regiment remained in the fighting line till their ammunition was completely exhausted. The regiment was frightfully reduced in numbers, but the men did their duty nobly, and made a name for themselves that gained for them the soubriquet of "The Fighting Thirteenth!"

In falling back to a position near the Chancellorsville house a number of them were wounded by the storm of shells and bullets through which I had passed, as previously described. The fighting continued all day, but although the Thirteenth was moved hither and thither, it did not again become actively engaged.

The battle was continued on the following morning in a desultory sort of a way, but pretty soon the rain began to interfere with the operations. The roads and fields became so deep with mud that the artillery and ammunition wagons could not be moved, and the river began to rise so rapidly that the current threatened to wash away the pontoon bridges. It was impossible to bring to the front any more ammunition or provisions, and a further delay might prevent the retreat of the troops to the other side of the river.

So, instead of following up the battle, the army had to retreat to the other side of the river to escape being hemmed in and cut up completely. This left the field in the possession of the enemy practically, although they were also cut up too badly to make any effort to follow us. The Northern army was in decidedly the best condition, and it was one of the greatest mishaps of the war that they were not in a position to follow up the enemy and annihilate them then and there, as might unquestionably have been done, but for the interference of the great storm.

As it was, the entire army was ordered back to the same camps they had occupied before starting out for the Chancellorsville campaign.

How different was that backward march from the one to the front only a few days before! The roads were heavy with mud. The rain came down in torrents, dampening both the bodies and spirits of the men. There were sorrowful hearts in the ranks as the comrades looked around and failed to see their former companions. No one knew the fate of his comrades, of course.

What had become of this one and that one, was the question that none could answer. They were last seen at this place or that place. Some remembered seeing some shot, but whether wounded or killed, no one could tell. To all intents and purposes all the absentees were killed. It took days before the real fate of the missing could be ascertained, and never was the fate of some of them discovered.

With thinned ranks, downcast, tired out, discouraged, what was left of the Thirteenth Regiment of New Jersey Volunteers filed into the same old camp they had occupied at Stafford Court House, and took possession of the same old log huts.

Those who participated in that return said afterward that it felt like coming home from a funeral. My faithful "pard," John Butterworth, had the whole bunk to himself, for I lay under that rain-soaked tent at Aquia creek and the report was in the regiment that I had been killed.

Indeed the first papers after the battle had my name among the list of the dead, and every once in a while when I feel in a peculiarly cheerful mood, and want something to amuse me, I get out the old files and read my own obituary!

CHAPTER LXXXI.

HOSPITAL SCENES.

The time I lay in the rain-soaked hospital tent at Aquia creek was about as tough an experience as I had yet passed through. It was impossible to go out without getting wet to the skin, while the inside of the tent was cold and damp, and it was so filled with wounded men that there was hardly room to get around.

The best thing that we could do under these circumstances was to remain in bed, and that is just what the most of us did. When I say "bed" of course I mean nothing more than the pile of straw on the wet ground upon which we lay.

The wounded men lay in a row along each side of the tent, leaving a sort of aisle in the middle through which the surgeons and attendants could pass. The wounds began to become very painful as the time passed, and the groans and moans of the poor victims were unceasing day and night. Every once in a while the doctors would have to amputate a leg or an arm or perform some other surgical operation in one end of the tent, and that added to our mental torture. Although wounded and feverish, the fare that we received was little better than the regular army rations out in the field, and taking it altogether it was a fearfully uncomfortable and painful experience.

After about three days, however, on a cold and damp night, although the rain had stopped, word was passed through the tent that a number of us were to be transferred to Washington, and I happened to be one of the men thus favored.

We were taken down to the dock and placed on board a steamboat. We were laid on the bare deck of the steamer, as closely together as we could lie, but it was a dry place, compared with the tent, although very draughty. Pretty soon the throbbing of the engines of the steamboat commenced. It was welcome music to my ears. It was the first sound of civilization. It was so different from the taps of the drum, the blast of the bugle, the rattle of musketry and the boom of cannon, that it sounded like veritable music, and it soon lulled me into a sound slumber.

I never awoke till morning. When I opened my eyes, the sun streamed into the windows at the side of the boat, and at a distance I could see some buildings. Getting up to take a more careful observation my eyes were delighted by the familiar sight of the unfinished dome of the National Capitol, and the half-completed shaft of the Washington monument.

I was again in Washington.

We were removed to the various hospitals that had been built at the capital. These were simply rough barracks built in wings, but commodious enough to accommodate many thousand wounded men. And from the way the wounded men were being taken into them it seemed that it would not take long to fill them all up. Wounded men arrived by the hundreds, by boat and by cars, and then for the first time we began to appreciate the vast number of soldiers that had been mutilated in the battle of Chancellorsville.

I was taken to the Lincoln hospital. There was a good deal of red tape in the army at all times, and it even extended to the operation of assigning wounded men to the different hospitals. I remember that it was late in the afternoon that I arrived at Lincoln Hospital, and it was night before I had been assigned to my particular ward and cot.

My name and regiment and the address of my friends at home were written on a piece of paper and stuck at the head of my cot on the wall. This was done in the case of all the men, and was of course for the purpose of identification in case anything happened that rendered it necessary to send word home or make a report to the regiment.

A sister of charity, God bless her!—a mere girl at

that, who would have been very pretty had she taken off her big white bonnet and fixed up her hair a little, came to me and calmly told me that she thought I had better go to bed. I am inclined to think that if my face was not too dirty to show it at the time, I actually blushed a little as I politely told her I would retire if she could manage to hide herself for a few moments. Smilingly she disappeared.

I proceeded to undress. Then it struck me that this was the first time that I undressed to go to bed since I enlisted. To tell the truth I felt rather ashamed. A soldier in the field never thinks of taking off all his clothing to go to bed, and there was a freedom or looseness about it, if you please, that felt very odd. When I opened the bed and saw the clean, white sheets, it seemed a sacrilege to muss them up.

But I hastened into the cot and pulled the clothes up around my chin, and oh! how comfortable it did feel! It was the first time in about nine months that I had been undressed and in bed, and the sensation seemed to be as strange as if it were the first time I had ever done it in my life.

Pretty soon the sister came along with a glass of something and told me to drink it. It was eggnog! Yum-yum-yum-yum! Did ever anything taste so good? It was nectar fit for the gods. I kept my lips glued to the edge of the glass as long as there was a drop of the precious stuff left. Then I felt as if I would like to swallow the glass.

The sister told me to go to sleep, and I think I obeyed this instruction in a few moments, for pretty soon the warmth of the liquor in the punch began to flow through my veins and I think that I never before nor since felt so supremely happy or comfortable.

Some time during the night I was awakened by a racket. The ward in which I was located contained a number of severely wounded men. The racket was caused by the efforts of the attendant to quiet a poor fellow who had become delirious. He had had both legs amputated just above the knees, and in his delirium had arisen from his cot and was trying to walk down the aisle on his mutilated stumps! The effort tore the bandages off and the blood flowed on the floor.

"Get that man quieted at once," exclaimed one of the surgeons, who had hastened out of his office to see what was the matter. "If you don't act quickly he will bleed to death."

"You're a liar," was the surprising answer from the wounded man. "You're a liar! You can't kill Jim Murphy. There isn't a —— rebel in the country that could kill Jim Murphy."

"But you'll bleed to death if you don't remain quiet and let these nurses attend to your bandages," said the surgeon.

"No, I'll be —— if I do," replied the wounded man. "I don't intend to die, and ye can't kill me. Jim Murphy's too tough for ye all!"

They got the plucky fellow back into his cot and tied him in, much to his disgust. There were other rackets in progress down the ward, for the wounds had begun to make the men feverish generally. I will only refer to one case as a contrast with that of "Jim Murphy." It was a fellow who had been shot through the thigh, and although it was a painful injury it was by no means dangerous. But the man was frightened half to death and had made up his mind to die anyway.

"I tell you, doctor," said he, plaintively, "I am going to die. I will never get over this. I have received a mortal wound."

"Oh, nonsense," replied the doctor. "You are not fatally hurt by any means. You are not half as badly wounded as this fellow with both legs off, and he says that they can't kill him."

"No, you spalpeen," replied the legless man, "they can't kill me. Don't ye be a baby. Brace up and don't die to satisfy the spalpeens."

But this did not pacify the other. The trivially wounded man lost his heart and made up his mind that he was going to die, and he did. He died that very night, and the doctors said that it was not from the wound at all, but from the fact that the fellow had lost his nerve and given up, and all the doctors on the face of the earth could not save a man under such circumstances.

The legless man, true to his word, kept up his pluck

and got well, and for all that I know he is living yet. Possibly he may be one of those who are scuffling along on the New York sidewalks, picking up a handsome living from charitably disposed people.

I simply relate this instance to illustrate a matter that had many parallels during the war. A grievously wounded man would invariably recover if he kept up his pluck and his nerve, while many a man, whose wounds should not have caused his death, died, simply because he gave up. The influence of the mind over the body was never more strongly shown than in such cases as these, and there is not an old army surgeon who could not relate hundreds of similar instances.

In a day or so my wound began to pain me fearfully, and swelled bigger and bigger till it became as large as my head. I grew feverish and somewhat delirious. The gentle sister who waited on me brought me many milk punches and cup custards, and if she had been my blood sister she could not have manifested greater solicitude for my welfare. My swollen hand was placed in an oil-silk bag and filled with ice, so that it was practically frozen.

But no use. Gangrene had set in, and old soldiers know what that means. One morning the doctor came to me and after examining my hand, shook his head and gravely remarked:

"It's no use, my boy; that hand has got to come off, if you want to live."

If the surgeon had given me a blow on the head with a sledgehammer I could not have received a greater shock.

CHAPTER LXXXII.

A SISTER OF CHARITY.

When the surgeon told me that he would have to cut off my hand to save my life, it was, as stated, a terrible shock. I had lain there and suffered, with my swollen arm incased in ice, frozen stiff and strapped to a chair beside my cot, and suffered untold tortures, but had not made a murmur. But the mental suffering occasioned by the startling information that I would have to go through the world for the rest of my life with only one hand, was a thousand times worse than anything that I had yet experienced.

As soon as I could recover my voice, I asked:

"Is there no hope of saving it, doctor? The loss of that hand would ruin me. It would make it impossible for me to ever work again at my trade."

"What is your trade?" he asked.

"A printer."

"Hump! That's bad. I'll see what can be done about it this afternoon."

"This afternoon?" I asked. It seemed a dreadfully short notice.

"Yes, my boy," answered the surgeon, kindly; "whatever is done must be done without further delay."

I shuddered at the idea of having my hand amputated, even though it was the left hand. I reflected how I would look going through life with one hand. How would I ever earn my living? I couldn't hold a composing stick and set type with one hand. Then I suddenly remembered my fiddle. How could I play the violin with one hand—and that instrument was one of the joys of my life. I am not saying how much joy it must have been to those who were compelled to listen to my practicing!

Then the good sister came along with another milk punch. It was a dandy. I imagined it must have been three-quarters brandy. In a few moments I felt so good that I didn't care if they cut off both hands and threw in one leg for good measure! I was soon sleeping the sleep of the just and virtuous, as soundly as if I had been given a dose of knock-out drops.

Some time during the afternoon I was awakened by the surgeon's assistant, who had come to take me to the operating-room at the end of the ward. Now the surgeons in the hospital in war times were no prohibitionists. They believed in the efficacy of good old whisky. And that it served a good purpose there can be no question.

The first thing the doctor did, therefore, was to pour out for me a regular old-fashioned bumper of Bourbon, a brimming glassful that would have made Weary Waggles' eyes glisten with joy. I swallowed it, and sent a chaser after it, and in a few moments felt as if I didn't care for all the surgeons' knives in the world.

The surgeon, and by the way he was a Dr. Brown, of Carlisle, Pennsylvania, and as expert a surgeon as ever lived, besides being a kind-hearted and humane gentleman, unwrapped the bandages off my swollen hand and arm and critically examined the wound.

"What do you think of it, doctor?" I asked, somewhat nervously.

"I may save the hand yet," replied the surgeon. "I can't tell, however, till I cut into it a little to see how far the gangrene has extended."

"Try and save it if you can," said I, mournfully. I had a terrible dread of losing the hand. Perhaps in the first excitement of the battle I would not have thought so much about it, but now that I had time to reflect it was different. And I had had an opportunity to notice the crippled and helpless condition of the other fellows who had been forced to part with that very necessary part of the human anatomy.

"Better try a little more of this, my boy," said the doctor, pouring me out another generous bumper of the whisky.

It struck me that the surgeon was determined that I

should get gloriously drunk. But I didn't care. If there ever was a time when I felt like getting a first-class jag, as it is called nowadays, it was just then and there. This, however, was not Dr. Brown's intention, as I discovered afterward. My system was run down, and it was necessary that I should be stimulated to go through with the operation.

I was strapped on the top of the operating table. The good sister stood at my side, holding a basin of water and a sponge. The surgeon's assistant got a sponge saturated with chloroform. It was the first time I had ever taken an anæsthetic.

A smothering sensation! A brief struggle for air. A feeling that I was going up, up, up! . . .

The next moment—so it seemed—I found myself in the grasp of three men. The table was upset, the sister, picking herself up from the floor with her face covered with blood and her usually white and spotless bonnet crumpled out of shape, and I struggling there with my wounded hand a mass of blood and gore, with the bandage knocked off.

I was completely bewildered. And what struck me the more strangely was the fact that everybody was laughing. Even the sister was smiling as she picked herself up from the floor. Dr. Brown said it was the "liveliest time he had since the war began."

It must have been, judging from my appearance and the looks of things about me!

It seems that the combined effects of the whisky and the chloroform had been too rich for my blood. As explained afterward to me, after the operation had been performed, and I was reviving from the effects of the anæsthetic, I had become delirious, and the first thing I had done had been to knock down the sister of charity with a blow of my wounded fist. This had torn off the bandages. The upsetting of the things in the little operating room was caused by the struggle the doctor and his attendants had in subduing me.

I knew nothing of what had occurred, of course. When I looked at my hand and saw that it was there yet, I imagined that the operation had not yet been commenced, and asked the doctor what was the matter that it had not been done?

"It's done," replied Dr. Brown. "The operation is finished——"

"But the hand's still there?" I asked, glancing at the bloody looking object.

"Yes," replied he. "I think we can save it. It is not so bad as we supposed. You will find that it is narrower than it was. I took out the bone on the side, below the base of the little finger, and got the end of the gangrene. You will be all right yet. Your hand will be saved."

"Thank God!" I exclaimed, fervently and thankfully. "Doctor, I'll never forget you for this."

"But you will have to have it fixed over again," said he. "You have knocked it all to pieces. The stitches have come out and I will have to sew it over again. Do you think you can stand that, or will I give you another dose of chloroform?"

"Oh, I can stand that, I guess," I replied. "No more chloroform for me, if you please. I think too much of the sister here to run the risk again."

The sister smiled. "Oh, that was nothing," she said pleasantly.

So the doctor proceeded to "sew me up." There were only three or four stitches, but fury! didn't it hurt! Those who have undergone surgical operations all agree that the most painful part of it is the sticking through of the needle and drawing through the silken thread. It is the most sensitive part of the body, the skin. But I got through with it all right.

Then I began to have an atrocious headache, and felt like completely collapsing. The doctor's suggestion that I take another drink of whisky almost made me gag. "No," I replied; "one drunk a day is enough for me."

I was put to bed, and pretty soon had a raging fever. For two days and night I lay there on the cot, not caring whether I lived or died. The afterclaps of the operation were worse than the operation itself, a thousand times.

But youth and health will triumph pretty quickly with a boy of nineteen years, and I rapidly came to myself again. Then I realized the inestimable service the good sister had rendered while I lay so low. She had sat by the side of my cot day and night and attended to my every want and desire. And anybody who has sat by a sick bed appreciates what that means.

When I got better the sister did not keep around me as much as while I was dangerously feverish. But she came now and then, with a glass of eggnog or a cup custard or some other dainty, such as they give convalescents. One night she came through the ward about 10 o'clock. She was on her last errand before retiring, and seeing me awake, stopped, took a seat at the side of the cot, and softly asked me how I felt?

The ward was very quiet. Everybody seemed to be asleep; with the exception of the lonely and half-asleep guard at the end of the room, there was no one there but the sister.

Now I had just about fallen half in love with that sister! And who would wonder? She was the first woman I had spoken to in months. She had treated me like a mother, and her kindness had been ceaseless. I felt more than grateful. I felt affectionate, as one would to his affianced. And as yet not a word had passed between us that was not strictly professional, so to speak. This time I decided to go a little further.

"I am glad that you have stopped here to-night," said I.

"Why?" she asked.

"Because you have been very kind to me, and I don't know how to thank you."

"It is my duty to be kind to these poor fellows," she replied.

"Yes, but I have been watching pretty closely, and I imagine that you have been specially kind to me."

The sister dropped her eyes—and blushed.

Now for a sister of charity to drop her eyes and blush is something out of the usual run. Generally they are as implacable and emotionless as marble. They are trained to be so. But here was an exception. I felt encouraged at the sign and proceeded.

"Sister," said I, "will you do me a favor?"

"What is it?" she asked, looking at me wonderingly.

"Will—will you please take off your big white bonnet?"

She blushed again.

"I can't do that," she said gently; "it's against the rules."

"Oh, never mind the rules," I said. "Take it off, and do me that little favor, won't you, please?"

"I—I——"

"Oh, please do."

She glanced about nervously, hesitated a moment, and then, with her face crimson with color, unfastened the broad white strings under her chin, and with a graceful movement threw back her bonnet.

In doing this it got caught in her hair somehow, and down to her very waist tumbled a luxurious mass of wavy brown tresses. I looked up and saw a vision of perfect loveliness!

CHAPTER LXXXIII.

"CRUSHED AGAIN."

"There's many a noble heart under a ragged coat," and there is doubtless many a handsome face masqueraded by an exaggerated and distorted white bonnet worn by a sister of charity, but never did I expect to find such an object of beauty in the little sister who now stood before me in all her loveliness.

To be sure, I had become acquainted with her gentle manner, her soft touch and her soothing voice, but I had all along imagined that she was naturally as homely as she looked in her solemn garb. Sisters of charity all look alike, owing to their peculiar dress, which seems specially designed to make them seem unattractive, but in this instance at least I discovered that there was beauty behind the plain exterior, and ever since when I have met one of them attired in the homely garb of the order I have involuntarily wondered how the sister would look if she were attired in ordinary costume.

Inasmuch as beauty is the pride of woman, what a sacrifice it must be for them to thus bury their charms and devote their lives to the mission of benevolence and the alleviation of human suffering! When one considers these things he must have a still higher regard for the self-sacrificing spirit of those who throw aside the pleasures of the world and devote themselves to an existence of slavery to good work, as it were.

When I saw the sister standing beside me that night in all her loveliness, with her flushed face, and her thick tresses hanging down her back, I was speechless with amazement. Embarrassed, she proceeded to readjust her hair, and as she did so her sleeves slipped back to her elbows, displaying an arm that would have set a sculptor wild with enthusiasm. I quickly put out my hand to stop her.

"Don't put it up, please," said I. "Let your hair remain as it is."

"But I must not," she said. "It is against the rules. But," she added coyly, "why do you ask that?"

"If you knew the difference it makes," said I, "if you appreciated how beautiful——"

"Sh," she interrupted. "You must not talk that way. You ought to be ashamed of yourself."

"But I'm not," I replied. "A young man who wouldn't admire you as you look now, ought to be ashamed of himself. But no one could help it, I guess."

"Sh, you mustn't," she repeated. But I noticed that she was not in a particular hurry to put up her hair again. She dallied in the operation. She was a woman, if she was a sister of charity.

"What is your name, sister?" I asked her.

"Sister Felicia. You know that."

"Yes, I know that. But what is your real name?"

"It would not be right for me to tell that."

"Oh, it wouldn't do any harm." I insisted. I reached out and took her hand. She did not withdraw it. I was making good progress, and my heart went pitty-pat. I had fallen in love with the sister!

"My right name—is—I don't suppose it will do any harm to tell, although it is against the rules—my right name is Nellie Carleton."

"Where do you live?" I asked her.

"I shouldn't answer that, but I will tell you that my home is in Philadelphia."

"Philadelphia, eh? That's where the soldiers are always so nicely treated. It is the city of Brotherly Love.

"Tell me," I continued, "what made you, such an attractive girl, perhaps surrounded with everything to make life enjoyable, lay aside your toilets and dresses of civil life, to put on that homely gown and devote yourself for life to such work as this? It does not seem natural."

"Excuse me," she answered. "I haven't devoted

my life to this, by any means. I am not a regular sister of charity. I have not taken the veil. I can leave and return home at any time I desire. I only volunteered, with some other girls, because the government wanted nurses. The men are doing their duty, and I thought it only right that the women should do their part, in the best manner possible, and I could not see any better way than to assist in alleviating the suffering of the sick and wounded."

"And then you are going back home when your services are no longer required?"

"Certainly. My father is a rich man, and my mother is not in good health, and I will return as soon as possible to look after my little sisters."

"Are they all as pretty as——"

"Sh," she interrupted. "No more flattery, please."

"I can't help that, but if you do not like it, I will stop."

To tell the truth she did not look as if she really wanted me to stop. She was a woman!

"Nellie," said I, but she promptly interrupted me:

"Sister, if you please."

"Well, then, sister," I said, smiling, "why have you been so kind to me since I have been here?"

"I have tried to be kind to all these poor fellows," she replied.

"Yes, but I have noticed carefully, and I think you have been specially kind to me."

She blushed deeply.

"Have I?" she asked quietly.

"Yes, you have. You know you have been." She seemed embarrassed considerably at this.

"I don't know that—that——"

"It makes no difference," I insisted. "You have been specially kind to me and you have made me feel very kind—I trust you will forgive me for saying it, but I think you have been almost affectionate in your treatment and kindness."

Her face turned crimson, and she proceeded to put up her hair and did not stop till she had pinned it up, and took up her ugly bonnet as if to put it on.

"Don't put that horrible headgear on just yet," I

said, taking her hand again. "I want to talk a little more with you."

"Then don't talk any more nonsense, or I will go away," she said coquettishly, just as any girl would have done. She was a woman!

I talked of various things, about her present life and the terrible strain it must be on a girl accustomed to ease and luxury, and complimented her on her noble conduct in giving her services to the good work in the manner she was doing, and all that. This seemed to please her and to re-establish the friendly relations between us. Finally I got back on the old strain again.

"Nellie," said I, once more—and this time she did not interrupt, to my great joy—"Nellie, why have you been specially kind and attentive to me?"

"Because—because—" she stammered hesitatingly.

"Well, 'because why?' " I asked her.

"Because—because I was attracted somehow to you the first time I saw you."

No girl could have made this winsome remark in a prettier way. I thought that every nerve in my body was afire with ecstasy. I was surely in love with her. I felt that she must have a warm feeling toward me.

"Why, Nellie, why did you feel that way?" I asked her, giving her hand a little—just a little squeeze.

"I have a brother in the army somewhere," she said.

A brother! What the dickens did I care if she had a dozen brothers in the army? What had that to do with me?

"Well?" said I, hardly knowing what was coming, and yet involuntarily suspicious.

"And," she continued, "my brother bears a remarkable likeness to you. When I first saw you I thought it was he, and my heart went into my throat."

"And when you found your mistake, you took me for a substitute, I suppose?"

"Hardly that," she replied blushingly. "But I thought perhaps my brother might some time be in the same situation as you are, and I hoped that some other sister would be kind to him. I treated you as I wished my brother to be treated should he be wounded."

"And I suppose when you saw a fellow that looked

like your brother you thought you would be specially kind to him?"

"Yes, that's it."

"You love your brother, don't you, Nellie?"

"Why, of course I do."

"And do you think you could love the fellow who looks like your brother?"

"Sir!" she exclaimed, pulling her hand from mine and drawing back.

"Well, I said it," said I, "and I repeat it. Do you think you could love me?"

"What do you mean, sir, by such talk as that?"

I immediately saw that I had put my foot in it—both feet, in fact! But I wasn't the fellow to back down in the face of the enemy—particularly if the enemy be one of the prettiest girls the Lord ever made.

"There's no use beating about the bush," I said. "I have said what I mean and I will stick to it. You know that I love you, and I simply wanted to know if you loved me. It was only a perfectly natural question to ask, after what we have said."

"I have made a mistake," she replied, half-sorrowfully, I thought. "I have let this interview go entirely too far. You have misconstrued all I have said and done."

"Then you do not care for me, after all?"

"Care for you!" she exclaimed, and here she was more womanlike than ever. "Why, you are the biggest fool I ever saw. Care for you? Of course not! I only thought I saw a resemblance to my brother, and that made me feel like taking special care of you while you were too feeble to take care of yourself."

"Then what you did was not for me, but for your brother?" I asked lugubriously.

"That's it exactly," she replied. "Good-evening!"

Crushed again!

As I caught the last glimpse of the pretty sister's gray skirt as it swished around the screen at the end of the ward, I was conscious of three separate and distinct sensations.

One was a sense of intense disappointment—a sense of having lost something on which I had fondly set my heart.

The next sensation was that I had made a great mistake—that I had been making a fool of myself. I had been entirely too precipitous. A girl's heart isn't captured in such a sudden manner as that. But I was young and inexperienced then! I learned more about "woman and her ways" later in life.

But as intimated, there was a third sensation. It was this: It was that if I should ever meet that homely brother of the sister's—the fellow that looked like me—I would kill him on sight.

The idea of falling in love with a girl who was kind to you simply because you resembled her big fool of a gawky brother! It was too much! One of us must die!

But fortunately for that homely brother of hers he has always managed to keep out of my way, and has thus escaped with his miserable life.

I did not see much of the sister the next morning. She passed through the ward a number of times, and always passed by without stopping or recognizing me. Toward noon she came to the side of my cot and calmly asked if I wanted anything.

I looked up into her face, but her eyes were averted. She acted as if she had never seen me before in my life. She was a woman!

Pretty soon I became somewhat convalescent and was able to be up and around, with my arm in a sling, and could help myself at meals, so that it was not necessary that I should be waited upon. Necessarily I met the sister daily and several times a day, but nothing except the most commonplace remarks ever passed between us.

We were apparently perfect strangers. I thought at times that she would make some reference to the interview that night, but she did not refer to it, and I was afraid to, for fear of some sort of an explosion.

Thus matters went on for three or four weeks, till one morning a number of us were notified that we were to be removed to a Northern hospital. Another big battle was expected, and all the convalescents were to be removed to make room for a fresh batch of mangled human beings from another bloody field of conflict.

It was one afternoon about 3 o'clock that we were

told to get ready, and an hour later the "invalid squad" was ordered in line to proceed to the depot. I was not at all averse to leaving Washington, but I still had a desire to have another word with Nellie, the pretty sister of charity.

The opportunity presented itself at the last moment, just as I was gathering up my few things from the side of the cot on which I had passed so many painful—and so many happy hours, it must be confessed.

The sister came to me to bid me good-by.

"So you are going away," said she. I thought that I noticed a tinge of regret in the inflection of her voice.

"Yes, we are going somewhere up North. Wilmington, I hear. Are you sorry to have me leave?"

The sister flushed a little, but replied coolly:

"Of course I am sorry. It is always sorrowful to part with friends."

"Then I am a friend of yours?"

"Of course. I am a friend of all the soldiers."

"That is altogether too general," said I. "Can't you say that you are especially sorry to part with me?"

"Well, yes, as I told you before, you look so much like my brother that I shall miss you more than some of the others."

Confound that brother again.

"Then you only care for me because I resemble your brother?"

"I told you that before."

"Yes, I know you did. But I wish that you cared for me for myself."

"There you go again. You men are such fools."

"Thanks. You are complimentary. But really, Nellie——"

"Sister, please."

"Well, then, sister, do you think we shall ever meet again? Could you consent to correspond with me?"

"Why can't you be sensible?" she asked in reply. "What is the sense of all this ridiculous talk? You know we are not likely ever to meet again. You know that our lives are to be apart, and that after you have gone you will forget me entirely or only remember me occasionally as the sister of charity that took care of you while you were wounded and helpless."

"No, you are mistaken in that," I replied. "I shall always remember you as Nellie, and not as the sister of charity."

"And I shall always remember you," she said, "as a great foolish boy, but," she smilingly added, "I hope that you will be successful and have good luck and be happy——"

"How can I be happy without you to——"

"Oh, you get out, you big goose," she said, laughing outright. "Good-by."

And then she turned away, and I had to fall in line, and was a moment later on the way to the depot with my companions. I turned and saw the sister standing on the steps of the hospital entrance, with a quizzical smile on her face, and so I remember her to this day, for I have never seen her nor heard from her since.

That was the first time I ever tried to make love to a sister of charity, and it was the last. It wasn't a success. But then as she said herself she was not a regular sister of charity.

From love making, however, I was suddenly precipitated into the stern realities of soldier life. We were marched up through the dusty streets of Washington—they were not the magnificent streets they are now by any means—and finally reached the depot. It was late in the afternoon. The miserable depot was crowded with wounded soldiers, northward bound.

Of course there was no train ready for us to take. There never was. Here were hundreds of wounded and feeble soldiers, waiting in that stuffy depot, in the hottest weather, and it seemed impossible to get even a drink of water. We had to remain there all night and till afternoon on the following day, and I don't think I ever put in a worse experience. After the luxuries and comforts we had enjoyed at the hospital, the contrast was terrible. We had some miserable black coffee and some of that tough "salt horse" dealt out to us, but none of us had the appetite to eat such stuff.

Finally we were embarked. They were not exactly cattle cars, but they were little better. The cars that used to be run on the Erie emigrant trains to the West were about the sort we had. The ride northward was not altogether unpleasant, for the breeze that came in through the car windows was a decided improvement over the stuffy and suffocating air that we had been breathing in that miserable depot.

Just before dusk the train stopped in the depot at Wilmington, Delaware, and we were removed to a hospital so finely located, so beautiful, and with such surroundings that we thought we had dropped into heaven.

But of this I will have to wait till the next chapt

CHAPTER LXXXIV.

IN PHILADELPHIA HOSPITALS.

As said before, we arrived at the hospital in Wilmington about dark on a beautiful warm day early in June, 1863. I don't remember at this late day what sort of a building it was, but I do remember that it was a beautiful place. To the best of my recollection it was a church that had been temporarily transformed into a hospital.

In those days everything was utilized for such purposes. The number of wounded men and soldiers who had become sick through the exposures of army life, was something terrible. Statistics show that ten times as many soldiers are disabled from sickness as from bullets. I have given some idea of the immense number of the wounded. Add the sick, and the number becomes frightful.

So everything possible was utilized for the purpose of hospital work, even to churches, and if my memory serves me right the hospital in Wilmington was an Episcopal church that had been turned into a hospital. It was a pretty, ivy-clad building of stone, surrounded by large shade trees, and the whole atmosphere was cool and pleasant. It was a great improvement in this respect on the rough board arrangement of wards that composed the Lincoln Hospital in Washington, which stood out on the flats, unprotected from the sun.

We were assigned to snowy white cots, and given a most excellent supper. But what struck us all was the number of pretty girls who seemed to have something to do with the place. There were no sisters of charity there. They were all women in ordinary dress of life, and a large majority of them were young ladies. And they were young ladies of refinement, of apparently the better walks of life.

During the evening we had a large number of lady visitors, and if all the soldiers felt as I did their hearts were beating with admiration. Now note the transition:

In Virginia the only specimen of women we saw were of the commonest class. They were what the darkies used to call "the poor white trash." They were women whose surroundings were those of the direst poverty. Their dresses, if dresses they could be called, were nothing more than old bed quilts sewed together. They were sunburned and untidy, and anything but attractive.

In Washington all the women we saw around the hospital were dresssed as sisters of charity, and although, as I have described before, there were some very pretty women disguised under that homely dress, yet the eye had become accustomed to the somber garb, and woman had somehow or other become associated with the idea of extreme plainness and simplicity.

But in Wilmington! There we for the first time since we left home were surrounded with ladies dressed in fashionable attire, and the light and bright-colored dresses that the ladies of the Southern cities wear in the month of June are bewitchingly fascinating.

White and pink dresses, straw hats trimmed with gay-colored ribbons, and all those delicate little nothings that go to make up the summer girl, were displayed before us, and delighted our hungry eyes. I remember thinking how pretty my little sister of charity friend in Washington would have looked thus attired, but, truth to tell, I almost forgot her in the presence of the handsome young ladies that flitted around the hospital ward that evening.

One of them, an extremely pretty girl of about my own age or perhaps a little younger, took a seat by the side of my cot, and we had a long and delightful talk. She was very friendly and unusually intimate for such a short acquaintance, but that was a pleasant way those Wilmington girls had, and as I looked around I saw that nearly every soldier in the hospital was similarly engaged in pleasant conversation with one of Wilmington's fair daughters.

I am rather inclined to think that my particular girl was somewhat of a flirt from the way she talked, but she found a match in me in that respect, I can assure the reader. Before she departed we had become quite chummy. She had told me the street and number where she lived, and said that she had two other sisters, and they would all be glad to have me call on them. I promised to get off the following day and call on them, and went to sleep to dream of pretty angels in white dresses and pink ribbons in their hair.

But alas! Wilmington was a sort of halfway house, a stopping place on the way to Philadelphia, where the principal hospitals were located. I did not get to see my fair visitor in the morning after all, for at an early hour we were ordered to fall in again, and to our intense disgust we were marched to the depot to take the train for Philadelphia. My girl was there, however, to bid us good-by. She said it was "really too bad" that we had to leave so soon, for she would "dearly have loved" to have me call to see her and her sisters.

I did not care a rap for her sisters, whom I had never seen, but I was really sorry that I had not the opportunity to accept her invitation, and told her so so warmly that she blushed. Just as the conversation was getting peculiarly interesting we heard the signal to get on the cars, and a moment later we were moving out of the depot amid enthusiastic cheers on the part of the men and waving of handkerchiefs by the ladies.

Nothing unusual or particularly interesting occurred on the ride to Philadelphia. It is only a short distance and the trip took but a short time. There were perhaps two or three hundred convalescent wounded men in the train besides some who were still in a dangerous condition. These were taken care of first, and carefully.

Here is where the beautiful ambulance system of Philadelphia came in useful. I think that I have referred to this feature somewhere before. Each engine company was equipped with an ambulance of the most elegant character. The exteriors of these vehicles were painted artistically to represent battle scenes and pathetic war episodes, and were of the most gorgeous character. They were arranged in, as it were, two stories or shelves, each of which would accommodate two soldiers lying flat, on a soft springy leathern mattress. These shelves were arranged to let down at the side and make seats for those who were able to sit up. I was one of the latter. Eight men could ride on the seats. The ambulance was very springy and comfortable and the ride to the hospital was extremely pleasant.

The hospital to which we were first taken was at Cherry Hill, a Philadelphia suburb, but I don't remember much about that place, for we only remained there for a day or so, till we were removed to the central hospital at the corner of Broad and Cherry Streets. This had been a big market or railroad station, I've forgotten which, and had been transformed into a first-class hospital, with accommodations for several hundred patients.

I was located on the third story, which perhaps contained a hundred wounded men. There was a great deal of red tape and form about this hospital, and the discipline was very strict. It was a good enough hospital, but at the same time it was a good deal like a prison.

Every morning at 10 o'clock the surgeon-in-chief would make his daily inspection. He was in full uniform, as was the big staff of assistants that always accompanied him. They marched through the different wards, past the cots, to inspect the wounded. We had to have the bandages removed from our wounds so that they could be seen as the doctors passed.

To us who were only comparatively slightly wounded not much attention was paid. Sometimes the doctors would stop and handle the wound in a perfunctory and at times rough sort of a way, but that was all. But when they came to a particularly bad case they would stop and give the matter more attention.

This was a sort of clinic. The head surgeon would examine the wound and perhaps do some probing, while the subordinates would stand around and watch the operation as the surgeon-in-chief would give a sort of a lecture on the character of the injury and its treatment. I will describe just one of these serious cases:

It was the case of a poor wretch who had been struck on the hip with a piece of shell. It had broken the hip bone into slivers, which of course made a running sore. Every morning the doctors would stop at this cot and after a great deal of probing, would remove one of the slivers of bone. For some reason they did not give the patient an anæsthetic, and from the way he yelled and howled it must have been excruciatingly painful.

This was kept up for a week or ten days. Every time the doctors would stop at the side of the poor fellow they would gather around while one of the surgeons fished under the sore flesh for another sliver of bone, and never stopped till they removed it. I remember one morning the surgeon-in-chief, after hacking at the fellow for some time and removing an infinitesimally small bit of bone, made the remark: "To-morrow we will perform the principal operation and see if we cannot remove the large piece that we feel." The poor fellow gave a groan over the prospect that echoed through the ward.

The next morning when the long string of doctors entered, and the patient referred to saw them coming, he gave vent to a series of shrieks and yells that made our hearts stand still. He was apprehending the operation that the doctors had been talking about the day before.

They did not give him ether, but began carving at him without much preliminary. I never heard a man cry and yell from pain as loudly as he did. It was terrible. We had to stuff our fingers in our ears so as to keep out the sound of his agonizing voice. He begged them to kill him outright and put him out of misery. Then he cursed them for a lot of devils and butchers. He prayed and cursed almost in the same voice, and so loud that it was simply a yell.

The doctors finally got the bone out, and left the suffering wretch writhing in agony and alternately praying and cursing. He kept this up for perhaps an hour and then suddenly all was ominously quiet.

Directly I saw a crowd of attendants around the cot. There was a brief consultation. Then somebody brought a sheet and spread it over the man. Then two men brought in a stretcher, and lifting the body on it carried it out. He was dead.

I must say that we all felt glad he was dead and out of his terrible suffering.

This is only one case of many. I simply relate this as an example of some of the terrible heartrending scenes in the hospital that we were continually witnessing.

After a week or so at the Broad and Cherry hospital I was removed to the one at the corner of Sixteenth and Filbert Streets. This was a large building, originally erected for manufacturing purposes. It was only one block from Market Street, on the corner of which stood a large market building.

I remained at this hospital till I got well. When able to be about I was put on light duties, such as standing guard at the door. Then when I could use my hand somewhat I was appointed as a sort of an assistant to the surgeons when they were operating. In this manner I learned considerable about surgery, and more than once personally applied an anæsthetic and did a little in the line of sewing up simple wounds. Then they put me in the dispensary and under instructions I put up many prescriptions. The doctor in charge took a fancy to me, and spent considerable time in explaining the uses of the different drugs and the fundamental principles of surgery.

All this, however, did not save me from a little duty in the line of standing guard. This duty was very light. I only had to stand on guard at the corner of Market and Filbert Streets from 9 to 11 o'clock every other night. What particular use we were there for I never discovered. Our only instructions were to stop the soldiers coming through Filbert Street and make them show their passes. If they had no passes we were to get their names and report them. But nothing was ever done with those who had no passes, so that I never saw any use for the service.

It should be explained that in Washington, Philadelphia and other cities where hospitals were located, no one could leave the institution without a pass. It was easy enough to get these passes, and the soldiers were practically free, between certain hours, but if they did not have the passes they were liable to be taken in by the provost guards.

There were many hospitals in Philadelphia in those days and the city was so filled with soldiers that it almost resembled a camp. There were as many soldiers as civilians, and perhaps more.

It was while I was in Philadelphia that the news came of the battle of Gettysburg. There had been intense excitement in the city for several days, for the news had arrived that the rebels were marching northward and it would not be surprising if they got as far as Philadelphia. Consequently there was an incipient panic all through the city, and the public nerve was on a great strain.

This was the state of affairs when the news came that General Meade had met and repulsed Lee at Gettysburg after a desperate three days' fight. Now it so happened that General Meade, who was in command of the Army of the Potomac at Gettysburg, was not only a Pennsylvanian, but a former resident of Philadelphia, and consequently there was a strong local pride in his conduct. When the news came that the army under General Meade had repulsed the Confederate army under General Lee, the entire city went wild with enthusiasm.

Flags were displayed everywhere, and one could not look a block through any street without seeing an elegant banner stretched across in honor of the occasion. The sale of soda water was superseded by the sale of "mead," a sort of root beer, which at once became the popular drink.

In the West General Grant had just achieved one of the remarkable victories that brought him into prominence, and this, coupled with General Meade's victory in Pennsylvania, filled the nation from one end to the other with enthusiasm; but nowhere was it more marked than in the city of Philadelphia. I remember one particular banner which happily referred to both the successful generals, and which read as follows:

"To our victorious commanders, we Grant the Meade of praise."

The author of that happy and appropriate expression

made the hit of his life, for it became a regular catch word, and was kept standing at the head of the editorial columns of the papers.

And, by the way, the principal paper read in Philadelphia in those exciting days was the *Inquirer*. The Philadelphia *Inquirer* and the Baltimore *American* were about the only newspapers that anybody in Philadelphia read then. We seldom or never saw a New York paper, although occasionally I came across a copy of the *Herald*.

Through these papers I read of the gallant part taken by the Thirteenth Regiment in the battle of Gettysburg. I rather kind of wished I was with them to share the glory, but on the other hand I rather think that I felt perfectly satisfied to be where I was.

It wasn't long before some of the wounded men of the Thirteenth Regiment turned up in the Philadelphia hospitals, and from them I got a full account of the part they took in the battle. When I heard this I was more than ever glad that I was not present on that occasion. And a year or so ago, when I went over the battle grounds and visited every one of the three hundred and sixty-six handsome monuments there, I was more than ever convinced that I was sensible in getting comparatively slightly wounded at Chancellorsville.

It was also while I was in Philadelphia that the great riot occurred in New York, when the *Tribune* building was partially wrecked, and when so many people were killed. That was the time when every negro who came in sight was hung to the nearest lamp post. Several regiments from the front had to be brought North from fighting the common enemy to suppress another rebellion that had started right in the principal city of the nation.

The anti-war feeling that was the principal incentive to that riot in New York had spread to a greater or less extent all over the country, and there were signs of its spreading. It might have become national, in fact, but for the prompt measures that were taken to suppress it in its incipiency.

This riotous sentiment spread even to Philadelphia, but the measures taken there were prompt and decisive,

Large bodies of armed men were stationed all over, in the market houses and other places and drilled in the riot tactics. Their guns were loaded with bullets and had the riot started there would have been some bloody work.

Philadelphia is a city gridironed with street railroads. It was even so in those days. Hastily the tops were torn off many passenger cars, and they were made into platform cars. On the platforms of these cars were placed howitzers, loaded with grape and canister. The cars, fully manned, were run into the depots of the street railroads, and remained there ready for instant emergency. There were not enough artillerymen in the city to man all these portable batteries, and infantrymen were pressed into the service.

To this duty I was assigned, greatly to my terror. I didn't want to be killed in a riot, after having passed through several battles in the front! But there I was. I was given a big wooden ramrod, with a brush arrangement on the end, and they told me it was a "swab." I was shown how to use it. Immediately after the cannon had been fired I was to clean out the barrel with the swab, and then step to one side for the next man to push in another cartridge—an arrangement that looked like a bag of salt.

But fortunately for the unruly element of Philadelphia, they did not break out into a riot and my services as chief swabber were not required. The chances are that I would have been so excited that I would have forgotten to pull out the wooden ramrod arrangement and some citizen of Philadelphia might have been hunting for a doctor with a thick wooden bar sticking through his stomach!

We had lots of good times in Philadelphia. The Chestnut Street and Walnut Street theaters were running and I visited them several times a week. I remember the spectacular play of "Joseph and his Brethren" in Walnut Street, and in the Chestnut Street theater I saw "The Duke's Motto" and Edwin Booth in "Hamlet," while in the Arch Street theater I saw the *début* of Caroline Richings in opera, under the management of the late Edmon S. Conner.

Taken altogether, therefore, our soldier life in Philadelphia was not unpleasant, and the several months we spent there were enjoyable.

Some time in the fall an officer came around to examine us to see if we were sufficiently recovered to be returned to our regiments. A good many were pronounced able to go back to the field. I can't say that I felt happy at this prospect, but I could only obey if so ordered.

But after my examination, I was informed that I was not to go back. I was to be transferred to the Invalid Corps.

And here is to be introduced another branch of army life, about which not much has been written. And it leads into a very interesting branch of the writer's military experience. But of that I will wait for another chapter.

CHAPTER LXXXV.

A BOLD STEP.

ABOUT the time the war was about half through, say the latter part of 1863, the government began to be confronted by an unprecedented condition of affairs. In the North the supply of volunteers was becoming too small to meet the calls for troops, and drafting was about to be resorted to. In the army large numbers of men were being disabled by wounds and from the sickness caused by exposure from service in the field.

Necessarily, many able-bodied men, who were capable of performing duty at the front, were being kept in the rear for duty as guardsmen, orderlies, clerks, etc., at the headquarters, around the provost guard posts, and other places, where the service required was indispensable yet not physically arduous.

It struck some one to use the wounded men for this reserve service, and after a good many different suggestions had been made and rejected, a branch of the army, called the "Invalid Corps," was organized.

The Invalid Corps, at first, was composed of two battalions, the first and the second. The Second Battalion was composed of men who had lost a leg or arm. They could elect whether to be discharged or remain in the service in the Second Battalion, and the most of them selected the service, for they began to appreciate the fact that a man minus one of the more important members of his body was lucky if he could get anything to do to earn a living. These men, however, could run errands, stand guard at gates and doorways, and do a thousand and one little things as well as a strong, able-bodied man, who might better be utilized at the front.

The First Battalion was composed of men less seriously injured, such as those with the loss of a part of a hand or foot, or who limped or suffered in some other way to such an extent that they were not able to do active duty at the front in the field. The latter had no class choice. They were put in the Invalid Corps whether they liked it or not, and could not elect to be discharged like those who went into the other battalion.

It was into this branch that I was drafted. I not only missed the part of my hand, but the wounds in my hip and foot made me limp considerably, and it was impossible for me to walk any great distance. At the same time I was able to do pretty good service in everything that did not involve marching or remaining out in the hot sun, for the effects of the serious sunstroke I had received at Rockville had begun to trouble me considerably more than they did at first.

And thus it was that I was transferred into the Invalid Corps during the latter part of the year 1863. This meant that I should serve my time out in this branch of the service, and never rejoin the regiment again. But my heart was with them and I closely followed the movements of my old companions wherever they went.

I should say right here that the name Invalid Corps did not stick to the organization very long. There was something about the name that was for some reason considered opprobrious, and ridicule was thrown on that branch of the service for no other reason than the title. So, at the suggestion of some of the leading officers of the organization, the name was changed to "Veteran Reserve Corps," and so it continued to the end of the war, and it became a very useful branch of the service.

The officers of the Veteran Reserve Corps were commissioned by the President of the United States instead of by the governors of the different States, as were the ordinary volunteers. In fact the commission of an officer in the Veteran Reserve Corps was the same as one of the regular army, and the rank was the same— that is, about one grade higher, rank for rank, than the officers of the volunteer service.

After the usual formalities of my transfer from the Thirteenth New Jersey to the Veteran Reserve Corps, I was assigned to Company D, Sixteenth Regiment, which was formed at Philadelphia, but immediately transferred to Elmira, New York.

At the latter place were located large military prisons for the confinement of rebel captives. The prisons, as well as the quarters for the men, were nothing more than rough barracks. The prisoners might have broken out at any time almost, but the security depended upon for their safety consisted in the cordon of guards stationed about the buildings, and the large reserve guard which was always kept on duty at the guardhouse to be called upon at any moment.

The rebel prisoners were a dirty, untidy, forlorn-looking lot of men, but as a whole tolerably good-natured and affording not the slightest trouble to keep under control. They were comfortably housed, notwithstanding the fact that the weather was cold (and there was snow on the ground all the time I was at Elmira), and they were better fed than they had been at any time during their service in the Confederate army. In fact there is reason to believe that some of them were better fed than they ever were at their homes in the South, for the class of men we had in our charge was not representative of the so-called aristocratic chivalry of the sunny South.

The rebels in our charge were prisoners in name and in fact, but they were a happy-go-lucky lot, and didn't seem to care for anything except to eat. In marked contrast with their condition was the horrible treatment received by the starved and illy treated Northern soldiers who were so unfortunate as to be confined in those death-holes, Libby and Andersonville.

Our life at Elmira during the late fall and early winter of 1863 was monotonous in the extreme. There wasn't much to be seen in Elmira in those days, for it was a comparatively small place. About the only place of amusement in the town was a little one-horse sort of music hall, where we occasionally went in the evening, and my recollection of the place altogether is that of its being intolerably stupid and uninteresting.

For some reason, perhaps from inspiration, but more likely because I had nothing better to do, I spent many of the long evenings in studying the revised army regulations, articles of war and tactics. Theoretically I had all these things at my fingers' ends. I don't know what ever took me to studying them, but as it turned out shortly it was a happy thing for me that I did so.

One evening while in the captain's office helping him make out some reports, I happened to pick up a circular issued from the office of Provost Marshal General James B. Fry, who at that time seemed to be at the head of the Veteran Corps. He was a sort of secretary of war for that branch of the service, as it were.

This circular was to the effect that examinations would be held in the city of Washington on January 27, 1864, for the appointment of sixteen lieutenants of the Veteran Reserve Corps, and it was desired that this examination be confined to members of the corps. The circular gave full instructions how to proceed.

My heart jumped into my throat at the sight of this. It seemed to be so presumptuous that I hardly had the nerve to mention it to anybody. But the more I thought of it the stronger did the feeling become, till at last, on the following morning, I went to the captain's office and informed him that I desired to make an application for examination for a commissioned officer.

The captain looked at me with a smile. He saw before him a boy not yet twenty years old, not at all imposing in appearance, in fact very youthful-looking, and anything in the world seemed more appropriate than to imagine him in the uniform of a commissioned officer. No wonder the captain laughed.

But I meant it, and soon impressed the captain with my earnestness. He at once took some interest in my case, and assisted me in writing my application. The circular, however, said that the application must be accompanied by a recommendation from my former company officers.

Then I remembered the conversation I once had with Captain Hopkins, of Company K. He had promised that if ever I wanted him to do anything for me he would do it, and it will perhaps be remembered at the time I told him I would remember the promise and call upon him to keep it. So I wrote to Captain

Hopkins and asked him to get the approval of my old officers, not only from Company K, but if possible from Colonel Carman as well.

I felt a little doubtful about the latter. The last time I had spoken to Colonel Carman was down near Wolf Run Shoals. The supply of provisions had run short and we were for two or three days in danger of being starved to death. It was all the result of blundering on the part of the officers. Being possessed of the penchant for newspaper correspondence, and having had two or three letters already published in the New York *Herald*, I sent that paper a very interesting account of our half-starved condition, which was published. In that letter I gave the officers the dickens, and pitched into Colonel Carman especially.

By some bad luck a copy of the *Herald* containing the letter fell into the hands of the colonel. He showed it to General Ruger, and the result of it was that I was clapped into the guardhouse. After being there several hours the colonel came to visit me. He gave me a scolding. There was no law that prevented a private from sending a letter to a newspaper, and that was the only punishment he could give me. But he exacted a promise from me that I would not write any more letters to newspapers, and not knowing any better at the time, I complied and stopped my correspondence.

That was the last conversation I had had personally with the colonel before I left the regiment a wounded soldier at the battle of Chancellorsville. I therefore had very little hopes of receiving the recommendation of Colonel Carman.

But nevertheless I did. In the course of a couple of weeks or so the answer to my letter to Captain Hopkins was received. The kind captain had more than kept his promise to me. The recommendation he sent was of the strongest possible character. It commended me for my intelligence, faithfulness to duty, and of all things in the world, for my bravery and courage in the field of battle in the face of the enemy. In fact the document was so extremely complimentary, that to use a modern expression I was "quite stuck on myself."

But, what was my surprise, on turning the recommendation over to find that it was signed by every officer of the Thirteenth Regiment. The document bore the signatures of some officers that I had never spoken to in my life, and who did not know the difference between me and a side of sole leather. But I could see through it all. They had all done this at the request of Captain Hopkins. Kind captain! How grateful I felt to him for this. I immediately sat down and wrote him my thanks, and as they were expressive of my feeling just at that particular moment they must have been very warm.

The next thing was to get a furlough for ten days to go to Washington to pass the examination. This was easily secured, under the circumstances. Not only does a commmissioned officer stand higher socially and otherwise than a private, but the very fact that a private stands a slight chance of being a commissioned officer puts him in a position to taste for the first time the privileges of a commission. Colonel Stephen A. Moore, the commander of the Sixteenth Regiment, V. R. C., at once granted me the desired furlough and kindly wished me every good luck on my journey.

"If you don't return wearing a pair of shoulder straps," said he good-naturedly, "I'll put you in the guardhouse."

Now that it began to look so much like business I began to be frightened. I almost felt like backing out. The idea of my going to Washington and undertaking to pass an examination to prove that I was able and qualified to hold a commission in a branch of the regular army was overwhelming. It seemed such a piece of cheek that I half-felt a mind to tear up the furlough and give the whole thing up.

But on the other hand I considered what a glorious thing it would be to be a commissioned officer, to wear shoulder straps, and to step into the other estate so high above that of the enlisted soldier. I concluded to go on, and face it through, whatever the result. And on the evening of January 26th, the day before that set for the commencement of the examination, I found myself in Washington again.

I put up at the old National Hotel. As I looked into the glass that night I was struck at my extremely youthful appearance, and more than ever was overcome with the cheek I had in thinking of being a commissioned officer. My mustache had just begun to show itself. It was a mere downy mass on my upper lip, hardly distinguishable to the naked eye! My hair was long, uncouth and scraggly. If I remember rightly the last time it was cut it was by one of my comrades in the barracks, and it looked as if it had been hacked off with a carving knife.

A happy thought struck me. I must do something with that mustache. Every officer wore a mustache, that is, every officer in Washington. The larger the mustache the more dignified and ferocious an officer looked. In fact to a certain extent the importance of a commissioned officer in those days was based on the size and impressiveness of his mustache.

I must do something to make my mustache show more plainly. At first I thought I would get a false one, such as they wear at masquerades, and paste it on my upper lip. But I discarded that idea as being too dangerous. Suppose the thing should drop off while I was undergoing the examination! That would ruin my chances at once. I would be ignominiously relegated to my regiment as a private for trying to get a commission under false pretenses.

But at last I solved the problem. I would go to the barber's and have that mustache dyed black. Then it would show more plainly. Further, I would get my hair cut to a crop, and the comparison would make the mustache still more prominent. I had solved the difficulty at once, and immediately proceeded to put it into execution.

I found a barber's shop on the first floor of the hotel, stretched myself back into the chair and gave the order. The barbers were all colored men in Washington in those days, and I remembered the smiling look my man gave his next companion as I gave the order to have my mustache dyed.

But it was accomplished at last. It cost me eighty cents for the job, but I never invested eighty cents that gave me greater satisfaction. When I surveyed myself in the glass, I straightened myself out with ineffable pride—for my mustache could be seen clear across the room. I squinted my eyes downward and could even get a glance of it below my nose. It was the first time in my life that I had been able to see my own mustache!

I took a short walk through Pennsylvania Avenue, clean gone on myself. I wondered if everybody did not notice that I was some distinguished personage, with such a big mustache! I felt at least a foot taller than I did before. With an air of importance I stalked into a saloon and asked for a cocktail!

"Can't sell liquor to enlisted men," said the barkeeper.

I had forgotten. I was only a private yet. I had forgotten that I still wore my dingy blue suit of a private in the Veteran Reserve Corps. If I had the shoulder straps I might have filled myself up with liquor till I could not stand. But none was sold to a private.

There was a feeling of humiliation about this. The idea that a man cannot buy what he wants when he has money in his pocket, simply because of his rank, is very galling to a native-born American. But such was the rule. Washington was under martial law, so far as the soldiers were concerned, and any saloon keeper who sold liquor to an enlisted man in uniform was liable to have his license revoked. Had I put on a citizen's suit I might have got all the liquor I wanted. But then, strange as it may appear now, it was against the law for an enlisted soldier to wear a civilian suit of clothes. It was regarded as a *prima facie* evidence that the man was disguising himself for the purpose of deserting. Another evidence of the degradation of low rank!

I really didn't want the drink. I had merely gone in because I just then felt my importance, and because it was a proper sign of importance for a man in my position to go into a saloon and order a drink. But I had come down like the stick of a used-up sky rocket. I had a mustache that could be seen, it is true, but the other necessity, the shoulder straps, were not yet visible. I had to go through something worse than a barber's shop before I got that insignia of rank.

The examination was to begin the next morning at 10 o'clock, and I was on hand bright and early. No sooner had I arrived, however, than I was almost paralyzed with the prospect.

As I said before, the circular of instructions said that there were sixteen appointments to be made. What was my horror to find that there were at least one hundred and fifty men there to be examined.

And some of them were very important-looking. Some looked as if they had already held commissioned offices. Many of them looked wise and important. Nearly every one was older than I. In fact I think that I was the youngest man there, and I imagined that some of the others looked at me with a disdainful air. Worst of all, most of the other candidates had mustaches ten times as formidable-looking as the miserable little black dyed outline of hair on my upper lip! What chances had I alongside such an array of formidable hirsute adornment!

An airish and important-looking officer came from another apartment into the room where we were huddled and read off the list of applicants, like a roll call. The list was made out in the order the applications had been received. Mine was nearly to the bottom. Another discouraging thing, I thought. The appointments would all be filled before my name was reached.

I took a note of the time it would take before my turn came, and from the time it took for the first ones to be examined, calculated that it would be quite late in the afternoon before my turn was reached. As I sat there looking over the circular of instructions again, I suddenly jumped at the sight of a name I had not noticed before. It was that of "Colonel M. N. Wisewell," an officer who held an important position in the office of the provost marshal general, and whose name was signed to the circular.

How well I recognized the familiar signature. Of all the men in the world, I could have wished for none more just then than Colonel Wisewell. Let me explain.

When I lived in Yonkers, New York, a boy, I went for a while to M. N. Wisewell's military academy. It was there that I received my first instruction. My father had only sent me there for the discipline, as he said, never imagining that it would be any particular benefit to me. But it was very fortunate for me just then. Colonel Wisewell, by the way, after the war, was the principal of the military academy at Eaglewood, near Perth Amboy, New Jersey.

I thought that I would at once try to see Colonel Wisewell at his office, and proceeded to the war department.

Now it was a hard thing in those days for a private soldier to get into the war department without a pass or order or some sort of an introduction. I was stopped at almost every turn of the hallways by a soldier on guard, but as I had had some newspaper experience in getting into places, I finally succeeded in reaching the office of the provost marshal general. Right at the entrance whom should I run right into but Colonel Wisewell himself!

The colonel was a remarkable-looking man. He was considerably over six feet high and had an eagle nose of the hookiest shape imaginable. He also had an eagle eye, that seemed to look straight through you. He was altogether a man of extraordinary, commanding appearance, and in his uniform he looked more commanding than ever. I remember being struck just then with the impression of how appropriate it was that a man with an eagle eye and an eagle nose, should wear eagles on his shoulder straps—a silver spread eagle being the insignia of a colonel.

"Colonel Wisewell?" I said quite bravely.

"Well, sir, what do you want?" he asked, very brusquely, not to say harshly.

"Do you remember me, colonel?" I asked, somewhat timorously, for his brusque manner had rather disconcerted me.

He turned his eagle eye at me, and his glance seemed to penetrate my innermost soul. I was terrified lest he should have forgotten his former humble pupil at Yonkers academy. For a moment he hesitated, and then said:

"Your face is familiar, but I can't place you. What is your name?"

My heart rather went down. But if I had stopped to think a moment I might have considered that it was quite improbable that he should have recognized me on the start.

I was a mere boy when I attended his school and it was several years previous. Furthermore how was it likely that he should have recognized me there, in that place and in that uniform? But I was a little shaky when I answered:

"My name is Crowell. I used to attend your academy at——"

"Oh, yes," he interrupted, "I recognize you now. You are Joe Crowell. But what are you doing here? I had no idea you were in the army."

Then I related to him the circumstances, and briefly went over my service in the Thirteenth, and explained how I had come on to be examined for a commission, but was afraid that with so many applicants there was little chance for me unless I had some influence. I frankly acknowledged that I had come to him to ask for his influence to help me through.

His answer was more than I could have expected. He gave me to understand then and there that if I could pass at least a creditable examination he would be able to help me through. And he very complimentary remarked that any one who had been a pupil at his school in Yonkers ought to know enough to answer the questions that would be propounded.

"When do you expect to be called before the examining board?" he finally asked.

"Some time this afternoon," I replied. "Judging from the way they are going I should think that I would be called about 3 o'clock this afternoon."

"All right," said he, "I will attend to the matter at once. You go and take your seat as you were and wait till you are called, and say nothing to any one about having seen me, for if it is heard that there can be any help, there will be no end to the applicants for assistance."

I went back to the rooms of the examining board with a much lighter heart. In a few minutes I noticed Colonel Wisewell enter the examination room, and directly he came out again. He gave me a significant nod of recognition as he passed me, but I had the sense not to stop him to ask any questions. I knew, however, from his glance that he had done everything he could do.

According to my calculations and judging from the number of candidates still ahead of me on the list, I thought that it would be at least two hours before my name was reached. But what was my surprise a few moments later to see one of the officers stick his head out of the mysterious apartment of torture, and looking around, ask:

"Is Private Crowell here?"

I arose and answered in the affirmative.

"All right," said the officer. "Come right in now."

I was so nearly paralyzed with astonishment and fright that I staggered like a drunken man. My shaking knees would hardly bear the weight of my body as I made my way into the mysterious chamber.

My self-possession was not in the least restored when I glanced around and saw the array of generals and colonels and majors gathered around the long table at the end of the room.

Then began the inquisition. I had come to the gulf that separates the privates from the commissioned officer.

CHAPTER LXXXVI.

CROSSING THE GREAT GULF.

NONE except those who have served in the army can fully appreciate the vast gulf that exists between the "enlisted man" and the "commissioned officer."

The former is the plebeian, the serf of the army, the latter the aristocrat, the autocrat of the service.

The difference between the master and a slave in the old times was hardly greater than that between the enlisted soldier and the commissioned officer. The former was compelled to do whatever the latter commanded, no matter what it might be. If an officer commanded a soldier to blacken his boots, brush his clothes, cook his breakfast, or even wash his shirt, to refuse or disobey would be regarded as mutiny. The soldier might subsequently make a protest, and perhaps—I say perhaps—it might be righted by instructions being given to the officer not to again put the soldier on such menial service.

But for the time being it was the soldier's duty to obey. In fact, the first thing a soldier is taught is to obey orders, no matter what they may be. And it were better for him to do so, for if there was a protest against some mean service, the officer could, by a system of petty tyranny, make that soldier's life forever after a hell on earth.

The best advice I can give to a soldier is to obey orders, no matter what they may be; and as far as possible keep on the right side of the officers.

This vast gulf I was about to cross, or to try to cross. It was therefore not an ordinary examination. The result was momentous. It was perhaps one of the most important steps I had ever taken. I was impressd with its importance, and naturally felt very nervous over the result. I had not the slightest idea of the nature of the questions to be asked, and so had not had the chance to make any preparation. I had more than a fair knowledge of the tactics and articles of war and military matters generally, but I had been given to understand that the examination would go a good deal further than that, although in what direction I was profoundly ignorant.

Seated around the table in the middle of the examination room were a lot of gold-laced, shoulder-strapped officers, whom I did not know at the time, but whom I subsequently learned were as follows:

There were Colonel Richard H. Rush, Colonel G. N. Morgan, Colonel F. D. Sewall, Colonel B. J. Sweet, Lieutenant-Colonel Dewitt C. Poole and Captain James R. O'Beirne. The latter is a prominent New Yorker at the present time. He is the same Colonel O'Beirne who was commissioner of immigration, who refused to vamoose the ranch when another man was placed in his position, on the ground that he was a veteran and that under the civil services rules he could not be removed except for cause.

The above-named officers were the official members of the examination board. I noticed a number of others sitting around, but they were there simply as spectators. They appeared to enjoy the torture of the innocents the same as the kings and emperors of old enjoyed the torture of the prisoners brought before them.

Well, the examination began promptly on time. Colonel Rush, the president of the board, sent the ball rolling in a kindly meant way by advising me not to be nervous and to keep cool, as the examination would not be a hard one. This was all right, but the idea that he should have considered it necessary to give me any such advice at all struck me as a preparation for something terrible, and, if anything, it made me all the more nervous.

The first question was of course my name and residence, occupation before enlisting, and all such things. Then came the time I had been in the army, the battles I had been in, and the nature of my wounds. When this part of the examination had been reached I had to undress and be examined by two surgeons who were present. I did not like the idea of stripping before so many big officers, but then I had come prepared to go through anything that might come along, the same as a fellow does when he offers himself as a candidate for initiation in a Masonic lodge.

This through, after being examined like a horse for all my "points," I resumed my clothing, and the questions were fired at me with lightning rapidity.

As I said before, I had posted myself on the regulations, articles of war, tactics, and such things, and could even draw from memory many of the blanks used in the service, thanks to my experience as company clerk. Then they commenced asking me questions touching my general intelligence.

Mathematics was my weak point always, and I felt sure that I would stumble on these things, but fortunately they did not go further than the computation of interest and the multiplication of plain fractions. If they had gone into the mixed and vulgar fractions I would have fallen by the wayside. They skipped over algebra, to my great satisfaction, for on that subject I never got further than to know that "x equalled the unknown quantity," and the rest has been an "unknown quantity" all my life. They asked me one question in geometry, and it happened to be about the only one I could have answered. It was the first problem in Book I of Davies' "Legendre," and I guess that must have been as far as any of my examiners had ever got themselves.

What under the sun all these things had to do with holding the commission of a lieutenant, perhaps the reader would like to know. So would I. I never did know.

Then they tackled me with geography, and here I made a pretty mess of it. "How long is the Mississippi River?" I was asked. How did I know? How many of my readers can tell, off-handed? "How many square miles are there in Lake Superior?" was fired at me. I began to get desperate.

"Gentlemen," said I, reaching for my hat, "I am a candidate for a position in the army, not in the navy."

I thought it was all up with me then. But instead of getting mad about it, my sally provoked a laugh, and they dropped the question of the areage of the great lakes.

Then they tackled me on grammar and spelling and literature, in which I did fairly well, I imagine, for there were approving nods passed round the board. And when I was asked to take a seat at the table and write an imaginary report of a street riot, I was right in my element, for I simply wrote it out as I would have done for a newspaper.

But I will not weary the reader by any further details of the examination. It lasted apparently a long while, but it was not so long after all, for when I was dismissed and got out into the other room I had not been before the board much more than half an hour.

Of course I did not know whether I had passed or not. I was told that I would receive word of the result in due time. From that moment I was on pins and needles. Now the prize seemed to be so near my grasp, I was more than ever anxious to secure it. I went to the hotel that afternoon in a very disconcerted state of mind over the feeling of uncertainty.

In the evening I met Colonel Wisewell at Willard's Hotel, where I had wandered somewhat aimlessly. The colonel was quite friendly.

"I have a room here," said he. "Come up."

And I went upstairs with the colonel. He rang a bell and the boy brought us some whisky. I felt that I needed something just then. Then I touched the bell. I had a little money and we had a good time!

During the evening two of the officers of the examining board dropped in. I was considerably surprised at their appearance.

"I was just treating my old friend and schoolmaster, Colonel Wisewell," I said. "If I were a commissioned officer I would ask you to join. I believe that it is contrary to the ethics of the service for a commissioned officer to drink with a private soldier."

"Oh, you needn't worry about that little thing, lieutenant," said Colonel —— (I won't mention his name).

"Lieutenant?" said I wonderingly.

"Yes, Lieutenant Crowell, permit me to congratulate you."

"You don't mean to say that I passed all right?" asked I, with ill-suppressed delight.

"That's just what I mean. You will receive formal notice in the morning. You are practically a second lieutenant now at this moment, for your commission dates from to day."

For a moment I was speechless. I could hardly realize it.

I rang the bell. There were no electric buttons in those days—only a sort of little brass crank fastened into the wall, which sounded a bell in the office. "Boy," said I, with all the air of a major-general, when the waiter stuck his woolly head into the door, "boy, bring up half a dozen bottles of wine."

Champagne was then five dollars a bottle, and small bottles at that. But what did I care for expense just at that moment? Thirty dollars in a momentary swoop, to be sure. One-third of the capital I had brought to Washington gone in a minute! But I never thought of the expense just then. I was getting one hundred and twenty-five dollars a month then, instead of the measly thirteen dollars that I had been receiving as a private.

We drank the wine, and one of the officers ordered some more. Then another officer ordered some more, and so on!

All the same I got back to my hotel about midnight without assistance!

I passed through the office of the "National" that night in the plain garb of a private soldier. "Only an enlisted man," is what any one would have said to see me. But I held a blessed secret in my heart that made me greatly enjoy the *incognito*.

There was little sleep for me that night. A commissioned officer! The dreams of every soldier are to be a commissioned officer. I had been accorded the distinction. I could hardly realize it. It seemed all so sudden that as I lay there on my bed that night I had to go over and over the facts to make myself believe that I had really been so fortunate.

I felt a little rocky in the morning and thought that a

cocktail would rouse me up. I forgot my uniform and ordered it with all the gusto of a general.

"Can't sell liquor to enlisted men," said the barkeeper.

I had forgotten. But then I wasn't an enlisted man. Would I tell the barkeeper? No, I guess not. He wouldn't believe me anyhow. And I rather enjoyed the disguise, as I had begun to regard my private's uniform. So I took a plain lemonade. I have an idea now that it did me a good deal more benefit than the cocktail would have done.

The next morning I received an official document setting all doubts at rest. Here is a copy of the original I have now before me:

> Office of the Board of Examination of Officers of the Invalid Corps,
> WASHINGTON, D. C., January 27, 1864.
>
> Report of the examination of Private Joseph E. Crowell, Co. D, 16th Regt. Inv. Corps, by the Board of Examination convened by Special Orders No. 9 (Ex. 26), War Dept., 1864.
>
> Having carefully examined Private Joseph E. Crowell, Co. D, 16th Regt. I. C. upon Tactics, Regulations, Articles of War, Field Service, Discipline, Disability, General Education, and capacity for holding a commission, upon mature deliberation decide to recommend Private Joseph E. Crowell, Co. D, 16th Regt. I. C., for the appointment of Second Lieutenant in the Invalid Corps and to do duty in the First Battalion.
>
> (Signed)
> Rich'd H. Rush, Col. 1st Regt. I. C., Pres't of Board.
> G. N. Morgan, Col. 2d Regt. I. C., member.
> F. D. Sewall, Col. 3d, 4th Regt. In. Corps.
> R. J. Sweet, Col. 8th Regt. I. C., member.
> Dewitt C. Poole, Lieut.-Col. I. C.

A true copy,
 James R. O'Beirne, Capt. I. C., on duty.

As before explained, the name of the organization at that time was the "Invalid Corps." It was subsequently changed to "Veteran Reserve Corps." The change was made between the time of my examination and the receipt of my commission from the president, so that the commission bore the new name, and I have been informed that mine was the first commission issued under the name of the "Veteran Reserve Corps."

I went up to the provost marshal general's office the same day and asked Colonel Wisewell what to do next.

He told me that there were certain formalities to be observed before I got my commission. I had to return to Elmira, where I would receive a formal announcement and the colonel of my regiment would also be similarly notified. And on the strength of that notice he would grant me a discharge as private.

So I returned to Elmira. I called on Colonel Moore and informed him of my success, and he congratulated me heartily.

"It's a good thing that you got through all right," said he good-naturedly, "for you will remember what I told you—that if you failed I would put you in the guardhouse."

I laughingly remembered.

For several days I waited for the official announcement of my appointment. As the days rolled by I began to get discouraged. What if after all there should be some mistake about it? The disappointment would have been terrible, after my ideas had been raised so high.

It was not till the 8th of February that I received the expected notification. It was dated February 2d, but there was so much red tape to go through in those days that there always was a delay in official documents. But the thing came at last, and I have it before me. It reads as follows:

"WAR DEPARTMENT,
"Provost Marshal General's Office,
"WASHINGTON, D. C., February 2, 1894.
"Second Lieutenant Joseph E. Crowell,
Invalid Corps,
Elmira, N. Y.

"SIR: Inclosed you will receive your appointment in the Invalid Corps. You will put yourself in uniform, according to the instructions contained in the inclosed circular, and report, in person, to the Provost Marshal General, Washington, D. C., with as little delay as possible. I am, very respectfully,

"Your obedient servant,
"M. N. WISEWELL,
"Colonel and Assistant to Provost Marshal General."

There was a little note attached to the effect that if I did not report in seven days it would be construed as a non-acceptance of the appointment. No danger of that! I would be there on time all right, you bet!

Colonel Moore, of the regiment to which I had been attached, received notice of my appointment at the same time, and he at once made out my discharge. I left Elmira the same day with the congratulations of my former companions and the envy of the men with whom I had been intimately associated in the menial duties of a private soldier.

The next thing was the uniform. I concluded to patronize home industry and made a bee-line for Paterson, and gave the order to a tailor of that city. The uniform was an expensive and elaborate affair. The overcoat alone cost $95. The sword and sash, which I have yet, cost $30. Altogether the outfit cost in the neighborhood of $250, and I had to borrow some money to make it up. But a jump from $13 to $125 a month and expenses paid was such an advance that the question of expense never entered my mind.

If ever I had a good time I had it on that occasion. I visited all my old friends and enjoyed myself immensely. I was regarded as a sort of hero, too, and I didn't let on to a single soul that I was anything else!

But I was surprised at the absence of so many of my old associates. I would ask for this one and that one, only to be told that he had enlisted in this or that regiment. It really seemed as if all my old friends had gone to the front. Paterson looked deserted. And my best girl had been married. If she had seen me in my uniform she never would have done it.

But there were still some people in town that I remembered well enough, including some of those whose speeches had instigated me and so many others to enlist. They never went themselves. Their course was like that of the dominie who said: "I want you to do as I say, not as I do." They fought the war with a chin— as did Samson of old, in his encounter with the Philistines!

Before the week was up I was ready, and started once more for Washington. There was lots of fun traveling in those days, for it cost nothing. All that it was necessary to do was to exhibit the order received to the nearest quartermaster (and there were quartermasters stationed in almost every city just for such purposes) and he would give you an order on the railroad, which was technically known as "transportation." This order presented at the ticket office would give a ticket for the trip, whether it involved one or a thousand men.

So I went to Washington in style. There were no Pullman cars in those days, or the officers would have patronized them. The officers always took the best there was to be had. I am speaking of the commissioned officer. Cattle cars were good enough for the enlisted men. But I had passed the great gulf and was now a commissioned officer.

The weather was very cold and I wore my big overcoat, a dark blue, navy cloth garment, with a wide cape, and the front all decorated with braids and loops instead of buttons. The number of braids in the decorations indicated the rank.

But they were not so noticeable as the bright new shoulder straps, and I remember throwing back my overcoat so that the shoulder straps would show. I only wished that my mustache was a little bigger. The dye was wearing off. I would have to patronize that Washington barber again as soon as I reached the capital!

I will digress a moment to say that while I had received my appointment, I had not yet my regular commission. I did not receive that for some time after. The commission was precisely the same as those given to the officers of the regular army. They were signed by the President of the United States. They were neatly engraved on real parchment, and highly prized by the recipients, more so in fact than the commissions of volunteer officers, for the latter were signed only by the governors of States, while those of the regular army and the Veteran Reserve Corps were signed by the President of the United States, the secretary of war and the adjutant general. My own commission, which I have carefully retained to this day, bears the names of Abraham Lincoln, Edwin M. Stanton and E. D. Townsend, the incumbents, respectively, of the three offices named.

I arrived in the evening, and went to the same hotel I had occupied before—the National. After I had been assigned to a room and left my valise and sword, I sauntered into the barroom. I didn't want a drink, but I thought I would just for once see what difference the shoulder straps would make.

"Make me a light cocktail," I said to the barkeeper.

"Certainly, lieutenant; what shall it be, whisky or gin?"

I was now convinced that I had crossed the great gulf!

CONCLUSION.

For nearly two years after promotion the writer served as a commissioned officer, but not in the field. It was on detached service, in secret government work, on commissions, etc. It was interesting, exciting, and replete with adventures. But that is, to quote a well-known author, "another story."

An answer to "The Story of An African Farm."
By ALIEN.
12 mo. Cloth, - - - $1.25.

(Neely's International Library.)

A FEW PRESS OPINIONS.

Christian World	"This is a fascinating and powerful story. We cordially recommend this book, which is as interesting as it is well written."
Aberdeen Free Press	"A novel of remarkable originality and power, and written in a style that is perfectly fascinating."
Daily News	"Striking passages * * * touches of pathos * * * a delightful scene in the opening portion."
Literary World	"An original and picturesque book. A very pretty bit of writing. The career of Florence offers some good problems for the student of life's philosophies."
Speaker	"Flashes of beauty * * * Some striking passages * * * Shows both originality and power."
Ladies' Pictorial	"This very original story; so good it is that its clever author is almost certain to have a great future before her."
Birmingham Daily Gazette	"Strong in thought, vigorous in expression. The character of Florence is drawn with sympathy and discrimination."
Methodist Recorder	"The conception is fine, splendidly worked up by a master hand. The work is full of artistic thought and deep feeling, and ranks high among present day tales. We warmly recommend it."
Church Family Newspaper	"A tale of considerable power, and with many thrilling incidents and pathetic details."

THE ONE TOO MANY
By E. LYNN LINTON,
Author of "Patricia Kemball" "The Atonement of Leam Dundas," &c

12 MO. CLOTH, - - - $1.25.

(Neely's International Library.)

Post Intelligencer	"Mrs. E. Lynn Linton is one of the very ablest from the group of brilliant writers of fiction. The charm of her style and the interest of the story are alike undeniable.
Commercial Appeal	"A work with a commendable mission. It is inscribed to the 'sweet girls still left among us who have no part in the new revolt but are content to be dutiful, innocent and sheltered.'"
Boston Courier	Finely worked up, buoying the interest of the reader on the highest surface level to the end.
Chicago Mail	"Although Mrs. Linton has a horror of the girl who jumps the home traces, she has built a plot in which the new woman has the best of the situation."
Boston Ideas	"The story as a story is a thoroughly interesting one and runs along with cultured smoothness and alertness."
Public Opinion	"The story is a notable one. The strength of character drawing is marked and the plot is developed with skill."

For Sale by all Booksellers, or sent on receipt of Price by the Publisher,

F. TENNYSON NEELY, Chicago. New York.

Neely's Prismatic Library.

GILT TOP, 75 CENTS.

"I KNOW OF NOTHING IN THE BOOK LINE THAT EQUALS NEELY'S PRISMATIC LIBRARY FOR ELEGANCE AND CAREFUL SELECTION. IT SETS A PACE THAT OTHERS WILL NOT EASILY EQUAL, AND NONE SURPASS."—E. A. ROBINSON.

A GUIDE TO PALMISTRY.
    By Mrs. Eliza Easter-Henderson.
THE BULLET. Max Nordau.
MONTRESOR. By Loota.
REVERIES OF A SPINSTER. By Helen Davies.
THE ART MELODIOUS. By Louis Lombard.
THE HONOR OF A PRINCESS.
    By F. Kimball Scribner.
OBSERVATIONS OF A BACHELOR.
    By Louis Lombard.
KINGS IN ADVERSITY. By E. S. Van Zile.
NOBLE BLOOD AND A WEST POINT PARALLEL.
    By Captain King and Ernest Von Wildenbruch of the German Army.
TRUMPETER FRED. By Captain King. Illustrated.
FATHER STAFFORD. By Anthony Hope.
THE KING IN YELLOW. By R. W. Chambers.
IN THE QUARTER. By R. W. Chambers.
A PROFESSIONAL LOVER. By Gyp.
BIJOU'S COURTSHIPS. By Gyp. Illustrated.
A CONSPIRACY OF THE CARBONARI.
    By Louise Muhlbach.
SOAP BUBBLES. By Dr. Max Nordau.

For sale everywhere, or sent, postpaid, on receipt of price.

F. TENNYSON NEELY, Publisher,

96 Queen Street,   114 Fifth Avenue,
LONDON.   NEW YORK.

IN THE QUARTER.

By ROBERT W. CHAMBERS,

Author of "The King in Yellow."

Neely's Prismatic Library.

50 cents.

A new novel by the author of that wonderful book, "The King in Yellow," is an event of considerable importance to the reading public; nor will a perusal of "In the Quarter" disappoint those critics who have predicted such a glorious future for Robert W. Chambers. As the title would indicate, the story deals with life in the Quartier Latin, in Paris, where the merry art students live and move and have their being, and over which the halo of romance ever hangs; a peculiar people with whom we have spent many an entrancing hour in company with such volumes as "Trilby" and "A King in Yellow."

PRESS NOTICES:

BOOK BUYER, New York:—"It is a story of a man who tried to reconcile irreconcilable facts. . . Mr. Chambers tells it with a happy choice of words, thus putting 'to proof the art alien to the artists.' . . It is not a book for the unsophisticated, yet its morality is high and unmistakable."

BROOKLYN CITIZEN:—"Full of romantic incidents."

BOSTON COURIER:—"Interesting novel of French life."

BOSTON TRAVELER:—"A story of student life written with dash and sureness of handling."

BOSTON TIMES:—"Well written, bright, vivid; the ending is highly dramatic."

NEW YORK SUNDAY WORLD:—"Charming story of Bohemian life, with its bouyancy, its romance, and its wild joy of youth . . vividly depicted in this graceful tale by one who, like Daudet, knows his Paris. Some pages are exquisitely beautiful."

PHILADELPHIA BULLETIN:—"Idyllic—charming. Mr. Chambers' story is delicately told."

NEW YORK EVENING TELEGRAM:—"It is a good story in its way. It is good in several ways. There are glimpses of the model and of the grisette—all dainty enough. The most of it might have come from so severe a moralist as George Eliot or even Bayard Taylor."

NEW YORK COMMERCIAL ADVERTISER:—"A very vivid and touchingly told story. The tale is interesting because it reflects with fidelity the life led by certain sets of art students. A genuine romance, charmingly told."

CONGREGATIONALIST, Boston:—"Vivid, realistic. There is much of nobility in it. A decided and excellent moral influence. It is charmingly written from cover to cover."

For sale everywhere, or sent post-paid on receipt of price.

F. TENNYSON NEELY, Publisher,

96 Queen Street, London. 114 Fifth Avenue, New York.

BLAIR'S PILLS.

Great English Remedy for
GOUT and RHEUMATISM.
Sure, Prompt, Effective.

Large Box, 34, $1; Small, 14 Pills, 50 Cts.

BOX MAILED ON RECEIPT OF PRICE.

Druggists and 224 William St., New York.

This wonderful and matchless Ointment has been a family standby and reliance of three generations, being one of the oldest household remedies in America, and those having once used it and experienced its wonderful curative powers, would not be without a box for its weight in gold. It can also be used with good results on horses and cattle for open wounds, sore neck, etc., etc.

THE CELEBRATED
R. CHINESE SKIN and TOILET POWDER.

For Preserving, Restoring and Beautifying the Complexion.

Sold by Druggists, Fancy Goods Houses and 224 William Street, New York.

Box mailed on receipt of 25 cents.

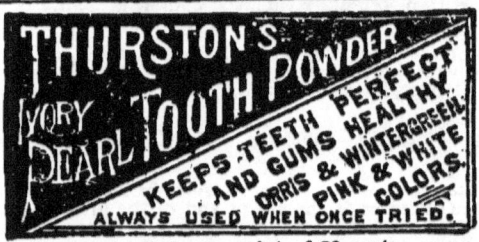

Box mailed on receipt of 30 cents.

This is a most excellent article for cleansing and preserving the teeth. It hardens the gums, sweetens the breath, and beautifies the teeth. It contains no acid or harsh, gritty substance—nothing that can injure the enamel in the slightest degree.

Sold by all Druggist, Fancy Stores and 224 William Street, New York.

DR. O. R. BAKER'S
PAIN ✻ PANACEA.

The Greatest Pain Curing Remedy Known.

Pain cannot long exist where this Remedy is faithfully used. For Pain in the Stomach, Back and Bowels; Flux, Colic, Burns, Bruises, Cuts, Swellings, Toothache, Headache and Earache.

Cures Almost Instantaneously.
Always keep a bottle in your Medicine Closet.
Three Sizes, 25c., 50c. and $1.00.

● DISCHARGE YOUR DOCTOR! ●

HOW TO LIVE,
WHAT TO EAT,
THE WAY TO COOK IT.

DR. CARLIN'S
UNIVERSAL
RECEIPT
BOOK AND FAMILY PHYSICIAN

MEMORIAL EDITION.

This wonderful compendium of practical information, pertaining to every branch of Social and Domestic Economy, embraces all that every mother and housekeeper need know. It gives general rules in regard to the proper selection of food, the best manner of preparing same, what should and should NOT be used under certain conditions, and all based on the excellent medical instructions also given. NO FAMILY SHOULD BE WITHOUT IT.

REDUCE YOUR DOCTOR BILLS.

This book is so arranged, written and illustrated, that it saves many times its cost to the purchaser every year. The best treatment in the world within the reach of all. The purchaser of Dr. Carlin's Physician invests his money at 1000 per cent. interest. Index of Symptoms. Index of Diseases. List of Medicines, their properties, how to prepare them and how to administer them.

"AN OUNCE OF PREVENTION IS WORTH A POUND OF CURE."

It will Save Many Times its Cost in One Year.
If your child is sick, consult it. If you are worn out, it suggests a remedy. If you want to start a garden, it tells you how. If your husband is out of sorts, it will tell you what he needs. If you need help in your cooking, nothing is better. If anything goes wrong in your household affairs,

OLD DR. CARLIN KNOWS ALL ABOUT IT,

and explains so you can make no mistake.

The work is voluminous in all its details, and written in such a way as to be readily understood by all. Any case of ordinary sickness is fully treated, and such remedies suggested as are easily obtainable and at small cost.

DR. CARLIN needs no indorsement. Born in Bedford, England, he acquired a reputation second to no physician in that country, which is a grand record. His grandfather, father and several brothers were eminent doctors, indicating a peculiar fitness of the family in this direction. His practical knowledge was of wide scope, much of which he has embodied in this great and indispensable book.

BOUND IN HANDSOME CLOTH, GILT SIDE AND BACK.
ALSO ENAMEL HERCULES MANILLA COVER.

Reg. Subscription Price, $6.00. Orders Solicited. Special Terms to Agents.

F. TENNYSON NEELY,
CHICAGO.   PUBLISHER.   NEW YORK.

Petronilla, the Sister.

By Emma Homan Thayer.

Cloth, $1.25.

Mrs. Thayer's art books have made for her a world-wide reputation as a writer, and an illustrator of the wildflowers of America. "Petronilla" is her first novel, and we can honestly recommend it as a most delightful story indeed. The gifted writer paints human loves and vanities with much the same dexterity she has exhibited as an artist in delineating the delicate hues of the modest wildflowers she so fondly worships. We take pleasure in recommending so chaste and interesting a story to the public. In this day of erotic literature such a book is doubly welcome, and "Petronilla" is of such a character as to hold the reader's attention to the last page. The scenes are laid in New York City, with a bright and spicy visit on a ranch in the mountains of Colorado, a region in which the writer is evidently at home. The illustrations, some forty in number, partly by the author, and ably abetted by the well-known artist, Remington W. Lane, add piquancy to the letterpress.

For sale everywhere, or sent post-paid on receipt of price.
F. TENNYSON NEELY, Publisher,
96 Queen Street, London.   114 Fifth Avenue, New York.

www.ingramcontent.com/pod-product-compliance
Lightning Source LLC
Chambersburg PA
CBHW021416300426
44114CB00010B/514